THE DARBAR OF THE SIKH GURUS

THE DARBAR OF THE SIKH GURUS
The Court of God in the World of Men

Louis E. Fenech

OXFORD
UNIVERSITY PRESS

OXFORD
UNIVERSITY PRESS

YMCA Library Building, Jai Singh Road, New Delhi 110 001

Oxford University Press is a department of the University of Oxford.
It furthers the University's objective of excellence in research,
scholarship, and education by publishing worldwide in

Oxford New York

Auckland Cape Town Dar es Salaam Hong Kong Karachi Kuala Lumpur
Madrid Melbourne Mexico City Nairobi New Delhi Shanghai Taipei Toronto

With offices in
Argentina Austria Brazil Chile Czech Republic France Greece Guatemala
Hungary Italy Japan Poland Portugal Singapore South Korea Switzerland
Thailand Turkey Ukraine Vietnam

Oxford is a registered trademark of Oxford University Press
in the UK and in certain other countries

Published in India by Oxford University Press, New Delhi

© Oxford University Press 2008

The moral rights of the author have been asserted
Database right Oxford University Press (maker)

First published 2008

All rights reserved. No part of this publication may be reproduced,
or transmitted, in any form or by any means, electronic or mechanical,
including photocopying, recording or by any information storage and
retrieval system, without permission in writing from Oxford University Press.
Enquiries concerning reproduction outside the scope of the above should be
sent to the Rights Department, Oxford University Press, at the address above

You must not circulate this book in any other binding or cover
and you must impose this same condition on any acquirer

ISBN 13: 978-019-569423-9
ISBN 10: 019-569423-6

Typeset in Naurang 10.5/12.7
by Excellent Laser Typesetters, Pitampura, Delhi 110 034
Printed in India by De-Unique, New Delhi 110 018
Published by Oxford University Press
YMCA Library Building, Jai Singh Road, New Delhi 110 001

For Christine

روز آنی پہ نہیں نسبت عشقی موقوف
عمر بھر ایک ملاقات چلی جاتی ہے

میر

ਸੋ ਮੁਖ ਕਰ ਕੇ ਚਾਰ ਅਸਥਾਨਾ ਬਿਖੈ ਮੈਨੂ ਦੇਖੇ ਅਰ ਜਾਣੇ। ਪ੍ਰਿਥਮੇ ਤੇ ਗਿਰੰਥ ਸਾਹਿਬੁ ਜੀ ਦੂਜੇ ਦਰਬਾਰ ਜੀ। ਤੀਜੇ ਗੁਰੂ ਖਾਲਸਾ ਜੀ ਚਉਥੇ ਸ਼੍ਰੀ ਭਗਉਤੀ ਜੀ ਅਰੁ ਜੋ ਕੋਈ ਏਨਾ ਤੇ ਵਖਰਾ ਆਪ ਨੂ ਗੁਰੂ ਸਦਵਾਵੇਗਾ ਸੋ ਜੋ ਵਾਹਗੁਰੂ ਕੇ ਘਰ ਕਾ ਮੁਰੀਦ ਸਿੰਦਕਵਾਨੁ ਸਿਖੁ ਹੋਵੇਗਾ ਸੋ ਨ ਮਾਨੇਗਾ।

Prashan Uttar, ms. 684, Punjab State Archives, folios 221a-b

Contents

Preface ix
Note on Orthography xiv
Note on Sources xv

1. The Sikh Darbar 1
2. (Re)forming the Early Sikh Court 49
3. Court and Sport 87
4. Spirit and Structure: The Court of Guru Gobind Singh 122
5. In the Tenth Master's Court: Bhai Nand Lal Goya 199
6. Conclusion 277

Bibliography 292
Index 314

Preface

बसा मेरे नैनन में नँदलाल[1]

Nand Lal dwells in my eyes

My interest in the court of the Sikh Gurus came about very gradually beginning with my first graduate class in South Asian Studies in January 1988 at the University of Toronto. In this remarkable class, conducted by J.S. Grewal, I was introduced to the Persian poetry of the premiere poet of the tenth Guru's darbar, Bhai Nand Lal Goya. Enthralled by Grewal's lecture and even more so by Nand Lal's poetry I decided that I would immediately begin the study of Persian in order to appreciate the sheer beauty of Nand Lal's compositions in the original. Discovering how little scholarship there was on Nand Lal, I set myself the task of eventually producing an article on our esteemed poet, or something more substantial. Three years later with hundreds of Persian ghazals tucked under my belt, I had translated into English Bhai Nand Lal's collection of ghazals, the *Dīvān-i Goyā* thanks to the patient help of Maria Subtelny, who introduced me to the study of classical Persian literature and taught me to read it. The time to write was at hand and I thus produced my first piece, an analysis of Nand Lal's third ghazal as a *javāb* or answer to Hafez Shirazi's famous first which was published in the premiere issue of the *International Journal of Punjab Studies* in 1994. By the time this article appeared though, my doctoral dissertation was beckoning.

My Nand Lal project was always in the background as I finished my dissertation and the first book which it became. It should elicit

x Preface

little surprise therefore that this book now in hand was originally intended to be a monograph on the life and poetry of Bhai Nand Lal. I began with this intention in mind and though many pitfalls were encountered I always kept to heart the remarks of the mother of the scooter-deprived protagonist in Bhisham Sahni's wonderful short story 'The Theft' which dealt with another, though less prolific Nand Lal: 'It is the *līlā* of Nand Lal [that this work be done].' But notwithstanding such sage prognostications, during the process of research I discovered that the court of the Sikh Gurus to which so many historians and Sikhophiles give voice had an almost silent one of its own in contemporary sources. Could I therefore discuss the poet without discussing the court in which he so lovingly toiled (or so tradition often claims)? I thought not and therefore spent a good deal of time uncovering sources that dealt with the Gurus' courts on the one hand and rereading well-used sources in a hopefully new courtly light on the other. It was at this time that Pashaura Singh sent to me for comment his manuscript copy of what would become *The Life and Work of Guru Arjan*, whose fourth chapter included many ideas regarding the fourth and the fifth Guru's court. The time for a further examination of the court of the Sikh Gurus thus dawned.

Ultimately the examination of the court and of Nand Lal introduced me to the courtly poetry of Nand Lal's fellow court poets in the darbar of Guru Gobind Singh. In so many ways the values and ideals enunciated in their poetry were commensurate with those of the imperial darbar, a point which I felt required analysis and so the book before us. The first chapter of this book thus asks many of these pertinent questions and begins to situate the court of the Sikh Gurus within a cosmopolitan Islamicate framework. It examines what Sikh scholars have said of the darbar of the Gurus since the mid-eighteenth century and also problematizes the study of the Sikh court and solicits answers to such questions regarding the Sikh court which are rarely ever asked by scholars of Sikh history. The second chapter begins with the history of the Indo-Persianite courtly culture from the time of Mahmud of Ghazna (eleventh century) until that of the Indo-Timurids (sixteenth century) beginning with Zahuruddin Babur. With this as base, I then situate the history of the courtly understandings surrounding Guru Nanak and his first four successors to Guru Arjan. Chapter 3, 'Court and Sport,' examines the courts and lives of the next four Gurus (Guru Hargobind to Guru Tegh Bahadar) while the fourth chapter suggests the underlying rationale of the Sikh court by examining the court of the Guru best known to the Sikhs, Guru Gobind Singh. The fifth chapter is dedicated solely to Bhai Nand Lal. After having placed him squarely within the august court of Guru Gobind Singh, the final section in this chapter attempts to answer why only Nand Lal's poetry, in a language little understood by nineteenth- and twentieth-century Sikhs in India, was transformed into sacred Sikh literature and placed on an equal footing with the utterances of the Gurus and the *var*s of Bhai Gurdas Bhalla. The final chapter concludes this text by briefly examining the history of the tenth Guru's court in his final years and after his death.

In the process of thus analysing and reconstructing the court of the Sikh Gurus, I have once again incurred vast debts which I can never truly repay. As the slightest of recompense therefore let me begin by noting the extraordinary contribution of my guide, teacher, and friend, a pioneering scholar for whom no word is too lofty in praise, Hew McLeod whose patient advice on individual and collective chapters over the long years of this text's preparation have been most enlightening and encouraging and indeed frustrating, causing me to rework passages late into the night. As well, to my friend, colleague, and mentor Pashaura Singh I send my heartiest thanks for his critical comments on earlier drafts of the manuscript. His example is also the ideal I strive to embody. Of course the usual scholarly disclaimers here apply.

I would also like to thank the institutions which allowed me to work regularly on this text. First, the University of Northern Iowa, a fellowship from which allowed me an uninterrupted summer of research in the various archives scattered throughout the Punjab and the Roy J. Carver Charitable Trust-funded Liberal Arts Core fellowships which familiarized me with much of the technology that went into producing this monograph. Thanks go out to the Vice Chancellor and Head Librarian of Punjabi University, Patiala for graciously hosting me on their campus and allowing me free access to both, the rare manuscripts in their possession and to Ganda Singh's exceptional collections of papers, manuscripts, and books. This was truly enjoyable for me as a keen student of Nand Lal Goya as no scholar of the Sikh tradition has exerted as much energy as Ganda Singh in xii Preface

the attempt to make Nand Lal's life and poetry known to the Sikh world. To him I owe a great debt indeed which I here acknowledge. Guru Nanak Dev University, Amritsar too deserves thanks for the number of weeks spent with their archival collections of manuscripts as does Kulwant Singh Bajwa who allowed me access to manuscripts at Khalsa College in Amritsar. Within Patiala, the librarians of the Central Library and those of the nearby Bhasha Vibhag Punjab collection assisted me. Patiala was also home to the manuscript collection of the Punjab State Archives of which I made much use before it shifted its location. I would also like to express my thanks to the Sahitya Academy in Ludhiana and to the seminary of the late Baba Sucha Singh of Gurdwara Gur-gian Prakash at Javvadi Taksal for access to rare manuscripts of the Adi Granth and for a CD recording of Nand Lal's ghazals, the first I discovered in well over ten years of attempts. Both Baba ji and the sevadars there received me graciously and while in Ludhiana treated me far better than I deserved. Baba Sucha Singh will be sorely missed. So too do I thank Sardar Harbans Singh and his family for allowing me to stay with them in Ludhiana.

Heroes often unsung in such epic works are the staff of the Interlibrary Loan Office of the Rod Library at the University of Northern Iowa which assisted me in every possible manner with regard to tracking down texts not in our possession. Without their support this work would have never been completed. I would also like to thank the students of my 2004 Mughal History seminar and those in my 2005 Sikh History seminar whose insightful questions gave me a great deal of food for thought.

I must not forget to thank Tony Ballantyne whose call to conference at the University of Otago in 2003 finally allowed me to bring together and share all my early thoughts about Nand Lal and his poetry; Toby Johnson and his wife Gita; N.G. Barrier; Robin Rhinehart; Gurinder Singh Mann; J.S. Grewal; Indu Banga; Shamsur Rahman Faruqi; Jack Hawley; Shinder Thandi; Harish Puri and his wife Vijay; and Maria Subtelny also deserve a note of thanks for their time, help, and patience. Let me also note that colleagues and friends in Cedar Falls deserve a most special mention: Ali Kashef and Farzad Moussavi and their families who spent far too much time scouring the book stores of Tehran hunting down items with my literary shopping list in hand; my colleagues and friends Greg Bruess,

Chuck Holcombe, Barbara Cutter, Brian Roberts, Betty DeBerg, Gabi Kuenzli, Wally Hettle, Konrad and Alijia Sadkowski, Tom Connors, Richard Utz, and Bob Martin and Jill Wallace all of whom made our History Department the ideal location for putting thought to paper. My friends Mark and Mary Grey, Isabella Varella, Beth and Steve Stofka-Davies, Hamid Amjadi and Michelle Buchan, Kamyar Enshayan, Jane Lewty, Thomas Newton, and Pedro Fernando Ribeiro also deserve many thanks for their help. Finally I would like to thank the people closest to home: my parents, of course, and my in-laws in Cornwall; my children, Agatha and Hanno, who have borne me with more forbearance than I deserve. Finally thanks to my wife Christine to whom this book is dedicated for a faith and support which defies expression.

NOTES

1. Parashuram Chaturvedi (ed.), *Mirānbāī kī Padāvalī* (Allahabad: Hindi Sahitya Sammelan, 1954), p. 3. Of course, the Nand Lal noted here is Krishna.

Note on Orthography

This book makes considerable use of Punjabi, Brajbhasha, and Persian and Arabic words. In many cases, the word is italicized when it first appears and then written without italicization in subsequent appearances. The use of nasalization is generally indicated with the letter 'n'. In almost every case, I have retained the original Punjabi/Gurmukhi spellings for words rather than their more popular Hindi/Devanagari spellings or Persian spellings. I have also adopted the less bulky transliteration of Arabic and Persian names and phrases: and so Jallaluddin rather than Jallal-ud-din. The Persian *ezāfah* is generally indicated with an hyphenated '-i' as in *Dīvān-i Goyā* while final *he-havvaz* is indicated as *-ah*. Most words are pluralized after the English fashion, by adding the final 's' to the word's ending. One prominent exception is the Perso-Arabic term *majlis* which when pluralized appears as *majālis*.

Except where noted, all translations from Punjabi, Brajbhasha/Hindi, and Persian are my own with editorial assistance from W.H. McLeod and Pashaura Singh.

Finally let me note my use of the term Persianite. This is very close to Shackle's use of Persian loan words but refers to more than simply vocabulary. Perisianite within the context of this book means any linguistic or cultural feature of north Indian culture which originates, either in reality or in popular understandings, in Persia.

Note on Sources

Many of the sources used in this book particularly in Chapter 5 are often unique hand-written manuscripts deposited into archives throughout the Punjab. I have also made use of one important internet source. As my personal collection of Santokh Singh's classic *gurbilās* work, the *Sūraj Prakāsh*, is incomplete I have often referenced the online resource at [http://www.ik13.com/online_library.htm#gurpartap]. There are, therefore, two styles of noting the *Sūraj Prakāsh* within this book. I have referenced the physical texts in my possession by their volume, chapter, sub-chapter, and verse numbers. And so Vir Singh (ed.), *Kavi Chūrāmani Bhāī Santokh Singh jī krit Srī Gur Pratāp Sūraj Granth* XII 3:25:26–8 (Patiala: Bhasha Vibhag Punjab, 1990), p. 5081 [or subsequently *SP* XII 3:25:26–8, p. 5081] means that the passage in question appears in the twelfth volume at *ritu* (chapter) 3, *ansu* (section) 25, lines 26 to 28 on page 5081. The exact same passage will be now referenced online: online *SP* 3:25: 26–8, pp. 254–5: Adobe Acrobat Reader 'SGPS Rut 3' at *http://www.ik13.com/online̦library.htm#gurpartap*. Within the digital text itself the passage in question appears on 'pages' 254–5. I have also made regular use of both the standard printed editions of the Adi Granth and the Dasam Granth of 1430 and 1436 pages respectively.

1
The Sikh Darbar

ਸਾਚਾ ਸਾਹਿਬੁ ਸਾਚੁ ਨਾਇ ਭਾਖਿਆ ਭਾਉ ਅਪਾਰੁ ।
ਆਖਹਿ ਮੰਗਹਿ ਦੇਹਿ ਦੇਹਿ ਦਾਤਿ ਕਰੇ ਦਾਤਾਰੁ । ਫੇਰਿ
ਕਿ ਅਗੈ ਰਖੀਐ ਜਿਤੁ ਦਿਸੈ ਦਰਬਾਰੁ ।[1]

True is the Lord and True is His Name. His speech is boundless love. [All people] speak and pray constantly repeating the refrain 'give [to us]'. As the True Giver gives [all] gifts what [offering] can we present before Him which will allow his court to appear?

Sikh tradition has for long painted a dazzling portrait of the court or *darbār* of the tenth Sikh Guru, Guru Gobind Singh (1666–1708 CE). Staffed by an impressive and auspicious number of poets, fifty two, as well as a smaller number of writers, the Guru's court produced a wide-ranging series of compositions. These include many current Sikh canonical works as found within the Dasam Granth and attributed to the Guru himself, the little-known *Sarab-loh Granth* (The Book of All-Steel, i.e., God), and other texts which are apparently no longer extant, such as the massive *Vidyā Sagar* or 'Ocean of Knowledge'.[2] The sole intent of this courtly literature was, we are told, to awaken India's oppressed masses to true heroism and to arouse within the Guru's Sikhs and all those suffering under the tyranny of Aurangzeb's Mughal regime, the desire for justice and righteousness: to live a life in accord with that righteousness and to ensure its stability, with one's life if need be. 'At that time,' contemporary tradition maintains,

> it was by no means an easy task to rouse the downtrodden servants (*ghulāmān*) of the Mughal empire. For this purpose the [Guru and the writers of his

darbar under his direction] treated their spiritual literature with strengthening agents, [a form of poetry manifesting] *bīr-rasī* [the heroic sentiment], and presented it in a novel way.[3]

Although this interpretation is discussed in the late Piara Singh Padam's relatively recent analysis, *Srī Gurū Gobind Singh jī de Darbārī Ratan* (The Courtly Jewels of Guru Gobind Singh), it is an understanding which was firmly in place by the early nineteenth century. For example, in the 1801–2 composition in praise of Bhai Mani Singh, the *Shahīd-bilās* (The Martyr's Splendour) attributed to Seva Singh Kaushish, we hear of the tenth Guru's court and the manifest effects of bīr-rasī:

Sangats from within and outside India came to obtain Guru Gobind's *darshan* (auspicious viewing). Fifty two [court] poets resided near the Guru in whose company was the gifted Mani Singh.[4] From the blessed mouth of the [tenth] Guru, the *kalgīdhar* [one who wears the aigrette's plume in his turban], was spoken a homily in *bīr-rass* [the heroic style of verse] taken from within the *Krishan Charitr* acknowledging the battle of Kharag Singh.[5] On hearing [this homily] timidity fled the hearts of all listeners [and in its place] a great desire to engage in righteous battle flared within.[6]

An apocryphal nineteenth-century text, the *Gurū kīān Sākhīān* (Narratives of the Gurus) explicitly shares this opinion of the effects of the heroic style.[7] Having just briefly read through Hirda Ram Bhalla's epic text, the *Hanuman Nātak*, the tenth Guru loudly exclaims:

O Brother Sikh! By reading this book [even] a cowardly and weak person can become a heroic warrior. This text is filled to the brim with the very essence of heroism (bīr-ras).[8]

For at least one of the poets who is supposed to have been associated with the tenth Guru, such sentiments doubtlessly achieved their lofty goals. In the epilogue to Kavi Kankan's *Das Gur Kathā* (The Story of the Ten Gurus) the Sikh Panth had itself become the sole repository of Hanuman's extraordinary strength:

After [the first] ten Rudras the eleventh [Rudra appeared and] was known as Hanuman.[9] And so in a similar manner after the ten [Sikh] Gurus the Sikh [Panth] was known as Hanuman[-like] because the Sikh [Panth] on its own [manifests] as much legendary strength as Hanuman possessed. It occurred to Kavi Kankan that in this there is no doubt.[10]

By the mid-nineteenth century Sikh authors were convinced that the court of the tenth Master prepared all manners of edifying courtly literature in order to strengthen those oppressed,[11] as the famous Nirmala Sikh author Santokh Singh makes clear in his voluminous 1843 CE *Gur-pratāp Sūraj Granth*:

The poets [of the Guru's court] wrote [new] poetic works and these very same works made evident the nine sentiments (*nav ras*) of literary adornment. Poets would come and go from the True Guru's presence writing and uttering beautiful poetry.[12]

While the general characteristics of Sikh poetry produced at the Guru's court cannot be readily distinguished from Sikh poetry fashioned outside the court, the category 'court poetry' is nevertheless convenient and will be used to describe both devotional and secular subjects written within the courts of the Gurus. In Sikh tradition the intent of such courtly literature was both altruistic and inclusivist, and its successful implementation (responsible in part for the 'heroic' period of Sikh history) made both the courtiers of the Guru and the products of their court unique, allowing them to clearly outshine the darbars of contemporary north Indian kings and princes—Mughal, Rajput, and Bijapuri amongst others—whose poets and artists selfishly exercised their arts solely for the edification and entertainment of their patrons and other courtiers. Piara Singh Padam once again captures this tone well, his Orientalism-istic rhythm notwithstanding:

[Through the production of literature at his court] the True Guru applied the [combined] power of knowledge and action in order to continue protecting Indian culture and the welfare of common people. When the kings and great kings of other courts [had] splendid literature created out of consideration for [their own] amusement they would display their pomp and splendour thus nurturing the bad habit of applying [this literary] art for interests purely personal.[13]

For Padam the patronage of obsequious poets and the praise of their encomiums, as well as the support of artists and architects who created such splendours as the Peacock Throne and the Taj Mahal with the sweat and blood of oppressed and unnamed Indian labourers are all representative of the hollow vanity and selfishness implied above.[14]

The Image(s) of the Sikh Court

This certainly presents a rather damaging image of the Mughal court and its contemporaries, but it is very interesting that Padam's criticism is generally directed to only one aspect of these darbars: their arts, especially their literature. Indeed, both Padam and contemporary Sikh tradition pass harsh judgement on these, but the disapproval of the Mughal court as a whole, however, remains a surprisingly qualified one, demonstrating Sikh tradition's ambivalence towards it.[15] While on the one hand, as we have seen, Sikh tradition strongly objects to its art and literature,[16] on the other it tacitly embraces, at least to limited degrees some of the standards of behaviour and comportment which Indo-Islamic and Mughal courtiers and kings were encouraged to display. It also adopted the aura of the ideal Indo-Timurid prince, a courtly image especially noticeable in the representation of the tenth Sikh Master, Guru Gobind Singh. Early Sikh tradition significantly accepted and displayed a number of Mughal symbols denoting power and royalty and thus legitimacy and authority, for example, kettledrums (Pbi: *nagārā*; Per: *naqqārah*); tents (Per: *khaimah, bārgāh*);[17] *khil'at*s or *siropā*s (Per: *sar o pā* '[from] head to foot'; robes of honour), and the production of books to name but a few.[18] These significant items were present and utilized throughout Western, Central, and Southern Asia as well as within the cosmopolitan ecumene around Byzantium well before the period of the Delhi Sultanate, but their semiotic potential was generally enhanced in the place and period under discussion by the court of the Central Asian conqueror Amir Timur (d. 1405 CE) and that of his successors, amongst whom are of course included the prominent Mughal emperors of India.[19] While pre-modern Sikh tradition has very little if anything to say about the panegyric literature of the royal court (probably because eighteenth-century Sikh authors were not directly familiar with it)[20] or its splendorous arts, its recognition of the symbolic forms, tropes, and imagery of the Indo-Timurids was based simply on precedents well-established since the very beginning of the Sikh tradition. This recognition appears even within early manuscript copies of the Adi Granth, such as the penultimate Kartarpuri *bir* or recension of the scripture and its earlier, celebrated draft copy, ms. 1245 at the Guru Nanak Dev University library.[21]

Fig. 1: Guru Gobind Singh seated in
royal regalia, fanned by courtier

One of the folios of ms. 1245, for example, bears the *shamsa* (Persian: 'sunburst'), a symbol long held dear in the preparation of manuscripts within the larger Islamicate whose presence was indicative of both divine glory (the *nūr* of the Qur'an)[22] as well as the divine light which God 'directly transfers to kings' (a 'divine stamp of authority' Abu'l Fazl 'Allami implies).[23] The existence of the shamsa raises questions about authority and implies that the scribes and artists who worked on the text were familiar with Islamicate manuscript standards, most likely receiving their training in Lahore. The shamsa folio also suggests that the manuscript was most likely intended for a royal patron which may tell us something further about the nature of Guru Arjan's court in which this text was produced.[24]

6 The Darbar of the Sikh Gurus

In many instances, moreover, the very image of the Guru is commensurate with glorious representations reserved for the Mughal emperors (and later Rajput ranas) themselves. Eighteenth- and nineteenth-century Sikh art, for example, including portraits struck onto Sikh coins and 'temple tokens' (fig. 2), is replete with images of the Gurus, particularly Guru Gobind Singh, painted and/or cast in a regal style reminiscent of Mughal miniatures. Figure 1, for example, that was found pasted into a very early manuscript copy of the Dasam Granth is perhaps the earliest such representation of Guru Gobind Singh, dated most likely to 1700 CE.[25] Significantly different from portraits found within the janam-sakhis[26] and various contemporary 'mythic' portraits of the tenth Guru most likely painted within the same region (fig. 3),[27] this painting may well provide a unique representation of Gobind Singh which, if the date is accurate, was painted very soon after the inauguration of the Khalsa Order in 1699 during a relatively calm period in the life of the tenth Master.[28] It may be for this reason that the Guru is here rendered very sensitively, as a *pādishāh* or emperor, in a very calm and relaxed pose. He is shown in portrait (rather than the three quarters profile common to Mughal illustrations) kneeling on a dais or *palkī*, hands gently holding an arrow, while a bow is placed before him and a sword in its magnificent sheath dangles on his left side. In his *kamarband* (cummerbund) is tucked a *katar* (punch dagger), the hilt of which appears to be overlaid with gold in *kundan* (Urdu: 'finest [gold]') technique and set with various gems.[29] He is being fanned with a peacock-feather fan by a bare-foot attendant who appears in a far more humble costume.

Fig. 2: 'Temple token' with Guru Nanak, Mardana and Bala on obverse; Guru Gobind Singh in royal regalia on reverse[30]

It should be made clear that this painting would never be mistaken as a Mughal illustration. The turban style is not late seventeenth-century Mughal and appears to suggest a Rajput influence, quite likely due to Anandpur-Makhowal's proximity to the various *paharī* or hill regions of the Punjab whose Rajput nobility traced their lineage to Lord Rama and his sons, Hindu gods of Rajput lore. Indeed, even the *jāmah* or robe is tied under the Guru's left arm, the more common Hindu style of dress as seen in Pahari paintings, and not under the right which was the accepted Mughal manner.[31] This leads one to conclude that the Pahari ateliers are the most likely origin of this artist's influence.[32]

This claim notwithstanding, clearly recognizable nevertheless are Mughal stylistic contributions. This stems most likely from the fact that mid-seventeenth to early eighteenth-century pahari Rajput portraits were very much affected by Mughal art and styles as recent scholarship has argued persuasively.[33] The emphasis in this portrait, for example, manifests that same stress we discover in Mughal painting during and after the period of Jahangir, an emphasis which 'consistently recognizes, acknowledges, and investigates the individuality and personal uniqueness of the people it portrays.'[34] It does this though with neither the shading nor the play on light characteristic of Jahangiri Mughal portraiture—which is here non-existent (the lack of shading for example is especially noticeable in the boldly drawn lines indicating folds on the jāmah of the attendant and the small white *rumāl* [handkerchief] which he holds in his left hand, as well as on the green *patkā* or sash tucked under the Guru's left arm)—but rather with vibrant colour.[35] To this end the landscape is bleak and in large part muted in tones of jade-apple green (though with a top band of vibrant blue and a line of light lapis lazuli-blue cloud shapes) while the Guru, in the middle of the painting, is clearly the centre of attention. He is boldly drawn and beautifully dressed in a bright red jāmah bespeckled with a five-dotted yellowish design which on very close inspection suggests paisleys.[36] The Guru also wears a necklace, bracelets, and earrings of pearls indicative of his importance while a cushion whose upholstery is dotted with what appears to be chrysanthemum blossoms supports his back. The skilful execution of textile patterns seen here on the cushion and the brown and blue patkā whose folds are gingerly draped over the Guru's bent knees,

8 The Darbar of the Sikh Gurus

as well as the intricate floral pattern on the sword's scabbard, follow very much an Islamicate stylistic sensibility underscoring the ubiquity of Islamicate standards.[37] The beauty of the scabbard so draws the viewer's attention that one is persuaded to think that the artist is here not just emphasizing the tenth Guru's imperial nature but rather Gobind Singh's reverence for the sword which is invoked in the prologue of the *Bachitar Nātak*, the so-called autobiography of the tenth Guru, as the supreme symbol of the divine.[38] This emphasis on the Guru and the divine suggests that the Guru's court was not as intensely conscious of style and fashion as the courts of both the Rajputs and the Mughals (at least before Aurangzeb's period). Indeed, here there is little show of the engagement which one often sees in lavish Mughalized courtly scenes.

A case in point would be the Guru's attendant whose waist is bound up with a cummerbund into which is placed a far less fancy katar. This figure blends into the background and foreground with his plain white finery and the focus lands upon the fanciful peacock-feathered *chaurī* or whisk (also known as a *morcham*) by which he is fanning the Guru. Frozen in time right above the tenth Guru's head, the whisk is reminiscent of the regal canopy or *chhattrī* to which we shall refer later.

Fig. 3: Guru Gobind Singh encounters Guru Nanak

'Mughalized portraits' of non-Mughal figures such as Guru Gobind Singh and the paharī rajas were subjected to such Islamicate styles, as Catherine Glynn claims in her analysis of the paintings of Bilaspur-Kahlur royalty (a royal family with whom Guru Gobind Singh was quite familiar as they find mention in writings attributed to the tenth Master), 'in order to project and mythologise' a reign and an image on the one hand and to retain a 'visual biography of persons critical to the development and advancement of the empire' on the other.[39] In this vein other portraits, though in a different style, picture the tenth Guru seated on a dais surrounded by courtiers and family in a type reminiscent more of later paharī Rajput miniatures (fig. 4). The painting in Fig. 4 is still clearly Mughalized as it depicts a courtly scene which seems to have much in common with mid-eighteenth century portraits painted in the paharī region of Mandi, just to the north of Bilaspur-Kahlur[40] although it also shares commonalities with Rajput paintings within the Rajput homeland to the south. According to Vishakha Desai, for example, 'heavily Mughalized Rajasthani pictures often depict courtly rather than religious or literary subjects.'[41]

These various adoptions in manuscripts and on canvas, particularly from areas of the Mughal court which contemporary Sikh tradition censures, imply that the nature of the Sikh court and its 'courtly culture'

Fig. 4: Guru Gobind Singh giving court to his sons

if any, particularly during the guruship of the tenth Master is not as altogether straightforward as modern Sikh scholars like Piara Singh Padam suggest. Despite the contemporary condemnation of the literature of the Islamicate courts and eighteenth-century Sikh tradition's vehemence towards certain members of the court, in particular Aurangzeb and other Mughal courtiers and officials who harmed the fortunes of the nascent Sikh Panth, it is in many ways by appropriating the imposing language and symbols of these courts and the 'grammar' of their rituals, particularly that of the darbar of the Mughals, that Sikhs describe in large part not only the tenth Master's darbar but indeed the courts of all the previous Gurus, beginning with Guru Nanak.[42] As this style of description occurs well before the very completion of the Adi Granth in the early seventeenth century it is very likely, as we shall see later, that the Sikh Gurus, especially Guru Gobind Singh, themselves adopted many such courtly symbols and features, and their accompanying Persianite terminology. This must have been a way to continue and buttress the Sikh legacy, a bequest of which the tenth Guru was particularly cognisant as the *Bachitar Nātak* makes abundantly clear.[43]

Such an awareness becomes manifest in the Sikh *bansavālī* and *gur-pranālī* (also: *gur-pranāvālī*), texts of the eighteenth and nineteenth centuries, that are concerned with tracing the proper lineage and legacies of the Sikh Gurus.[44] Put simply, the Sikh Gurus and their disciples embraced the very 'grammar' of the Mughal court, its rituals, symbols, and ceremonies to convey power and authority as would be understood in the sixteenth and seventeenth centuries;[45] became adept in its use; and adapted it accordingly to reflect their particular situations and fulfil their own unique and multiple interests.[46] Clearly this was no mere mimicry nor was it simply the mechanical functionalism of 'legitimation'. As Sumit Guha notes in the context of the sixteenth-century Marathi-speaking courts of the Deccan, 'Total assimilation to the glorious imperial court was dangerous, if not tempting.'[47] In the end therefore, Islamicate courtly precedence was one feature albeit an extremely important one which provided in part the framework for what was a much larger, uniquely Sikh construction, a Sikh 'courtly "world",' 'which is coherent in its own terms.'[48] It was perhaps during the time of the tenth Guru that the Sikh community became most adept at such revisions.

A Quest for Rationale

The above statements are meant to strike a note of caution. One must be vigilant in any attempt to delineate the Sikh court as this is a formidable task given the nature of the historical record. Nowhere in it do we find, for example, a source equal to the autobiography of the seventeenth-century Kayastha Hindu, Bhimsen Burhanpuri, the *Tārīkh-i Dil-kushā* (The Heart-revealing History) which specifies in part the court life and behaviour and beliefs of the Mughal nobility of Aurangzeb's time from the perspective of one of its minor members, which details the prerequisites for membership to the Sikh court.[49] Nor does one discover guidebooks along the lines of the late-seventeenth century *Mirzā-nāmah*s (The Gentleman's Guide), which supply information on the standards, behaviours, restraints, and etiquettes cultivated by Sikh courtiers which bound them together, thereby separating the Sikh court from the wider Sikh Panth of its respective periods.[50] One could argue that the rahit-namas most certainly serve in this capacity as guides to Sikh refinement but these important texts are not contemporary and even the earliest that is dated (1719 CE) deals more with the collective Sikh memory of the Guru's court rather than with the court itself. The rahit standards were, moreover, not restricted to a select few disciples but open to all Sikhs.[51] For the actual details of the Sikh court, we must therefore search elsewhere. That disciples surrounded the Sikh Gurus and performed selfless service both for the Guru's benefit and for the Panth seems a very reasonable conclusion to draw, in the light of both contemporary evidence and the testimony of tradition. To this very day Sikh sants, babajis, and in some cases bibijis within the Punjab are often seen surrounded by a coterie of loyal followers and disciples who selflessly serve them and their respective communities in a variety of ways.[52] But did such Sikh men and women of the sixteenth and seventeenth centuries form the Guru's court? Did they collectively give shape to a social formation coherent in its own terms as suggested above? The answer to this question depends upon how one interprets the phrase 'coherent on its own terms' as the evidence, both Sikh and non-Sikh, as we shall see, is simply unclear.

Although the Gurus probably held court (that is, presided over receptions or gatherings of Sikhs) it is far more difficult to ascertain whether or not they possessed a formal court with designated attendants, advisors, newswriters, agents, canopy-bearers, and so on, who were regularly in attendance and formed a hierarchy bound together by a precise etiquette.[53] The contemporary evidence which is available makes clear that the Sikh court was not the 'first household of the extended royal family', a characteristic shared by most royal courts generally, European and Asian alike.[54] This same evidence nevertheless suggests, as we shall see, the existence of some of the court personnel noted above (contemporary Sikh accounts make no attempt to distinguish between particular sections of the Sikh 'nobility').[55] Both these implications precipitate the following statement: If the Sikh Gurus were indeed surrounded by a panoply of courtiers and court officials, the darbar to which the latter belonged was far less exclusive and formal during the period covering the guruships up until Guru Tegh Bahadar's, than the others we discover in northern India. Bhai Gurdas may well be referring to the Sikh darbar generally in the following *paurī* in which we find loyal servants, scribes, and musicians within the retinue of the Guru:

Precious are the hands of the *gurmukh* (Guru-facing Sikh) who does the Guru's work in the sadh sangat, the congregation of true believers. He draws drinking water [for the faithful]; fans [the sangat]; grinds the flour; washes [the feet of the Guru] and takes amrit, sanctified water, from the Guru's feet. He writes the Guru's hymns and [binds the pages together as] books (*pothīān*), and plays the cymbals, drum, and rabab.[56]

We speak in the subjunctive above because of the confusion engendered by the ambiguous nature of the language used. Terms such as *sevā* for example, which can refer to the courtier's pledged service to the sovereign, an entirely worldly idea, relied upon views which developed in the religious arena, connoting in Sikhism generally selfless service in the soteriological sense used by the Sikh Gurus.[57] The above passage from Bhai Gurdas is thus very much in line with the many general references we discover in the Adi Granth in which Persianite terms for 'royal court' appear and in which the royal courtier is sparingly defined. One may cite Guru Nanak's *Sirī rāg* 18 as example:

Through hearing (lit., 'acquiring') the sacred utterances which are unspoken self-centredness is eliminated. Forever am I a sacrifice to those who selflessly serve their True Guru. They are clothed [in robes of honour] (*paināiai*) [while] standing (also: 'having been brought') in the Court (*dargah*) of the Lord. [Indeed] the very Name of Hari the Divine Master has its abode on their lips.[58]

Although lacking in concrete description, Guru Nanak here speaks of the otherworldly court of the Supreme Lord in which the gurmukh is gifted with robes of honour, a recurrent theme in the bani of Guru Nanak, underscoring the reward for the name-conscious individual. Certainly Bhai Gurdas had this court in mind while preparing his paurī but the sixteenth-century northern Indian context in which he wrote also saw the rise of Amritsar as an important centre of commerce, the increasing importance of the Sikhs as a political and economic power, and the rising significance of the office of the Sikh Guru (about all of which more will be said) under both Guru Ram Das and Guru Arjan. Therefore, there was more that exercised our revered theologian's imagination.

The sentiments in both *var* 6:12 and the hymns of the Adi Granth suggest that upon the Islamicate framework we noted above were placed features modelled along the same patterns as the Sikh sangat of the period of the Gurus. As such the Sikh darbar was a more open, fluid court in the sense that Sikh values and standards of refinement, love, loyalty, beauty, service, etc. idealized by courtiers inhabiting other courts were to be cultivated by all Sikhs and potential gurmukhs alike in their self fashioning and were not simply the prerogative of a restricted, talented, well-born few who ultimately formed a powerful and prestigious elite.[59] Although sources attributed to the ninth Guru, Tegh Bahadar, suggest a courtly hierarchy, it is nevertheless difficult to imagine a closed and limited Sikh court presided over by the Sikh Gurus, especially because their message was self-consciously inclusivist and available to everybody regardless of caste; creed; or, indeed, sex.[60] This fluidity is clearly evident during the period of Guru Gobind Singh, the Sikh Guru who most certainly possessed a court (albeit a limited one), to whom the *Akāl Ustati* (In Praise of the Timeless Lord) is attributed. This is a portion of the Sikh canon which highlights the inclusive nature of humanity (Sikh tradition claims that the tenth Guru prepared this bani in the Sikh court over a number of years). Its rudiments of membership and the etiquette prescribed were relaxed and far from formal as they were not to be found so much in one's dress,[61] appearance, gestures, knowledge of the outside world, and ability to consume conspicuously (crucial factors in classical Indian, Delhi Sultanate, and Indo-Timurid courts),[62] or in various court ceremonial (all of which Guru Nanak claims are supremely inferior to meditation upon the divine name),[63] but more in an individual's love and loyalty to the Guru and the nascent Panth. More important was the ability to cultivate the qualities of the Guru-oriented Sikh, one whose character and practices were eventually outlined in both the Adi Granth and the *vārān* of Bhai Gurdas. One particular Brajbhasha *kabitt* (a quatrain with 31 or 32 syllables) by Bhai Gurdas puts the matter in a quintessentially Sikh way, contrasting general characteristics and symbols of Indic and Indo-Timurid courtly culture with what our esteemed amanuensis considered their more virtuous equivalents:

> Make moderation and truth the throne; balance and contentment the minister; righteousness and forbearance the royal banner; and so the empire will be steadfast. Make bliss' abode the home and embrace mercy as the wife. Make good fortune the treasurer and fear [of God] the nourishment and the aim [of life] will be fulfilled. Make contemplation your wealth and the highest of all wealth (knowledge of the divine) your diplomacy. Make forgiveness your king (*chhatrpati*) and the shade of his canopy will grace [the world] with gracefulness. Bliss for all and peace for your subjects will be the delight while the divine light in all things will be made apparent and the unstruck melody will sound [securing salvation].[64]

Let us note however that these qualities for membership were relaxed in only this sense, for as Guru Nanak implies, the Sikh courtier must walk the same path as that travelled by all pious Sikhs, 'a narrow lane as thin as the edge of a double-edged sword'.[65]

Although ideally the Mughal court too was an open one in the sense that an individual's ability was a criterion for entry, its members were nevertheless drawn from only certain social groups whether Muslim or Hindu, ensuring that membership was indeed constrained.[66]

Of course the nature of the Sikh court did change, most likely from guruship to guruship, in response to the new circumstances in which the Gurus and the Panth found themselves over the roughly two-hundred year Guru Period of Sikh history (*c.* 1500–1708). The ideal criteria for inclusion may be gathered from the famous eleventh var of Bhai Gurdas in which are revealed, by name, specific

Sikhs from all walks of late fifteenth- and early sixteenth-century life, Sikhs who are so mentioned in part because of their abilities to embody the qualities of the gurmukh.[67] Amongst the valued traits are devotion to and absorption within the *nām* (Name) or within *gurbānī* (11:14:5; 11:13:8), contemplation of the Word (*sabad vīchārā* 11:18:7), a detached nature (*udāsī* 11:13:1), benevolent altruism (*paraupkārī* 11:15:4), and bravery (*sūrmā* 11:24:5). All these are meant to be brought together harmoniously with perhaps the most important quality for Bhai Gurdas, selfless service to the Guru and the Panth, the attribute most often repeated in his descriptions.[68] The many Sikhs who manifested these were the Sikhs who had found honour in the court of the Guru, thus forming an implied Sikh nobility: these were the true courtiers of the Guru whose example other Sikhs who wished to rise to a courtly stature could most hope to imitate.[69] In many ways, therefore, it may well appear that the activities at the Sikh court in an important sense were the activities which all Sikhs were encouraged to emulate.[70]

Kalu [the Khatri who] humbly faced [his Master] placed his hope in the sacred utterances of the Guru and achieved honour [lit., 'congratulations'] in the court [of the Guru].[71]

and

Mallia and Saharu, who were proficient calico printers [and who resided in the village of Dalla] were/became courtiers (*darbārī*) in the court of the [third] Guru (*gur-dargah*).[72]

It is certainly worth mentioning that the context in which Bhai Gurdas prepared this important var is significant. It seems that Bhai Gurdas is doing far more than simply outlining the characteristics of the gurmukh and the darbari. Once again he reminds seventeenth-century Sikhs of the qualities which constituted the true Sikh of the Guru's court, an understanding which was most likely open to question by our theologian's time thanks to the activities of the Guru's masands (to which we shall return in the next chapter). The masands were the second generation who mainly inherited their positions from their fathers, and were most likely assuming the elite airs of royalty which ultimately led to their offices' end under the tenth Sikh Master.[73] We assume for example that when Guru Hargobind shifted his headquarters to Kiratpur thus absenting himself from the central Punjab, his hold over the masands—whose offices were now hereditary just like that of the Guru—was considerably weakened, a weakening no doubt exacerbated by the sixth Master's more assertive stance.[74] This is perhaps why Bhai Gurdas emphasized the idea of selfless service and outlined in var 11:22 the characteristics that constitute the 'great/best masands' (*vadde masand*).[75]

Narrativizing the Sikh Court

Under the loving hand of tradition, however, circumstantial references to a Sikh court are transformed into genuine ones. What seems instructive for our purposes is that the traditional narratives of the Sikh court to which we shall intermittently refer appear at a rather confusing time in Sikh history, the eighteenth century. Certainly Khalsa Sikhs under Banda (d. 1716) had been the first Sikhs to strike that most regal of symbols, the coin.[76] The reasons for such an unprecedented step may be fathomed from a hukam-nama attributed to Banda in which he claims, '*Asā sat yug vartāiā hai*' ('We have established the Age of Truth').[77] Banda and his Sikhs struck this coin to mark a new era, a point underscored by the edict's date of 12 Poh, year 1 (12 December 1710 CE).[78] However, this age was precipitated not by Banda himself and the Khalsa Sikhs under his general direction but rather by the Sikh Gurus (despite its beginning with Banda's rule). It seems only natural that Sikhs saw the sovereignty and the empire which such symbols evoked originating with the Gurus and their courts, easily the source of Sikh authority. The so-called *Gobindshāhī* couplet cast on Banda's seal whose imprint can be clearly seen in his hukam-namas, and slight variations of which were also struck upon many eighteenth- and nineteenth-century Sikh coins thereafter, made those sentiments abundantly clear.[79] Eighteenth-century references to the earlier Sikh courts of the Gurus therefore may be apocryphal attempts to demonstrate both the symbolic legitimacy of the sovereignty of the Sikhs under Banda, the later Sikh misls, and, under Ranjit Singh too.

To this we may add other factors which highlight the fondness for the court of the Gurus. Although contemporary tradition still maintains the exciting though simplistic nature of eighteenth-century Sikh history as a time in which righteous Sikhs as a uniform power confronted the forces of evil and despair, it was in reality a phase during which the Panth was clearly divided (perhaps severely).[80] The first half of the eighteenth century witnessed Jat Sikh zamindars support the depredations of Banda against Muslims and non-Jat, particularly Khatri, Sikhs, and Hindus. Threatened by such Khalsa Sikhs, Khatri Sikhs, especially around the Ganges Basin and within Delhi itself, sided with Mughal forces to protect their more vested interests, an alliance which is implied in Sainapati's *Srī Gur-sobhā* (1711 CE) and made explicit in early eighteenth-century Persian chronicles, especially the *Akhbārat-i Darbār-i Muʿallá* (News from the Exalted Court) of Emperor Bahadar Shah (r. 1707–12 CE).[81] Indeed, in some cases it seems that Sikhs even became Muslims (at least superficially) in order to avoid becoming targets of Mughal wrath.[82] It seems clear that Banda's coin casting activities in themselves suggest that the Sikh Panth was by no means united. Apart from broadcasting a message of Banda's power and intentions to the Mughal emperor himself (the passages on both the seal and the extant coins were in Persian after all) such actions most likely attempted to quell at least one dimension of Sikh dissent which followed in Banda's wake. Later in the eighteenth century the situation did not improve much. The late 1720s for example, saw the beginning of internecine battles which were somewhat relaxed during the period of Nawab Kapur Singh (1733–53 CE), only to be taken up again after the establishment of the Sikh misls (confederations) in the mid-eighteenth century. These mutually destructive struggles were dramatically muted when the misls were brought together under the auspices of Ranjit Singh in the late eighteenth century.[83]

Although such anomalies certainly appeared during the time of the Gurus as the occasional hymn highlighting the infamous detractors of Sikh history implies,[84] later Sikh writers had the benefit of chronological distance. Conflicts between what Sikhs did and the ideal actions prescribed within Sikh writings such as the Adi Granth, the janam-sakhis, and the rahit-namas were just too evident. Writers such as Kirpal Das Bhalla and Kesar Singh Chhibbar amongst others, looked back upon a now-mythicized past in the light of an anomalous present and assigned to that golden age a greater simplicity, grandeur, and morality. While the Sikhs of the early to mid-eighteenth century were thus involved at times in internecine disputes and were very much a marginalized community with little power and wealth to support a courtly life that could sustain Sikh writers such as the brahman Chhibbar Sikhs,[85] the earlier courts of the Gurus were presented by our Sikh authors in a very significant way. They were presented as grand and influential centres of largesse whose nobles were selfless Sikh warrior/servants fighting on behalf of their Guru and Master, and all those threatened by oppression on the one hand, and pious and devoted Sikhs writing and reciting poetry, and singing shabads on the other, all of whom provided examples of the ideal Khalsa Sikh.[86]

This is a later eighteenth-century tradition however, for although the earliest of these traditional accounts, *Srī Gur-sobhā* does make reference to both the kingly and divine nature of Guru Gobind Singh and his possession of a Sikh darbar, its concerns are focussed on the character of the nascent Khalsa and the villainy of its detractors. Its allusions to the court therefore generally serve this purpose, describing the arms which such Khalsa Sikhs carried to the court and the seva that they performed without detailing the comportment of its members or the structure of its membership.[87] As such, Sainapati's references to poets such as himself and his contemporaries in this text are negligible (though we shall later note references to his fellow poets in other works attributed to him).

Despite Sainapati's economy of words on the court of the tenth Master, it was the Sikh court of Guru Gobind Singh, the latest in the recent memory of our mid-eighteenth century authors, which easily became the court upon which they most prolifically exercised their art. This was in large part possible because Guru Gobind Singh did indeed have in his possession a number of regal courtly symbols, having requested these from his Sikhs in his hukam-namas or written instructions (to which we shall return in Chapter 4). It is no surprise therefore that eighteenth and nineteenth century Sikh authors note these royal items and incorporate them into a kingly and courtly paradigm. In his early-nineteenth century gur-bilas text for example, Koer Singh alludes to such royal possessions as those found in both princely tentage and textiles when he describes a young Gobind Singh about to leave Patna to the sorrow of his Bihari disciples:

The [young] Guru Sahib was prepared [to leave]. He fixed his baggage which consisted of countless items, accessories [virtually] without number. [These included] tents (*tambū*) and *qanāts* (tent enclosures), and very lovely canopies.[88] As well were found *jājams* (Per: *jājim,* a flat woven rug of Turkic origin), a *shataranj* (Per: shatarnjī, a type of carpet)[89] and *sudhārī* (a type of sharp weapon), a chariot and palanquin, prized horses (*bājar*) and camels. Upon [the backs of] a number of these animals [and within the confines of the chariot and palanquin] the Guru's equipment was secured.[90]

According to Persian authors, both contemporary with and later than the period of the tenth Master, Guru Gobind Singh's continued possession of these created the impression that he comported himself like a raja, a behaviour for which Aurangzeb (and, as the *Bachitar Nātak* makes clear, those rajas whose domains adjoined the Guru's territory at Anandpur–Makhowal) sought to chastise him.[91] According to Grewal and Bal,

Gobind seems to have been so fascinated by a court with kingly appearances that later he maintained it even when that was likely to result in Aurangzib taking some stern action against him.[92]

The adoption of such symbols seems to have made more than simply a passing impression on our Persian authors as in a *hasbulhukam* (Arabic: 'as commanded,' ornately written imperial communications) dictated by the emperor Aurangzeb to the secretary 'Inayatullah Khan. In this communication the tenth Guru is referred to as the *ra'īs* or 'leader' of the Sikhs, a citation which seems to indicate a Mughal recognition of the tenth Guru's authority.[93]

It appears that the tenth Guru took it upon himself as a leader to give out *sanad*s. Early in the year 2000 just such a document, claimed to have been issued by Guru Gobind Singh as he made his way to Nander in southern India, was discovered in the possession of a brahman family in Harda, Madhya Pradesh. Within India, sanads (from the Arabic *isnad* referring to the chain of narrators which established the legitimacy of a hadith (tradition) of the Prophet Muhammad) were documents forming contractual obligations between the issuer and the person(s) to whom the sanad was issued. Usually these granted the people named within, the rights over certain territories or the authority for holding an office and meant that the resources of the power issuing the sanad would back the legitimacy and the rights of the holder. Although only recognized Mughal officials could grant such sanads, the system of issuing these documents began to fragment in the eighteenth century as the nature of Mughal power changed. If this is indeed a genuine document then it demonstrates that the tenth Guru and his Sikhs adopted this form of courtly authority.[94]

It appears, moreover, that among those surrounding the Guru were a number of poets who wrote in both Brajbhasha and Persian (the most prominent of whom was Nand Lal Goya) some of whom were most likely living while our mid-century authors were writing.[95] Within the extant court poetry of these men we often discover self-references and sobriquets as well as indications that they wrote specifically within the darbar of Guru Gobind Singh. On the eighteenth folio of his composition dealing with *ras*, the *Bhāv Panchāshikā* (Five Doctrines Regarding the [Poetic] Sentiments) for example the poet Brind (Vrnd) states that

Bhai Brind the poet composed a large number of poems in the [august] presence of Guru Gobind Singh.[96]

The poet Kuvaresh notes within his *Rati Rahass Kok* (The Secret of Love according to Koka), a Brajbhasha rendition of the famous *kāmashāstra* attributed to Pandit Koka (the *Koka-shāstra*):

May the poet Kuvresh always remain within the court (lit., *dvār* 'gate') of Guru Gobind.[97]

The stories of these poets and perhaps their poetry were most likely circulating among pious sangats in large part because of their proximity to their departed, beloved Guru (whom they regularly praise in their poetry).[98] It is the presence of these poets in particular (and the scribes and messengers we discover in both the hukam-namas and contemporary Sikh literature as well as the musicians—dhadhis and ragis—implied)[99] rather than the more observable symbols of regal courtliness which allows us to take the tenth Guru's possession of a formal court for granted.[100] Indeed, as is well known, since the eleventh century a court's grandeur (and thus its reputation) throughout the Islamicate was known for the poets in its employ.[101] This is probably the reason why the tenth Guru may have sought poets out and why his court is the best described in traditional Sikh history.

In this description we discover many of the personnel who were a part of the general courtly retinue of the Mughal darbars. In the narrative portions of his rahit-nama, for example, Chaupa Singh Chhibbar claims such status for many of his family members to demonstrate his household's intimate association with the darbar of the tenth Master. Although he mentions in passing service to the courts of the seventh and eighth Gurus[102] and more intimate ties with the court of the ninth Guru, he reserves his lengthiest praise for those Chhibbar Sikhs, himself included, who were in the courtly service of the tenth Guru:

[Guru Gobind Singh] commanded Sadhu Ram, a Sikh, to bring a robe of honour. Sahib Chand [Chhibbar] was draped [with this garment,] the Divan's siropa. Dharam Chand [Chhibbar then] received the siropa of stewardship and the treasury and both [Chhibbar brahmans] took to their duties. The Guru then had written instructions dispatched to the masands.[103]

We have here the office of the exchequer as well as the offices of the treasury and of the secretary. So too implied (and made explicit in line 174) are the scribes whose task it was to write down the Guru's instructions.[104] In eighteenth- and nineteenth-century Sikh accounts such as these it was not uncommon to observe warrior and scribal devotees stressing their undying loyalty to Guru Gobind Singh, their true padishah, whose concern for their welfare was simply undivided thus expressing 'the high profile codes of martial honour widely shared amongst specialist military communities [in Indo-Islamic northern India].'[105] We witness too the tenth Master himself lavishly awarding poets for a particularly clever composition in grand Indo-Timurid fashion. Santokh Singh, for example, whose own attempts to seek patronage from the courts of the various subordinate rajas under Ranjit Singh were at times limited or unsuccessful, claims that one of the tenth Master's court poets, Hans Ram Bajpei, himself refers to a reward he had received for versifying a portion of the great Sanskrit epic the Mahabharata:

[The poet] translated into the common language [from Sanskrit] the *Karna Parab* (Skt: *Parva*), the section [of the Mahabharata dealing with] Karna, [the son of Mother Kunti and the Sun God Surya]. [As] the versification took on a beautiful tempo the poet obtained a reward amounting to a hundred thousand [rupees]. Through the mercy of the Guru the poet Hans Ram [who] wrote the chapter was honoured.[106]

It is very likely that Santokh Singh had read a number of works produced at the Guru's court (many of which were not swept away in the

Sirsa River in 1705 as tradition claims) as the authors of a few of these do indeed mention in their introductions (*muddh*) gifts and rewards which the Guru had given to them. The prologue of Hans Ram's sammat 1752 (1696 CE) Brajbhasha translation or rendition of the *Karna Parba* which is referred to by Santokh Singh above, mentions the Guru's gifts in what we may assume is an overstated fashion,

Guru Gobind [Singh] first generously patronised [this poet] through his mercy and then rewarded [him] with sixty thousand [rupees].[107]

Comparing this passage with Santokh Singh's allows us to see first-hand the nineteenth-century author's further refinement in his version of events. This is, however, an embellishment which is quite justified in the light of the contemporary hyperbole we discover in the words of the tenth Master's court poet Mangal Rai, who in sammat 1753 (1697 CE) completed his translation of Book Nine of the Mahabharata, the *Shalya Parab*. We discover this passage in the epilogue to his translation:

The segment dealing with Shalya [the king of Madras slain by Yudhishthira] was translated into the common language [of Brajbhasha] during the rule of Guru Gobind. He gives abundantly huge amounts of money (*arab kharab*, lit., 'billions and trillions') in return for the poets' work.[108]

In more instances it seems that compensation for a poet's work was not monetary but rather material. Mangal Rai, Santokh Singh mentions, further claims that the tenth Guru 'satisfied his poets' with the gift of a Kashmiri shawl among other items:

To [the poets] Shyam, Set, and Piri Guru Gobind gifted an expensive [Kashmiri] shawl (*pāmarī*) which was yellow, red, and green in colour.[109]

The first two hemistiches within the prologue of the *Jang-nāmā Gurū Gobind Singh jī kā* written by the court poet Ani Rai (who is mentioned in both the hukam-namas of Guru Hari Krishan and Guru Tegh Bahadar),[110] moreover, tell us that

Ani Rai met with the Guru and he was blessed. 'Come' [the Guru] himself said and he rewarded [Ani Rai] greatly. The Guru gave [him] a stunning golden and jewel-embedded token and had a hukam-nama specially written [in which] he expressed a delightful affection towards him.[111]

From contemporary accounts such as these and traditional accounts mentioned earlier, we infer that the Sikh court of the tenth Master was clearly different from that of the Mughal emperors'. At the centre of the Sikh court was the one true spiritual king of the universe, an emperor who was not so concerned with impressing upon his courtiers 'the magnitude of imperial prestige and authority' the principal object behind Mughal courtly etiquette but rather the magnificence of the Divine.[112] This was perhaps why Mangal Rai can claim that the Guru distributes 'wealth amounting to the billions and trillions,' a clear exaggeration intented to impress upon readers and listeners that the gifts one principally received from the Guru were spiritual rather than material.[113] This was a court in which humble grass cutters (*ghāhī*) like Bhai Dhanna Singh could rival imperial poets in their erudition and versifications.[114] Such claims to uniqueness notwithstanding, the delineating practices of the Sikh darbar were nevertheless the very stuff of Islamicate courts: tradition notes, for example, that the Guru held *majālis* or 'poetic jousts', a regular pursuit of Indo-Islamic courts since the eleventh century. This was a characteristic of the Guru's court which was often lauded, as Piara Singh Padam makes clear:

One general feature [of the Guru's court] was the contest of a poet's dexterity (lit. 'contest of the poets' poetic art'). In order to demonstrate their excessive skill several poets experimented (*parakh karde*) with poems (*chhand*s) of many varieties while several [others] endeavoured to demonstrate these greater abilities in 'answering' (*javāb*) theirs [perhaps a reference to the modification of a poem by a 'rival' poet, a process known as *javāb* in Persian ghazal poetry].[115] Such [a development] is apparent for example in the poetic contest between [the proud poet] Chandan and [the humble grass cutter] Bhai Dhanna Singh.[116]

To this too we may add tradition's insistence that the Guru gave and received robes of honour; was treated and referred to as a king and master; gave audience to visiting dignitaries who included Bhim Chand, the raja of Bilaspur–Kahlur, as well as both Rajas Fateh Shah of Garhwal and Medini Prakash of Nahan–Sirmur—within whose districts was situated Paunta Sahib. The Guru also undertook various other courtly duties such as overseeing the majalis of his poets.[117] A glance through the surviving compositions of Guru Gobind Singh's many poets suggests that such courtly procedures were carefully observed. Indeed, one could argue that such images and practices associated with Islamicate courts in general persist well into modern-day Sikhism as the very gathering of Sikh sangats in a gurdwara, anywhere in the world, with its court-like ceremony is reminiscent of the Mughal darbar: entering the darbar and approaching the Guru Granth Sahib; prostrating oneself before the text[118] and presenting an offering, and finally sitting down before a throne-like dais called a *pālkī* (palanquin) under the canopy of which the Guru Granth Sahib is placed on a *manjī* while an attendant granthi waves a whisk over the sacred text.[119]

It is in part for these reasons that Sikh tradition makes a series of underlying assertions in regard to the Gurus' court, ones which may appear justified given the Persian Islamicate origins of Sikh courtly terminology, a vocabulary for example which includes certain key Sikh terms such as *khālsā* and *hukam* both of which had very strong Mughal court connotations.[120] One of these assertions which most studies on courtly societies make is that the court was an extension of the state (and vice versa) and as such possessed a stature and all-India importance affecting the very direction of Indian history.[121] Clearly this was not the case for a number of reasons. While the reach of the individuals who made up the Mughal court (including the emperor himself) was clearly vast, the Sikh court's sphere of influence was severely limited in many respects. Firstly, it could not affect or influence any non-Sikhs outside of its relatively small geographical sphere even when one takes into consideration the institution of the masands and their followers and the various building projects undertaken by the Gurus, details to which we shall return (one could argue that its effect even within this singular domain was not overwhelmingly strong, a point to which tradition itself tacitly agrees in its attention to detractors such as Prithi Chand, Dhir Mal, and Ram Rai). Secondly, it was very much subject to the outside force of Indo–Timurid Mughal power, a fact of which Guru Arjan and his successors were most certainly cognizant and which was, moreover, made dramatically manifest in both the Mughal executions of Guru Arjan and Guru Tegh Bahadar and in the Mughal attempt to decide the successor to the guruship in the late seventeenth century.[122] The nobles and emperor who made up the Mughal court were of course subject to no one and nothing outside of the norms and etiquettes through which they themselves constructed their own subjectivity. It was through their own coherent forms of 'sociability' that their self-identity was formulated.[123]

Despite the testimony of tradition, the Islamicate understanding of both the court and courtly culture on the part of Sikh poets and authors and indeed the Gurus should nevertheless elicit little surprise. The harsh tone towards most things Mughal that eighteenth-century Sikhs would adopt, demonstrates that it was the Persianized courts of the eastern Islamicate with which they and earlier Sikhs along with the greater part of northern India had been most familiar. This was by no means an intimate familiarity (it seems clear, for example that although seventeenth- and eighteenth-century Sikh writers may have had some passing acquaintance with such Mughal courtly phenomenon as 'devoted, familial hereditary service to the emperor' or *khānzādī* or just simply devoted service to the court and *javān-mardī* [lit. 'youngmanishness'] they were most certainly not privy to their detailed inner workings)[124] but rather a more general awareness of the Mughal court based on second-hand reports and gossip and long residence within northern India. This was most likely supplemented in the late sixteenth century when Guru Arjan (and perhaps Guru Amar Das earlier and Bhai Gurdas later) had met with the emperor Akbar. Since there is very little contemporary evidence regarding the courts of the first five Gurus, let us begin by turning our attention to these and setting them and later courts within their proper Indo-Islamic context.

NOTES

1. Guru Nanak, *Japjī* 4, Adi Granth, p. 2.
2. Background on the *Vidyā Sāgar* appears in Piara Singh Padam, *Srī Gurū Gobind Singh jī de Darbārī Ratan* (Patiala: New Patiala Printers, 1976), pp. 56–8. For concise articles on the Dasam Granth and the *Sarab-loh Granth* see Harbans Singh (ed.), The *Encyclopaedia of Sikhism* (Patiala: Punjabi University Press, 1992, 1998), I, pp. 514–31; IV, pp. 57–8. [Hereafter *EoS*]. Background on the contemporary Sikh canon appears in W.H. McLeod (ed. and trans.), *Textual Sources for the Study of Sikhism* (Manchester: Manchester University Press, 1984), pp. 38–70.
3. Padam, *Darbārī Ratan*, p. 23. For Padam this intent is both commensurate with, and an extension of the objective behind Guru Nanak's singing of

sacred hymns. See pp. 17–22. Padam also reproduces both brief excerpts from the more technical secular compositions of the Guru's poets, works on Brajbhasha prosody known as *pingal*s, works on diplomacy (*rājnīti*), and works on astrology (*sāmudrik-shāstra*). To this he adds passages from the encomiums of Nand Lal Goya (which we will discuss in Chapter 5), and a sizeable amount of the poetry of less martially inclined poets like Nanua Vairagi. All these counter the implication that the tenth Guru's poets produced only heroic verse. Padam explains (p. 82):

> It is known from his [Nanua's] bani that poets who wrote works manifesting the heroic sentiment were not the only such poets within Guru Gobind Singh's darbar. Indeed, there were also apparent tender, peaceful, and devotional poets like Nanua whose poetic compositions stressed matters spiritual and moral [rather than militant].

4. The number 52 is auspicious since it derives from the number of letters of the Devanagari alphabet in which classical Sanskrit is generally written. It is auspicious of course because both Sanskrit and Devanagari (literally, 'script fashioned in the city of the gods') possess divine origins according to Hindu traditions. Such allusions to the number 52 appear even within the Adi Granth (whose traditional script is not Devanagari but Gurmukhi) in compositions by both Guru Arjan and Kabir in *rāg gaurī* titled *Bāvan akharī* or 'The Fifty Two Letters' (Adi Granth, pp. 250–62; 340–3). Sewa Singh Kaushish's reference is an early one to which we may add Santokh Singh's:

> There were fifty two poets surrounding the Guru every one of whom brought bani to light.

and

> Within the Guru's court [lit., 'In the presence of the Guru'] there were 52 poets. They were always right by his side. Several of them came and went eulogising the Guru. In return for which they were rewarded (*len dhann rās*).

See online edition of Vir Singh (ed.), *Kavi Chūrāmani Bhāī Santokh Singh jī krit Srī Gur Pratāp Sūraj Granth* VII (Patiala: Bhasha Vibhag, Punjab, 1990), [Hereafter *SP*] 3:41:47, pp. 459; and 5:52:1, p. 498. The late eighteenth-century Sikh poet Sukha Singh also tells us that the tenth Master's court was staffed with a number of writers who were not poets:

> Near the Ocean of Mercy [Guru Gobind Singh] resided thirty six talented writers. That which the Guru ordered was written in both a grand and intelligent manner.

Gursharan Kaur Jaggi (ed.), *Gurbilās Pātishāhī Dasvīn* 17:12 (Patiala: Bhasha Vibhag, Punjab, 1989), pp. 250–1.

5. For the narrative of Kharag Singh see *Krishanavatār* 1370–1717, *Srī Dasam Gurū Granth Sāhib jī* (Amritsar: Bhai Chatar Singh Jivan Singh, 1988), pp. 434–73. A brief description of Kharag Singh appears in Kahn Singh Nabha, *Gur-shabad Ratanākar Mahān Kosh* (Patiala: Bhasha Vibhag Punjab, 1981), pp. 368, 370 [hereafter *MK*].

6. Garja Singh (ed.), *Shahīd-bilās (Bhāī Manī Singh) krit Sevā Singh* (Ludhiana: Punjabi Sahit Academy, 1961), canto 47, pp. 62–3. A history of Bhai Mani Singh appears in Garja Singh's text. A far more brief account may be found in *EoS* III, pp. 39–41.
7. The heroic style of writing and indeed singing begins, according to tradition, during the guruship of the sixth Master, Guru Hargobind. Recent research has shown, however, that is it more likely to have begun with Guru Arjan. See Pashaura Singh, *The Guru Granth Sahib: Canon, Meaning and Authority* (Delhi: Oxford University Press, 2000), pp. 208–10. For more on bir-ras in Sikh traditional history see Vir Singh's footnote marked with an asterisk in Santokh Singh's version of the construction of the Akal Takht. Vir Singh (ed.), *SP*, pp. 2403–4. Also see Dharampal Ashta, *The Poetry of the Dasam Granth* (New Delhi: Arun Prakashan, 1959), pp. 33 ff. The Sikh understanding of bir-ras develops principally from Sanskrit poetics in which the idea originates as *vīra-ras* as first expressed by Bharatamuni in his *Nātyashāstra* (circa 4th–6th century CE) to be later refined in Anandavardhana's *Dhvanyāloka* (9th century CE), though it is apparent that the development we see in both the poetry of the Guru's court and the Dasam Granth moves into slightly alternate directions commensurate with those being established in the early seventeenth century by Hindu writers of the same type of courtly Brajbhasha we find in the Dasam Granth. For Brajbhasha literature and courts of the seventeenth and eighteenth centuries see Allison Busch, 'The Anxiety of Innovation: The Poetic Practice of Literary Science in the Hindi/*Riti* Tradition', in *Comparative Studies of South Asia, Africa and the Middle East* 24:2 (2004), pp. 45–59. Background on the ras theory in Sanskrit poetics appears in Sushil Kumar De [with notes by Edwin Gerow], *Sanskrit Poetics as a Study of Aesthetic* (Berkeley: University of California Press, 1963), pp. 48–61. For vira-ras itself see the discussion in S.K. De, *History of Sanskrit Poetics* II (2 volumes in 1, second revised edition, Calcutta: Firma K.L. Mukhopadhyay, 1960), p. 273, n. 28.
8. Piara Singh Padam (ed.), *Gurū kīān Sākhīān krit Bhāī Svarūp Singh Kaushish* (2nd edn., Amritsar: Singh Bros., 1991), p. 91. That the tenth Guru enjoyed this work is attested to by the large number of Gurmukhi manuscripts of the *Hanuman Nātak*.
9. *MK*, pp. 1042–3 notes the eleven Rudras although Hanuman is not included amongst them.
10. *Das Gur Kathā* 232–3, Khalsa College ms. 1797A, f. 32. The importance of Hanuman to the nineteenth-century Panth may be divined from the fact that an image of this devoted servant of Lord Rama occassionally appeared on Sikh flags along with Shiva, Chandi, and Kartikya. W.H. McLeod, 'Reflections on the *Prem Sumārag*', in *Journal of Punjab Studies* 14:1 (Spring 2007), pp. 126, 132.

28 The Darbar of the Sikh Gurus

11. The passage within the Dasam Granth to which all Sikh commentators allude to support this point appears in the *Krishanavatār* 2491 (Dasam Granth, p. 570):

> The tenth story of the Lord has been written in the common tongue for no purpose other than [inspiring] righteous battle.

See for example Padam, *Darbārī Ratan*, p. 23 and Grewal and Bal, *Guru Gobind Singh: A Biographical Study* (Chandigarh: Panjab University Press, 1967), p. 77.

12. See online *SP* 4:2:50, p. 379. A significant portion of the entire chapter or *ansū* (50:1–43, pp. 379–85) deals with the attempt to strengthen oppressed Hindus with the various poetic sentiments.

13. See Padam, *Darbārī Ratan*, pp. 33–4. Padam easily explains away the existence of courtly literature which does indeed praise the tenth Guru (*gur-ustati*), much of which he supplies in Part Two of his text:

> ...but this praise was only insofar as the Guru was the leader of a singular revolution, [a leader] who certainly empowered the movement for the public good.

Darbārī Ratan, p. 37. Some of this gur-ustati literature will be noted later.

14. Padam, *Darbārī Ratan*, p. 34. Aurangzeb certainly lacked such conceit, Padam explains, but his deficiency in this regard was made up by his contempt for such 'delicate arts' (*komal kalā*). Because of Aurangzeb's reputation for tyranny, moreover, Padam to a certain extent excuses the seventeenth-century Rajput rulers of western India for not implementing a literary scheme as progressive as the Guru's. He claims (p. 35):

> In the state of affairs [engendered by Aurangzeb's destruction of Hindu temples] how could a poet become a revolutionary?

Padam's view of Mughal 'courtly' literature conforms to many of the misconceptions which often equate Persian courtly literature with 'artificial, lush, and over-ingenious' tastes. A critique of these misreadings appears as Julie Scott Meisami, *Medieval Persian Court Poetry* (Princeton: Princeton University Press, 1987), pp. viii–ix, 11–13.

15. Padam's *Darbārī Ratan* as noted focusses principally upon the poets of the Guru's court, their works, and what we may crudely call the court's literary life, poetic jousts (Persian: majālis) and the like. He may thus be excused for failing to describe other than very briefly non-literary aspects of courtly life such as comportment. Indeed, as we will note scholars of Sikhism have never delineated how the Gurus and their contemporaries understood the idea of the court nor what membership to the Sikh court actually entailed. Padam's work in this regard therefore captures the general trajectory of scholarly literature dealing with the court of the tenth Guru, a literature which is likewise generally silent on courtly life outside of the literary. One assumes that Sikh studies on the subject simply take for granted the belief that other Sikhs of the court, particularly its later Khalsa component, manifested the ideals and values on which the poets

The Sikh Darbar 29

and writers of the darbar dwelled. Padam like most scholars tacitly notes that there is a missing dimension in his study of the court specifically by dividing the darbar of the tenth Guru into two portions:
> The Guru's court at Anandpur was the central location for both those who wielded the sword (*shastrdhārī*) and those who wielded the words of divine authority (*shāstrdhārī*) [warriors and poets].

Piara Singh Padam, *Darbārī Ratan*, p. 33. The double classification is reminiscent of one we discover in the famous Persian text written in 1235 CE, the *Akhlaq-i Nasirī* (The Ethics of Nasir) of Nasiruddin Tusi, who based on earlier precedents recognized in the third section of his Third Discourse the *ahl-i qalam* (men of the pen) and the *ahl-i saif* (men of the sword) along with 'men of negotiation' (*ahl-i mu'āmlah*) and 'men of husbandry' (*ahl-i muhāl*). G.M. Wickens (trans.), *The Nasirean Ethics* (London: George Allen and Unwin Ltd., 1964), p. 230. A contemporary reading representative of the dominant 'literary' understanding of the Guru's court is Gurinder Singh Mann, *Sikhism* (New Jersey: Prentice Hall, 2004), pp. 75–7.

16. One could argue as a counterpoint that Padam and Sikh tradition generally seem to deny the very Sikhs they praise agency, laying that power at literature's door (a denial which seems commensurate with the Sanskritic understanding of the sentiments or rasas for which one may consult Edwin Gerow's masterful treatment in his *Indian Poetics* [Wiesbaden: Otto Harrassowitz, 1977], pp. 245–58). This may then account for the negative judgement of the whole of the Mughal court: Mughal courtly literature was of a vain variety *ergo* the Mughals themselves and their courts were self-centred and arrogant. Such reproach however misguided notwithstanding it is the symbols and styles of the Mughal court which Sikhs welcomed.

17. Tradition claims the possession of these items engendered an infamous envy within the hearts of the Hill Rajas neighbouring Guru Gobind Singh's Anandpur which led to the early battles described in the *Bachitar Nātak*. M.A. Macauliffe, *The Sikh Religion: Its Gurus, Sacred Writings and Authors* vol. 5 (Oxford: Clarendon Press, 1909), pp. 5, 8. For the tent as a symbol of royalty see P.A. Andrews, 'The Tents of Timur: An Examination of Reports on the Quriltay at Samarqand, 1404', in Philip Denwood (ed.), *Arts of the Eurasian Steppelands* (London: SOAS, 1977), pp. 143–88; esp. p. 144 and his fascinating *Felt Tents and Pavilions: The Nomadic Tradition and its Interaction with Princely Tentage* 2 volumes (London: Melisende, 1999), especially volume 2, pp. 847–1286. Also Dominic P. Brookshaw, 'Palaces, Pavilions and Pleasure-gardens: the Context and Setting of the Medieval *Majlis*', in *Middle Eastern Literatures* 6:2 (July 2003), p. 204. Background on the kettledrum appears in Bonnie Wade, *Imaging Sound: An Ethnomusicological Study of Music, Art, and Culture in Mughal India* (Chicago and London: University of Chicago Press, 1998), pp. 129–30; Khwandamir, *Qanun-i-Humayuni* (Also known as *Humayun Nama*), Baini Prashad (trans.) (rpt, Calcutta: The Asiatic Society, 1966), pp. 27, 82; and

Khaliq Ahmad Nizami, *Royalty in Medieval India* (Delhi: Munshiram Manoharlal, 1997), p. 54.

18. In another of his hukam-nāmās Guru Tegh Bahadar himself wrote sometime in the 1660s that he had sent a robe of honour to Bhai Dayal Das and the sangat of Patna for the service and money they had donated to the celebrations of the future Guru Gobind Singh's birth. S.S. Sagar, *Hukamnamas of Guru Tegh Bahadur: A Historical Study* (Amritsar: Guru Nanak Dev University Press, 2002), pp. 90–1 (Pbi.); p. 128 (Eng.).

19. The best reference on such Mughal standards remains J.F. Richards, 'Norms of Comportment among Imperial Mughal Officials', in Barbara D. Metcalf (ed.), *Moral Conduct and Authority* (Berkeley: University of California Press, 1984), pp. 257–89. For Timurid arts and royal symbols see Thomas W. Lentz and Glenn D. Lowry, *Timur and the Princely Vision: Persian Art and Culture in the Fifteenth Century* (Los Angeles: Los Angeles County Museum of Art, 1989). Among many of the important features and symbols of the imperial Mughal court that the Sikh court of Guru Gobind Singh's period did not acknowledge, however, were the minting of coins in the ruler's name (*sikkah*, 'casting') and the possession of a harem. Another though far less significant was the Guru's rejection of _khutbah_ or the sermon read in the name of the emperor for obvious reasons while another still was portraiture.

20. These Sikh authors however were most likely familiar with famous Islamicate literature, particularly poetry. These texts would include the *Dīvān* of Hafez, the works of Shaikh Sa'di (to which the author of the *Zafar-nāmah* alludes), the *Shāh-nāmah* and Rumi's famous mathnavi amongst others. Works by the poets of the Mughal court, however, were most likely unknown although the *Zafar-nāmah* (The Epistle of Victory) attributed to the tenth Guru may tacitly criticize some aspects of this literature. See Chapter 4.

21. For background on ms. 1245 see Pashaura Singh, *The Guru Granth Sahib*, pp. 41–53.

22. Qur'an 24:35 for example explicitly compares the two.

23. The quote is found in the *Ā'īn-i Akbarī* of the famous Abu'l Fazl 'Allami (d. 1011/1602). Milo C. Beach and Ebba Koch, *King of the World: the Padshahmana, an Imperial Manuscript from the Royal Library, Windsor Castle* [trans., Wheeler Thackston] (London: Azimuth Editions, Sackler Gallery, 1997), p. 24.

24. Shamsas were not the only styles that Sikh manuscriptists adopted. So too did they utilize the '*unvān*, the highly ornate blue and gold Islamicate lettering technique. Jeevan Singh Deol, 'Illustration and Illumination in Sikh Scriptural Manuscripts', in Kavita Singh (ed.), *New Insights into Sikh Art* 54:4 (Mumbai: Marg, 2003), p. 53. Interestingly, the beautiful floral spray which appears on the first folio of the Lahore recension manuscript found in Deol's 'Illustration', p. 50 is reminiscent of a Mughal stylistic technique

which came into vogue during the reign of Shah Jahan (d. 1666 CE). Although this technique originated with and on textiles it was eventually incorporated by the artists of the royal atelier into Mughal miniatures and manuscript decoration. See Rebecca Wells Corrie, 'The Paisley', in *The Kashmir Shawl* (New Haven: Yale University Art Gallery, 1975), pp. 24–51, esp. p. 27. According to Corrie, the floral ornamentation of textiles became 'increasingly stylized' throughout the eighteenth century after the death of Shah Jahan (p. 24). Also see Pashaura Singh, *The Guru Granth Sahib*, pp. 41–2; and Yves Porter, *Painters, Paintings and Books: An Essay on Indo-Persian Technical Literature 12–19th Centuries* (trans. S. Butani) (Delhi: Manohar, 1994). Beautiful shamsas appear in the *Padshāhnāmah* manuscript found in the Royal Library at Windsor Castle. Beach and Koch, *King of the World*, pp. 14, 22–3. As Akal Purakh is often likened to a divine light (*joti*) such symbols may prefigure the later Sikh idea of Guru Granth. Such Islamicate influence dwindled considerably by the late eighteenth century. Pashaura Singh's claim that Sikh scribes self-consciously rejected such Islamicate styles of manuscript preparation (assuming those scribes understood such style as 'Islamic' or 'Islamicate') in the early seventeenth century as a result of Guru Arjan's execution by Mughal/Islamic/Islamicate authorities is therefore questionable. Pashaura Singh, *Life and Work of Guru Arjan* (New Delhi: Oxford University Press, 2006), pp. 113, 138.

25. This painting appears as a black and white reproduction in Gurinder Singh Mann, *Sikhism*, p. 43 from which I received the date 1700 CE. It also appears in *Darbārī Ratan*, p. 13. I would like to thank Dr. Mann for sharing his copy of the colour portrait with me. Background on Sikh art appears in Hew McLeod's delightful *Popular Sikh Art* (New Delhi: Oxford University Press, 1991). Other similar images of the tenth Guru may be seen in W.G. Archer's *Paintings of the Sikhs* (London: Her Majesty's Stationery Office, 1966) figure 7, p. 198. This *c.* 1830 CE image has an attendant running behind the Guru on horseback while holding the chhatri over the Guru's head. An Islamicate-style angel in Guler-style clothing fans the Guru with both a yak-tail and peacock-feather whisk while two hunting dogs keep pace.

26. See as example Surjit Hans, *B-40 Janamsakhi Guru Baba Nanak Paintings* (Amritsar: Guru Nanak Dev University Press, 1987).

27. This too is an early eighteenth-century Sikh painting titled 'Guru Govind Singh Encounters Guru Nanak' and is taken from Archer's *Indian Paintings from the Punjab Hills: A Survey and History of Pahari Miniature Painting* II (Delhi: Oxford University Press, 1973), p. 264. The style here is an example of a painting within the Mandi atelier which is far less Mughalized.

28. The two years between the establishment of the Khalsa and the first siege of Anandpur in 1701 by the forces of Bhim Chand the Raja of Bilaspur-Kahlur was an 'extended interval of peace' during which Guru Gobind Singh was 'left to consolidate his new position.' Grewal and Bal,

32 The Darbar of the Sikh Gurus

      Guru Gobind Singh, p. 128. Sainapati moreover tells us of two years of relative calm after the first battle of Anandpur and its evacuation (1702–4). Ganda Singh (ed.), *Kavī Saināpati Rachit Srī Gur-Sobhā* (Patiala: Punjabi University Press, 1987), 11:1–4, p. 116.

29. This style of jewellery-making is discussed in Manuel Keene, 'The *Kundan* Technique: the Indian Jeweller's Unique Artistic Treasure', in Rosemary Crill *et al.* (ed.), *Arts of Mughal India: Studies in Honour of Robert Skelton* (London, New York, Ahmedabad: Victoria and Albert Museum and Mapin Publishing, 2004), pp. 191–202, especially Fig. 1 which portrays a similarly styled katar.

30. The temple token here is in my personal collection. The right side with Guru Nanak, Mardana, and Bala is the obverse while the left side is the reverse. The latter has the date sammat 1804 or 1747 CE. To the left and right of the tenth Guru's haloed head on the reverse side are the words *sat kartār* or The Creator is Truth in Devanagari script. The similarity between the image of the Guru on the reverse and Fig. 1 suggests that the painting of Guru Gobind Singh and his attendant may well have provided the template for such token and other numismatic renderings. Other temple token images appear in Hans Herrli, *The Coins of the Sikhs* (Nagpur: Indian Coin Society, 1993), pp. 237–8; and Irwin F. Brotman, *A Guide to the Temple Tokens of India* (Los Angeles: Shamrock Press, 1970), pp. 142–53. Unfortunately, neither of these texts mentions the purpose of such tokens. Surinder Singh claims that these tokens were the Sikh equivalent of religious medallions, 'passed on to a pilgrim for a few rupees…[the purchase of which] may [have been] an act of religious devotion….' Surinder Singh, *Sikh Coinage: Symbol of Sikh Sovereignty* (Delhi: Manohar, 2004), pp. 201–4. This is certainly plausible though it is also likely that such temple tokens were bought at gurdwaras and could be exchanged for karah prashad which Sikhs queuing to take darshan of the Guru Granth Sahib would place into the common cauldron (*degh*)—shown below Guru Nanak on the obverse—in the Prakash Asthan, an exercise which still exists at the Golden Temple. Herrli claims that this token may have been cast in this year to commemorate the invasion of Ahmad Shah Durrani. I find this difficult to imagine when one considers the sheer destruction the Dur-i Durrani perpetrated throughout the Punjab, especially his involvement in the Chhota Ghalughara or Lesser Massacre of Sikhs. Herrli, *The Coins of the Sikhs*, p. 238. Surinder Singh has conjectured that the date 1804 cast here may simply be fictitious. Surinder Singh, *Sikh Coinage*, p. 206.

31. Catherine Glynn's 'Early Painting in Mandi', *Articus Asiae* XLIV:1 (1983), pp. 21–64, esp. pp. 23–4. Note, incidentally, that at least two later rahit-namas insisted that Sikhs fasten their jamahs at the front rather than at the side since the authors of these texts probably considered side-fastening a Muslim proclivity. The author of the rahit-nama attributed to Chaupa Singh Chhibbar for example tacitly makes this point in the late 1740s:

The Kesdhari [Sikh] who fastens his jamah at the side is worthy of punishment.
W.H. McLeod (ed.), *The Chaupa Singh Rahit-Nama* (Dunedin, New Zealand: University of Otago Press, 1987), line 380, pp. 104, 180. [Hereafter *CSRn*]. The other rahit-nama is the *Prem Sumārag* as McLeod notes in *CSRn*, p. 236.

32. I should note immediately that I have not seen the original portrait nor do I know where the original resides. Nor alas am I privy to information regarding the painter, the patron, nor their relationship if any. A number of stylistic features suggest however that this painting was most strongly influenced by the styles of the Mandi and possibly Bilaspur–Kahlur ateliers, perhaps painted by an artist from within one of these Pahari workshops who was a Mughal or received his training under the Mughals. The Mandi atelier seems the more likely origin since within this hill principality the Sikh Gurus, especially Guru Gobind Singh, were highly respected while generally within Bilaspur–Kahlur they were not. The jade-apple green background framing the Guru, the sky of blue and lapis lazuli-blue cloud formations all suggest this as these colours and the shape of these clouds were often used in Pahari painting from this region according to both Catherine Glynn's 'Early Painting in Mandi', pp. 55, 58, 60, 61; and her 'Further Evidence for Early Painting at Mandi', *Articus Asiae* LV:1/2 (1995), pp. 183–90, esp. p. 189. So too does the turban style (which was most likely adopted by Pahari painters after 1630 CE) and perhaps the fact that the dot pattern on the Guru's *jāmah* is the same as that found on the carpet upon which he sits [the latter feature is noted in Catherine Glynn, 'Mughalized Portraits of Bilaspur Royalty in the Second Half of the Seventeenth Century,' in Rosemary Crill *et al.* (ed.), *Arts of Mughal India*, p. 241]. Finally the textile design on the cushion is reminiscent of later Pahari paintings dealing with the Sikh Gurus. See for example the cushions in figures 6, 7, 8, 9, 11 in B.N Goswamy, 'A Matter of Taste: Some Notes on the Context of Painting in Sikh Punjab', in *Mārg: Appreciation of Creative Arts under Maharaja Ranjit Singh* (December 1980), pp. 45–62. There is a great deal of scholarship on the Pahari Schools of painting. A brief reference to the most famous works from the Pahari ateliers is Milo Cleveland Beach, *Mughal and Rajput Painting* (Cambridge: Cambridge University Press, 1992), pp. 168 ff., 190 ff. Pahari Rajput-style turbans appear in every figure referenced in Catherine Glynn, 'Mughalized Portraits', pp. 234–47. Also see the 1730 CE painting of Raja Medini Pal of Basohli in Beach, *Mughal and Rajput Painting*, p. 201. If this is indeed an early Sikh painting from Mandi as I believe this would bring into question W.G. Archer's claim that 'in no other styles of painting in the Punjab Hills does this subject [i.e. Sikhism or the Sikh Gurus] occur until the nineteenth century and then only in Guler.' W.G. Archer, *Indian Paintings from the Punjab Hills*, p. 354. For Guler portraits, see Roy C. Craven, Jr.,

'The Reign of Raja Dalip Singh (1695–1741) and the Siege of Lanka Series of Guler', in *Mārg: Ramayana: Paintings from the Hills* (September 1990), pp. 4–56. Sikh Pahari paintings from the janam-sakhis are noted in Dalbir Singh Dhillon, 'Development of Illustration on the Sikh Sacred Writings', in *Punjab History Conference, Sixteenth Session, March 12–14, 1982, Proceedings* (Patiala: Punjabi University, 1982), pp. 156–61.

33. Catherine Glynn, 'Mughalized Portraits of Bilaspur Royalty.'
34. Milo Cleveland Beach, *Mughal and Rajput Painting*, p. 82.
35. For the use of colour by Mughal artists near the end of Akbar's reign see Linda York Leach, 'Pages from an *Akbarnama*', in Rosemary Crill *et al.* (eds), *Arts of Mughal India*, p. 51.
36. Rather difficult to make out the yellowish design is a triangular pattern of five yellow dots strung together with a very slender thread of yellow. This same pattern though with blue dots appears on the carpet (perhaps a jājim) on which the Guru sits.
37. See Catherine Glynn, 'A Rājasthānī Princely Album: Rājput Patronage of Mughal-Style Painting', in *Articus Asiae* LX: 3/4 (2001), p. 224.
38. *Bachitar Nātak* 1:1, Dasam Granth, p. 39:
    I salute the sword (kharag) with my whole being and invoke you to assist me in completing this text.

    There is little more that can be said about this portrait. It is most likely unique for it seems to me that although Guru Gobind Singh most likely possessed a *kitab-khānah* (perhaps the same *pothī mahal* referred to in the janam-sakhis, a place at which the Gurus kept written collections of bani) it seems unlikely that the same could be said of a *tasvīr-khānah* or painting workshop as it is quite likely that the Guru would have realized the potential for self-aggrandizement which such portraits as seen here imply. The simple fact that there is no contemporary evidence to suggest the existence of a coterie of painters within the Guru's court seems to support such a conclusion.
39. Catherine Glynn, 'Mughalized Portraits of Bilaspur Royalty in the Second Half of the Seventeenth Century', p. 235. This would also hold true of Mughal images themselves. Images of Maharaja Bhim Chand at times Guru Gobind Singh's nemesis while at others an ally, appear on pp. 237, 240. It is difficult to say whether the artists who painted such images were influenced by Mughal portraiture directly or by Mughalized paintings of Rajput figures by Pahari artists. If the latter is true then this may perhaps be an example of the 'rajputization' of the Guru although this pithy term must be questioned in the light of the debt Rajput iconography has to Indo-Timurid styles. For the idea of Sikh 'rajputization' see Doris Jakobsh, *Relocating Gender in Sikh History: Transformation, Meaning and Identity* (New Delhi: Oxford University Press, 2003), pp. 221, 236, n. 8. For the effects and ramifications of rajputization amongst Rajputs themselves see Dirk H.A. Kolff, *Naukar, Rajput and Sepoy: The Ethnohistory of the Military Labour*

Market in Hindustan, 1450–1850 (Cambridge: Cambridge University Press, 1990), pp. 69–74; 117–58.

40. This image is taken from Ajit Singh Baagha, *Banur Had Orders* (Delhi: Ranjit Printers and Publishers, 1969), p. 84. Although Baagha dates it to 1698 CE its stylistic features suggest a date of c. 1720–30 CE. Compare it for example to figure 33 in Catherine Glynn, 'Early Painting in Mandi.' The shields held by the courtiers and attendants are similar to those carried by Raja Shyam Singh's attendants as too are the turban styles and the plumes in the turban of Shyam Singh and those lodged on the top of the turbans of the Guru and his sons. Also see Catherine Glynn, 'A Rājasthānī Princely Album', pp. 222–64; and her 'Mughalized Portraits', pp. 235–47, esp. pp. 245–6. A similar portrait, this typically Guler style shows the Guru in portrait while the whisking attendant is portrayed in three quarters. It appears opposite the title page of Grewal and Bal, *Guru Gobind Singh*. For Rajputs paintings of the Pahari region see Milo C. Beach, *Mughal and Rajput Painting*, pp. 168 ff., 190 ff and the now-classic work of W.G. Archer, *Indian Paintings from the Punjab Hills*.

41. Vishakai N. Desai, 'Painting and Politics in Seventeenth-Century North India: Mewār, Bikāner, and the Mughal Court', in *Art Journal: New Approaches to South Asian Art* 49:4 (Winter, 1990), p. 371.

42. This basically holds true of all the Sikh literature prepared in the eighteenth and nineteenth centuries. I do not mean to suggest that the Sikhs adopted the Persian language as their courtly language but rather adopted certain Persian words which had become loans even before the writing of the hymns of the Adi Granth. Certainly the Persian language played a role in this Sikh courtly culture as the works of Bhai Nand Lal Goya will make clear.

43. Grewal and Bal, *Guru Gobind Singh*, pp. 109–10. The *Bachitar Nātak* appears at Dasam Granth, pp. 39–73. Guru Gobind Singh's familiarity with these symbols may be discerned from the many writings attributed to him.

44. This concern with lineage appears in numerous eighteenth-century accounts. For the gurpranali see Randir Singh (ed.), *Bābānī Pīrhī Chalī Guru-Pranālīān* (Amritsar: Shiromani Gurdwara Prabandhak Committee [Hereafter *SGPC*] 1964) and *EoS* II, pp. 191–4. Also Piara Singh Padam (ed.), *Bhāī Kesar Singh Chhibbar krit Bansāvalīnāmā Dasān Pātshāhīān kā* (Amritsar: Singh Brothers, 1997). [Hereafter *BSVN*].

45. I do not mean to suggest that such standards of comportment were static throughout this hundred year period. Indeed, with the emergence of a more complex stratified urban society in the late seventeenth century new nuances were added to older meanings. A discussion of one such, the standard of 'manliness', appears in Rosalind O'Hanlon's 'Manliness and Imperial Service in Mughal North India,' in the *Journal of the Economic and Social History of the Orient* 42:1 (1999), pp. 47–93.

46. Stewart Gordon interprets such assimilation on the part of Indian rulers of the South Asian Islamicate rather differently, but with the same ultimate

conclusion. See his discussion of the robing ceremony as a 'meta-language' in Stewart Gordon, 'Introduction: Ibn Battuta and a Region of Robing', in Stewart Gordon (ed.), *Robes of Honour: Khil'at in Pre-Colonial and Colonial India* (New Delhi: Oxford University Press, 2003), pp. 23–5.
47. Sumit Guha, 'Transitions and Translations: Regional Power and Vernacular Identity in the Dakhan, 1500–1800', in *Comparative Studies of South Asia, Africa and the Middle East* 24:2 (2004), pp. 23–31, esp. p. 26. He makes this observation in regard to the Baghul kingdom in northern Maharashtra which ultimately failed as a result of its close assimilation with the Mughal court. Background in Sumit Guha, *Environment and Ethnicity in India c. 1200–1900* (Cambridge: Cambridge University Press, 1999).
48. Daud Ali, *Courtly Culture and Political Life in Early Medieval India* (Cambridge: Cambridge University Press, 2004), p. 5.
49. This is despite the fact that Bhimsen's text (also known as *Nuskhah-'i Dil-kushā* [The Exhilarating Sourcebook]) makes a brief and passing reference to Guru Gobind Singh just prior to the latter's death in Nander. In this reference the existence of a court is implied, but not made explicit (clearly the tenth Guru as we shall see did possess a court). A translation of the relevant portion of Bhimsen's text appears in J.S. Grewal and Irfan Habib (eds), *Sikh History from Persian Sources: Translations of Major Texts* (New Delhi: Tulika, 2001), pp. 104–5. A partial English translation of the text appears as Bhimsen Burhanpuri, *Nuskha-i Dilkusha* [Jadunath Sarkar (trans.)] in V.G. Khobrekar (ed.), *Sir Jadunath Sarkar Birth Centenary Commemoration Volume: English Translation of Tārīkh-i Dilkasha (Memoirs of Bhimsen Relating to Aurangzeb's Deccan Campaigns)* (Bombay: Maharashtra State Archives, 1972). John Richards has analysed this text's references to the comportment of Mughal court personnel in his 'Norms of Comportment Among Imperial Mughal Officers', pp. 270 ff. As Richards notes, Bhimsen though a Hindu, was a Mughal deputy and an officer in the court of the Rajput Dalpat Rao Bundela, and as such thought of and referred to himself as a khanzada.
50. Aziz Ahmad, 'The British Museum Mirzānāma and the Seventeenth Century Mirzā in India', in *Iran: Journal of the British Institute of Persian Studies* 13 (1975), pp. 99–110. The idea of *mirzā'ī* upon which these texts elaborate means 'gentlemanliness' or 'gentility'. The 'manly' dimensions of Delhi Sultanate and Mughal court life which is in part brought out in the *Mirzā-nāmah* texts is examined in Rosalind O'Hanlon's 'Manliness and Imperial Service in Mughal North India', pp. 70–84.
51. As such the Rahit believed prescribed by Guru Gobind Singh was open to manipulation by later Sikh authors as is evinced in the rahit-namas. Nripinder Singh speaks of the eighteenth-century rahit literature as a refinement literature along the lines of the earlier Dharmashastras of the Hindu tradition. See Nripinder Singh, *The Sikh Moral Tradition* (Columbia, MO: South Asia Books, 1990), pp. 102–208.

52. See for example W.H. McLeod, 'The Meaning of "Sant" in Sikh Usage', in Karine Schomer and W.H. McLeod (ed.), *The Sants: Studies in a Devotional Tradition* (New Delhi: Berkeley Religious Studies Series and Motilal Banarsidass, 1987), pp. 251–64; and Daniel Gold, *The Lord as Guru: Hindi Sants in the Northern Indian Tradition* (New York: Oxford University Press, 1987). The only bibiji with whom I am familiar is a Sikhni known as Mata Dev ji whose residence is close to the wonderful Sri Guru Nanak Dev ji Gurdwara at Manikaran Sahib, Himachal Pradesh. I should add that the vast majority of these sants do not confuse their positions with those of the traditional Sikh Gurus.
53. Notwithstanding the existence of the *pakkhāwalā* in the courtly image of Guru Gobind Singh noted earlier. The Persian and Persianite term darbār also carries both connotations.
54. Norbert Elias, *The Court Society* (trans. Edmund Jephcott) (Oxford: Basil Blackwell, 1983), pp. 1, 80.
55. The Indo-Timurid Mughal court was tied to, and at the apex of a number of courtly societies within later Indo-Islamic India. Around the person of the emperor there were lesser courtiers (the emperor was after all the ultimate courtier) known as the *umara'* (sing. *amīr*) who were bound to the emperor through their hereditary service to the court and by the wealth of their families. These court personnel claimed to have a voice in the governing of the empire and as such may be referred to as nobles. The court was also made up of a number of officials or lesser nobles who had no say as to governance. These personnel were court chroniclers, scribes, advisors, musicians, attendants and so on concerned with broadcasting the power and authority of the emperor and those nobles close to him. They too were part of a court nobility but of a much less influential sort. Under the Mughal emperors since the time of Akbar a noble's status was reflected in the military ranking granted him by the emperor, his *mansab*, which was divided into the number of footsoldiers and cavalrymen and horses he could supply at any given instant. The higher the number the greater the noble's status at the Mughal court. The highest numbers were reserved for Mughal princes (with rare exceptions) though even scribes were sometimes possessed of a small mansab. A more detailed explanation of the mansab, the mansabdar and the nobility appears in M. Athar Ali, *The Mughal Nobility Under Aurangzeb* (London: Asia Publishing House, 1966), pp. 32–68.
56. Vir Singh (ed.), *Srī Gurū Granth Sāhib jī dī Kunjī: Vārān Bhāī Gurdās Satīk Bhāv Prakāshanī Tīkā Samet Mukammal* (New Delhi: Bhai Vir Singh Sahit Sadan, 1997), var 6, pauri 12, lines 1–3 [i.e. 6:12:1-3], p. 106 [Hereafter *BG*]. The text of line three has *tān* while Vir Singh's notes indicate *tāl*. The latter is correct.
57. Daud Ali alludes to such ambiguity in his *Courtly Culture and Political Life in Early Medieval India*, pp. 237–41. Sikh views on sevā are quite

38 The Darbar of the Sikh Gurus

straightforward. Guru Nanak claims this in his *Sirī rāg* 3–4 (33), Adi Granth, pp. 25–6:
> [When] the sacred utterance permeates the body one finds joy performing selfless service. All the world transmigrates yet doing selfless service in its midst one shall be given a place [of honour] in the Lord's Court. Says Nanak, swing your arms [about] in joy.

58. Guru Nanak, *Sirī rāg* 3 (18), Adi Granth, p. 21.
59. In his own way Piara Singh Padam implies this in his discussion regarding the traditional 52 poets surrounding the Guru:
> In history books dealing with the Sikhs the number of poets placed within the darbar at Anandpur is given as 52 while that of writers is placed at 36. But this does not mean that there were *only* 52 poets in the darbar of the True Gurus. In many cases poets came and poets went so that their [overall] numbers would at times increase and at others decrease. At certain times there would be 52 poets residing [with the Guru]...

Piara Singh Padam, *Darbārī Ratan*, pp. 44–5. A short list of characteristics to be cultivated by the courtier of Indic-period courts appears in Daud Ali's *Courtly Culture*, pp. 76–7.
60. Pashaura Singh details these inclusivist Sikh principles in his *Guru Granth Sahib*, pp. 167–74. The feminine dimension of this inclusivity is underscored convincingly in Nikky-Guninder Kaur Singh's *The Birth of the Khalsa: A Feminist Re-Memory of Sikh Identity* (Albany: State University of New York Press, 2005), pp. 35–67.
61. One could argue that the *banā* or dress (also *bastar*) of the Khalsa eventually did become a criterion for inclusion. The existence of non-Khalsa Sikhs in Guru Gobind Singh's court, however, suggests that it did not.
62. These external factors were meant to manifest internal qualities such as knowledge of the world outside of India and gentility. See Daud Ali, *Courtly Culture and Political Life* and Rosalind O'Hanlon, 'Manliness and Imperial Service,' pp. 68, 69, 70 ff.
63. Guru Nanak, *Sirī rāg* 2 (4), Adi Granth, p. 15 for example. Also *Sirī rāg* 3 (6), Adi Granth, p. 16 may be further cited as representative of Guru Nanak's derisive view of the splendours which he notes again in his *Sirī rāg* compositions (Adi Granth, pp. 14–26):
> Some come while others arise and depart. Some take on [lofty] names such as Salar [i.e. Sultan Salar Masud 'Ghazi Miyan' of Bahraich]. Some are born beggars, and some hold vast courts (*darvār*). Departing for the next world everyone will know that all such things are worthless without the [True] Name.

64. *Kabitt* 246 in Onkar Singh, *Kabitt Savaiye Bhāī Gurdās: Pāth, Tuk-Tatkarā, Anukramnikā ate Kosh* (Patiala: Punjabi University Press, 1993), p. 64. See also kabitt 46, p. 13 which ends:
> Within this court (*sabhā*) all riches and all treasuries exist; it is the abode of bliss possessed of a wonderful fragrance and the most brilliant beauty

effulgent, all of which pervade the world. Its maxims and manners are love which makes all of its subjects joyous. Its intentions are all fulfilled and its success in all matters assured.

65. Guru Nanak, *Mārū solhe* 10(8), Adi Granth, p. 1028.
66. M. Athar Ali, *The Mughal Nobility*, pp. 11–33. Also Douglas Streusand, *The Formation of the Mughal Empire* (New Delhi: Oxford University Press, 1989), pp. 123–53; Rosalind O'Hanlon, 'Manliness and Imperial Service', p. 61; and, by implication, Linda T. Darling, '"Do Justice, Do Justice, For That is Paradise": Middle Eastern Advice for Indian Muslim Rulers', in *Comparative Studies of South Asia, Africa and the Middle East* 22.1–2 (2002) 3–19, p. 10.
67. *BG* 11:13–31, pp. 182–96. Legendary narratives of the individual Sikhs mentioned in var 11 appear in Tarlochan Singh Bedi (ed.), *Sikhān dī Bhagatmālā* (Patiala: Punjabi University Publication Bureau, 1994) [Hereafter *SBM*]. This text is attributed to Bhai Mani Singh.
68. We also discover the theme of *sevā* and altruism within Bhai Gurdas' less popular kabitts. See kabitt 103 and 295 for example in Onkar Singh (ed.), *Kabitt Savaiye Bhāī Gurdās*, pp. 28, 76.
69. It is therefore not surprising that according to tradition Bhai Mani Singh produced a text detailing the lives of the many Sikhs mentioned in var 11, the *Sikhān dī Bhagat-mālā*. One is here reminded of Norbert Elias' ideas that the values of the court ultimately trickled down to society in general. See his *Court Society*.
70. Daud Ali makes the claim in regard to Classical Indian courts generally that the activities of the court in fact were the activities of the state. Since the Sikhs possessed no state the activities of their court were far more curtailed. Daud Ali, *Courtly Culture*, p. 7.
71. *BG* 11:13:8, p. 183. For Kalu the Khatri of Sultanpur noted here see the third definition supplied for the term '*Kālū*' in *MK*, p. 325.
72. *BG* 11:16:7, p. 186. Bhai Saharu is noted in '*Sahārū*', *MK*, p. 139. Vir Singh's notes indicate that all of the Sikhs mentioned in this pauri resided in Dalla.
73. There is a later tradition, tacitly repeated in Sukha Singh's gur-bilas text, which suggests that the masands were also understood as forming a segment of the tenth Guru's court prior to their collective corruption and banishment. Such is implied in the following passage, set within the well-known narrative of the Khalsa's creation:

> Immediately upon hearing the news [of Guru Gobind Singh's intent to create a new order] the selfless servants (*dās*) of the Guru [who surpasses [all gurus] rushed from both home and abroad with their lord's written request stating that they come and appear in his presence (*hazūr*) with the hair on their head [intact and] unshorn. Some time after [the order's creation] the Guru had such a thought: having now created the Khalsa, both special and effective (*khās kārī*), the cleansing and refinement of the [Sikh] royal court (*sarkār darbār*) and the purification

40   The Darbar of the Sikh Gurus

of sangats [generally by the removal of the masands must follow]. The masands adhere to nefarious and foolish tenets. They are deceivers. They arrogantly (*adhak bhārī:* 'with additional weight') become envious of the Guru (*sarīkat*). Their own selves they devour by taking far more of the offerings (*lacchamī*) given [to the Guru] in devotion than is their due (*adhik hī*). As such they have destroyed the [most basic] teaching [of the Guru which prompted the creation of their office in the first place].

Gursharan Kaur Jaggi (ed.), *Gurbilās Pātishāhī Dasvīn* 11:2–3, p. 160.
74. Grewal and Bal, *Guru Gobind Singh*, p. 28.
75. *BG* 11:22, p. 189. In this pauri Bhai Gurdas mentions in the final line that the great masands often competed amongst one another to demonstrate the superiority of their selfless service. The entire pauri though does describe the ideal masand who if we read this pauri in the same context as the following one is also understood as the ideal Sikh.
76. Three such coins are known extant at this point in time. Surinder Singh, *Sikh Coinage*, pp. 39–40.
77. Ganda Singh (ed.), *Hukamnāme: Gurū Sāhibān, Mātā Sāhibān, Bandā Singh ate Khālsā jī de* (Patiala: Publication Bureau Punjabi University, 1985), pp. 194–5.
78. Ibid. This was both the first year of the rule of the Khalsa Sikhs and Banda as well as the first year of the new Age of Truth. Jeevan S. Deol, 'Eighteenth Century Khalsa Identity: Discourse, Praxis and Narrative', in Christopher Shackle *et al.* (eds), *Sikh Religion, Culture and Ethnicity* (London: Curzon, 2001), pp. 25–46.
79. Ibid., pp. 192, 194:

Abundance, might, victory, and instant support are the bequest of [Guru] Nanak and Guru Gobind Singh.

This couplet though considered for many decades to have been the bait which appears on Bandai coins actually differs considerably from those first cast by Banda and his Khalsa. The first to third runs of such coins appeared with the following inscription (with slight refinements after the initial casting) on the obverse:

[This coin] was struck in both this world and the next [with] the munificent [help] of [Guru] Nanak's sword. [Guru] Gobind [Singh], the king of kings, is victorious through the grace of the True Lord.

The reverse also emphasizes not Banda's rule but rather that of the Khalsa:

Struck at the refuge of the world, the protected place, the quintessentially beautiful town in which the glorious throne of the Khalsa resides.

The word '*sinah* 2' or 'year 2' also appears on second year coins. Surinder Singh, *Sikh Coinage*, p. 41 has facsimiles of the second and third year coins.
80. Compare for example Harbans Singh, *The Heritage of the Sikhs* (Delhi: Manohar, 1985), pp. 124–43 with the more sober claims of J.S. Grewal, *The Sikhs of the Punjab*, pp. 88–95.

The Sikh Darbar 41

81. Ganda Singh (ed.), *Ma'ākhiz-i Tavārīkh-i Sikhān jild avval*: 'Ahd-i Gurū Sahibān [Sources of Sikh History volume 1: the Age of the Sikh Gurus] (Amritsar: Sikh History Society, 1949) reproduces a small number of these news reports one of which mentions (on page 85) a clash between the 'community of Khatris' (*qaum-i khatrīyān*) and the *sikhān-i khālsah* (Sikhs of the Khalsa) which first began in Anandpur (*Chakk Gurū*). I would like to thank Hew McLeod for sharing his copy of this text with me. Also see Muzaffar Alam, *The Crisis of Empire in Mughal North India, Awadh and the Punjab 1707–48* (New Delhi: Oxford University Press, 1986), pp. 134–203; Ganda Singh (ed.), *Srī Gur-Sobhā*, chapters 5 and 6, pp. 78–96. Traditional accounts of this period are commonplace and are generally summed up in my *Martyrdom in the Sikh Tradition*, Chapter 3.
82. Sikh conversions are mentioned in an *akhbarat* or news report of 1712 during the rule of Jahandar Shah. In this we are told, according to Muzaffar Alam, that
    In 1712 only seventeen persons of the entire non-Muslim population of Thanesar could be identified as Sikhs. Fourteen of them were willing to become Muslim to avoid torture and death.
    Muzaffar Alam, *Crisis of Empire*, p. 154.
83. Detailed examinations of the latter part of the eighteenth century, especially the policies of the Sikh misls appear as Indu Banga, *Agrarian System of the Sikhs* (Delhi: Manohar, 1978) and Veena Sachdeva, *Polity and Economy of the Punjab During the Late Eighteenth Century* (Delhi: Manohar, 1993). Helpful too though mired in traditional understandings is Bhagat Singh's *A History of Sikh Misls* (Patiala: Punjabi University Publication Bureau, 1993).
84. For example, Guru Ram Das, *Vār gaurī* 9 and Guru Angad, *Asā vār* 1(23), Adi Granth, pp. 304; 474–5. Also see J.S. Grewal, 'Dissent in Early Sikhism', in *Punjab History Conference Fourteenth Session March 28–30, 1980 Proceedings* (Patiala: Punjabi University Press, 1980), pp. 109–20.
85. Both Chaupa Singh Chhibbar and Kesar Singh Chhibbar deride large sections of the contemporary Khalsa Sikh population. *CSRn*, p. 18; lines 596, 618–19, pp. 121, 126; *BSVN*, 10:140–7, pp. 137–8.
86. This last paragraph was inspired in part by James W. Laine, *Shivaji: Hindu King in Islamic India* (New York: Oxford University Press, 2003), p. 61.
87. Although, of course, Sainapati would most likely concede that only Khalsa Sikhs could belong to such a structure. *Srī Gur-sobhā* 9:14–15, p. 109 may be here cited as representative of the text's understandings of the court, an understanding which as we shall later see echoes requests we find in the tenth Guru's hukam-namas:
    Sangats from various cities all over India came and [ultimately] arrived at the [Guru's] court. Then in attendance before the Lord they performed service at the court. They presented [themselves to the Guru] (*mujre līne*) with all of their weapons girded.

42 The Darbar of the Sikh Gurus

As we shall later note the tenth Guru often, especially after 1699 CE, had written instructions sent to his Sikhs to come into his presence with weapons girded about the waist.

88. Although it here appears as *miāne* the Persian term is <u>shamiānah</u> and in India after 1400 CE refers to an awning pitched between two tents. P.A. Andrews, *Felt Tents and Pavilions* II, p. 1338.
89. For such carpets see Abu'l Fazl's description at *AA* I, p. 57.
90. Shamsher Singh Ashok (ed.), *Gurbilās Pātshāhī Dasvīn krit Kuir Singh* 2:30 (Patiala: Punjabi University Press, 1968), p. 33. The *Prem Sumārag Granth* which was written before Ranjit Singh's period prescribes the use of the accoutrements of the court such as kettle drums whenever a maharaja holds court (8:19:4) and when the army is out marching (8:19:7). For these and further descriptions of courtly gatherings and processions and marches see W.H. McLeod (trans.), *The Prem Sumārag: The Testimony of a Sanatan Sikh* 19 (New Delhi: Oxford University Press, 2006), pp. 100–1. The issue of dating the *Prem Sumārag* is discussed in the introduction to McLeod's text, pp. 3–7 although a recent article by McLeod himself now clearly situates the *Prem Sumārag* in the period before Ranjit Singh, the late eighteenth century. W.H. McLeod, 'Reflections on *Prem Sumārag*', in *Journal of Punjab Studies* 14:1 (Spring 2007), pp. 123–4.
91. The evidence for this, as we shall note, appears in both the tenth Guru's hukam-namas as well as later Persian accounts, particularly the 1723 CE '*Ibrat-nāmā* of Muhammad Qasim Lahori. J.S. Grewal and Irfan Habib (ed.), *Sikh History from Persian Sources*, p. 113. A glowing report of the Guru's court underscoring its regal appearance may be found in the online edition of *SP rut* 1, *ansū* 24, pp. 191–7 which the editor Vir Singh titles *ranjīt nagārā banavāunā* 'constructing the battledrum Ranjit Nagara.'
92. J.S. Grewal and S.S. Bal, *Guru Gobind Singh*, p. 206, n. 22. As we made clear above, however, this was not a simple mimicry of Mughal standards. Indeed, a number of features considered quintessentially courtly in the seventeenth and eighteenth centuries find no place in the early Sikh narrative of the Guru's court, especially, for example, the haram. For a recent insightful exploration of the haram's history during the period of the first three Mughal emperors and its proper place within Mughal society see Ruby Lal, *Domesticity and Power in the Early Mughal World* (Cambridge: Cambridge University Press, 2005).
93. Ganda Singh (ed.), *Ma'ākhiz-i Tavārīkh-i Sikhān*, p. 74:
   In these times of great victory the world-ruling order has been issued that a note be despatched to his ministerial highness to the effect that Gobind, the *ra'īs* of the Nanak-parastān, has along with a representative sent a petition ('*arz dāsht*) to this sky-glorious court, expressing a desire to kiss the imperial threshold (*astān būs*) and make a plea for the issuance of an order in his favour.

The term ra'īs is derived from the same roots as rāi and rāja. It is possible as we shall later see that the petition which was sent to Aurangzeb was the famous *Zafar-nāmah* attributed to Guru Gobind Singh.

94. See the 4 March 2000 and the 8 August 2006 online edition of the Chandigarh *Tribune* (*www.tribuneindia.com*). The latter article claims that the sanad was found to be genuine by the Archaeology Department of Madhya Pradesh. I have yet to see the actual document in question. For a brief history of Mughal sanads and sanads in later Mughal history see Stewart Gordon, 'Legitimacy and Loyalty in Some Successor States of the Eighteenth Century', in John Richards (ed.), *Kingship and Authority in South Asia* (Madison: South Asian Studies, University of Wisconsin, 1978), pp. 286–303, esp. pp. 288 in which it is claimed that a sanad was a 'dated document' which 'stated the holder's name, rights and recompense, duties and length of tenure; such a document was signed and sealed by the appropriate Mughal official.'

95. Although tradition claims that the poet Nanu Rai (later Bhai Nanu Singh) was martyred at Chamkaur Sahib, his son Darbar Singh, known to Sikh history as Divan Darbar Singh, was a jathedar 'after the period of Banda but before the period of Kapur Singh.' Padam, *Darbārī Ratan*, p. 229.

96. Bhasha Vibhag Punjab Library ms. 201, folio 18 as noted in Padam, *Darbārī Ratan*, p. 167. The poet Brind was said to have been the teacher of Raj Singh of Kishangarh. For Brind's Brajbhasha poetry see *Darbārī Ratan*, p. 167 and R.S. McGregor, *Hindi Literature from its Beginings to the nineteenth century* (Weisbaten: Otto Harrassowitz, 1984), pp. 195–6.

97. Padam, *Darbārī Ratan*, p. 143. Interestingly, it seems that the *Koka-shāstra* was very well known within the court of the tenth Guru as it is often referenced within writings attributed to the tenth Master. Not only is it expectedly found in the lengthy set of narratives known as the *Pakhyān Charitr* (*Pakhyān Charitr* 13:10, 64:3, Dasam Granth, pp. 828, 893 amongst many, many others) but also in what I will call less explicit and more theological texts such as the *Akāl Ustati* 18, Dasam Granth, p. 13. Such references to patrons were not uncommon in courtly Brajbhasha compositions. Rupert Snell notes the last couplet of Satiram Tripathi's *Phūlmañjarī* as just such an example:

On Jahangir's command, while residing in the city of Agra the poet Satiram created this 'garland of flowers' using all of his wit.

Rupert Snell, *The Hindi Classical Tradition: A Braj Bhāshā Reader* (London: School of African and Oriental Studies, 1992), p. 49. The translation is Snell's.

98. For example the poet Girdhar Lal writes in his treatise on prosody (*Pingalsār*) that:

Gobind Singh is the revered true Guru, the soldier and the saint who is adorned with joy. During his rule Girdhar Lal continuously wrote the *Pingalsār*.

44 The Darbar of the Sikh Gurus

Ms. 129 Bhasha Vibhag Library, Patiala as noted in Padam, *Darbārī Ratan*, pp. 170, 173.
99. Padam notes that there were rababis, dhadhis, likharis (scribes), and other 'artists' (*kalākār*) within the Guru's darbar. He names the rababis Bhai Sadu and Bhai Madu—who are noted in *Sūraj Prakāsh* (online SP 5:27:11, p. 253) and the dhadhis Mir Mushki and Chhabila. Padam, *Darbārī Ratan*, p. 210. The names of a number of scribes and other with similar duties are found scattered throughout the manuscript record. In a bir of the Adi Granth dated sammat 1745 (1688 CE) for example we discover the following note
   Ik onkar. Dated sammat 1745 in the month of Magh.... The writing of this Granth was completed. The scribe was Pakhar Mall Dhillon, resident of Chambhal, grandson of the Chaudari of Langah. [Reflect on it and say] Vahiguru.
Padam, *Darbārī Ratan*, p. 255–6.
100. Although very few of these works of the tenth Guru's poets have been published a number of manuscript copies exist in libraries, private collections, and archives scattered throughout the Punjab, Rajasthan, and Bihar. These include translations of the *Hitopadesha* and numerous chapters from within the Mahabharata such as the Draupadi Parba, the Karna Parba, and the Ashvamedha Parba to name a few. Padam also attributed an original *Triā Charitr* to the poet Kavi Chand. Piara Singh Padam provides brief biographies of each poet and small samples of their works in his *Darbārī Ratan*, pp. 63–262. Also see Harmahendr Singh Bedi, *Gurmukhī Lipi men Upalabdh Hindī Bhakti Sāhitya kā Alochnātmak Adhyayan* [A Critical Study of Hindi Devotional Literature Available in the Gurmukhi Script] (Amritsar Guru Nanak Dev University Press, 1993), pp. 242–7 for a side by side match up of the particular poet and his authored works.
101. See for example Muzaffar Alam, 'The Culture and Politics of Persian in Precolonial Hindustan', in Sheldon Pollock (ed.), *Literary Cultures in History: Reconstructions from South Asia* (Berkeley: University of California Press, 2003), p. 138.
102. Kesar Singh Chhibbar also alludes to Chhibbar Sikhs who served specific functions in the courts of the seventh and eight Gurus. Dargah Mal Chhibbar for example served as the Diwan, the exchequer, in the courts of both Guru Hari Rai and Guru Hari Krishan:
   Dargah Mall was the Divan of Guru Hari Rai ji. A Chhibbar brahman by caste Dargah Mall was the very embodiment of understanding.
BSVN 8:22, p. 106. Also *BSVN* 9:24 and 10:303, pp. 111, 152. 10:303, p. 152 claims that Dargah Mall Chhibbar was the Divan of Guru Tegh Bahadar.
103. *CSRn* lines 171–4: Punjabi text, pp. 81–2. My translation here is slightly adapted from that of McLeod, p. 169. Kesar Singh also lauds the Chhibbar brahmans in the service of the tenth Guru. Indeed, after having been marked with the tilak of investiture Guru Gobind Singh himself commands the Chhibbar Sikhs to come forward and accept courtly positions since their

household has long served the family of the Sikh Gurus. The exchange between Sahib Chand, Dharam Chand, and the tenth Guru in the *Bansāvalīnāmā* is positively delightful. In this version it is Chaupa Singh who is requested to drape the robe of honour on his cousins. See *BSVN* 10:25–8, p. 127. There are apparently a number of hukam-namas attributed to the tenth Guru held by descendants of these Chhibbar brahmans which corroborate these narratives. These are, however, of a questionable nature as Balwant Singh Dhillon has implied. See Balwant Singh Dhillon, 'Some Unknown Hukam-namas of Guru Gobind Singh', in *Punjab History Conference Proceedings* 13 (March, 1979), pp. 103–9.

104. *CSRn* line 174, p. 82 (English, p. 169).

[Guru Gobind Singh] had written instructions sent to his Sikhs for which purpose he kept Sikh scribes in attendance.

Such scribes are also mentioned in *BSVN* 10:55–6, p. 130. That the Gurus possessed a number of scribes is simply beyond doubt. Indeed, a number of these penned their names into manuscripts they had copied. See Padam, *Darbārī Ratan*, pp. 247–56. Chaupa Singh also mentions the presence of a *naqīb* an assistant whose task it was to issue proclamations, *CSRn* 571, pp. 117, (English, p. 191). Another feature of the Guru's court on which eighteenth-century Sikh authors dwell is the presence of brahman pandits. For these consult Sarup Das Bhalla, *Mahimā Prakāsh* 2 volumes [ed. Gobind Singh Lamba and Khazan Singh] (Patiala: Bhasha Vibhag, Punjab, 1971). [Hereafter *MP*]. The relevant passage appears in volume 2, chapter 10:11: 1–5, pp. 794–5.

105. Rosalind O'Hanlon, 'Manliness and Imperial Service', p. 51.
106. Online *SP* 5:26:6–7, p. 245. Further references to the poets and poetic court of the tenth Guru comprise *SP* 5:51–2.
107. Padam, *Darbārī Ratan*, pp. 29, 134.
108. Ibid., p. 129.
109. Online *SP* 5:52:9, p. 499. Also Padam, *Darbārī Ratan*, p. 133.
110. Hukam-namas 6 and 22 in Ganda Singh (ed.), *Hukamnāme*, pp. 72–3, 104–5.
111. Ani Rai's composition is amongst one of the rare courtly epics to have been published. It appears within a collection of 'battlebooks' prepared by Shamsher Singh Ashok, *Prāchīn Vārān te Jangnāme* (Amritsar: SGPC, 1971), pp. 17–32. The passage above appears as lines 1–2, p. 17 and is reproduced in Padam, *Darbārī Ratan*, p. 157. The final line implies that already in the late seventeenth century the handwriting of the Guru, even on simple written instructions, was considered precious and worth preserving. It seems likely that such a document issued by the Guru which recognized certain individuals named within would have generated status, importance, and legitimacy. Padam, *Darbārī Ratan*, p. 157. For further background on Ani Rai see Harmahendr Singh Bedi, *Gurmukhī Lipi men*, p. 251.

46 The Darbar of the Sikh Gurus

112. M. Athar Ali, *The Mughal Nobility*, p. 139.
113. The passage by Mangal Rai is well in keeping with (and may perhaps allude to) a shabad by Guru Arjan with similar wording:
    When the Name of Hari is lodged within the heart this amounts to the merit accrued from ten million ablutions as too that from gifting hundreds of thousands, and billions and trillions [in charity].
    Guru Arjan, *Rāg gaurī guāreri chaupad dupade* 1(111), Adi Granth, p. 202. Also note *Rām Avatār* 48, Dasam Granth, p. 192 which speaks of King Dasaratha's generosity in this manner.
114. Online *SP* 5:26:9–27, pp. 245–9. Also Padam, *Darbārī Ratan*, pp. 39–40 and H.S. Bedi, *Gurmukhī Lipi men*, p. 249. Both Dhanna Singh and eventually Chandan, the learned poet bested by Dhanna Singh, became poets in the tenth Guru's darbar. Padam, *Darbārī Ratan*, pp. 206–8.
115. For the javāb ghazal as a crucial element of Persian ghazal poetry see Ricardo Zipoli, *The Technique of Ğawāb: Replies by Nawā'ī to Hāfiz and Ğamī*. Quaderni del dipartimento di Studi Eurasiastici 35 (Venice: Università degli Studi di Venezia, 1993). The example which Piara Singh mentions however differs from classical Persian javāb types as it describes a scene in which a poetic riddle is recited and its 'answer' sought.
116. A majlis (plural: majālis) refers to both an assembly or meeting hosted by a patron and the audience hall in which such gatherings were held. As is well known it was largely within the majālis that a large amount of the intellectual, cultural and social life of culturally elite Muslims took place from the eleventh century onwards. Brookshaw, 'Palaces', p. 199. Piara Singh, *Darbārī Ratan*, p. 39. For majlis settings in which the Guru oversees the work of his poets, at times bothering to question them and in turn provide answers to their queries see the online edition of *Sūraj Prakāsh* 5:24, pp. 217–27 which is aptly titled by Vir Singh *kaviān nāl prashanuttar*, 'Question and Answer Time with the Poets.' Another venue forms the narrative supplied in the 66th sakhi of the mid nineteenth-century *Sau Sākhīān*. Gurbachan Singh Naiar (ed.), *Gur Ratan Māl: Sau Sākhī* (3rd edition, Patiala: Punjabi University Publication Bureau, 1995), pp. 80–2.
117. Numerous eighteenth and nineteenth-century texts note the many royal and spiritual visitors to the Guru's darbar. See for example *MP* II, 10:3:17, p. 761. In some cases court protocol was observed outside the royal darbar. See for example the fourth chapter of Sukha Singh's late eighteenth-century text, Gursharan Kaur Jaggi (ed.), *Gurbilās Pātishāhī Dasvīn* 4: 38–42, p. 51 especially the last line (42).
    He then came down from the palanquin (*jhamphān*) and went to catch his foot (*qadam*). He performed the *sijjadah* (full prostration) in front of [Guru] maharaj and clung to (*lapatāi*) his feet.
    Also see the fifth *adiāi* of Koer Singh's gur-bilas text. Shamsher Singh Ashok (ed.), *Gurbilās Pātshāhī Dasvīn krit Kuir Singh* 5:167, p. 80; and *Sūraj Prakāsh* online edition *rut* 1, *ansu* 28, pp. 219–25. Also sakhi 62 in

Gurbachan Singh Naiar (ed.), *Guru Ratan Māl: Sau Sākhī*, p. 71 and M.A. Macauliffe, *The Sikh Religion* V, pp. 7–8.

118. This is not prostration proper though the spirit of the sijjadah is certainly prevalent in the Sikh ritual of *matthā tekanā* or touching the forehead upon the ground in obeisance.

119. A diagram of a typical darbar appears in Hew McLeod's *Sikhism*, p. 137. A description of Sikh worship at the Darbar Sahib or Golden Temple in which, too, one discover numerous courtly themes is narrated in Patwant Singh, *The Golden Temple* (New Delhi: Time Books International, 1989), pp. 145–64. The photos here clearly demonstrate the courtly nature of Sikh veneration.

120. The Emperor Aurangzeb for example often issued instructions which were then written up and distributed as hasbulhukam. A small sampling of these concerned with the Sikhs of Guru Gobind Singh appears in 'Inayatullah Khan Ismi's collection of commands, the *Ahkām-i'Ālamgīrī* [The Orders of Aurangzeb] reproduced in Ganda Singh (ed.), *Ma'ākhiz-i Tavārīkh-i Sikkhān*, pp. 72–5. As we shall note a number of the Gurus had issued hukam-nāmās, what may well have been the equivalent to the Mughal hasbulhukm.

121. This is brought forth in Piara Singh Padam's *Darbārī Ratan*, p. 44:
The Guru's darbar was a unique assembly of skilled people amongst whom spiritual matters were discussed while at the same time national issues were pondered which deserved to be so. It was [within this darbar] that suitable plans were regularly made for solving these problems.
For one interpretation of the structure of the Mughal court and the state see Stephen Blake, 'The Patrimonial-Bureaucratic Empire of the Mughals', in the *Journal of Asian Studies* 39 (November 1979), pp. 77–94. Earlier Indian courts are noted in Daud Ali, *Courtly Culture*, pp. 5, 51–6. For European courtly societies generally see Elias, *The Court Society*.

122. Mughal interference in the succession is implied as early as 1643 CE the year in which Shah Jahan granted land around the area of Kartarpur to Baba Gurditta's eldest son, Dhir Mal (d. 1677). The original grant is still held by the Sodhi descendents of Dhir Mall in Kartarpur while a Persian facsimile of it appears in Ganda Singh's compilation of Persian sources dealing with the Sikhs: Ganda Singh (ed.), *Ma'ākhiz-i Tavārīkh-i Sikhān*, pp. 51–2.

123. For these standards see John Richards, 'Norms of Comportment among Imperial Mughal Officials', in Barbara D. Metcalf (ed.), *Moral Conduct and Authority* (Berkeley: University of California Press, 1984) and Douglas Streusand, *The Formation of the Mughal Empire*, pp. 123–53. Also Norbert Elias, *The Court Society*, p. 35.

124. The author of the *Bachitar Nātak* refers to the son of Dilawar Khan the *faujdār* of Kangra as khānzādā. See *Bachitar Nātak* 10:10, Dasam Granth, p. 65. Although khānzād means the 'progeny of slaves' it was the term used for many mansabdārs—those who held a military rank. The description of khānzādī appears in both John Richards' 'Norms of Comportment',

48 The Darbar of the Sikh Gurus

pp. 262–7 and M. Athar Ali, *The Mughal Nobility*, pp. 11–12. Whether k͟hānzādī was as all-embracing as Richards suggests, however has been perceptively questioned in Stephen Blake's analysis of Shahjahanabad. For those who were not khanzadas at the Mughal court it seems there nevertheless existed a code which bound them and their fellow courtiers together. Stephen Blake, *Shahajahanabad*, p. 150 n. The idea of javānmardī is found in Rosalind O'Hanlon 'Manliness and Imperial Service', p. 59. Here she defines javānmardī as 'a particular ideal of generosity, bravery, and spirit.' Court etiquette did alter over the rule of the famous Mughal emperors. For a description of such etiquette in the darbar of the Emperor Aurangzeb see M. Athar Ali, *The Mughal Nobility*, pp. 137–9.

2
(Re)forming the Early Sikh Court

ਤੇਰੇ ਭਗਤ ਸੋਹਹਿ ਸਾਚੈ ਦਰਬਾਰੇ । ਗੁਰ ਕਾ ਸਬਦਿ
ਨਾਮਿ ਸਵਾਰੇ ।[1]

> Your devotees shine in the Lord's True Court as they are [immersed in] the Guru's shabad and adorned with the nām.

Since the time of Guru Nanak the majority of Sikhs have traditionally inhabited what was and continues to be the northwestern Indian frontier, an area composed principally of the 'Land of the Five Rivers' which has been on the margin of one cultural complex (the eastern Islamicate) adjoining another (Indic civilisation).[2] Certainly one may assume that India's pre-Islamic dynastic past played a very important role in shaping understandings of the royal court. Though the scholarship in this regard has only begun to describe this phenomena we can say that certain practices, such as the adoption of the elephant as a royal symbol, have their origins in the royal ceremonies and the Sanskritic culture of the north Indian inscriptions and literatures of the first millennium CE. So references to poets and courtiers as 'courtly jewels' and various understandings surrounding accoutrements such as the canopy and the whisk.[3]

The Punjab of the Sikh Gurus was nevertheless a frontier whose dominant political, martial, and royal culture was largely shaped by the Persianite Islamicate traditions brought to northern India in the tenth century by Mahmud of Ghazna.[4] And it was largely shaped by these traditions because Mahmud and his successors had imposed themselves and their cultural proclivities by an overwhelming force of arms. Peter Hardy makes the point succinctly: 'Muslim rulers were there in northern India as rulers because they were there—and they were there because they had won.'[5]

THE PERSIANITE COURT OF THE EASTERN ISLAMICATE

These victories in India had earned Mahmud an infamous reputation at least within traditional Indian historiography. Known principally as an intolerant conqueror in such orientalist readings of India's past, Mahmud was the first nominally Muslim ruler to bring the nascent Persianite traditions of the eastern Islamicate to India, transforming both Ghazna and later Lahore into cosmopolitan centres of Islamicate culture for which they were famous at the beginning of the Common Era's second millennium.[6] Islamicate (and more contemporary) readings of Mahmud's past therefore are far more forgiving than orientalist ones or the new histories of India prepared by today's Hindu chauvinists. It is in eleventh-century Lahore, for example, that the famous Sufi master, Shaikh Hujwiri Data Ganjbakhsh prepared his manual of Sufi mysticism the *Kashf-ul-Mahjūb* (The Discovery of the Hidden), a text which up until the nineteenth century was regularly referenced throughout the entire Islamic world.[7] It was to Mahmud's court, moreover, that scholars such as Hakim Sana'i and poets such as 'Unsuri Balkhi, Manuchihri Damaghani, and Mas'ud Sa'd Salman were summoned and employed in the tenth and eleventh centuries in the Ghaznavid's attempt to bolster his own reputation and the status of his court at faraway Ghazna in the eyes of the Arabic-speaking Caliph in Baghdad. In this, Mahmud certainly succeeded as a popular representation of the Ghaznavid has him proudly slipping on a robe of honour presented to him by the emissaries of the 'Abbassid Caliph.[8]

By the latter part of Mahmud's career his reputation for patronizing poets, the conviviality of his many majālis, along with the grandeur of his poetic garden parties earned him an enviable standing within the Islamic world.[9] Indeed, his status was such that the famous Persian litterateur, Ferdausi (d. 1019–20 CE), author of the Iranian epic the *Shāh-nāmah*, came to the Ghaznavid's court seeking support. This in itself should have been enough to ensure Mahmud's Islamicate legacy but the memory of Mahmud was further enhanced within the Persianized Islamic world when he was ultimately transformed, first by Jallaluddin Rumi in the thirteenth century and later by other Persian poets, into the archetypal lover found within the widely popular Sufi literary tradition. Here Mahmud loves and is enamoured by his slave Ayaz.[10]

Mahmud's glorification on the part of Persian poets was perhaps deserving (and not just because tradition claims that he employed well over 400 of them) since he is said to have been the first Muslim ruler to have formally coined the title and established the office of the *malikushshu'arā*', 'poet laureate [of the royal court]', first applied to the court poet 'Unsuri Balkhi.[11] Mahmud's bestowal of this title certainly resonated with political and cultural subtexts which were not lost on the later Delhi Sultanate or the Timurid courts of Central Asia (that is the area covering *Māvarā'annahr* 'The Area which is behind and beyond the Oxus River', i.e. Transoxiana, Balkh, and Khurasan in Perso-Arabic sources) and India. Nor were these implications overlooked, I believe, by the court of the tenth Guru.[12]

These traditions of patronage and other facets of Persianite Islamicate courtly styles, norms, and values often including classical Persian as the dominant literary and courtly language would be for the most part embraced by succeeding sultanates of the eastern Islamicate and northern India and their conquered elite from the twelfth to the mid-seventeenth centuries. These would be further buttressed when Chinggis Khan (d. 1227 CE) invaded the Perso-Islamic world, a incursion which saw the migration of numerous scribes, scholars, and Sufis to northern India. Subsequently the styles adopted and encouraged by the splendid court of Amir Timur Gurgan after the late fourteenth century, particularly after Timur's invasion of the subcontinent in 1398 CE also saw Islamicate norms and values make their way eastwards.[13] In Herat, Isfahan, and within Samarqand and Bukhara these styles and values reached their pinnacle in the fifteenth- and sixteenth-century courts of the Uzbek and Shibanid Sultanates while in India these standards became gloriously manifest under the Indo-Timurid emperors beginning with Zahiruddin Babur (r. 1526–30) and ending with Aurangzeb 'Alamgir (r. 1658–1707), the latter period perfectly corresponding with that of the Sikh Gurus.[14] These were styles and values, moreover, which did not restrict themselves only to the court and the cultural elite but found their way into the subcontinent's most humble corners through Persianite sermons (*tazkīr*) in good Persian prose, that were recited in army camps, public places, and bazaars. Such sermons peppered with baits from classical Persian poetry allowed commoners and soldiers alike to become familiar with the great variety of Persian literary classics including works by Jallaluddin Rumi, Shaikh Sa'di, Hafez Shirazi, and Nizami to name a few. Contact with Sufi *khānqāhs* or centres also helped popularize Persian and later Indo-Timurid culture within both urban and rural India.[15] The khanqahs, moreover, would have also served to introduce pious north Indians to the Sufi *malfūzāt* literature, the endearing table-talk records of Sufi shaikhs and pirs collected by the disciples of masters such as Nizamuddin Auliya.[16] Indeed, it is quite likely that Guru Nanak himself may have heard a number of these Persian sermons or excerpts from the malfūzāt as he toured northern India, preaching and singing his message of emancipation. The janamsakhis suggest this, as do traditions associated with the more Persianite hymns of the first Master.

All this is not to suggest that Persian and Persianite culture in any way displaced more regional languages, identities, and cultures such as Punjabi or Braj. Alam states that there were certainly times when the empire and its dominant courtly language were threatened by more regional ethnicities, but

the increasing cultural affirmation of the region expressed in its linguistic diversity had to be accommodated in more meaningful ways. [The Mughals] recognized the need to culturally integrate and accommodate with, and not to simply dominate, the regions. This could be illustrated from the interest they showed in Hindawi.[17]

By the seventeenth century, in both northern and southern India,

the relationship between Persian and the vernaculars seems to have been one of complimentarity and even synergy rather than of conflict.[18]

Keeping in mind the fluidity of the Islamicate culture of the sixteenth century, therefore, one may conclude that by the time of Babur, a direct descendant of both Timur and Chinggis Khan, and that of the first Sikh Guru there existed in northern India a cultural and conceptual universe, especially prominent amongst but by no means limited to the ruling elite, which included Central Asian concepts of sovereignty, law, and imperium that date back to the period of Chinggis Khan to which were assimilated ideas and notions of Perso-Islamic kingship and ceremonial reaching back to Sassanid Iran (224– 651 CE) as well as models indigenous to India.[19] This was a particularly dynamic mixture of cultural and courtly elements which may have helped engender Indo-Timurid Mughal India's reputation for wealth, artistic patronage, and extravagant courtly culture, a status which became proverbial throughout the then Islamic world.[20]

PERSIANITE TERMINOLOGY OF ROYALTY

It is the very Persianite terminology of royalty and of the royal courts at Samarqand, Bukhara, Herat, Kabul, and later Agra which permeates the hymns and the understandings of royalty and court found within the Adi Granth. As Christopher Shackle makes clear in his now-classic essay, 'Approaches to the Persian Loans in the *Ādi Granth*,' Persian loans of a courtly nature 'can be used to form a mirror reflecting the impression made by Islamic political dominance on at least one section of non-Muslim society in sixteenth-century Panjab.'[21] This is in line with Peter Hardy's earlier statements but is to an extent all that Shackle provides by way of the context in which the hymns were written. The rarity of non-Persian loans to describe the court and its symbols allows us to significantly supplement Shackle's conclusion for our purposes.[22] Indeed, by the time of Guru Nanak and his Sikhs, the eastern Islamicate Persian terminology of the court (as well as Persianite terms for 'royal court', *darbāru* or *dīvānu/dībānu* respectively) and its accompanying 'grammar' and symbols, particularly its martial symbols, were so pervasive as to be considered indigenous. And so, for the Sikhs of the sixteenth century, describing Guru Nanak in terms borrowed from Persianized Islamicate culture was simply commonplace. This is made abundantly clear by the so-called Goindval Pothis, the earliest sources which were later incorporated and edited into the Adi Granth. At one point in the Pothis, the arranger(s) or scribe(s) of the extant text enthusiastically declare(s) that

Baba Nanak [is] the Bedi Patshah [who is] the support of both this world and the next.[23]

Such an image of the Guru, drawn almost exclusively from Persianite Islamicate terminology (*pātshāhu dīn dunīā*), is one which sixteenth-century Sikhs, particularly Bhai Gurdas Bhalla and the bards whose compositions also appear in the Adi Granth, would repeatedly use. This imagery was used to describe the first Guru and his successors, especially Guru Ram Das and Guru Arjan under whom many of the bards (both Muslim and Hindu) took direction.[24] The Pothis may have set this trend (at least in Sikh literature), as the first Guru is not the only Guru whom the compilers or scribes of this manuscript enthusiastically describe. The 'blessing' which is found on both folios one and nine of the Pothis ends as follows, glorifying Guru Nanak and his first two successors:

O Supreme Being! O Imperishable Lord! O Baba Nanak, Angad, [and] Amar Das! O True King! (*sache patishāh*). Fix my mind upon the sacred utterances of Baba [Nanak as] there is no gift loftier than this. That person to whom you grant [your acceptance, O Lord,] will meet Baba [Nanak] Patishah [at life's end].[25]

The Gurus frequently use this terminology for themselves. Guru Nanak appropriates the word patishah, for example, in a number of senses: patishah as the worldly king and its adjectival declension, *pātishāhī* 'sovereignty' to indicate both the transitory nature of human rule or the metaphorical reward awaiting the truly pious disciple who remembers the nām, the Name of the divine; and the Patishah as Akal Purakh, God, the great true king of all beings.[26] Amongst Guru Nanak's successors, the latter usage is the most common though other usages mentioned above do appear.[27] By the early to mid-seventeenth century this trend continues. Bhai Gurdas (d. 1637), in words which echo the Goindwal Pothis, claims the following of the fourth Sikh Guru, Guru Ram Das:

The Sodhi Patishah, [Guru] Ram Das, is [now] seated [upon the throne of guruship] and is called the True Guru.[28]

And of the sixth Sikh Master, Guru Hargobind, he states:

[Guru Hargobind] is the emperor of both this world and the next (*dīn dunī dā pātisāhu*) as well as the unwavering emperor of emperors (*pātisāhān pātisāhu adolā*).[29]

Likewise, the famous Zoroastrian traveller who authored the celebrated *Dabistān-i Mazāhib*, the 'School of Religions' in Persian claims that,

...the Sikhs refer to [their] Gurus as *sachā pādshāh*—that is to say 'true kings' (*pād<u>sh</u>āh haqīqī*)...[30]

The most extensive use of Persian terms and understandings that originated within the Islamicate court has been made by the *bhatts* (a group of brahmans from the Malwa area who were versifiers by profession) and *mirāsīs* (Muslim minstrels). Their hymns that describe the Sikh Gurus and their entourage appear within the scripture. These bards praise the various Sikh Gurus in their shabads, most of which portray them in a kingly fashion. As Pashaura Singh notes, their hymns 'modelled on the genre of [panegyric] court poetry' provide an image of the Gurus and their courts which is inscribed onto the collective memory of the Sikhs. Regular recitation of the *Bhattān de savaīe* (panegyrics of the bards) at the Golden Temple, and its broadcast throughout the world via satellite television has helped in the popularization of these images.[31]

For our purposes, let us take a famous Adi Granth hymn, known popularly as 'The Ode of the Investiture Mark' (*Tikke dī vār*) composed by Rai Balwand and Satta the Dum, Muslim rebek players (rabābīs) associated with the darbar of Guru Arjan, the fifth Sikh Guru. The entire hymn is extremely significant, as Pashaura Singh has recently noted, as it allows the reader to glimpse how the bards and Sikhs generally (by extension) understood and described the nature of the Guru's court in this period.[32] In this we repeatedly hear of Guru Angad being seated on the throne (*ta<u>kh</u>at*) of Guru Nanak, who applies the coronation mark of sandal paste (*tikkā*) to Guru Angad's forehead.[33] We are also told of the investiture of the successive Gurus until that of the fifth Guru with whom the bards worked. All of these descriptions follow the pattern outlined in stanza one. Let us then quote the sixth stanza as representative of the entire hymn, which describes some of the ceremonial surrounding the Guru's court and the investiture of the new Guru.

How can I praise you, O True King (sache pātishāh), when you are so wise and all-knowing? Those blessings granted by the pleasure of the True Guru—please bless Satta with those gifts. Seeing Nanak's canopy (chhataru)

waving over your head, everyone was astonished. The same mark of investiture (tikkā), the same [throne on which] to sit, and the same royal court (dībānu; Persian: dīwān). Just like the father and grandfather, the son is approved [by the Lord].[34]

The chhattar, the canopy or umbrella often placed over the emperor's head in Mughal miniatures, is an accoutrement mentioned by Abu'l Fazl 'Allami as one of the principal 'ensigns of royalty', as it represents the king's protection of his subjects as well as a device which separates the king's light from that of the divine effulgence. The chhattar which is spread over the heads of the Gurus (either by God or by the previous Guru) appears repeatedly within this particular hymn and as well within other Sikh hymns and writings.[35] The investiture itself is structured as a royal crowning ceremony, but in its simplicity is unlike that of the Mughal emperors.[36]

While it is the investiture of Guru Amar Das which Satta and Balwand describe above, Bhatt Haribans chooses to narrate the coronation of Guru Arjan:

The whisk [of sovereignty] (chavaru) waves over his head and he [the fifth Guru] utters the nectar-like Name. The Supreme Lord has himself spread the royal canopy (chhataru) over Guru Arjan's head.[37]

Like the chhattar, the whisk or chavar (Pbi: chaurī) too has a long history of royal associations in India which predates the birth of Islam. Like the elephant and the canopy/umbrella it was also later incorporated and assimilated into the fluid Islamicate culture noted earlier.[38] As Pashaura Singh notes, this hymn and others like it offer 'an eyewitness account of how the early Sikhs started venerating the Gurus in a most dignified way...marked by the symbols of royalty such as the canopy, throne, and the waving of a whisk over their heads.'[39]

I would like to pause here to make two points. Firstly, shabads like the *Tikke dī Vār* and panegyrics such as the *Bhattān de savaīe* should by no means suggest that the bards and other Sikh writers describe the royal nature of the Gurus and their guruships solely in an 'Islamicate' way. This is certainly the dominant pattern of royal description but a patient look through the Adi Granth would demonstrate that it was not the only one. The bards of the Adi Granth sometimes refer to the Gurus in a terminology which alludes to kings from India's mythological past, comparing the Gurus from Guru Nanak to Guru Arjan to Raja Janak, who was noted for adopting the Sant axiom that one must live in the world in a detached manner.[40] Bhatt Kirat, for example, refers to the second Sikh Master, Guru Angad as an avatar of the detached King Janak:

[Guru Angad,] you are Raja Janik newly descended to earth as the contemplation of your shabads, [whose message contains] the essence [of life] (*saru*), allows all of creation to remain pure like a lotus surrounded by the water of worldliness.[41]

These descriptions of the Sikh Gurus suggest that Sikh bards and later Sikh writers drew from a vast store of descriptive metaphors and tropes among which are the ones that originate from the eastern Islamicate.

Secondly, it is worth noting that despite the appropriation of royal Persianite terminology both the bards and the Gurus, as well as Bhai Gurdas, do not question or contest the worldly authority of the Mughal emperors. The Gurus condemned neither monarchy nor the monarch per se within their many shabads. Rather, they denounced the abuse of the sovereignty given to the monarch by God.[42] The bhatts, moreover, make metaphorical references to the glory which surrounds both the man and the institution of the Guru. Such Persian and Persianite descriptives were commonly used well before the period of the Gurus and the Sikh bhatts by the members of the many Sufi *silsilah*s (lit., succession) throughout northern India after the thirteenth century to describe their spiritual masters (*shaikh*s or *pīr*s).[43] Certainly both the Sikh Gurus and Sufi pirs possessed authority over their respective followers and though this authority differed from that of the mundane ruler it was nevertheless believed to be intimately tied to it. In Sufi hagiographies generally known as *tadhkirah/tazkirah*, as well as within the later Sikh hagiographies, the *janam-sākhī*s (which were partly modelled along the lines of the popular tadhkirah),[44] the worldly authority of the Islamicate rulers of the Delhi Sultanate and the later Mughal empire derived principally from the blessings of the revered master who was the object of the hagiographer's attention. As Simon Digby says, 'In the opinion of their followers [Sufi pirs] held powers for the making and unmaking of kings and kingdoms.'[45] These opinions were no doubt enthusiastically supported through the activities of Jalaluddin Akbar who was most certainly cognizant of such blessings as his regular royal pilgrimage to the tomb of Khwaja Muinuddin Chishti at Ajmer made clear. 'These recurring ceremonies [demonstrated],' John Richards asserts, that '[r]oyal heirs, royal victory, and royal authority flowed from [Akbar's] devotion to the Chishti [Sufi] saints.'[46]

The same understandings very much held true for the disciples of Baba Nanak. By the mid-seventeenth century, the awareness of Guru Nanak as the force behind Babur's victories over the Lodi Sultanate was popular enough to have been narrated to the author of the *Dabistān-i Mazāhib* in which the narrative was retained for posterity:

> One [of the miracles] attributed to [Baba] Nanak [by his disciples] is as follows: having been afflicted by the Afghans [Baba] Nanak delivered them over to the Mughals so that in the year [Hijra] 932 [1526 CE] Hazrat Firdaus Makani [He Whose Place is Paradise (Babur's posthumous title)] Babur Padishah defeated Ibrahim [Lodi] the Afghan.[47]

Within Sikh accounts too, Babur's fame and wealth and later that of his descendants resulted principally from Guru Nanak's blessings.[48] In a later, mid-nineteenth century Sikh text of the gur-bilās (The splendour of the Guru) genre, the *Gur-panth Prakāsh* of Ratan Singh Bhangu (known popularly as the *Prāchīn Panth Prakāsh*), the Mughal emperor Farrukh Siyyar (d. 1719 CE) would himself remind his courtiers of this debt to the Sikh Gurus.[49]

THE COURT OF THE EARLY SIKH GURUS

Let us now return to Pashaura Singh's earlier statement that the *Bhattān de savaīe* provide an 'eyewitness account' of the way Sikhs began to venerate the Gurus. Certainly there is validity in this point of view. The Sikh Gurus were surrounded by disciples, poets, and perhaps singers in a style which could easily evoke regal comparisons. Bhai Gurdas, for example, through a characteristically Persianite terminology describes Guru Nanak's minstrel companion Mardana in a way that suggests the existence of a number of such musicians as early as the period of Guru Nanak:

> Mardana the Mirasi expertly played the rebek within the majlis.[50]

But Bhai Gurdas' statements here were most likely based on impressions he received in the courts of the fifth and sixth Sikh Gurus implying that majālis were indeed held in this later period. After all, Persian literary soirées such as the majlis and the *mahāfil* had become, by the time of Bhai Gurdas, an important if not integral part of Indian culture, according to the many Persian tazkirahs of seventeenth- and eighteenth-century India.[51] This says nothing about the many millions of people in India who did not know the language but there is a great deal of evidence to suggest that such poetic gatherings were not restricted to Persian poets and writers. Although different in name, majālis-like assemblies (*kavi-samāja*, lit., 'society of poets') were held in which poets of classical Hindi, Brajbhasha, and other regional languages likewise demonstrated their skill, learned from one another, and perhaps gave form to nascent communities based on a common linguistic identity.[52] But whether Sikh versions of this experience existed during the first Master's time is far more difficult to ascertain. Certainly as we shall see, the very structure of the Adi Granth possesses in certain respects a majlis-like structure, a fact of which Guru Arjan and Guru Gobind Singh were likely aware.

There seems little doubt that both Bhai Gurdas and the bhatts did understand and help perpetuate an image of the early Gurus and their disciples as kings surrounded in their courts by poets and courtiers, but whether these hymns are descriptive or idealistic (at least in terms of outward appearance) remains unknown. So also unknown is whether the early Gurus understood themselves in the royal manner that the bhatts describe. It seems that Guru Arjan must have seen nothing untoward with such kingly associations: not only was he the ultimate authority in regard to the inclusion of the hymns of the bhatts within the Adi Granth but the 'proportionately stronger Brajbhasha element in [Guru] Arjan's [own hymns]... appears to reflect the vogue of that dialect for devotional and court poetry in the late 16th century.'[53]

That the hymns of the bhatts were primarily descriptive nevertheless seems unlikely as such an understanding would run counter to the overwhelming message of humility one regularly encounters within the entire Sikh canon. As we had earlier noted, mid-eighteenth century Sikh tradition draws upon these bardic images to suggest that the early Gurus comported themselves in a way commensurate with the bhatts' descriptions, in other words, behaved like the very kingly figures who the bhatts made famous, though with the very important caveat that theirs (the Gurus') was principally a spiritual kingdom which was superimposed upon the secular realm (an understanding anticipating the development of the *mīrī/pīrī* 'doctrine'— that is, secular/spiritual sovereignty—which took place under the sixth Guru and which would not compromise Guru Nanak's constant references to personifying humility).[54] The foundation of Goindwal under the auspices of the third Sikh Guru, Guru Amar Das prompted this description by Bhatt Nalh:

Gobindval is the City of God built on the banks of the Beas River.[55]

This was the city of God not the city of Guru Amar Das. It is by the time of Guru Ram Das, however, that tradition buttressed in large part by the descriptions of the bhatts claims that the fourth Master held court like a *rāj-yogī*, a saintly king surrounded by 'his bards and holy congregation'.[56] Contemporary Sikh art illustrates this by conflating the images of the padishah and the yogi into a single portrait, thus providing a rather crude amalgamation of both miri and piri respectively.[57] Although the actual hymns of Guru Ram Das say very little of substance in regard to the existence of a Sikh court, we may extrapolate from their principal concerns.

A careful analysis of the hymns of the fourth Guru led Surjit Hans to conclude that both the founding of the town of Ramdaspur and the growing size of the Sikh community (and its feeding) were developments prompted by the Guru himself.[58] As the founder of a new town concerned with attracting both wealth and people to its environs, Guru Ram Das would require some sort of administrative set up to ensure the collection of contributions from pious Sikhs and their proper distribution. He would, moreover, need such an infrastructure in order to reach out to the increasing number of Sikhs in rural tracts, the peasants to whom the fourth Guru pays a great deal of attention in his shabads.[59] It is likely that the founding of Ramdaspur was a way to serve the spiritual needs of rural Sikhs and others. Ramdaspur was most likely envisaged as a pilgrimage centre since it was built around the sacred tank which gave the city its later name, Amritsar—the pool of nectar. Such activity would easily suit the enlightened religious policies of emperor Akbar, who it seems, may have been familiar with the work of the early Gurus prior to his meeting with Guru Arjan in 1598. This most likely led to the large growth of Sikh numbers later noted by both the author of the *Dabistān* and the emperor Jahangir in his memoirs.[60] Simultaneously, the town would also help to economically alleviate the plight of such peasants. As Chetan Singh has claimed in his study of seventeenth-century Punjab, the inefficiency of transportation in Indo-Islamic northern India necessitated the emergence of towns in well cultivated regions, towns which could provide a large urban market for various commodities and raw materials which could in turn stimulate production in the surrounding countryside.[61] He continues,

If these towns were dependent upon villages for their survival it can also be suggested that the supply of commodities to urban centres ensured the prosperity of some social sections of the countryside.[62]

Such an inclination and its successful deployment therefore enhanced the Guru's reputation amongst these Punjabi peasants. It may well hold true as it did for cities such as Fatehpur Sikri and Shahjahanabad among other imperial centres, that the very presence of the Guru and his close disciples and also the dharamsalas within the newly created city would have been enough to entice a number of people to settle there, employed in the service and maintenance of the Sikh Guru and his followers.[63] Such an environment would doubtlessly have appealed to Khatri merchants and traders, who as is well known, often took on the 'externals of the Indo-Islamic' lifestyle (a point, it seems, Guru Nanak criticized).[64] Such emigrations would also have provided employment opportunities for those many armed peasants who spent time hiring themselves out to protect the conveys of such merchants and traders.[65]

The system of administration, organization, and tribute collection which the fourth Guru eventually developed for these purposes was based in large part upon the earlier *manjī* system established by his predecessor, Guru Amar Das. Most likely derived from the Punjabi term for 'cot' (*manjā*), *manjī* (literally, a 'diminutive cot' in the sense that it was placed below—or its legs were shorter than— the cot on which the Guru himself sat) referred to the office or title of a respectable Sikh on whom the Guru had conferred the responsibility of collecting the offerings made by distant sangats.[66] There were twenty-two such manjis which, according to early to mid-nineteenth century Sikh tradition, was purposefully meant to reflect the number of *subā*s or provinces into which the Mughal empire under Akbar was divided.[67] This office was most likely transformed under Guru Ram Das to accommodate on the one hand, the much larger and more scattered sangats to which he alludes in his hymns, and on the other, the future prospects of the new Sikh centre initially known as *Gurū kā chakk*; then Ramdaspur; and finally under the fifth Guru, Amritsar.

It is very instructive for our purposes that Guru Ram Das also chose to modify the name of this new office from manji to *masand*, a word derived from the Persian term *masnad-i 'ālī* or simply the *ezāfah*-less *masnad*, 'elevated cushion/chair'. This term may appear to be a straightforward change from the Punjabi word for cot to the Persianized one, but the masnad implied far more than a simple cot as the term was traditionally used to describe the raised platform or cushion on which nobles sat in the presence of the sultan, either in an actual building or within a tent. Its use could prefigure the more commonly used Punjabi term *gaddī*, 'cushion', to describe the seat or 'throne' of guruship.[68] As early as the fourteenth century, these masnads as 'cushions of state' were given to newly created khans by sultans themselves as a symbol of the khans' new authority.[69] In the time of Jalaluddin Akbar (r. 1556–1605 CE), moreover, the masnad could also indicate a royal platform, pile of cushions or even a throne.[70] The title thus reflected the Persianized language of nobility, royalty, and authority used by the Timurids and later by the Mughals, thus engendering an image of the Guru's court very much akin to that of Islamicate rulers if not in actuality at least in spirit, in which the Guru is surrounded by loyal disciples, courtiers, and nobles. Although we cannot know for certain how the fourth Guru conducted the nascent Panth's affairs, it seems to me unlikely that Guru Ram Das would not have been aware of the semantic range of the term masnad/ masand and all of its implications.[71] The existence of a courtly image is no doubt enhanced by the fourth Guru's hymns implying the presence of the Sikh equivalent to the Mughal kitāb-khānah or atelier (the Sikh pothī mahal perhaps) which would most certainly have been expanded under the aegis of Guru Arjan who had actually seen first-hand such a 'production house' when he met with the emperor Akbar on 4 November 1598 CE:

Fortunate and approved are those eyes, my soul, which gaze upon the holy True Guru, the divine being. Sacred and pure are those hands, my soul, which write the resounding praises of the Lord Hari who is Ram.[72] I worship continually the feet of that humble being, my soul, who walks along the laneways of dharma, the path of righteousness. My soul, Nanak is a sacrifice to those beings who [mystically] hear the Lord Hari and believe in His Name.[73]

In these cases as well we may assume the existence of ragis or those singers who sang the shabads composed by the Gurus.[74] The construction of Ramdaspur also suggests the existence of a Sikh kār-khānah or workshop.[75] Sevā or the Sikh concept of selfless service most certainly played a fundamental role in the construction of Ramdaspur,[76] but even a brief stroll through the old walled-city of Amritsar suggests a well-organized form of urban planning which in turn suggests dedicated planners, builders, and perhaps merchants attached to the retinues of Guru Ram Das and Guru Arjan. In this light therefore, it seems fitting that later Sikh tradition does indeed describe the fourth Master as the first of the Gurus to adopt a kingly posture.[77]

Reasons for the semantic shift undertaken by the fourth Guru may once again underscore the familiarity which most Sikhs had with Indo-Timurid Mughal courtly culture (they were after all the rulers of the most of the subcontinent). It may have been aimed at engendering within the group a more firm loyalty to the spiritual office of Guru Ram Das and his spiritual lineage (without compromising their fidelity to the Mughal emperor),[78] plagued as it was in the mid-sixteenth century by detractors (*nindak*s), a situation which is often brought to our attention in the hymns of the fourth Sikh Master.[79] Although the Adi Granth tells us nothing about the masand system per se, the royal and authoritative images invoked by the term masand were not lost on the author of the *Dabistān-i Mazāhib*, a companion at one point of both Guru Hargobind and Guru Hari Rai, who spends some time describing the system established by Guru Ram Das and continued by Guru Arjan in his famous text.[80] The description alludes to the missionary activities of the masands and their collection of offerings, and also references the noble origins of the term: *bāyad dānast dar 'ahd-i salātīn-i āfghān āmorā' rā masnad-i 'ālī mīnavashtand* ('It should be known that during the period of the Afghan sultanate the nobles were known as *masnad-i 'ālī*'). It finally makes very clear that the system was inherited by the fifth Guru and concludes with the following informative statements regarding Guru Arjan's treatment of individual officers:

In the month of Baisakhi when the sun is in the sign of Taurus (*saur*) the masands gather together at the court of the Guru (*dargāh-'i gurū*). Whichever of their deputies (*melīān*) desires to see the Guru and has the means of transportation [to do so] will go with the masand to the Guru. At the time of their departure the Guru confers upon each masand a turban (*dastār*).[81]

THE DARBAR OF THE FIFTH PADISHAH, GURU ARJAN

Here we see clear parallels to rituals and activities performed not just within the larger Mughal court but within the more cosmopolitan courts from China to Byzantium. Certainly, the granting of the turban (in a court it seems) invokes the symbolism associated with the granting of garments such as the *khil'at*, the robe of honour: it bound the donor to the recipient through the transferal of the Guru's/sovereign's *baraka* or 'essence' (perhaps as a way to influence the behaviour of the receiver as in the Sufi granting of robes). It cemented both loyalty and fealty between the two, and in this case the turban granted was also a sign of the Guru's authority to scattered Sikh sangats, an indication perhaps that the Guru was indeed mystically present within the person of the masand. In some ways such activities may foresee the placement of small *gutkā*s (breviaries) within the turbans of particularly pious Sikhs, a practice which one still encounters in Punjab today, keeping the True Guru nearby if you will. This is perhaps why the author of the *Dabistān* makes a point of underscoring the successful missionary activities of the masands and their agents. This simple ritual gifting suggests that by the later sixteenth century the Sikh Gurus were following and adapting at least some of the principles of conduct and ritual whose origins (at least for northern India) lie in the Persianite Islamicate.[82] What was most likely a metaphorical reference to robing in honour in the bani of Guru Nanak became the actual gifting of garments under Guru Arjan.

This understanding is reinforced by another reference to the practices of Guru Arjan that we discover in the *Dabistān*. The text also tells us that the organization of masands was used in part to collect voluntary contributions which the author refers to as *bhet*, the Punjabi term for 'offering' or 'present' which were then taken *beh sarkār-i gurū*, 'to the Guru's *sarkār*.'[83] The term *sarkār*, as Irfan Habib reminds us, 'signified in the seventeenth century the establishment, financial or fiscal of the king, prince or noble.' He also notes, however, that the use of this term 'did not necessarily mean a sovereign government.'[84] This was most certainly the situation in Guru Arjan's case, as we shall note, and it seems very likely that the author of the *Dabistān* who was able to personally view the Sikh situation in the early 1640s under both Gurus Hargobind and Hari Rai would have understood sarkār in Irfan Habib's second, sovereignless sense. One may nevertheless here assume a touch of ambiguity on our Persian author's part when we consider, among other things, the fifth Guru's administrative arrangements (that is the masands which he inherited from Guru Ram Das who most likely possessed a number of followers in their own respective districts), the compilation of the Adi Granth (a fact which tradition claims was brought to the emperor Akbar's notice),[85] and the reverence in which the fifth Guru was held by the Sikhs, all of which were lovingly communicated to him by his Sikh informants. Certainly to the sceptical mind all this appeared to be the stuff of sovereignty.

Perhaps nothing seemed more so than Guru Arjan's foundation of the towns of Kartarpur (between the Beas and Sutlej Rivers), Taran Taran, and Amritsar. As Guru Arjan was the principal force behind Amritsar's rise as an economic, commercial, and spiritual centre for Sikh sangats distant and proximate, one can further justify the sense of ambiguity that we infer from the *Dabistān*. Yet within the very hymns of Guru Arjan himself is the statement which puts an end to any such uncertainty. While Amritsar's significance increased (alongside that of nearby Taran Taran), Guru Arjan makes a point to emphasize that the new situation in which both he and his Sikhs found themselves in the late sixteenth century need not compromise their fidelity to the Mughal court and its emperor. It is this caution, I believe, which partly informs both Guru Arjan's renaming of the city from Ramdaspur—the City of Guru Ram Das—to Amritsar and Guru Arjan's famous statement in his *Sirī rāg* 13(2), a concern which in the light of later developments under the new emperor Jahangir was most justified.

The merciful Lord has now ordered [everyone] to live and let live (lit. 'no one chase after and attack anyone'). Let everyone abide in peace, under this [new] rule of humility (*halemī rāju*).[86]

Habib's interpretation of the *Dabistān*'s use of sarkār was thus most likely our Persian author's privileged understanding of the term. But the association between Amritsar and halemi raj is worth further scrutiny. Guru Arjan's insistence on this 'rule of the meek' (Per: halemī, 'meek' or 'gentle') accentuates Guru Nanak's steadfast commitment to humility (and so the translation above), an attitude which fortifies many of the shabads we discover within the Sikh canon.[87] Unlike the majority of grand Mughal edifices and cities which were constructed in part to amplify and broadcast the power and authority of the emperor and his nobles (in this instance one is very much reminded of both Akbar's Fatehpur Sikri and his grandson's Shahjahanabad),[88] Guru Arjan's Amritsar would be the dwelling place of peace, justice, and modesty. It would be, as the contemporary sign above the entrance to the modern city's Hall Bazaar proclaims, the *siphatī dā ghar* or the 'home of praise.'[89] Here we have a prominent facet of Mughal courtly culture, the construction of cultural artefacts such as buildings and cities resonating with the power and authority of the Mughal darbar and the Mughal sovereign himself as the apotheosis of the divine, refashioned to serve both the spiritual and economic needs of Guru Arjan and the growing Sikh Panth.[90] Indeed, we may observe that the Guru's emphasis on humility was very much at the heart of both this and other meticulously organized building schemes. Perhaps it was with such humility in mind that the town planners built thirteen gates around the wall enclosing the original city. The word thirteen in Punjabi, *terāh*, is as is well known from stories about Guru Nanak's early days in Sultanpur Lodhi, a word which sounds very much like the word *terā*, '[This is all] Yours' a common epithet for Akal Purakh in the bani of the Sikh Masters.[91] This emphasis on humility is also demonstrated in what was not constructed, an absence as significant as material presence. Although Guru Arjan had towns, wells, and other structures built throughout the countryside to benefit both rural and urban Sikhs, nowhere do we find the commissioning of any building for his personal use. Among these we may include forts, palaces, mansions, or less grandiose structures for his immediate kin. It seems clear in light of his hymns that this was a conscious and deliberate decision, a clear departure from Indo-Timurid courtly precedent seen, for example, in stunning detail in the construction of both Fatehpur Sikri and Shahjahanabad.[92] Amritsar itself and the building for which Guru Arjan is best known, the Darbar Sahib or the Royal Court (that is the Harimandir which contains the *prakāsh asthān* in the centre of the sarovar in the Golden Temple complex), glorifies not the personal Guru but rather the Divine Guru and, in a Durkheimian way, the Sikh Panth under the Supreme Lord's guiding hand.[93] The purpose of these thus seems to reinforce what Pashaura Singh in his examination of the fifth Sikh Master calls, Guru Arjan's 'proactive approach' in that 'the compilation process of the Adi Granth went hand in hand with other major institutional developments in the Sikh tradition.'[94] There is in other words, a symmetry, a harmony of form, between the Adi Granth, its structure and message, and other historical and institutional enhancements within the Sikh tradition and the court of the tenth Sikh Guru. It seems clear that Amritsar as the home of halemi raj was to be included in this assessment. So also can be included the fifth Guru's kitab-khanah/pothi-mahal, the work shop which he certainly possessed and most likely inherited from his father.

This kitab-khanah/pothi-mahal would have possessed a resident staff of paper makers, calligraphers, illuminators, gilders, illustrators, inkmixers,[95] and scribes. Late sixteenth- and early seventeenth-century manuscripts of the Adi Granth provide evidence that some of these workers had earlier worked on Mughal Islamicate texts, probably at Lahore, since the emperor Akbar resided in this city between 1585 and 1598. Akbar was particularly keen on producing such hugely illustrated and entertaining manuscripts like the famous *Dastār-i Amīr Hamzah* known generally as the *Hamzah-nāmah* (produced between *c.* 1562 and 1577 CE).[96] Under the guidance of the fifth Guru, these scribes, among whom we may include Bhai Gurdas, helped prepare both drafts of the Sikh scripture and in due course its penultimate text, now known as the Kartarpuri Bir.[97]

It seems clear that in some respects the preparation of these early manuscripts of the Adi Granth were in line with standards established in the Mughal atelier. In the latter, for example, both the emperors and/or the overseers of the kitab-khanah would often write or impress 'inspection notes' (*'arz-dīdah*) onto the initial or final folios or within the manuscript margins. Such notes were very common and quite short, rarely more than two lines, and recorded the date of the inspection, its month, and regnal year.[98] In many instances, moreover, inspection notes were not simply concise 'arz-dīdah but took the form of directives which relegated the various tasks involved in painting and calligraphy to specific artists and calligraphers or, as often, specified the subjects of illustration ensuring that the portraits corresponded to the Persian calligraphy found on the respective folio or one very near by.[99] In other cases, inspections 'were carried out primarily to verify the physical presence and well-being of the manuscripts' as the possession of beautiful books added prestige and authority to the Mughal court and its emperors.[100] Like the Mughal emperors, Guru Arjan would too approve of correctly transcribed and written texts of the scripture by recording the word *sudh* or 'correct' in the margins. In manuscripts which were not initially so approved, we discover the words *sudh kichai* 'make corrections.'[101] The Mughal equivalent to such directives was the single Persian word *sahī* or 'sound', an inscription which may, for example, be seen in a flyleaf of the *c.* 1440 CE Timurid *Shāh-nāmah* found in the Mughal library which includes the seals of the emperors Babur to Aurangzeb.[102]

According to Pashaura Singh, it is quite likely that such procedures as placing inspection notices into manuscript copies of the Sikh scripture were put into place and such guidelines followed only after the fifth Guru's meeting with the emperor Akbar and his inevitable contact with the ensemble of artists, poets, calligraphers, and musicians which generally accompanied the great emperor's train.[103] As the emperor's cortége moved through Goindwal it is also very probable that Guru Arjan may have seen a number of earlier manuscripts from the Mughal library which travelled with the emperor.[104] One is very tempted to suggest with this in mind that the Sikh Gurus also adopted the habit of autographing manuscripts handed down to them by their predecessors after Indo-Timurid Mughal practice.[105] Once again we note, however, that while the principal concern of the artisans employed within the Mughal kitab-khana was to magnify the power and authority of the emperor and his court, the Guru's kitab-khana/pothi-mahal, based on the little evidence at our disposal, was devoted to the production of manuscripts which glorified the greatness of Akal Purakh, the True Guru.[106]

Notes

1. Guru Amar Das, *Rāg mājh ashtapadīān* 1(23), Adi Granth, p. 122.
2. My understanding of the 'Islamicate' is modelled along Hodgson's definition. See Marshall G.S. Hodgson, *The Venture of Islam: Conscience and History in a World Civilization I: The Classical Age of Islam* (Chicago: University of Chicago Press, 1974), pp. 57–60. It should be noted that I do not mean to imply that the culture of the Islamicate was a stable one, but rather, as Stewart Gordon has insightfully proposed for fifteenth and sixteenth-century India, 'a rapidly changing mix of influences from Central Asian nomadic war band life, Persia, Rajputs, and other local peoples in service.' See his 'Conclusions', in Stewart Gordon (ed.), *Robes of Honour: Khil'at in Pre-Colonial and Colonial India* (New Delhi: Oxford University Press, 2003), p. 146. As a clearly marginal group in sixteenth-century Islamicate Mughal India, it was unlikely that the Sikhs would add to this mixture on the larger scale.
3. The Punjab has been a shifting and fluid boundary since time immemorial. The Islamicate's familiarity with—and incorporation of—such symbols as the elephant (which incidentally Arabic and Persian poets outside the subcontinent considered quintessentially Indian) may have come simply from the porous nature of Islamicate culture which gradually and eventually made its way to the Punjab or rather from the Delhi Sultanate's patronage of Sanskrit learning or, the most likely, from both. See Chintaharan Chakravarti, 'Muslim Patronage to Sanskrit Learning', in D.R. Bhandarkar *et al.* (eds), *B.C. Law Volume* part 2 (Poona: Bhandarkar Oriental Research Institute, 1946) and K.A. Nizami, *Royalty in Medieval India* (Delhi: Munshiram Manoharlal Publishers Pvt. Ltd, 1997), p. xviii. For pre-Islamic royal courts and courtly culture consult Daud Ali's fascinating *Courtly Culture and Political Life in Early Medieval India*. A descriptive account of the courts of the Delhi Sultanate is Nizami's *Royalty in Medieval India*. Both the elephant and the canopy or chhatri may be seen on both pre-Gupta and Gupta-period (approx. 320–600 CE) coins. The successor of the empror Kanishka, for example, Huvishka (126–64 CE) is shown riding an elephant on a coin cast during his rule.
4. There were less formal contacts between India and Persianite Islamicate culture before the establishment of Mahmud's kingdom in the eleventh century. For these contacts see Muzaffar Alam, 'The Culture and Politics of Persian in Precolonial Hindustan', pp. 131–98, esp. p. 132.
5. Peter Hardy, 'Growth of Authority over a Conquered Political Elite: Early Delhi Sultanate as a Possible Case Study', in J.F. Richards (ed.), *Kingship and Authority in South Asia* (Madison: South Asian Studies, University of Wisconsin, 1978), p. 207.
6. For the history of this Islamicate movement eastwards and its adoption of both Persian/Sassanian bureaucratic and courtly norms there are a number

of sources which may be consulted. Brief accounts are Robert Canfield, *Turko-Persia in Historical Perspective* (Cambridge: Cambridge University Press, 1991), pp. 1–21 and Richard Frye, *The Golden Age of Persia: The Arabs in the East* (New York: Barnes and Noble Books, 1975), pp. 150–74. Also Meisami, *Medieval Persian Court Poetry*, p. 5:
> The emerging Arab Caliphate, stimulated by the demands of the new, urban society that was rapidly displacing the old tribal one, drew heavily on Persian models of court conduct and etiquette.

Meisami bases her conclusions in part on what Hodgson refers to in this context as a travelling *adab*, 'the worldly culture of the polite classes.' Hodgson, *The Venture of Islam* I, p. 239; also pp. 280–4.

7. Reynold A. Nicholson (ed. and trans.), *The Kashf al-Mahjūb: The Oldest Persian Treatise on Sufiism* (1911; 2nd ed. 1936, rpt London: Luzac, 1970).

8. Stewart Gordon, 'Introduction: Ibn Battuta and a Region of Robing', in Stewart Gordon (ed.), *Robes of Honour: Khil'at in Pre-Colonial and Colonial India*, p. 1. It appears that Mahmud was quite cognisant of his status as an upstart and wished to obviate his past by making his capital a cultural centre. Also see Marshall G.S. Hodgson, *The Venture of Islam*, pp. 39–42.

9. Dominic P. Brookshaw, 'Palaces, Pavilions and Pleasure-gardens', p. 199. Citing archaeological fieldwork in Afghanistan, Brookshaw states (p. 203),
> Just as the 'Abbāsid caliphs had numerous palaces and audience halls, so Ghaznavid sultans kept many gardens in which they staged *majālis*. Their capital city, Ghazna, sported several garden suburbs beyond the city proper....

10. Annemarie Schimmel, *Mystical Dimensions of Islam* (Chapel Hill: University of North Carolina Press, 1975), pp. 291–2.

11. Meisami, *Medieval Persian Court Poetry*, p. 11 and Jerome W. Clinton, *The Divan of Manūchihrī Dāmghānī: A Critical Study* (Minneapolis: Bibliotheca Islamica, 1972), p. 29.

12. Background on Mahmud and the Ghaznavids and the culture they ushered into India appears in C.E. Bosworth, *The Ghaznavids: Their Empire in Afghanistan and Eastern Iran, 994–1040* (2nd ed., Beirut: Librairie du Liban, 1973); see especially pp. 131–5 for the patronage of poets and poetry. Also C.E. Bosworth, *The Later Ghaznavids: Splendour and Decay* (New York: Columbia University Press, 1977). In the latter see pp. 74–7 for courtly life. For Ghaznavid poets one may consult the first ever anthology or tazkirah in Persian the *Lubābulalbāb* (Essence of Wisdom) by the thirteenth-century author Sadiduddin Muhammad 'Aufi. There are, moreover, a number of accessible monographs dealing with the lives and poetry of poets and scholars attached to the courts of both Mahmud and his successor Masud of Ghazna. Jerome W. Clinton, *The Divan of Manūchihrī Dāmghānī*; J.T.P. de Bruijn, *Of Piety and Poetry: The Interaction of Religion and Literature in the Life and Works of Hakīm Sanā'ī of Ghazna*

(Leiden: E.J. Brill, 1983); F.D. Lewis, 'Reading, Writing and Recitation: Sanā'ī and the Origins of the Persian Ghazal' (unpublished PhD dissertation, University of Chicago, 1995); and Sunil Sharma, *Persian Poetry at the Indian Frontier Mas'ud Sa'd Salman of Lahore* (New Delhi: Permanent Black, 2000). Also see Julie Scott Meisami, *Medieval Persian Court Poetry*. We should also note finally that although the term was coined by Mahmud the significance of both poets and minstrels to the royal court considerably predates his arrival in India. References to pre-Islamic court poets and minstrels may be found in Mary Boyce, 'The Parthian *Gōsān* and Iranian Minstrel Tradition', in *Royal Asiatic Society of Great Britain and Ireland* 18 (1957), pp. 10–45.

13. I am cognizant of doing grave injustice to the complicated and convoluted history of the twelfth to sixteenth-century courts of northern India as the shaping of these courtly cultures, especially that of the Delhi Sultanate and its contemporaries was by no means uncontested, unproblematic, nor was it one-sided. Indeed in many instances in the sixteenth century and before, we find 'the enhancement of regional literary cultures, largely by those very individuals and institutions that promoted Persian' (Muzaffar Alam, 'Persian in Precolonial Hindustan', p. 157). See for example, Irfan Habib, 'Formation of the Sultanate Ruling Class of the Thirteenth Century', in Irfan Habib (ed.), *Medieval India 1: Researches in the History of India, 1200–1750* (New Delhi: Oxford University Press, 1992), pp. 1–21; Iqtidar Husain Siddiqi, 'Social Mobility in the Delhi Sultanate', in Irfan Habib (ed.), *Medieval India 1*, pp. 23–49; Peter Hardy, 'Growth of Authority over a Conquered Political Elite: Early Delhi Sultanate as a Possible Case Study,' in J.F. Richards (ed.), *Kingship and Authority in South Asia*, pp. 192–214 and his 'The Authority of Muslim Kings in Mediaeval India', in Marc Gaborieau (ed.), *Purushārtha*, vol. 9, *Islam et société en Aise du sud* (Paris: Ecole des Hautes études en sciences sociales, 1986), pp. 37–54. Farther east and to the south the situation was not dissimiliar: Richard Eaton, *The Rise of Islam and the Bengal Frontier 1204–1760* (New Delhi: Oxford University Press, 1994), pp. 1–70; Phillip P. Wagoner, '"Sultan Among Hindu Kings": Dress, Titles, and Islamicization of Hindu Culture at Vijayanagar', in the *Journal of Asian Studies* 55:4 (1996), pp. 851–80; and James W. Laine, *Shivaji Hindu King in Islamic India* (New York: Oxford University Press, 2003), pp. 36–42. For a brief view of early courtly Hindi literature of this period see R.S. McGregor, *Hindi Literature From its Beginnings to the Nineteenth Century* (Weisbaden: Otto Harrassowitz, 1984), pp. 10–44.

14. The principal literary representatives of the Uzbek courts of the fifteenth and early sixteenth century include among others Daultatshah Samarqandi, 'Ali Sher Navai and 'Abdurrahmani Jami. While Mughal representatives, all Iranian born, included Fayz Fayyzi, Abu'l Fazl, and Bayram Khan-i Khanan, among many others. The scholarly literature dealing with them

and the courts and courtly styles of the Timurids and their successors, especially the fifteenth-century Uzbeks and sixteenth-century Mughals is vast. Some examples include Lentz and Lowry, *Timur and the Princely Vision*; Maria Eva Subtelny, 'Art and Politics in Early 16th Century Central Asia', in *Central Asiatic Journal* 27 (1983), pp. 121–48; Bonnie Wade, *Imaging Sound: An Ethnomusicological Study of Music, Art, and Culture in Mughal India* (Chicago and London: University of Chicago Press, 1998); and Douglas E. Streusand, *The Formation of the Mughal Empire* (New Delhi: Oxford University Press, 1989). Needless to say this is but a small sample. A far more robust bibliography is Stephen F. Dale, *The Garden of the Eight Paradises: Bābur and the Culture of Empire in Central Asia, Afghanistan and India (1483–1530)* (Leiden and Boston: Brill, 2004), pp. 471–94.

15. These ideas generally follow those found in Muzaffar Alam, 'Persian in Precolonial Hindustan', pp. 147–9. See particularly his intriguing discussion on page 148 in regard to the Arabic translation of the Panchatantra, the Kalīlah va Dimnah.

16. For malfuzat and other Sufi literature, see S.A.A. Rizvi, *A History of Sufism in India* 2 vols (Delhi: Munshiram Manoharlal, 1983). Another genre of Sufi literature which may be included here are the famous *maktubats* or collections of letters written by Sufi masters to their disciples which were often distributed amongst the pir's murids.

17. Muzaffar Alam, 'The Pursuit of Persian: Language in Mughal Politics', in *Modern Asian Studies* 32, 2 (1998), p. 349. One may also here include Akbar's patronage of Sanskrit poets. M. Athar Ali, 'Translation of Sanskrit Works at Akbar's Court', in Iqtidar Alam Khan (ed.), *Akbar and His Age* (New Delhi: Northern book Centre, 1999), pp. 171–80.

18. V.N. Rao, David Shulman, and Sanjay Subrahmanyam, *Textures of Time: Writing History in South India 1600–1800* (New York: Other Press, 2003), p. 225.

19. Slightly adapted from Gavin R.G. Hambly, 'The Emperor's Clothes: Robing and "Robes of Honour" in Mughal India', in Stewart Gordon (ed.), *Robes of Honour*, p. 35. Some of these Indian models included issues of bodily comportment promoted by specific forms of Sufi devotionalism, Hindu ascetic *sampradāyas*, and brahmanic traditions of *brahmachāryā* all of which were easily assimilated into the comportment of nobles and courtiers. As well let us keep in mind that Indian Persian was also slightly 'Indianized' especially in part because of the many Persian translations of Sanskrit texts. According to Muzaffar Alam, 'Persian in Precolonial Hindustan', pp. 142–7, esp. p. 149: 'The indigenous imagery thus gradually became a part of Persian literary style [in India] through the translation of Indian texts.' Also p. 154, n. 73 which expands this theme.

20. According to Muhammad Ali Quli Salim Tehrani (d. 1057/1647–8), one of the Iranian poets in Shah Jahan's court, for example:

In Iran there exists no instrument by which one may acquire perfection:
Henna does not develop its colour until it makes its way to India.

This famous and oft-repeated couplet is taken from Shibli's Urdu work the *Shir ul-Ajam* (The Non-Arab Poets) and appears in E.G. Browne, *A History of Persian Literature*, p. 166. A History of the large-scale emigration of court poets from Iran to India is found in Ahmad Gulchin-i Ma'ani, *Kārvān-i Hind: dar ahvāl va āsār-i shā'irān-i 'asr-i Safavī keh beh Hindūstān raftah and* [The India-bound Caravan: The Circumstances and Traditions Regarding the Poets of the Safavid Age who had Gone to India] 2 vols (Mashhad: Astan-i Quds-i Razavi, 1369/1990–1). For Salim specifically (although the bait above is absent) see vol. 1, pp. 566–82.

21. Christopher Shackle, 'Approaches to the Persian Loans in the *Ādi Granth*', in *the Bulletin of the School of Oriental and African Studies* 4:1 (1978), pp. 85–6.

22. Such terms are indeed rare but they do nevertheless exist within the scripture. One such, for example, is the word *singhāsan* which originates in Sanskrit (literally, 'the Lion's Seat') and may be translated as 'throne' (also 'heart' as implied in Guru Nanak's *Rāmkalī chaupade* 4(7), Adi Granth, p. 878: *jāpai jiu singhāsani loi*). The term occurs nine times in total twice in the bani of Guru Nanak (both in *ramkalī rāg*), once in Guru Ram Das (*rāg kanrā*), and once in Guru Arjan (*savaīe mahale panjve ke*). It is also used twice by Kabir (*āsā* and *rāmkālī*), once by Ravi Das (*sorāth*), and appears twice in the *bhattān de savaīe*. Gurcharan Singh (ed.), *Ādi Granth Shabad-anukramnikā* I (Patiala: Punjabi University Press, 1971), p. 377.

23. Bedi is the *zat* or caste to which Guru Nanak belonged. Gurinder Singh Mann, *The Goindval Pothis: The Earliest Extant Source of the Sikh Canon* (Cambridge, Mass.: Harvard University Press, 1996), p. 97. Mann claims that these pothis predate 1595 CE, the traditional date of their writing. Also see Gurinder Singh Mann, *The Making of Sikh Scripture* (New York: Oxford University Press, 2001), pp. 32–50; and Pashaura Singh, *The Guru Granth Sahib*, p. 103 regarding the term patishah within the Jalandhar Pothi.

24. For a similar example but in Persianized Marathi, see the *Hindu turk samvad* of the sixteenth-century sant Eknath. Sumit Guha, 'Transitions and Translations', pp. 25–6.

25. Gurinder Singh Mann, *The Goindval Pothis*, p. 193. My translation is slightly adapted from Mann's (p. 19).

26. Guru Nanak, *Japjī* 11, 25 and *Siri rāg* 4(7), Adi Granth, pp. 3, 5; 17 for example. Also Guru Nanak, *Basant ashtapadīān dutukīā* 5(3), Adi Granth, p. 1188:
> There is only one throne (*takht*) and there is only one Patishah. The [Lord,] independent [of all,] (*veparvāhu*; Persian: *be-parvā*) is everywhere present.

27. Guru Angad for example appropriates the term in a derisive way to explain the Kali yuga's chaotic effect upon the world. Guru Angad, *Vār malār* 22:1, Adi Granth, p. 1288:
   The name of the poor beggar is patishah and the name of the fool is pandit. See also Guru Amar Das, *Gaurī guarerī chaupad* 11(31), Adi Granth, p. 161; Guru Ram Das, *Gaurī kī vār* 10, Adi Granth, p. 305; and Guru Arjan, *Rāg Āsā* 3:105, Adi Granth, p. 397.
28. Vir Singh (ed.), *Srī Gurū Granth Sāhib jī dī Kunjī: Vārān Bhāī Gurdās Satīk Bhāv Prakāshanī Tīkā Samet Mukammal* (New Delhi: Bhai Vir Singh Sahit Sadan, 1997), var 1, pauri 47, line 2, p. 38. [Hereafter *BG*]. Guru Ram Das was a member of the Sodhi zat.
29. Var 39:3:2, *BG*, p. 602.
30. The author of this text met with the Sikhs in the mid-1640s. I have relied principally upon a relatively recent printed Iranian edition of the *Dabistān* which the editor, Rahim Rizazadah-'i Malik, credits to neither the Mohsin Fani nor to the Mirza Zu'lfiqar of popular tradition, but rather to one Kaykhusrau Isfandyar, apparently the son of Azar Kaiwan, a *mobad* or Parsi priest who founded the Yazdani sect of the Parsi tradition. Like the two authors of tradition this one as well seems to have adopted the penname 'Mobad'. See Mobad Kaykhusrau Isfandyar, *Dabistān-i Mazāhib* I [ed. Rahim Rizazadah-'i Malik] (Tehran: Kitabkhanah-'i Tahuri, 1362/1983), p. 206. This edition does not incorporate portions found within the recently surfaced Aligarh manuscript of the *Dabistān*, the Sikh section of which has been translated into English by Irfan Habib in his 'Sikhism and the Sikhs, 1645-6 From "Mobad", *Dabistān-i Mazāhib*', in J.S. Grewal and Irfan Habib (eds), *Sikh History from Persian Sources*, pp. 59-84. For an interesting discussion as to the actual identity of the author of the *Dabistān* see M. Athar Ali's posthumous, 'Pursuing an Elusive Seeker of Universal Truth—the Identity and Environment of the Author of the *Dabistān-i Mazāhib*', in the *Journal of the Royal Asiatic Society* 3:9:3 (November 1999), pp. 365-73. This article assumes Mirza Zu'lfiqar is the author and makes claims as to this regard by noting the very problematic passage in which the *Dabistān* author asserts that the good Mirza Sahib was called 'Nanak' by Guru Hargobind. Compare the statements in 'An Elusive Seeker,' p. 372 with *Sikh History from Persian Sources*, pp. 71-2, 82, n. 46. It seems to me that Habib and Grewal's interpretation of this dilemma is the more likely.
31. Pashaura Singh, *The Life and Work of Guru Arjan*, p. 85. This image of the Gurus as maintained by the bhatts is also noted within popular Sikh art. See for example figure 29 in W.H. McLeod, *Popular Sikh Art*, p. 100. The caption above Guru Amar Das is a shabad in praise of the third Master by Bhatt Bhikha.
32. Pashaura Singh, *The Life and Work of Guru Arjan*, pp. 84-5. The *Tikke dī vār* is not a part of the *Bhattān de savaīe* which appear at the end of the Adi

Granth. This hymn appears after those of Guru Arjan in *rāmkāli kī vār*. This peculiar placement, Gurdharam Singh notes, 'in the main body of the text lends weight to the authority of the passage...' Gurdharam Singh Khalsa, *Guru Ram Das in Sikh Tradition* (New Delhi: Harman Publishing House, 1997), p. 37.

33. The entire *Tikke dī vār* contains eight stanzas and appears in Adi Granth, pp. 966–8.
34. Rai Balwand and Satta the Dum, *Tikke dī vār, Ramkālī rāg* 6, Adi Granth, p. 968.
35. For example, Guru Arjan, *Gaurī bāvan akharī* 37, Adi Granth, p. 258: [The Lord] is the king over whose head is situated the royal canopy. O Nanak [apart from the True Guru] there is no other, there is no second. For more examples see Gurcharan Singh (ed.), *Ādi Granth Shabadanukramnikā* vol. I, p. 947. The chattar was probably assimilated into Islamicate standards via the Islamicate contact with the Indic culture of the eighth to the tenth centuries. An image of the royal chattar appears in Blochmann's translation of the *Ā'īn-i Akbārī*. Abu'l Fazl 'Allami, *The A-in-I Akbari* I [trans. H. Blochmann] (New Delhi: Low Price Publications, 1997), illustration across from p. 52 [Hereafter *AA*]. Images of the chattar are commonplace in Mughal miniatures. Further background appears in K.A. Nizami, *Royalty in Medieval India*, pp. 50–3.
36. Although there were instances in which the Mughal adopted simple coronation ceremonies this was rarely so. See for example the glorious two-folio frontispiece painted *c*. 1618 commemorating the accession of Jahangir by Abu'l Hasan. Milo C. Beach, *Mughal and Rajput Painting*, pp. 98–9 (a reference to Jahangir receiving this painting appears in the emperor's memoirs. Wheeler H. Thackston (trans.), *The Jahangirnama: Memoirs of Jahangir, Emperor of India* (Washington, D.C.: Smithsonian, 1999), pp. 267–8.) Other elaborate coronations were the famous crowning of Shivaji and the earlier kings of the Delhi Sultanate. James Laine, *Shivaji: Hindu King in Islamic India* (New York: Oxford University Press, 2003), pp. 30–1; and K.A. Nizami, *Royalty in Medieval India*, pp. 76–8.
37. Bhatt Haribans, *Savaīe mahale panjve ke 5* 1(20), Adi Granth p. 1409.
38. For the fly-whisk as a symbol of royalty see Daud Ali, *Courtly Culture*, p. 45 and especially p. 117: 'The ultimate submission to another king [in ancient India] was signified by fanning him with fly-whisks.'
39. Pashaura Singh, *The Life and Work of Guru Arjan*, p. 87.
40. Pashaura Singh, *The Life and Work of Guru Arjan*, pp. 88–9. That this belief was a part of earlier Sikh tradition is clear as it is also noted in the *Dabistān-i Mazāhib*. Persian text appears in Isfandyar, *Dabistān-i Mazāhib* I, p. 200, lines 11 ff. while an English translation is Irfan Habib, 'Sikhism and the Sikhs,' p. 65.
41. Bhatt Kirat, *Savaīe mahile dūje ke* 3, Adi Granth, p. 1391. This hymn was brought to my attention by Pashaura Singh. The lotus is the symbol of

detached existence par excellance as its flower floats atop the water while its roots are stuck within the muddy bottom.
42. Eleanor Nesbitt, 'Sikhism', in Peggy Morton and Clive Lawton (eds), *Ethical Issues in Six Religious Traditions* (rpt, Edinburgh: Edinburgh University Press, 1999), p. 103. As we shall see the same holds true for Guru Gobind Singh.
43. A list of such Sufi masters and their Persian poetry appears as Bruce Lawrence, *Notes from a Distant Flute: The Extant Literature of pre-Mughal Indian Sufism* (Tehran: Imperial Iranian Academy of Philosophy, 1978).
44. Simon Digby, 'The Sufi Shaikh as a Source of Authority in Mediaeval India', in *Purushārtha*, vol. 9, *Islam et société en Aise du sud* (ed.), Marc Gaborieau (Paris: Ecole des Hautes études en sciences sociales, 1986), pp. 57–77, esp. p. 60. The term tazkirah was also used to describe texts dealing with the lives of poets. These usually took the form of a brief biography of the poet with a number of his or her poetic samples. Tazkirahs would both praise and criticize depending upon the author's proclivities.
45. Simon Digby, 'The Sufi Shaikh', p. 62.
46. John F. Richards, *The Mughal Empire* (Cambridge: Cambridge University Press, 1993), p. 31. Akbar's reverence for the Chishti Sufis is beautifully brought out in the first few minutes of the classic film *Mughal-e-Azam* [The Great Mughal] (directed by K. Asif, 1960).
47. *Dabistān-i Mazāhib* I, p. 198.
48. The story of Babur and Guru Nanak's meeting may be found in Macauliffe, *The Sikh Religion*, vol. I, pp. 113–15. Early to mid-eighteenth century accounts narrating this meeting are W.H. McLeod (trans. and ed.), *The B40 Janam-Sakhi* (Amritsar: Guru Nanak Dev University Press, 1980), pp. 74–80 and Kesar Singh Chhibbar's *BSNV* 6:124–6, p. 98.
49. Jit Singh Sital (ed.), *Srī Gur-panth Prakāsh krit Bhāī Ratan Singh Bhangū Shahīd* (Amritsar: SGPC, 1994), p. 186. Even before Sarup Das Bhalla wrote his *Mahimā Prakāsh [Kavitā]* (The Glorious Effulgence [in Poetry]) in 1776 CE the idea had been put forward that the appropriation of such terminology may have played a role in the downturn in Sikh fortunes after the accession to the Mughal throne of the emperor Jahangir. We find for example in the twenty-second sakhi of the fifth chapter of *Mahimā Prakāsh* that the wicked Chandu Shah tells the emperor that

[Guru Arjan] has [people] call him sacha patishah [yet] he shows consideration to no one.

in the hope that such statements would incite Jahangir to take action against the Guru. *MP* II, 5:22:7, p. 411. The same understanding also appears in the narratives of Guru Tegh Bahadar as in the early nineteenth-century Persian text of Khushwant Rai, the *Tavārīkh-i Sikhān*. In regard to the period of Guru Tegh Bahadar such royal appellations may have certainly inspired Aurangzeb to take a dislike to the ninth Guru. Although Sikh accounts suggest this as early as the 1740s (see *MPV* sakhi 125, p. 174) the first instance I have found in Mughal sources appears within the 1723 CE text of Muhammad Qasim Lahori, the *'Ibrat-nāmah*. See Grewal and Habib (eds), *Sikh History from Persian Sources*, p. 113. But that such use provoked Jahangir is another matter entirely. It is certainly possible but questionable as this sort of terminological appropriation had been commonplace well before the time of Guru Nanak's birth. Certainly all of the Mughal emperors and their governors were cognizant of the Sufi use of royal terms to describe pirs and shaikhs and may have felt a little uneasy at such, but the Timurid emperors beginning with Babur and most certainly including Jahangir nevertheless continued to venerate specific Sufi pirs (and even Hindu gurus)—see for example the Smithsonian's famous portrait of Jahangir painted by the artist Bichitr, *Jahangir Preferring a Shaykh to Kings*—and chose to accept the use of such terms of royalty for what these were. Indeed, the Persian baits inscribed above and below Bichitr's famous painting suggest as much:

...Jahangir...is the monarch of both external form and inner intrinsic meaning/Although outwardly kings stand before him, inwardly he always keeps his gaze upon dervishes.

It seems unlikely that the use of such Persianite terms could have lead to the execution of a spiritual figure as highly venerated as Guru Arjan. A reproduction of this painting appears in Thackston (trans.), *Jahangirnama*, pp. 257, 476–7 which is also responsible for the above translation. Interestingly, in the *MPV*, Jahangir claims that Guru Hargobind rather than himself is the sacha patishah. *MPV* sakhi 84, p. 128 an anecdote one also finds in Macauliffe, *The Sikh Religion* IV, p. 19.

50. Var 11:13:4, *BG*, p. 183. Of course the term majlis may simply mean a gathering of Sikhs around the person of Bhai Gurdas or it may also mean the place at which such gatherings are held.

51. Muhammad Tahir Nasrabadi, *Tazkirah* (ed. Vahid Dastgirdi) (Tehran: Armaghan, 1938). Also Muzaffar Alam, 'Persian in Precolonial Hindustan', p. 177.

52. Just such a gathering took place in Agra in 1737 CE as noted in the Brajbhasha text of Rai Sivdas, the *Sarasasara*. Allison Busch, 'The Anxiety of Innovation', pp. 53–4. Also relevant is the fact that Jayarama Pinday's *Rādhāmadhavavilāsachampu* includes in its seventh canto a description of a literary competition which is very much like the majlis gathering (as noted in Sumit Guha, 'Transitions and Translations', p. 28). Also see Edwin Gerow, *Indian Poetics*, p. 220, esp. n. 8 which refers one to classical Indian examples of such literary one-upmanship. He states,

[*Samasyāpūrtī* ('pandit relaxations') occur] where scholars compete, more or less ad libitum, to complete a verse part of which has been fixed as a "problem" (*samasyā*); the Bhojaprabandha (sic) [attributed to Ballala] has may examples, including several fabulous ones about Kālidāsa....

78 The Darbar of the Sikh Gurus

53. The quote is R.S. McGregor's. See his *Hindi Literature*, p. 55. For further references to courtly Brajbhasha consult pp. 74, 118ff.
54. This is suggested in a number of mid-eighteenth century Sikh texts. Of the fifth Guru, for example, the *Mahimā Prakāsh Vārtak* (1741 CE) attributed to Kirpal Das Bhalla notes that

    At one time during which Guru Arjan was seated upon his throne (singhāsan) holding court, the entire sangat seated [before him], Bhai Gurdas arrived. He came before the True Guru and placed his forehead onto the floor. The Guru [then] instructed him: 'Bhai Gurdas, you have composed bani. Please recite [a line] for us.'

    Bhai Gurdas then recited a line from his var 35:20. Although this is probably the first time in Sikh literature that we hear of the vars of Bhai Gurdas described as bānī or sacred utterance it is more with the image of the Guru holding court (*dīvān lagā thā*) that we are concerned. Indeed, the lines *singhāsan par baithe the dīvān lagā thā* above do occur in other sakhis of the *Mahimā Prakāsh Vārtak*, usually at the beginning of individual anecdotes. Kulvinder Singh 'Bajwa' (ed.), *Mahimā Prakāsh (Vārtak)* sakhi 77 (Amritsar: Singh Bros., 2004), p. 121. [Hereafter *MPV*]. Others appear at sakhi 61, p. 105; sakhi 64, p. 108; and sakhi 67, p. 110–11 respectively. In the contemporary *CSRn*, line 589, p. 120 we discover the similarly phrased *darbār lagā hoiā sī*, 'The Guru's court was being held.' Other texts likewise illustrate the royal facets of the Gurus. We noted directly above the rahit-nama of Chaupa Singh Chhibbar (*c.* 1740–65 CE), but there is too the *Bansāvalī-nāmā* (1769 CE) of Kesar Singh Chhibbar and the *Mahimā Prakāsh [Kavitā]* (1776 CE) of Sarup Das Bhalla. See *CSRn* lines 171–4, pp. 81–2, 169; *BSVN* chapter 10, and Sarup Das Bhalla, *Mahimā Prakāsh* 2 vols [ed. Gobind Singh Lamba and Khazan Singh].
55. Bhatt Nalh, *Savaīe mahale chauthe ke 4* 6(10), Adi Granth, p. 1400.
56. Gobind Singh Mansukhani, *Guru Ramdas: His Life, Work and Philosophy* (New Delhi: Oxford and IBH Publishing Company, 1979), pp. 160–2. Also see *Bansāvalī-nāmā*, pp. 69–72 and *Mahimā Prukash* II 4:1:1–13, pp. 273–5. See too Bhatt Nalh, *Savaīe mahale chauthe ke 4* 4, Adi Granth, p. 1399.
57. Gurudharam Singh Khalsa, *Guru Ram Das in Sikh Tradition* (New Delhi: Harman Publishing House, 1997), p. 62. Also see W.H. McLeod, *Popular Sikh Art*, p. 103 for a bazaar print which does as much. Here, on the mat immediately above the footstool are embroidered the words of Bhai Gurdas noted earlier regarding Guru Ram Das as the Sodhi Patishah.
58. Surjit Hans, *A Reconstruction of Sikh History From Sikh Literature* (Jalandhar: ABS Publications, 1988), pp. 96, 104. These views should be supplemented with those of Pashaura Singh. See his *The Life and Work of Guru Arjan*, pp. 67–72; also pp. 105–11 for the later development of Amritsar.
59. Hans, *A Reconstruction of Sikh History*, p. 104.

60. Gurudharam Singh Khalsa, *Guru Ram Das in Sikh Tradition*, pp. 23–5. Tradition firmly holds that Akbar had met Guru Amar Das. Although Pashaura Singh has deftly argued the case for this 'incidental' meeting the fact remains that there is no contemporary textual evidence to support it. Pashaura Singh, *The Life and Work of Guru Arjan*, pp. 66, 107, 291–2. However, Akbar most certainly met with Guru Arjan in 1598 as this is noted in Abu'l Fazl 'Allami's *Ā'īn-i Akbārī*. See Grewal and Habib (eds), *Sikh History from Persian Sources*, p. 55. Jahangir comments upon the growing size of the Sikh population in Thackston (trans.), *Jahangirnama*, p. 59.
61. Chetan Singh, *Region and Empire: Panjab in the Seventeenth Century* (New Delhi: Oxford University Press, 1991), p. 173. See also Irfan Habib, *The Agrarian System of Mughal India 1556–1707* (second revised edn, New Delhi: Oxford India Paperbacks, 2002), pp. 85, 89–90.
62. Chetan Singh, *Region and Empire*, p. 173.
63. François Bernier made just such an observation a century later whilst living in Shahajahanabad. François Bernier, *Travels in the Mughal Empire, 1656–68* [Archibald Constable (ed.)] (New Delhi: S. Chand and Co., 1972), pp. 280–1.
64. See Guru Nanak, *Āsā dī vār* 13(1), 16(2), pp. 470, 472. For merchants and cities in Mughal India see Blake, *Shahjahanabad*, pp. 110–12. For Khatris and the economic prosperity of cities like Amritsar see Shireen Moosavi, 'Economic Profile of the Punjab (sixteenth-seventeenth centuries)', in Reeta Grewal and Sheena Pall (eds), *Precolonial and Colonial Punjab: Society, Economics, Politics and Culture* (New Delhi: Manohar, 2005), pp. 108–9.
65. Dirk Kolff, *Naukar, Rajput and Sepoy*, pp. 1–31.
66. Fauja Singh, *Guru Amar Das: Life and Teachings* (New Delhi: Sterling Publishers, 1979), pp. 116–29.
67. *SP* V 1:7:20, p. 1334:
    There were two plus twenty nobles (*umarāv*) [at the court in Delhi]. The same number of Sikhs were appointed as manjis.
    Santokh Singh here implies that nobles headed the provinces. Also see M.A. Macauliffe, *The Sikh Religion* II, p. 151.
68. Kirpal Das Bhalla uses this in the compound term *gur-gaddī* in *MPV*, sakhi 62, p. 106. The term gaddī was also used by Rajputs to denote a throne and was most likely borrowed by the Sikhs from this use. M. Athar Ali, *The Mughal Nobility*, p. 25.
69. Peter Andrews, *Felt Tents and Pavilions* II, p. 845.
70. Douglas E. Streusand, *The Formation of the Mughal Empire*, p. 126.
71. There is some debate as to whether or not Guru Ram Das is the originator of the masand system. In truth, we can never really know if he was though it is clear that by the time of the *Dabistān* (1640s), Sikhs believed the system to be in place during the guruship of the fourth Guru's son, Guru

80 The Darbar of the Sikh Gurus

Arjan. J.S. Grewal states that that there are 'indications in the compositions of Guru Ram Das that he authorized some of his Sikhs to act as his representatives and to collect offering from those Sikhs who could not come personally to the Guru.' J.S. Grewal, *The Sikhs of the Punjab* (Cambridge: Cambridge University Press, 1988), p. 52. Gurudharam Singh Khalsa notes (after Gobind Singh Mansukhani) that it is indeed likely that the *Dabistān* alludes to Guru Ram Das as the creator of the masands when it regularly refers to the masand officeholders by the alternate title 'Ram Das' in honour of the Guru, we are told, who founded the system. 'The evidence [of the *Dabistān*] is slim,' he rightly states, 'but it does lend support to the claim...' Gurudharam Singh Khalsa, *Guru Ram Das in Sikh Tradition*, pp. 109–10. Also Isfandyar, *Dabistān-i Mazāhib* I, p. 206.

72. The implication here is the existence of scribes (*likhārī*) in the entourage of Guru Ram Das. According to Piara Singh Padam:

Since the very time of Guru Nanak there has existed the custom of keeping scribes.

Padam, *Darbārī Ratan*, p. 248. Although he mentions the names of a number of scribes who served under both Guru Nanak and Guru Angad he states that

The sons and grandsons of Guru Amar Das were skilled in all of these [scribal] tasks and Guru Ram Das himself was the practitioner of the writing of bani.

73. Guru Ram Das, *Bihāgarā Chhant* 3(4), Adi Granth, p. 540. Although in contemporary Persian the term kitāb-khānah (lit.: 'book-house') means 'library' it meant far more to the Timurids and the later Mughals. It was rather an atelier. Apart from the production of all-important books as signifiers of power, prestige, and culture, the artisans of the kitab-khanah were also responsible for binding books, paintings (although painting production was often a department most likely within the kitab-khanah namely the tasvīr-khānah), engravings, calligraphy, etc. Guru Arjan's meeting with Akbar and the impression this may have affected on the fifth Guru and the later development of the Sikh Panth is insightfully noted in Pashaura Singh's *Life and Work of Guru Arjan*, p. 140. Guru Arjan's meeting with Akbar was recorded by Abu'l Fazl in his *Akbar-nāmah* a translation of which appears in Grewal and Habib (ed.), *Sikh History from Persian Sources*, p. 55.

74. Pashaura Singh, *The Guru Granth Sahib*, p. 136.

75. For a thorough description of late seventeenth and eighteenth-century karkhanahs, see R.K. Saxena, *Karkhanas of the Mughal Zamindars: A Study in the Economic Development of 18th Century Rajasthan* (Jaipur: Publication Scheme, 2002).

76. Tradition certainly claims that it did so. Madanjit Kaur, 'The Harimandir', in Fauja Singh (ed.), *The City of Amritsar: A Study of Historical, Cultural, Social and Economic Aspects* (New Delhi: Oriental Publishers & Distributors, 1978), p. 27.

77. Guru Ram Das was the first Guru to appoint a Sodhi family member to the guruship, a trend which continued until the human guruship was dissolved, according to tradition, by Guru Gobind Singh. Sikh tradition claims that in these cases it just happened that the family members were the best qualified candidates for the job but the context of Guru Ram Das suggests a different explanation to my mind. Clearly as a result of many factors including the larger number of Sikhs the significance and consequence of the guruship had increased dramatically by the time of the fourth Master. As Gurinder Singh Mann claims in the context of the naming of Ramdaspur:
  It was not Kartar or Govind—epithets for God in Sikh literature—but was the town of Guru Ramdas. Such naming may indicate a strengthening of the authority of the guru [sic], who was believed to be God's representative on earth.
Gurinder Singh Mann, *The Making of Sikh Scripture*, p. 12. Portrayal as a sacha padishah may then have prompted in part Guru Ram Das' decision. After all the worldly sovereigns did indeed appoint successors based upon such time-honoured precedents. There is one caveat to observe in this regard and that is that it seems unlikely that Guru Ram Das could have prognosticated the future development and future successors to the guruship.

78. What strongly supports this contention is that there is no evidence to suggest that the Sikh Gurus of the sixteenth and seventeenth centuries contested the royal court's administration of justice, an important facet of Indo-Timurid Mughal courtly procedure. Guru Nanak certainly condemns corrupt kings who 'must be bribed to administer justice' (*rājā niāu kare hathi hoi*, Guru Nanak, *Āsā chaupade* 3(4), Adi Granth, p. 350), but it is unlikely that this would have proscribed Sikhs from seeking redress through official channels. Sikhs who sought justice in this period still petitioned the local zamindars, village panchayats, and as a last resort the royal court or the emperor himself. Indeed, it appears that during Akbar's visit to Goindwal in 1598, Guru Arjan sought redress from the royal court in regard to the high taxes assessed on Punjabi peasants (Pashaura Singh, *Guru Arjan*, pp. 81–3) and too, as we shall see, Guru Gobind Singh himself made use of this feature of the Mughal court when he issued just such a petition to the Mughal emperor Aurangzeb in early 1705, most likely seeking the emperor's justice in regard to the Pahari Raja annexation of his residence of Anandpur. Certainly the Mughal emperors were very keen to ensure the propagation of their public image as the grand dispensers of justice even though in reality they were far more concerned with the needs of their nobility on whom their power and prosperity rested. See Linda Darling, 'Middle Eastern Advice for Indian Muslim Rulers', p. 13.

79. Hans, *A Reconstruction of Sikh History*, pp. 106–7.

80. Isfandyar, *Dabistān-i Mazāhib* I, p. 206; *Sikh History from Persian Sources*, pp. 66–7.

81. Isfandyar, *Dabistān-i Mazāhib* I, p. 206.

82   The Darbar of the Sikh Gurus

82. Gavin R.G. Hambly, 'The Emperor's Clothes: Robing and "Robes of Honour" in Mughal India', in Stewart Gordon (ed.), *Robes of Honour: Khil'at in Pre-Colonial and Colonial India*, p. 35 and his 'From Baghdad to Bukhara, from Ghazna to Delhi: the *Khil'a* Ceremony in the Transmission of Kingly Pomp and Circumstance', in Stewart Gordon (ed.), *Robes of Honor: The Medieval World of Investiture* (New York: Palgrave, 2001), pp. 193–222. Although generally outside the scope of our present concerns Bernard Cohn deals with turbans in a later period in his 'Cloth, Clothes, and Colonialism: India in the Nineteenth Century', in his *Colonialism and Its Forms of Knowledge* (Princeton: Princeton University Press, 1996), pp. 106–62. Very close Sikh male friends within India to this day exchange turbans as a sign of friendship. As well, it is not uncommon for leaders of the SGPC to grant siropas to particularly deserving Sikhs and non-Sikhs. The first tying of a turban (*dastār bandī*) is as well an important coming of age ritual for Sikh boys. Hew McLeod, *Sikhism* (New York: Penguin, 1997), p. 143.
83. Isfandyar, *Dabistān-i Mazāhib* I, p. 206.
84. Grewal and Habib (eds), *Sikh History from Persian Sources*, p. 80.
85. *EoS* I, p. 62.
86. Guru Arjan, *Sirī rāg* 13(2), Adi Granth, p. 74. This hymn was suggested to me by Pashaura Singh.
87. Pashaura Singh, *Life and Work of Guru Arjan*, pp. 118–27, esp. p. 121.
88. S.A.A. Rizvi and V.J.A. Flynn, *Fatehpur-Sikri* (Bombay: Taraporevala, 1975); Michael Brand and Glenn D. Lowry, *Akbar's India: Art from the Mughal City of Victory* (London: Sotheby Publications, 1985); and Stephen Blake, *Shahjahanabad: the Sovereign City in Mughal India, 1639–1739* (Cambridge: Cambridge University Press, 1991). Also note John Richards' particularly important discussion on the placement of the tomb to Shaikh Salim Chishti within the great congregational mosque at Fatehpur Sikri. John Richards, *The Mughal Empire*, p. 30. Akbar's city of Fatehpur Sikri we are told,

> was a political operation implemented to achieve two very precise aims. The town was conceived as a seat for the court...centralizing the court in order to keep the nobility firmly under control. It is perfectly possible that Akbar set about controlling the various tribes [*sic*] (Rajputs, Turks, Afghans, and Persians), who were continually at war with each other, by the simple expedient of uprooting them either from their territories or from an economic centre such as Agra. That Fatehpur-Sikri is a residential city, a "gilded prison" for the court...is demonstrated by the insufficiency of its military defenses.

Attilio Petruccioli, 'The Geometry of Power: The City's Planning', in *Mārg: Akbar and Fatehpur Sikri* XXXVIII:1 (March 1985), p. 57. See also Carla M. Sinopoli, 'Monumentality and Mobility in Mughal Capitals', in *Asian Perspectives* 33:2 (Fall 1994), pp. 293–308, esp. p. 300.

(Re)forming the Early Sikh Court 83

89. The statement on this particular sign reproduces Guru Amar Das' *Slok vārān te vadhīk* 28, Adi Granth, p. 1412.
90. For Mughal city planning as a nexus of political and cultural power see Attilio Petruccioli, 'The City as an Image of the King: Some Notes on the Town-Planning of Mughal Capitals in the Sixteenth and Seventeenth Centuries', in *Mārg: The Mughals and the Medici* XXXIX:1 (December 1985), pp. 57–68. Here on page 61 we find a description of the 'theatrical scheme of arrangement' that undergirds Fatehpur Sikri which transformed Akbar into a semi-divine being:

    The Anup Talao fountain and the Diwan-i-Khass, which embody complex symbols, make up at the same time an allegory of spiritual pilgrimage on the part of the Sufi Akbar from the terrestrial world towards Universal and Celestial harmony, the centre of which is placed Akbar in the role of Cosmocrat. A subtle play of equivocation between Cult of the Throne and Cult of the Divine spreads out from this strange building at Fatehpur-Sikri across the entire Mughal domain.

    Also see Attilio Petruccioli, 'The Geometry of Power', pp. 49–64; and Douglas Streusand, *The Formation of the Mughal Empire*, pp. 91–4. For individual buildings such as Mughal palaces and sub-imperial palaces (belonging to governors generally) as sites onto which the power of the sovereign is inscribed see Catherine Asher, 'Sub-Imperial Palaces: Power and Authority in Mughal India', in *Ars Orientalis* 23 (1993), pp. 281–302. A thorough discussion of Mughal and Mughal-style architecture appears in her *Architecture of Mughal India* (Cambridge: Cambridge University Press, 1992).
91. The anecdote regarding Guru Nanak falling into a trance when he reached the number thirteen while weighing items in the shop in which he was employed in Sultanpur is found in Macauliffe, *Sikh Religion* I, p. 33. Also *GNSR*, p. 107 n. Although this story is noted in the later Puratan janamsakhi it most likely had a long oral history prior to its recording one with which perhaps Guru Arjan was familiar. Incidentally, it was during the period of Maharaja Ranjit Singh that the wall and the gates were erected. *EoS* I, p. 109. Thirteen gates may be seen in the map of Amritsar supplied in Kahn Singh's *MK*, p. 76.
92. For the construction of Amritsar see Pashaura Singh, *Life and Work of Guru Arjan*, pp. 107–18. The details of Shahjahanabad's cityscape are particularly intriguing in this regard. See Stephen Blake's *Shahjahanabad*, pp. 26–82.
93. This is very much unlike previous courts within India which were housed in specifically developed palaces whose form often represented their function. A study of such palaces as narrated in Sanskrit literature such as the Arthashastra appears in Daud Ali's *Courtly Culture*, pp. 38–51. The Prakash Asthan of Harimandir Sahib is perhaps the equivalent to the *jharokā* or viewing balcony/window of Mughal palaces. Compare for example, the

jharoka of Shah Jahan in his public audience hall (*daulat khānah-'i khass va 'amm*) with the Darbar Sahib's prakash asthan in which we find the Guru Granth Sahib on a palki. An image of the jharoka appears as figure 5 in Catherine Asher, 'Sub-Imperial Palaces', p. 297. Of course today's Prakash Asthan is different from the Prakash Asthan of Guru Arjan's time.

94. Pashaura Singh, *Life and Work of Guru Arjan*, p. 144. Perhaps then we may thus see the term *mahallā* in a different light. The word appears at the end of a particular hymn or set of hymns followed by a number (1–5, 9) to designate the respective Guru author. The term in this context is unique to the Sikh scripture and means something like 'form' (according to Balbir Singh Nanda it is a Punjabized version of the Arabic *halūl* or 'descending': see his '*mahala*' in the *EoS* III, p. 12.). In its Perso-Arabic form however it means 'ward of a city', 'palace', and even metaphorically 'heart'. Steingass, *A Comprehensive Persian-English Dictionary* (Beirut: Librairie du Liba, 70), p. 1182. Also A.A. Dehkhoda's '*mahallā*' in his *Lughat-nāmah*, CD-ROM edition.

95. Perhaps the appearance of formulas to mix ink within manuscript copies of the Adi Granth suggests that a number of such manuscripts were prepared by copyists employed by various sangats or individual patrons. Within the rahit-nama attributed to Chaupa Singh Chhibbar for example the necessity of reading these formulas is laid bare:

    When the Sikh of the Guru reaches the conclusion of a reading of the Granth Sahib he should read the ink formula.

    CSRn, pp. 76, 163. Also worth noting are McLeod's comments to the note of his English translation of this line: *CSRn*, pp. 224–5. According to Gurinder Singh Mann Sialkot was a centre of papermaking.

96. Milo C. Beach, *Mughal and Rajput Painting*, p. 56. The text which is also known as the *Qissā-ye Amīr Hamzah* deals with the adventures of the Prophet Muhammad's uncle, Amir Hamzah. See J.W. Seller *et al.* (eds), *The Adventures of Hamza: Painting and Story Telling in Mughal India* (Washington, D.C.: Freer Gallery of Art and Arthur M. Sackler Allery, 2002). There were a number of illustrated texts for which Akbar's atelier is justly famous including both the *Razm-nāmah* (Book of Battles) which includes Fayzi's Persian rendering of the Sanskrit Mahabharata and the *Timur-nāmah* detailing the adventures of Akbar's ancestor, Amir Timur. This line of thought also appears in Pashaura Singh's discussions in his *Life and Times of Guru Arjan*, chapter 6.

97. The names of the many scribes who populated the Sikh court from the times of Guru Nanak to Guru Tegh Bahadar are in Padam, *Darbārī Ratan*, pp. 248–9. Within the darbar of Guru Arjan the scribes Bhais Haria, Sukha, Sant Ram, and Manasa Ram were under the direct supervision of Bhai Gurdas according to Padam, *Darbārī Ratan*, p. 248. Incidentally, I refer to the Kartarpuri Bir as the second to last one because it does not include the hymns of Guru Tegh Bahadar. Draft copies of the Adi Granth

have been examined by Pashaura Singh in both his *Guru Granth Sahib* and *Guru Arjan*.

98. John Seyller, 'The Inspection and Valuation of Manuscripts in the Imperial Mughal Library', in *Artibus Asiae* 57:3/4 (1997), pp. 243–335, especially p. 274.

99. See John Seyller's fascinating 'Scribal Notes on Mughal Manuscript Illustrations', in *Artibus Asiae* XLVIII (1987), pp. 247–77, especially p. 254 and figure 7 which mention that folio 382a of the British Library *Baburnāmah* for example has the following directive along the folio's outer edge: *sūrat-i ahū khar u...kah āmnah...kūh mīshavad bāyad kashīd*, 'A picture of an antelope...who...the mountains must be drawn.'

100. Seyller, 'The Inspection and Valuation of Manuscripts', p. 248.

101. This discussion is based in large part upon Pashaura Singh, *The Guru Granth Sahib*, pp. 122–3 and his *Life and Work of Guru Arjan*, pp. 160–1.

102. The only seal not seen here is Akbar's. This photo of this manuscript held by the Royal Asiatic Society (ms. 239) appears in Michael Brand and Glenn D. Lowry, *Akbar's India*, p. 90. The word sahī impressed by the deputy or secretary of the atelier is seen in the upper left-hand corner just to the right of Babur's bold seal in *thuluth* (Per: *sulusī*) script and the left of Humayun's nastalikh seal and below the term *avval dovum* indicating that this manuscript was 'First Class, Second Grade'. There is no scholar who has expended as much effort as John Seyller in analysing the dates and inspection notices found on Mughal-period manuscripts. A number of his works in this area may be consulted. Amongst others the two mentioned directly above as well as his 'For Love or Money: The Shaping of Historical Painting Collections in India', in Mason *et al.*, *Intimate Worlds: Masterpieces of Indian Painting from the Alvin O. Bellackj Collection* (Philadelphia: Philadelphia Museum of Art, 2001), fn. 35–7; and 'A Mughal Code of Connoisseurship,' in *Muqarnas* 17 (2000), pp. 178–203. A painting of a Mughal atelier in which just such a kitab-khanah overseer is portrayed appears in Milo C. Beach, *Mughal and Rajput Painting*, figure one, a detail from an *Akhlāq-i Nasīrī* (The Nasirean Ethics) manuscript across from the title page.

103. Pashaura Singh, *Life and Work of Guru Arjan*, pp. 137–41. As the trip and residence in Lahore took a great deal of time and energy on the emperor's part the processional train or courtly retinue of Akbar, according to the Jesuit Father Antonio Monnserrate reached a length of two and a half kilometres. J.S. Hoyland (trans., with annotations by S.N. Bannerjee), *The Commentary of Father Monserrate, S.J., on his Journey to the Court of Akbar* (London, Bombay: Oxford University Press, 1922). Abu'l Fazl too notes the length of the train though his estimation was approximately half that of Monseratte or about 1230 metres (i.e. 1540 *gaz illāhī*). See H. Blochmann (ed.), 'The Encampment on Journeys', in *AA* I, pp. 47–9. For the emperors processions generally see H. Beveridge (ed.), *The Akbar Nama* III, p. 549.

104. Pashaura Singh, *Life and Work of Guru Arjan*, pp. 81, 137–41. This seems a likely conclusion as it was through contact with Akbar's atelier in Lahore in 1590 CE that the Raja of Bilaspur, Tila Chand, was exposed to Mughal painting and probably Mughal manuscripts finished before 1590. See Catherine Glynn, 'Mughalized Portraits', pp. 236, 246–7, fn. 10. It is possible (though unknown) that the raja brought some of the artists along with him to Bilaspur. That manuscripts often travelled with the Mughal emperors is noted in an account of Humayun found within the *Akbar-nāmah*. H. Beveridge (ed. and trans.), *The Akbar Nama of Abu-L-Fazl* I and II (Delhi: Low Price Publications, 1998), pp. 309–10.

105. Pashaura Singh *Life and Work of Guru Arjan* too suggests this. A wonderful autograph of Shah Jahan exists in the very same <u>Shāh</u>-*nāmah* manuscript noted earlier (Brand and Lowry's *Akbar's India*, p. 90). This signature appears along with the various *nishāns* or seals of the previous emperor-owners beginning with Babur. For more autographs and the manuscripts on which these are found see John Seyller, 'The Inspection and Valuation of Manuscripts in the Imperial Mughal Library', figures 1–27, pp. 257–68. Nishans and autographs of the Gurus likewise populate a number of Adi Granth manuscripts.

106. Seyller, 'The Inspection and Valuation of Manuscripts', p. 277. Here, according to Seyller, '[inspection notes and autographs] seem to have been essentially markers of proud ownership, akin to the practice of modern museums of assigning hypothetical market values to irreplaceable objects.' Background on Akbar's kitab-khanah and the ideology and royal lineage it privileged is found in Michael Brand and Glenn D. Lowry, *Akbar's India*, pp. 57–106. Beautiful Persian miniatures of the kitab-khanah artisans at work appear on pp. 58, 59. The large number of autographs and statements penned by the emperors make clear that the emperors were very proud of their collections of manuscripts so much so that for the sake of underscoring their authority they had their manuscripts valued. See John Seyller, 'The Inspection and Valuation of Manuscripts in the Imperial Mughal Library', pp. 255 ff. Also see Shireen Moosvi, 'Making and Recording History—Akbar and the *Akbar-nāma*', in Iqtidar Alam Khan (ed.), *Akbar and His Age* (New Delhi: Northern Book Centre, 1999), pp. 181–7. A novel depiction of the activities within Akbar's kitab-khanah is the fictional account by Kunal Basu whose protagonist is named after the most famous Timurid Persian painter of the late fifteenth and early sixteenth centuries, Bihzad (d. circa 1525 CE). See Kunal Basu, *The Miniaturist* (London: Orion Books, 2003).

3

Court and Sport

ਹੁਕਮ ਨਾਮ ਅਤਿ ਦੇਸ ਸਿਧਾਏ । ਸੰਗਤ ਕੀ ਚਿੰਤਾ ਮਿਟਵਾਏ ।[1]

Written instructions were dispatched [by the Guru] throughout the entire land easing the anxieties of his sangats.

We may now turn to the life of Guru Arjan's successor, his son Guru Hargobind. Although Guru Hargobind is the first of the Sikh Gurus to have no shabads within the Adi Granth, there are a small number of works attributed to him. These are, however, of a variety that scarcely qualify as hymns or scripture since these are neither inspiring nor edifying but are rather in the form of commands collectively known as hukam-namas or Written Instructions.[2] Unfortunately the two extant hukam-namas attributed to Guru Hargobind make, surprisingly, no references to any of the accoutrement, royal or military, which the author of the *Dabistān* claims the sixth Master possessed.[3] This is in strong contrast to Sikh tradition's oft-repeated claim that Guru Hargobind's hukam-namas include requests for arms and horses and not for money.[4] Instead these contain simple requirements which seem rather mundane for a Guru whose reputation as a *sant-sipāhī* or 'saint-soldier' was already well established in the mid-seventeenth century—a point the *Dabistān* makes clear. In these the Guru asks his Sikhs to constantly repeat the name of the divine and to abstain from eating both meat and fish, requests which prompted Hew McLeod to include these hukam-namas within his discussion of the 'proto-rahit' and which cause others to question their authenticity as it seems unlikely that the sixth Guru whom tradition claims did eat meat would have advised his Sikhs to do otherwise.[5] These instructions also ask Sikhs to send draft notes (*hundī*) for money and to dispatch textiles such as a bag (*bāslā*) full of *ilāiche* [cloth] 'costing ten *mathas*' [so-called because this woven cotton and silk cloth looked like cardamom (*ilāichī*)], and birds such as a pair of Indian cuckoos (*koel*) and, in one case, a pair (*jorā*) of a special type of expensive pigeon apparently found only in Patna (*patne de kuko kabūtar*).[6]

The mention of the pigeons above is a reference which merits some further comment. Although pigeons were kept by the Mughals for what the emperor Akbar affectionately referred to as '*ishqbāzī* or pigeon-flying (literally, 'love-play'), a 'dull kind of amusement,' as Abu'l Fazl notes, that is associated with 'the ordinary run of people,' the request by Guru Hargobind makes no allusions to such common entertainments.[7] We can only assume, in the light of his more documented activities, that his need for pigeons was intended for such a pursuit. Secondly, it is true that the hukam-nama contains one reference to the Guru's court (gurū dī dargah). But this may be ambiguous. It suggests either the divine court of Akal Purakh and so is in line with the numerous allusions to the court we regularly discover within the Adi Granth, or it may allude to the court of the sixth Guru himself. There is a possibility, as well, that the Guru refers to both:

He whose rupees are obtained in the service of the Guru will find his place in the court of the Guru (gurū dī dargah).[8]

Finally, just above the reference to the Guru's court, Guru Hargobind refers to the sangat of Patna as the Guru's Khalsa.[9] What is significant here is the adoption of the Persianite term khālsā, perhaps the first in Sikh history, connoting the crown lands directly under the emperor's control to describe a Sikh community at some distance from Guru Hargobind. This may be a veiled allusion to the increasing prominence of the masands though such understandings may seem rather anachronistic.[10] Certainly the masands were gaining a reputation for selfish activities by this time as Bhai Gurdas seems to imply, but whether such disaffection was as widespread as it would be in the final years of the ninth Guru, is difficult to say.

GURU HARGOBIND AND THE HUNT

Although Guru Hargobind's hukam-namas are not particularly helpful, contemporary mid-seventeenth century sources, however skeletal in nature, do provide us with a point to begin a reconstruction of the sixth Guru's court. The two principal texts are the vars of Bhai Gurdas Bhalla which are strongly supplemented by the *Dabistān*. Both these authors were closely associated with the Guru's court. While Bhai Gurdas was also knowledgeable about the sixth Master's father, the author of the *Dabistān* was a companion of Guru Hargobind's grandson, Guru Hari Rai. Bhai Gurdas first describes Guru Hargobind in the forty-eighth paurī (stanza) of his first vār (ode). At the pauri's beginning we note that Bhai Gurdas is perhaps attempting to place the first five Gurus within a common Punjabi folk framework: Gurus Nanak to Arjan are now the famed *Panch Pīrs* or 'Five Spiritual Masters' of Punjabi folklore, thus superseding (for Sikhs) the legendary five Sufi pirs known and revered throughout the Punjab.[11] The original structure is further displaced with the sixth Guru who is not only the very image of Guru Arjan (1:48:2) but, according to Bhai Gurdas, is

The Guru [who is] the vanquisher of armies, the hero [who is] both very brave and benevolent.[12]

With such a description Bhai Gurdas is certainly breaking new ground. Although his twenty-fourth var (24:24–5)[13] does revert back to standard imagery in its depiction of the sixth Master, the martial theme is elaborated once again two vars later.

In its entirety pauri 24 of var 26 may be seen as an endeavour to address the anxiety which the Sikhs of Guru Arjan may have felt towards the new Guru's more martial demeanour, an apprehension which was perhaps understandable in the light of the emperor Jahangir's earlier execution of their spiritual Master.[14] In this pauri we are told that while the earlier Gurus had remained seated in a dharamsala this Guru wandered about freely; while other Gurus listened to the sacred utterances, Guru Hargobind neither recited nor heard such.[15] Bhai Gurdas concludes his var by claiming that despite these superficial differences Guru Hargobind was still the Guru in whom the joti of Guru Nanak shone and that as such his is a burden unbearable by most. The tacit statement here is that Sikhs must therefore end their misgiving as there is no cause for it.

There is a line, however, which is particularly significant for our purposes:

> [The earlier Gurus] were seated on a cot (manjī) blessing [their devotees] while this Guru keeps dogs and hunts.[16]

Although one may assume that Bhai Gurdas here exercises his poetic licence in an attempt to underscore the Guru's clear differences from his more-spiritually inclined predecessors by alluding to a pursuit considered particularly worldly, his claim is corroborated by the *Dabistān*, which also notes Guru Hargobind's fondness for the hunt in two separate instances:

> Afterwards, [Guru] Hargobind the son of [Guru] Arjan Mal ate meat and hunted prey (*shikār kard*) and the majority of his disciples adopted his practices.[17]

and

> [Guru Hargobind] adopted the manner of soldiers and, contrary to his father's practices, donned a sword, maintained servants (*naukārān nigāh dāsht*), and took to hunting (*shikār kardan gereft*).[18]

The fact that the Guru's disciples took so easily to hunting as the first *Dabistān* passage points out suggests that his followers were a part of the 'armed peasantry' we recognize in the work of Dirk Kolff.[19] In the latter passage we hear echoes of the concerns to which Bhai Gurdas (as a close friend of Guru Arjan's) must have been subjected by anxious Sikhs. These concerns notwithstanding statements such as these certainly created an image of the sixth Guru as an expert huntsman which Sikh tradition most enthusiastically embraced. We are told, for example, in the *Bansāvalī-nāmā* of Kesar Singh Chhibbar (1769 CE) that Guru Hargobind, seemingly echoing the words of the *Dabistān* above, went hunting along with his Sikhs after the birth of his daughter Bibi Viro:

> In the year sammat 1674 [1617 CE] Mata Nanaki gave birth to Bibi Viro. [Guru Hargobind] Sahib seized the sword and began to keep servants (*chākar*).[20] He took his Sikhs along with him hunting.[21]

Both the earlier *Mahimā Prakāsh Vārtak* attributed to one Bawa Kirpal Das (or Singh) Bhalla (*c.* 1741 CE) and the later *Mahimā Prakāsh Kavitā* of Sarup Das Bhalla (1776 CE) likewise refer to the Guru's hunting activities.[22] So does a text, dated to the early to mid nineteenth-century, *Gur-bilās Pātshāhī Chhevīn* (also known as the *Gur-bilās Pātshāhī 6*) that is usually cited as the principal text describing the sixth Guru's life. We discover, in one instance, an adolescent Hargobind who has arrived at his father's side after an invigorating hunt and just before the young Sodhi's marriage to the daughter of the particularly pious Sikh Narain Das:

Hargobind came at this time. He arrived, smiling, after having been hunting and [appeared] remarkably splendorous, his body positively bristling with energy (*tej su pāvati*).[23]

We focus specifically on Guru Hargobind's inclination to the hunt because one of the favourite royal amusements of the Indo-Timurid Persianite court was in fact hunting, often combined with another pastime, feasting.[24] There were many styles of royal hunting and depending upon which format was used for a particular hunt, it included a number of well-known symbols which were once again indicative of the royal personnel who most actively engaged in its pursuit.[25] At times even the animals who were used in the hunt received, literally, a royal treatment as was the case with Akbar's favourite cheetah, Samand-manik, whose servants sounded the kettledrum to announce its arrival.[26] Such dealings with hunting animals and their glorious descriptions by bards and chroniclers such as Abu'l Fazl provided an opportunity to indirectly narrate the qualities of the royal hunter himself.[27]

One should not however think of hunting merely as sport or leisurely activity, a point which both the author of *Gur-bilās Pātshāhī Chhevīn* and late sixteenth-century Mughal precedent explicitly note.[28] The praise and fondness for hunting in our texts may stem from the sport's symbolic associations, as hunting was a discipline, indeed a ritual, through which one exercised control and mastery over both oneself and one's environment. It was in a sense, a form of battle, a type of war (and so the presence of martial symbols such as the naqqara) which during Zahiruddin Babur's lifetime and well before 'blended almost seamlessly into military campaigns'.[29] This is in continuity with the determined exhortations we discover in both the Islamicate 'mirror' or advice literature as well as the later Sikh rahit-nama texts towards self-mastery, discipline, and humility.[30] Abu'l Fazl claims, for example, that while some 'superficial, worldly observers' thought of hunting as simply 'a sort of pleasure,' the more knowledgeable

> see in hunting a means of acquisition of knowledge, and the temple of their worship derives from a peculiar lustre. This is the case with his Majesty [Akbar]. He always makes hunting a means of increasing his knowledge... and uses hunting parties as occasions to inquire... into the condition of the people and the army... Short-sighted and shallow observers think that his Majesty has no other object in view but hunting; but the wise and experienced know that he pursues higher aims.[31]

Sikh tradition also implies that Guru Hargobind's hunting was not simply a one-sided endeavour nor merely an engaging pastime, that its goal too was the pursuit of lofty aims. In its case however the aims are far more lofty, indeed, heavenly. In one particularly interesting association the author of the *Gur-bilās Pātshāhī Chhevīn* sets the activity within a soteriological paradigm common to both the Sikh and Hindu traditions. Our author begins by describing the splendour of the nine-year-old Guru Hargobind's appearance (5:45) and ends by claiming that the sixth Master

> beautifully adorned his body by tying various weaponry to his waist band (*kamar*).[32] While hunting in the forest all [the prey] requested (*nivedai*) him to come [and dispatch them so that they may thus secure their liberation].[33]

It is most improbable that such understandings played any part in the Mughal fascination with the sport. Akbar's son, Prince Salim and then Jahangir, certainly took note of his father's disposition towards hunting. This is perhaps best summed up in his memoir, the *Jahāngīr-nāmah*, in which, during his eleventh regnal year (mid-1617 CE), he has his overseers of the hunt tally the number of animals which he (Jahangir) has hunted from age 12 in 1580–1 until March 1617. The end result, Jahangir states, was a staggering 17,167 animals of which 86 were lions.[34] Shah Jahan too enjoyed the activity and was depicted doing so in a number of Mughal miniatures.[35] Since Guru Hargobind's association with Jahangir later in the emperor's life and his service to Shah Jahan soon after the former's death are clearly noted in the *Dabistān*, it is quite likely that the sixth Guru accompanied Jahangir on the occassional hunt and while so doing became cognizant of the fact that hunting was a royal activity and that such activity provided a multifaceted arena for the display of both martial and courtly qualities.[36] Indeed, at times hunting parties may well have appeared to onlookers as the royal court itself, especially when we note how mobile the court of Akbar was on occasion. On one simple hunt, for example, we are told that Akbar was accompanied by a veritable battalion of courtiers and followers along with 100 elephants, 500 camels, 400 wagons, and 100 bearers. This extensive list continues with 1000 *farrāshī*s (officers who supervise the pitching of tents or the chamberlains who spread carpets or cushions),[37] 100 water carriers, fifty carpenters, and at least 150 common workmen and 500 pioneers.[38] It seems likely given Jahangir's more sedentary nature that his hunts, although held more often, were far less extravagant affairs and involved fewer personnel, especially when we consider the emperor's dislike of noisy beaters.[39] The progress of the court through the countryside thus served many functions apart from the mere display of kingly wealth. Amongst these we may include an opportunity to offer humble subjects access to the king, an occasion to enquire into the affairs of local residents, and an exhibition of the king's ability to protect his people.[40]

Sikh tradition tells us that Guru Hargobind did at times accompany Jahangir on his hunts, in one instance, saving the emperor from a particularly aggressive tiger, according to Santokh Singh's mid-nineteenth century *Sūraj Prakāsh*.[41] Although Sikh writers are here most likely exaggerating as neither Jahangir's memoirs nor contemporary Persian accounts make any reference whatsoever to this incident, it is nevertheless an embellishment which helps underscore the royal nature of hunting and the royal, perhaps manly, bearing of the Guru, a demeanor far superior to that of the emperor himself as it was the sixth Master who kept his head about him when the tiger attacked.[42] Such anecdotes moreover seem to suggest the tension which must have manifested itself between the sixth Guru and the emperor responsible for his father's demise.[43] Sikh tradition here mirrors a reality as hunting and other outdoor activities did provide, as Peter Hardy suggests for thirteenth-century hunting in India, a theatre for contact between Muslims and Hindus, and it seems in this case Sikhs.[44] One may therefore assume that such activities allowed both Guru Hargobind and Jahangir to share their many ideals about bravery, appropriate comportment, and perhaps courtliness.[45]

Since the evidence for the sixth Master's hunting activities is certain we may infer that he possessed many of the royal trappings and accessories generally used in the endeavour.[46] These would include tents, kettledrums, servants to act as beaters, and 'nobles' who had accepted service with Guru Hargobind and demonstrated such in the hunting camp.[47] It is perhaps for the hunt that Guru Hargobind is claimed by the author of the *Dabistān* to have had a large retinue including 700 horses, 300 horsemen, and 60 musketeers which he kept ready at Kiratpur.[48] It is most likely this reference that prompted William Irvine to suggest that the sixth Guru held a significant position in the Mughal court.[49] Moreover, the fact that these numbers neatly correspond to those maintained in the contingents of Mughal mansabdārs (that is, a similar 1:5 ratio of horsemen and infantry) suggests, as Iqtidar Alam Khan has conjectured, that the armed bands led by the sixth Master 'were organized on the pattern taken from [his] adversaries [i.e. the Mughals].'[50] We earlier noted this Mughal to Sikh correspondence in Guru Amar Das's creation of manjis and subsequently the masands of Guru Ram Das.

Tradition also claims that Guru Hargobind often made use of hunting-birds, hawks in particular, and although the *Dabistān* fails to mention this point, it may be implied in its references to hunting.[51] According to Sikh tradition, it was this partiality which initiated a change in the sixth Guru's relations with the emperor Shah Jahan. In one version of what has become a very popular Sikh tradition, Chiman Khan (Asman Khan in later accounts), the son-in-law of Guru Hargobind's servant Painda Khan, captured the sixth Master's rare white hawk and ultimately gave it to the emperor (in return for a jagir or landholding) whose retainers had refused to return it to the Guru.[52] This incident, however, cannot be corroborated with contemporary evidence though hawks were, to be sure, amongst the favourite royal hunting birds of the Mughals.[53]

Guru Hargobind as King

Tradition has appropriated these evident interests which were generally the prerogative of royalty and interpreted them as components within the kingly and courtly attributes of the sixth Guru. As in both epic and Mughal courtly literature we find eighteenth- and nineteenth-century Sikh descriptions of the sixth Guru's appearance, his daily routine, as well as his comportment among other such descriptions. This was perhaps on the one hand, in an attempt to provide an *imitatio*, or ideal blueprint for pious Sikhs as to how to live a life most 'Guru-oriented' while on the other, to demonstrate that the sixth Guru had a personal presence which generated loyalty and devotion in his troops and his Sikhs.[54] Such descriptions are still recited to pious Sikhs by *kathākārs* throughout India and abroad.[55] As a harbinger of interpretations to come we are told in the *Gur-bilās Pātshāhī Chhevīn* that the martial Guru's birth was itself heralded by instruments usually associated with the royal court:

The *turhī* (a type of aerophone), the small drum (*dhol*) and the kettledrum (*nagāra*) were all sounded. The gods created the collyrium made from flowers while Sikh sangats from all over India came [and gathered together].[56]

Such announcements were meant to elicit little surprise among Sikhs as Guru Hargobind was a little later in his life the Guru responsible for the building of the Akal Takht or Throne of the Immortal [Lord] which inhabits the precincts of the later-day Golden Temple. Built, according to tradition, in the year of the Guru's investiture it was

a simple platform, 3.5 metres high, on which the Guru would sit like a king at court, surrounded by the insignia of royalty such as the parasol and the flywhisk, and perform kingly tasks of receiving petitions and administering justice.[57]

The kingly and martial demeanour of the Guru is also implied in his construction of far less sanctimonious structures such as the fortress of Lohgarh just outside of the old city of Amritsar and the nine-storied tower of Baba Atal Rai on the precincts of today's Golden Temple, and in his foundation of the town of Sri Hargobindpur along the western bank of the Beas River in district Gurdaspur, the pattern of which, according to Gurmeet Rai and Kavita Singh, 'has its roots in the organization of military encampments.'[58] While such a project seems likely to have provided the Guru with the potentially vast hunting ground just outside of the town, it also seems clear that the sixth Master encouraged Sikhs to settle within Sri Hargobindpur perhaps offering to merchants, as tradition claims, 'free land if they built a house, and free bricks if their built a two-storied house.'[59] The construction of Sri Hargobindpur and Guru Hargobind's hunting expeditions seem therefore to have provided to Sikhs, who were anxious after the emperor's execution of the previous Guru, a symbol of the protection and refuge they most likely sought. According to Sikh tradition the many tours of the sixth Guru's son Guru Tegh Bahadar in the 1660s and 70s had this aim very much in mind.

Funds for these building projects were most likely collected from the various offerings given to both the Guru and his masands, a point which is implied in the *Dabistān*'s references to and anecdotes about loyal masands of the sixth and seventh Gurus such as Jhanda [*sic*. Chanda], Bidhita [*sic*. Bidhia], Sadha, and Debi Chand, son of Pirana the Jat.[60] We may once again assume that this particular building project was as well commensurate with the values and ideals of the Adi Granth in the same way as that of both Amritsar and Taran Taran.

The *Dabistān* thus provides us with some insight into both the Guru's conduct and his court. Circumstantial evidence moreover proclaims that a court was in place: as the most recent incumbent to the guruship it seems clear that Guru Hargobind would have been surrounded by professional musicians and pious Sikhs at the least. Since the *Dabistān* does allow us to clearly infer that during Guru Hargobind's tenure, the message of Guru Nanak remained unchanged,[61] we may thus assume that the Guru would have maintained the ragis, bards, minstrels, and scribes implied in the compositions of the bhatts and the Gurus. So too we may conjecture the continued existence of the kitab-khanah/pothi-mahal which most likely began with Guru Ram Das and was sustained by Guru Arjan. The fact that the sixth Guru's autograph appears on the Kartarpuri Bir as a sign that he had inherited the text from his father, implies this among other things.[62] Interestingly, the author of *Gur-bilās Pātshāhī Chhevīn* mentions that not only did Guru Hargobind keep a retinue of ragis or reciters of the sacred scripture within his court along with the various soldierly personnel noted by Bhai Gurdas but that he also kept near him 'martial' minstrels, dhādhīs, the most famous of whom were Mir Abdul and Natha.[63] In his court both groups sang in front of the Akal Takht, playing many of the instruments which were generally played by the musicians of Mughal nobility.[64] In one instance, for example Dhadhi Abdul takes up the long membrophone known as the *nishān*[65] and the naqqara-like drum called the *shutrī* which was played on the back of the camel from which this specific instrument received its name (Per: shutar, 'camel').

Baba Buddha spoke as follows, 'Listen to the Lord and happiness shall be obtained.' A dhadhi fetched both the shutri and the nishan. The dhadhi who did so lived [in] Sur Singh [Nagar in Amritsar district] in a home of talented [individuals] (*gun sadnā*). Abdul was his name and his heart had become free from both delusion and pride.[66]

And in another both Abdul and Natha, witnessing for the first time the splendour of the Akal Takht, compose and sing a panegyric in praise of Guru Hargobind, commemorating the completion of the Akal Takht's construction:

This true throne has been put down by the revered Guru [who] is pleasing. Its magnificence cannot be described. Tell [me]: what can I sing of it? Having seen this glorious sight the very brightness of both the sun and the full moon is dimmed [in comparison]. The revered Guru reposes (*birāje*) on the throne and contemplates the True Lord. Mir Abdulla and Nattha have adorned him with glory (*jas*).[67]

This last tradition is not a part of the contemporary seventeenth-century Sikh record but it is nevertheless very much in line with general Indo-Timurid courtly standards. It was certainly not uncommon for poets, professional and amateur alike, to prepare literary works to commemorate the construction of particularly magnificent monuments and palaces as well as the unveiling of a particularly outstanding regal accoutrement (such as the Peacock Throne of Shah Jahan) with the 'purpose-poem'. The best known and perhaps most beautiful Mughal edifice, the Taj Mahal, for example had a number of contemporary poets put their hand to its praise, the most noted of whom was Shah Jahan's poet laureate Abu-Talib Kalim.[68]

Thus we have in both, the contemporary record and within later narratives of the sixth Guru, an image which is clearly royal and courtly in nature: a kingly Guru surrounded by warrior/servants, court musicians, scribes, and perhaps poets who possessed the 'liberty of the manor'. Tradition claims that the next two successor Gurus, Hari Rai and Hari Krishan, continued to display these standards of kingliness. Although contemporary evidence regarding the guruship of Guru Hari Krishan is virtually non-existent we may once again reference the *Dabistān* for anecdotes regarding the seventh Guru.[69] These merit perhaps the most serious consideration as our author claims that he was very closely acquainted with this Guru whom the Sikhs referred to as *mahall haftam*, the seventh mahal.[70]

A Less Martial Guru

As we have seen the author of the *Dabistān* was certainly aware of the royal imagery which permeated the Sikh descriptions of the previous Gurus to which he had been privy. It is not surprising therefore that he adopts this style of portrayal in regard to Guru Hari Rai. It bears repeating that this depiction seems somewhat more significant than the similar ones of the previous Gurus as our author most likely witnessed events unfold before Guru Hari Rai first-hand. We hear, for example, of Guru Hari Rai's departure to Thapal in the territory of Sirmur soon after his succession to the guruship in 1644 (*sic* 1055 H.).[71] Although Thapal proper has yet to be identified, the migration to it is nevertheless a fact which may be corroborated by the information given on folio 3b of the Jograj manuscript copy of the Adi Granth completed in 1667 CE (Punjabi University Museum ms. 2).[72] It is, however, the description of the seventh Master's investiture which I would like to note. The *Dabistān* here states that

At the time of [Guru Hargobind's] own death [in 1644 the sixth Master] installed him [Hari Rai] onto his own place and arranged the robe of honour of succession (*khil'at-i khilāfat*) over his body.[73]

This description of the successor Guru's investiture with the robe of honour in an almost Sufi-like way[74] is unique as all previous Gurus most likely succeeded the previous incumbent in the ways enthusiastically narrated in the *Tikke dī vār* or *Bhattān de savaīe*. That Guru Hargobind 'robed' Guru Hari Rai in this clearly Islamicate manner is plausible, particularly in the light of the later Puratan Janam-sakhi narrative which claims that the first Master was himself draped with the robe of honour (*sirupāo*) by Akal Purakh while immersed in the Bein River, the primal Sikh myth.[75] But this reference in the *Dabistān* is impossible to verify. It may well be that for our Zoroastrian author the description of the installation was simply an echo of standard stereotypical Persian vocabulary. Guru Hari Rai's comportment may likewise be gleaned from other references in the *Dabistān* but ultimately these too are based solely on inference. We may only assume for example that the seventh Guru, in much the same way as his grandfather, continued to hunt and that he also kept a retinue of soldiers with him, assumptions that are strengthened by tradition.[76] Such inference is based principally upon the *Dabistān*'s claim (in the context of the hunt) that *aksar az murīdān-i īshān tarīq-i ū pīsh gereftand* 'most of [Guru Hargobind's] disciples adopted his practices.' We may assume that disciples who happened to be blood relatives also participated in such activities. Unfortunately the *Dabistān* says nothing about a court although certain manuscript copies of the Adi Granth produced during the period of Guru Hari Rai (1644–61 CE) do imply some sort of Sikh group surrounding the seventh Guru as well as suggest the existence of a kitab-khanah/pothi-mahal. In a seva-panthi manuscript dated sammat 1710 (1653 CE) for example our scribe refers to this group simply as the *Gur Har Rai jī kī sangat* 'the sangat of Guru Hari Rai.'[77] By the early twentieth century these groups became a court as implied, for example, in Rose's glossary:

Less warlike than his grandfather, Gurú Har Rái still maintained the pomp and circumstances of a semi-independent military chieftain.[78]

In the next passage Rose mentions the seventh Guru's association with the eldest son and intended successor of Shah Jahan, Dara Shikoh (d. 1658). Since the mid-eighteenth century, Sikh tradition has highlighted this meeting between the two men as responsible in part for the eventual enmity between the Sikhs of the Guru and emperor Aurangzeb, ultimately resulting in Ram Rai's presence at the darbar of 'Alamgir.[79] Contemporary sources regarding this event are however silent. As far as I know it is first noted some forty years after the alleged event in Sujan Rai Bhandari's Persian chronicle *Khulāsatuttavārīkh* (The Essence of History) completed in the fortieth year of Aurangzeb's reign (1696 CE), the same year that Prince Mu'azzam (later Bahadar Shah) was sent to the Punjab to discipline the Hill Rajas whose territories lay adjacent to the tenth Guru's at Anandpur-Makhowal.[80] A Persian inscription found in Dehradun, the residence of Guru Hari Rai's wayward son, Ram Rai, dated 1699 CE (1110–11 H.) supports Sujan Rai's conclusions claiming in one instance that, 'After lowering his banners throughout the empire, Dara Shikoh made it known that he was going to join the service of the Guru.'[81]

THE PERIPATETIC GURU AND HIS ENTOURAGE

While we remain unsure as to Guru Hari Rai's meeting with Mughal noblemen and princes we are quite certain that his uncle, Guru Tegh Bahadar, did indeed count such personages among his many acquaintances. And this knowledge is due, in part, to the fact that Guru Tegh Bahadar unlike his predecessors wrote a large number of hukam-namas (thirty-one genuine hukam-namas are extant) which he had dispatched to numerous sangats throughout eastern and western India. In one hukam-nama, for example, the ninth Master instructs his Sikhs to send gifts (caskets, pitchers, and bowls of good workmanship) to Nawab Saif Khan (d. 1685 CE), a scholar, poet, patron, and mansabdar who according to Shah Nawaz Khan's *Ma'āsirulumara'* (Contemporary Nobles) was born in India to a father (Saifuddin Mahmud Khan) of Central Asian descent (i.e., Turani) and possessed a rank of 1000/300.[82] According to Sikh tradition Nawab Saif Khan, residing very close to modern-day Patiala, was a great friend of the Guru who had often invited Tegh Bahadar to reside with him as the latter travelled through northern and eastern India. During one of their partings, tradition claims, Saif Khan had gifted Guru Tegh Bahadar with a horse, Siri Dhar, which would become the ninth Master's beloved companion.[83]

There are, moreover, references to an unnamed raja whom the ninth Guru accompanies during his travels eastwards. This raja, it appears, is most likely the Rajput courtier, Raja Ram Singh Kacchawaha of Amber whose rank was rather more impressive than the good nawab's.[84] Received at Amber by the emperor Shah Jahan in 1643 CE when he was a mere eight years old,[85] by the latter part of his career Ram Singh was possessed of an extraordinary mansab of 5000/5000 (*do-asp seh-asp*).[86] Though a highly placed Mughal courtier Ram Singh did run afoul of the emperor Aurangzeb both for supporting Aurangzeb's rival Dara Shikoh during the war of succession and for his implication in the daring escape of the Maratha leader, Shivaji Bhonsale, from Mughal custody in 1666 CE.[87]

Sikh tradition also claims that Ram Singh's fondness for the ninth Guru, an affection which prompted him to intercede on the Guru's behalf and then release him from confinement when the ninth Master was first presented to the emperor in 1665 CE also increased Aurangzeb's distrust.[88] This explains why the emperor posted the Kacchawaha Rajput to the very inhospitable Assam in late 1667 where he would squander the next nine years engaged in a fruitless campaign. It was here that he would spend two years with Guru Tegh Bahadar until the Guru began his return to the Punjab in March 1670. Although Ram Singh was relatively disgraced, he was nevertheless the patriarch of an exceptionally important Hindu lineage. His father, Jai Singh (d. 1667 CE) had been given the Timurid title *mirzā* (from *amīrzāda*, 'progeny of Amir [Timur]') by Shah Jahan in March 1639, underscoring his extraordinary standing within the Mughal courtly hierarchy. The granting of this title thus symbolically and verbally incorporated the Kacchawahas into the Mughal courtly sphere in a way similar to the Mughal emperors' own incorporation into the religio-cultural sphere of the Rajputs.[89] This implies, as Catherine Glynn explains in her analysis of Mewari Rajput painting, that the close proximity to

> the Mughal way of life, whether at the Imperial court or with the Mughal rulers in the field, exposed the Rajput upper class, and especially the Kachhwahas, to numerous examples of imperial taste, a taste that must have appeared elegant and refined.[90]

It is impossible to say how Guru Tegh Bahadar would have felt in regard to such courtly tastes but it is nevertheless safe to assume that the ninth Sikh Master's ties to and gift exchanges with these and other rather lofty representatives of the Mughal nobility suggest a familiarity with the Mughal darbar and the followers who surrounded such prestigious noblemen, that was seconded only by that of the ninth Guru's father, Guru Hargobind.

This broad interaction with Mughal nobility is also clear by other references found in the hukam-namas, particularly in the items requested by the Guru as well as those objects which he conferred upon members of the various sangats addressed, implying a cognizance of Indo-Timurid courtly propriety. In one of his written instructions, for example, the ninth Guru asked Bhai Dayal Das and the sangat of Patna to procure tents from Sahazadpur for the Guru's camp:

Brother, we want to write to Sahazadpur [to purchase] tents (*kheme*) for our camp.[91]

The Punjabi/Brajbhasha term here used for tents, *kheme*, is derived from the Persian <u>kh</u>aimah (pl. <u>kh</u>aimah-hā) which may suggest the tent as the royal symbol, but the context of the request seems a casual one, without any royal or symbolic connotations. The term khaimah was after all sometimes used during the fourteenth century and afterwards to simply describe the tents of the soldierly.[92] However, in another hukam-nama addressed to the same sangat, the Guru again desires a tent from one Bhai Raja but this is the *ravātī* (also *rā'ūtī*), the smaller quadrangular tent or pavilion with a pyramidal roof,[93] originally associated with lesser Indo-Timurid nobles (but known later in the seventeenth century as a retiring tent). This suggests that the Guru was aware of the symbolism behind the former.[94] Certainly, the ninth Guru was quite familiar with items specific to Indo-Timurid princely tentage for in this hukam-nama we too find Guru Tegh Bahadar requesting tently accoutrements such as the *qalandarī*, the ridged fly of waxed cloth pitched above a large tent, in this case for the kitchen (*rasoi*); the qanāt, the section of canvas screen for an enclosure; and the latrine (*sehat-khānā*; Per: *si<u>hh</u>at-<u>kh</u>ānah*). We also find the term *suhelā* which seems to indicate a rather large commodious kind of canopy though this is not found in references to either Turkic or Timurid princely tentage.[95] In the hukam-nama which names Saif Khan, moreover, we find the terms *navāb* ('a girth of webbing used to restrain a trellis wall or the frame of a wooden pavilion') and *tanāvā* (Arabic: *ṭanāb*) which is a tent or a guy rope.[96] Tradition claims that Guru Tegh Bahadar spent a number of years travelling throughout central and eastern northern India, tours which would in many instances have required the use of tents and other outdoor gear thus allowing us to assume the presence of the <u>sh</u>agirdān and <u>sh</u>āgird-pī<u>sh</u>ah, 'tent-raisers' and 'a camp following' respectively. The references to tents and tentage therefore, like the many allusions to the Guru's darbar noted in these written instructions are ambiguous: they may be courtly in nature or they may not. The ninth Guru's cognizance of the language and specific items of princely tentage, moreover, may simply stem from the assumption that one of the Sikhs of the Patna sangat, Bhai Raja, was a tent dealer by trade.[97]

But courtly evidence is certainly supplied in another reference. In a hukam-nama dispatched to Bhai Dayal Das and the sangat of Patna sometime after December 1666, Guru Tegh Bahadar mentions a siropa he had gifted them for the service and money they had donated to the celebrations of the future Guru Gobind Singh's birth:

> Respected brothers, a robe of honour (*sarpāu*) has been sent. Patna is the home of the Guru [and as such] the sangat [here] is blessed.[98]

Gifting a siropa for such services rendered is a feature of khil'at found all over the seventeenth-century Islamicate and beyond.[99] Guru Tegh Bahadar's action here, at some distance from Patna, allows us to witness one of the principal features of such giving. 'Robing,' according to Stewart Gordon,

> was the ceremony that recognized successful service, whether in war or peace, and was especially used to maintain ties when distance precluded face-to-face contact.[100]

It was most likely that such gifting accounts for the Guru's repeated requests for both cloth and turbans as we discover in another hukam-nama sent to the Patna sangat by the ninth Master: *do kauriā paggā bihār kī bhejanī ek korī paggā kī chālīs rupaye kī bhejanī*, 'send forty (2 *kaurīs*) Bihari turbans which are worth two rupees each (i.e., 'forty rupees per twenty') while in another still we find a request for homespun cotton cloth (*reje khārve*) and a hundred yards of unbleached cloth (*korā*).[101]

Such requests strongly imply that Guru Tegh Bahadar's principal intent (like that of his grandfather, Guru Arjan) was the maintenance and further strengthening of ties, and that he chose to do this in a way most familiar to Sikhs scattered across northern and eastern India, the gifting of garments and repeated visits in which he made himself available to his Sikhs.[102] Maintaining such links is most likely the reason for the construction of another town in 1665 CE, this one situated on the lower edges of the Shivalik Hills and initially called Chakk Nanaki and later Anandpur Sahib, upon land he had purchased from the raja of Kahlur-Bilaspur. The same reason can be imputed to tradition's insistence that Guru Tegh Bahadar had numerous wells sunk throughout the north Indian countryside to help alleviate the plight of Indian peasants and farmers.[103] Such strengthening and the optimism which tradition claims accompanied it[104] was an especially important act on the Guru's part when one considers the more orthodox bent of emperor Aurangzeb and his support for Sikhs such as Ram Rai who contested the ninth Guru's office.[105] It is no surprise, in this light, that one of the most oft-repeated phrases written in the ninth Guru's own handwriting was: *sevā kī velā hai*, 'This is the time to tender service [to the Guru].'[106]

According to S.S. Sagar, the repeated use of this phrase suggests an early 'crisis of guruship' which may well be true as the ninth Guru had to deal with a number of contenders for the gur-gaddi. Unfortunately, as Grewal and Bal have made clear, the contestation would only come to an end with the execution of Guru Tegh Bahadar in November 1675, an act on the Mughal emperor's part which assured the legitimacy of the guruship of the ninth Guru's son and Sikh loyalty to the new, young Guru and his uncle Kripal.[107] There was perhaps no Sikh amongst the disciples of the Guru who more embodied the call to seva than Bhai Ded Mal, a member of the sangat at Patna. In a number of hukam-namas addressed to this sangat, Bhai Ded Mal's position in Guru Tegh Bahadar's ranking of disciples moves a number of places, from eleventh initially to fourth ultimately.[108] This rise of individual Sikhs in the Guru's estimation may be the equivalent of a promotion which may in turn suggest the existence of a court. Bhai Batha for example, a Sikh mentioned in a hukam-nama attributed to Guru Hari Krishan who is to receive the offerings of the Pattan sangat and convey them to the Guru is in one instance elevated to the status of head of the sangat of Pattan by the ninth Guru, and at times identified as the 'Guru's son'.[109] Such elevations (and, indeed, demotions) and the regular recognition of important disciples at the beginning of each hukam-nama suggest a 'hierarchy of power' which 'culminates in the authority of the Guru...[a] hierarchy [that] is asserted [within the Guru's written instructions] time and again.'[110]

Tradition, as we have seen takes such structures for granted, going so far as to claim that Guru Tegh Bahadar even maintained his interest in the hunt while visiting various sangats throughout northern India and transforming the revered Bhai Mati Das into the ninth Guru's principal treasurer.[111] The very structure of the hukam-namas (in which we sometimes find the instructions in the Guru's own hand alongside repeated directions in a scribe's hand) may ultimately support tradition's avowal as these do indicate the existence of court personnel which in turn implies, as Sagar claims, both the 'institutional character' of the hukam-nama as well as the legitimacy of Guru Tegh Bahadar's claim to the guruship since the preparation of hukam-namas was principally the prerogative of the Sikh Gurus.[112]

The hukam-namas of the ninth Master therefore allow us a glimpse of the Sikhs surrounding Guru Tegh Bahadar. One can be certain that the Guru travelled throughout India with a group of close companions, as tradition claims, many of whom would have performed functions similar to those performed by Mughal courtiers. A number of these followers performed various scribal duties.[113] Such an entourage would have most likely further impressed upon the Sikhs the legitimacy, authority, and ultimately the benevolent nature of the ninth Guru. Whether this group constituted a formal court is an understanding which is certainly open to question. What we do not find in these hukam-namas is evidence for the claim put forward by Kahn Singh of Nabha and repeated by Dharampal Ashta in his English-language analysis of the Dasam Granth, that Guru Gobind Singh inherited a darbar populated by poets from his father, Guru Tegh Bahadar.[114] Both Grewal and Bal second this claim[115] and one can well imagine that the tenth Guru's fondness for and skill in writing verse would have most likely originated with those tutors and perhaps poets who surrounded his father, forming—especially in retrospect—an informal court. Let us now turn to this only son of Guru Tegh Bahadar, Guru Gobind Singh whose fascination with the royal court and 'regal appearances' is implied in his own hukam-namas and finds mention in the works of his poets and near-contemporary Persian chronicles, as well as later Sikh tradition.

NOTES

1. Shamsher Singh Ashok (ed.), *Gurbilās Pātshāhī Dasvīn krit Kuir Singh* 1:48, p. 21.
2. Kirpal Das Bhalla claims that Guru Arjan also sent hukam-namas. If he did these are no longer extant. See *MPV* sakhi 71, p. 113.

106   The Darbar of the Sikh Gurus

3. Isfandyar, *Dabistān-i Mazāhib* I, pp. 207–8.
4. Examples of this claim abound in Sikh histories. See for example Gian Singh's famous Punjabi *Tavārīkh Gurū Khālsā* I (Patiala: Bhasha Vibhag Punjab, 1993), p. 440. In English there is Gurbachan Singh Nayyar, *Guru Hargobind in Sikh Tradition (Based on Acknowledged Conventional Sources)* (New Delhi: National Book Organisation, 1998), p. 66. It seems to me that this tradition concerning the requests found within the sixth Guru's hukam-namas may originate with Santokh Singh's *Sūraj Prakāsh*. In *rās* 4 *ansu* 42 lines 17–18 (*SP* VII, p. 2404) we are told:
   Have hukam namas written and send these out everywhere there are masands. On these write out our instruction (*āisu*) that the Sikh who comes with both weapons and horses (*turang*) will please the Guru and will [himself] be united [to him] in joy (*sukh sangā*).
   That Guru Hargobind despatched hukam-namas is also noted in the earlier works of Kirpal Das Bhalla and Sarup Das Bhalla: *MPV* sakhi 90, p. 136 and *MP* II 6:11:10; 6:12:6–10; and 6:12:13–14; pp. 478, 483, 484 respectively.
5. W.H. McLeod, *Sikhs of the Khalsa* (New Delhi: Oxford University Press, 2003), pp. 33–40.
6. Ganda Singh (ed.), *Hukam-nāme: Gurū Sāhibān, Mātā Sāhibān, Bandā Singh ate Khālsā jī de* (Patiala: Publication Bureau Punjabi University, 1985), pp. 62–7. Since tradition claims that Guru Har Rai established a zoo in which all sorts of animals were kept (*MP* II 7:18–19, pp. 545–6) it may be significant that Guru Hargobind also requests that a pair of young cuckoos (koel) which had just begun to sing be placed in a cage and then sent to him (*pinjre vichi pāke bhejne*).
7. *AA* I, pp. 310–15 deals exclusively with pigeons. The quote appears on p. 310.
8. Ganda Singh (ed.), *Hukam-nāme*, pp. 66–7.
9. Ibid., pp. 66–7:
   The eastern sangat [of Patna] is the Khalsa of the Guru.
   We will have more to say about this term when we turn our attention to the court of Guru Gobind Singh who uses it often in his hukam-namas.
10. Surjit Hans, *A Reconstruction of Sikh History from Sikh Literature*, p. 270.
11. Var 1:48:1, *BG*, p. 39:
    The five pirs [drank from] the five cups [*sat* (truth), *santokh* (contentment), *dayā* (compassion), *dharam* (righteousness), *dhīraj* (discernment)]. The sixth pir [is now] sitting [on the throne] bearing the weight of guruship.
    The names of the Five Pirs, as William Crooke noted in the nineteenth century, were subject to change depending upon their locale but almost always included Khwaja Khizr, a pan-Islamic deus ex machina. William Crooke, *The Popular Religion and Folk-Lore of Northern India* I (rpt, New Delhi: Munshiram Manoharlal, 1968), pp. 205–6. Also Aziz Ahmad, *An Intellectual History of Islam in India* (Edinburgh: Edinburgh University

Press, 1969), pp. 48–9. It is also likely that Bhai Gurdas is here attempting to dissuade Sikhs generally from venerating the five Muslim pirs thus playing a fundamental role in the formation of a separate Sikh identity.
12. Var 1:48:4, *BG*, p. 39.
13. Var 24:24–5, *BG*, pp. 387–8.
14. How Sikhs reacted to the Guru's execution is still unknown. Two contrasting opinions are Louis E. Fenech, 'Martyrdom and the Execution of Guru Arjan in Early Sikh Sources', in the *Journal of the American Oriental Society* 121.1 (2001), pp. 20–31 and Pashaura Singh, 'Understanding the Martyrdom of Guru Arjan', in the *Journal of Punjab Studies* 12:1 (Spring 2005), pp. 29–62.
15. It may be that Bhai Gurdas is here exaggerating as there are early manuscript copies of the Adi Granth which contain Guru Hargobind's autograph pasted into the folios suggesting that he had indeed read the bani. See, for one example, Pashaura Singh, *The Guru Granth Sahib*, p. 69. Tradition's insistence on the sixth Guru's daily routine likewise demonstrates the good Bhai ji's understatement. See Pashaura Singh, *The Guru Granth Sahib*, p. 54.
16. Var 26:24:4, *BG*, p. 417.
17. Isfandyar, *Dabistān* I, p. 198.
18. Ibid., p. 207. *Dabistān* I, pp. 208–9 also tells us that Guru Hargobind recited an anecdote regarding a king who went on a hunt using the famous *qamarghah* technique of capture 'in which thousands of drivers would enclose the game within a vast circle and the Emperor would bring the animals down from on horseback.' Milo C. Beach and Ebba Koch, *King of the World*, p. 193. Qamarghah is lucidly explained in M.N. Pearson, 'Recreation in Mughal India', in the *British Journal of Sports History* 1(3), pp. 335–50, esp. p. 342. An image of the qamarghah appears in Stuart Cary Welch, *Imperial Mughal Painting* plate 14 (New York: George Braziller, 1978), p. 66.
19. Dirk H.A. Kolff, *Naukar, Rajput and Sepoy: The Ethnohistory of the Military Labour Market of Hindustan, 1450–1850* (Cambridge: Cambridge University Press, 1990). For martial sports such as hunting and various others see especially pp. 28–9. It is likely that the sixth Guru made use of the military labour market which is the principal feature of north Indian history discussed in Kolff's work.
20. There is a very interesting connotation present in both Kesar Singh's account and that of the *Dabistān*, and this deals with the terms used for 'servants'. Both *chākar* and *naukār* are Persian/Persianite terms and both in Indo-Islamic India had a definite martial connotation. *Naukārī* for example was understood during the periods of both the Delhi Sultanate and Mughal empire as 'honourable service in the warband, the retainership of the lord's companion' (even the verb *nigāh dashtān* used in the *Dabistān* implies 'maintaining guard'); while chākar especially amongst the Rajputs

indicated 'military retainers.' Most English translations of the Sikh portion of the *Dabistān* seem to simply ignore this element (that is Ganda Singh and Irfan Habib). For naukari see Dirk Kolff, *Naukar, Rajput and Sepoy*, p. 20; for chākarī note Stewart Gordon, *Marathas, Marauders, and State Formation in Eighteenth-Century India* (Delhi: Oxford University Press, 1994), p. 186.

21. *BSVN* 6:107, p. 96. Tradition claims that Bibi Viro was born in 1672 CE and that her mother was Mata Damodari. See *MK*, p. 879. Other *BSVN* references to hunting appear at 6:58, 115, 138, pp. 92, 97, 99.

22. *MPV* sakhi 84, p. 128 and *MP* II 6:5:2, p. 439:

The Guru [in Ramdaspur] enjoyed himself immensely [as] he went hunting everyday.

Also see *MP* II 6:6:48, p. 452. According to Sarup Das Bhalla the Guru's son, Tegh Bahadar likewise enjoyed the hunt:

[The young] Tegh Bahadar was the very personification of proper knowledge: The appearance of a king but a heart supremely detached. Possessed of steadfastness and extraordinary generosity he daily went hunting in the company of the true Guru.

MP II 6:5:4, p. 439. Similar sentiments are expressed in *MP* II 9:2:2, p. 658 and are very well in keeping with the general tenor of the ninth Guru's bani which, according to G.S. Talib, stresses the idea of *vairāg* or detachment. Fauja Singh and G.S. Talib, *Guru Tegh Bahadar: Martyr and Teacher* (Patiala: Punjabi University Press, 1975), p. 117.

23. Inder Singh Gill (ed.), *Kavi Sohan jī krit Srī Gur-bilās Pātshāhī Chhevīn Tipanīān Samet* 5:55 (Amritsar: Vazir Hindi Press, 1968), p. 98. Although Surjit Hans has claimed a mid-nineteenth century date for the text of *Gur-bilās Pātshāhī Chhevīn* based in part on its references to the gilding of Harimandir Sahib with gold leaf (Hans, *A Reconstruction of Sikh History*, p. 270) Gurbachan Singh Nayyar refers to the older, early eighteenth-century date by claiming that the text is actually composite in nature and that such anachronistic statements are actually the products of a later author. G.S. Nayyar, *Guru Hargobind in Sikh Tradition*, pp. 2–7. Two recent versions of *Gur-bilās Pātshāhī Chhevīn* have appeared both of which claim that the actual author(s) of the work were neither the Kavi Sohan noted in the title of Inder Singh Gill's edition nor the Bhais Gurmukh Singh Akalbungia and Darbara Singh, to both of whom Kanh Singh Nabha attributed the text in the early twentieth century [Kanh Singh Nabha, *Gurmat Sudhākar* (5th ed., Patiala: Bhasha Vibhag Punjab, 1988), p. 216, n. 1)]. The first, edited by Gurmukh Singh, ascribes the text to one Bhagat Singh while the other edited by Joginder Singh Vedanti attributes it to the unknown servant of the Bhai Dharam Singh who heard Mani Singh recite the text of *Gur-bilās Pātshāhī Chhevīn* to the Bhagat Singh to whom Gurmukh Singh attributes the text. Reasons for the new ascriptions are noted in Gurmukh Singh (ed.), *Gur-bilās Pātshāhī Chhevīn krit Bhagat Singh*

Court and Sport 109

(Patiala: Punjabi University Publication Bureau, 1997), pp. 1–3 and Joginder Singh Vedanti (ed.), *Gur-bilās Pātshāhī Chhevīn* (Amritsar: Dharam Prachar Committee of the SGPC, 1998), pp. 55–6.

24. Dominic Brookshaw, 'Palaces, Pavilions, and Pleasure-gardens', p. 205. Also see Ibn Battuta's description of a hunt in which he accompanied Muhammad bin Tughluq as noted in K.A. Nizami, *Royalty in Medieval India*, p. 74. See also M.N. Pearson, 'Recreation in Mughal India.'

25. Some of the numerous styles of hunting are explained by Abu'l Fazl in the *Ā'īn*. *AA* I, pp. 292 ff. by the late seventeenth and early eighteenth centuries, however, hunting was no longer the sport of royalty alone. The *Mirzā-nāmah* explains that even Mughal gentlemen or mirzas (holding ranks less than 1000 zat) could engage in the pastime. See Aziz Ahmad, 'The British Museum Mirzānāma and the Seventeenth Century Mirzā in India', pp. 105–6.

26. *AA* I, pp. 298–9: Here we are told that the cheetah was carried on a palanquin-like conveyance called a *chau-dol* and flanked by servants who 'fully equipped, run at his side; the *naqqarā*... is beaten in front and sometimes is carried by the two men on horseback.' The role and importance of cheetahs during such sport is highlighted in a wonderful illustration found in the Akbar-namah prepared for Akbar's mother, Hamida Banu Begum. In the bottom portion of the painting we may actually see the palanquin on which a cheetah was carried. See Linda York Leach, 'Pages from an *Akbarnama*', figure 7 'Akbar enthroned during a hunting expedition by Narsingh', p. 50. Sikh tradition also claims such bonds of affection between the sixth Guru and his hunting animals, especially his horses and goes to great lengths to demonstrate the royal lineage of such animals. See, for example, the famous story of Bhai Bidhi Chand Chhina and the sixth Guru's horses Dilbagh and Gulbagh. *MPV* sakhi 89, pp. 135–6. It is perhaps with his father as an example that the ninth Guru too shows an intimate concern for his horse, Siri Dhar whom he mentions in his hukam-nama to the sangat of Benares. Sabinderjit Singh Sagar, *Hukam-namas of Guru Tegh Bahadar*, pp. 66–7; 116.

27. Rosalind O'Hanlon, 'Issues of Masculinity in North Indian History: The Bangsh Nawabs of Farrukhabad', in the *Indian Journal of Gender Studies* 4:1 (1997), p. 14.

28. I am quite aware of M.N. Pearson's comments about the nature of play and amusements in sixteenth-century Mughal India: games and such were not leisure in the contemporary and economic sense of the term. Pearson relies primarily upon the statements of Abu'l Fazl in regard to sport. We shall note one such statement in a moment. M.N. Pearson, 'Recreation in Mughal India', pp. 339–40.

29. Stephen F. Dale, *The Garden of the Eight Paradises: Bābur and the Culture of Empire in Central Asia, Afghanistan and India (1483–1530)* (Leiden and Boston: Brill, 2004), p. 222. Of course such attitudes to hunting animals were common amongst the Mongolians of Chinggis Khan. It was he,

Dale tells us, who 'institutionalized customary hunts as training exercises for the massive encircling maneuvers his armies conducted on the treeless Mongolian steppe' (p. 221).

30. Islamicate advice literature begins with two famous eleventh-century texts: the *Qābūs-nāmah* (1082 CE) of Kaykā'ūs bin Iskandar bin Qabus and the *Siyāsat-nāmah* (1091–2 CE) of the Seljuq Nizam al-Mulk. Hubert Drake (trans.), *The Book of Government or Rules for Kings: the Siyāsat-nāma of Siyar al-Mulūk of Nizām al-Mulk* (New Haven: Yale University Press, 1960), and Reuben Levy (trans. and ed.), *A Mirror for Princes: The Qābūs Nāma by Kai Kā'ūs ibn Iskandar Prince of Gurgān* (London: Cresset Press, 1951). Mughal mirror literature and various other forms of advice literature are rather commonplace. A readily accessible translation of an advice text intended for the emperor Jahangir is Sajida Sultana Alvi (ed. and trans.), *Advice on the Art of Governance: Mau'izah-i Jahāngīrī of Muhammad Bāqir Najm-i Sānī: An Indo-Islamic Mirror for Princes* (Albany: State University of New York Press, 1989). For the rahit-nama literature see W.H. McLeod, *Sikhs of the Khalsa*, pp. 1–58 and Nripinder Singh, *The Sikh Moral Tradition*, pp. 102–208. Another branch of Islamicate and Mughal literature which is worth noting here is that dealing with ethics or morality, '*ilm al-akhlāq*. For these texts and their exhortations see Muzaffar Alam, '*Akhlāqī* norms and Mughal Governance', in M. Alam *et al.* (eds), *The Making of Indo-Persian Culture: Indian and French Studies* (Delhi: Manohar, 2000), pp. 67–95.

31. *AA* I, p. 292. Also Beveridge (ed. and trans.), *The Akbarnama of Abu-L-Fazl II*, p. 232:

   Secretly [Akbar] was testing the sincerity, the large-mindedness, and business-capabilities of men; ostensibly, he was prosecuting hunting and elephant-fights which the ignorant regard as a kind of neglect of the duties of sovereignty but which the wise regard as the cream of practical skill.

32. Rosalind O'Hanlon, 'Manliness and Imperial Service', p. 64 speaks about the waistband in the context of [hyper] masculinity. *Kamar kasāi* 'waist [band] tightened' is thus the Punjabi equivalent to the Persian *kamar band* 'waist bound up.' In both phrases the implication of self-control such as that found in the colloquial English expression 'tighten your belt' is very much present.

33. Inder Singh Gill (ed.), *Srī Gur-bilās Pātshāhī Chhevīn* 5:47, p. 97. Also see *MPV* sakhi 107, pp. 153–5. Santokh Singh also relates a story about the seventh Guru, Guru Hari Rai which is constructed along similar lines. In this tale the seventh Guru while hunting kills a snake which had been a Hindu pandit in an earlier life who had slandered the hymns of Guru Nanak. The Guru's killing of the snake, it is implied, granted the serpent liberation from the cycle of existence. Online *SP* 9:4:22–31. Also Macauliffe, *Sikh Religion* IV, pp. 282–3. A parallel story initially told in the Bhagavata Purana

invloving Krishna and the brahman Sudarshan appears at *Krishanavtār* 757–67, Dasam Granth, pp. 354–5. Within Hindu epic literature being slain by a divine being such as Krishna, Rama, or the goddess Durga assures the slain of salvation. Note, for example, this passage from the *Vār Srī Bhagautī jī kī* attributed to the tenth Guru:
>As the demon adversaries [of Durga] were adept in the arts of battle they did not even think of fleeing. Killed by the goddess [on the battlefield] they went [directly] to heaven [as a result of being the focus of her attention].

Vār Srī Bhagautī jī kī 1:14, Dasam Granth, p. 121. Also *Rāmāvtār* 622, Dasam Granth, p. 238 at which point Ravana's ten heads 'go to Shiv Lok' after having been chopped off by Rama.

34. Thackston (trans.), *Jahangirnama*, p. 216. This prolific number may perhaps be why Jahangir eventually chose to take a vow of non-violence though he often broke it because of his love for the sport. See Elison Findly, 'Jahāngīr's Vow of Non-Violence', in the *Journal of the American Oriental Society* 107 (1987), pp. 245–56. Lions could only be hunted by the royal line.

35. Beach and Koch, *King of the World: the Padshahnama*, pp. 84–5 and 110–11.

36. *Dabistān* I, p. 207:
>[Guru Hargobind] always accompanied the victorious camp (*rikāb-i zafr* lit., 'the stirrup/household of victory') of Jahangir… After Jannat Makani's ['He whose place is the garden of heaven,' Jahangir's posthumous title] soul left his body [Guru Hargobind] remained in attendance on the Commander of the Faithful, Abu'l Muzzafar Shihabuddin Muhammad Sahib Qiran-i Sani Shah Jahan Padishah Ghazi.

That the sixth Guru accompanied Jahangir while hunting is implied in the use of the term *rikāb-i zafr* suggesting that the sixth Guru followed the emperor while he was on the hunt. For the association between the term rikāb and hunting during Aurangzeb's period see Jamshid H. Bilimoria (trans.), *Ruka'at-i-Alamgiri or Letters of Aurangzebe [with Historical and Explanatory Notes]* (London: Luzac & Co., 1908), letter 38, p. 42, n.2.

37. According to Abu'l Fazl (*AA* I, pp. 55–6),
>The *Bārgāh* [regal tent], when large, is able to contain more than ten thousand people. It takes a thousand *farrāshe*s, a week to erect with the help of machines.

38. Attilio Petruccioli, 'The City as an Image of the King,' p. 64. For an idea of the vast size of these followings a great deal of which was concerned principally with raising, decorating, and taking down tents see *AA* I, pp. 47–50. A diagram of the emperor's imperial camp appears as plate I opposite p. 48.

39. A sizeable number were still included as is made clear in the emperor's memoirs. A series of hunts held between September and November 1607, for example, imply a large number of such personnel present though

112 The Darbar of the Sikh Gurus

nowhere near the numbers noted during Akbar's period. Jahangir himself also claims that on occasion 'my sisters and inmates of the harem were along.' W.H. Thackston (trans.), *Jahangirnama*, pp. 86–7.
40. Though in a completely different context one may here consult John Mackenzie, *The Empire of Nature: Hunting Conservation and British Imperialism* (Manchester: Manchester University Press, 1984), p. 175.
41. *SP* VII 4:55, pp. 2457–61, especially lines 24–38, pp. 2459–61 in which we have described amongst other things the various animals and trappings which accompanied the Guru, Jahangir, and the *mīr shikāran* or hunt master. The Sikh narrative is in many ways reminiscent of the famous incident which occurred in the eleventh regnal year, when Jahangir was saved from a lion by his 'intimate servant' Anup Rai who was granted the title Ani Rai Singhadalan in return for his bravery. The account appears in Thackston (trans.), *Jahangirnama*, pp. 117–18. Another incident of a tiger scaring Jahangir appears at *SP* VII 4:61, pp. 2481–5. A brief account appears in Macauliffe, *The Sikh Religion* IV, p. 18. Santokh's Singh's account may have partly relied on a narrative we discover in the *Pakhyān Charitr* of the Dasam Granth in which Jahangir is once again saved from a lion but in this case by a woman in Jahangir's hunting party known as Jodha Bai, the Rajput daughter of the raja of Jodhpur. See *Pakhyān Charitr* 48:18–19, Dasam Granth, p. 872.
42. A similar hunting anecdote in which both a Sikh Guru and Mughal emperor are involved is found in Sukha Singh's late eighteenth-century gur-bilas. Here, while the tenth Guru and the emperor Bahadar Shah are hunting, the emperor sends his soldiers out to confront a tiger (*pasurāi, pasu nāik, and mirgīshar* here) who are themselves killed by the animal. The emperor looked to the tenth Master in frustration at which Guru Gobind Singh sends out a solitary Sikh who blocks the tiger's attack on his shield and then guts him with his katar. Gursharan Kaur Jaggi (ed.), *Gurbilās Pātshāhī Dasvīn* 26:190–205, pp. 410–11. Such would most certainly have 'caught the emperor's eye.' See M.N. Pearson, 'Recreation', 343.
43. Sikh tradition also highlights the allegedly tenuous relationship between Jahangir and Guru Hargobind (albeit unknowingly) implied in this tiger-hunt anecdote in its claim that the emperor bestowed a robe of honour upon the Guru. See *MP* II 6:10:8, p. 471 in which the Guru is so honoured near Kartarpur with a robe, it is implied, that Jahangir takes off of his own back. Also, *SP* VII 4:55:15, p. 2459. This is in good keeping with the general ambiguity of the robing ceremony and robing in general. For this last point see Stewart Gordon, 'Introduction: Ibn Battuta and a Region of Robing', pp. 18–19 and his 'Robes, Kings, and Semiotic Ambiguity', in Stewart Gordon (ed.), *Robes and Honor*, pp. 379–85.
44. Peter Hardy, 'The Growth of Authority Over a Conquered Political Elite: The Early Delhi Sultanate as a Possible Case Study', p. 208. Note for example that in an attempt to teach the young Rajput prince of Mewar

Karan Singh the ideals of courtliness Jahangir took the prince along with him while hunting in the tenth regnal year (1615–16 CE). Thackston (trans.), *Jahangirnama*, p. 174. For other facets as part of this attempt see p. 167.

45. Is it plausible that Jahangir may have ultimately felt some regret for his orders to execute Guru Arjan and may have thus allowed his son Guru Hargobind to attend him, especially at the hunt, as a way to atone for his earlier command? Perhaps in an attempt to get to know the Sikhs and their Guru better? This is simply impossible to prove but nevertheless seems in accordance with Elison Findly's interesting psychological assessment of the emperor and his relationship with his father Akbar (Elison Findly, 'Jahāngīr's Vow of Non-Violence,') and, moreover, finds echoes in Pashaura Singh's recent discussions of Jahangir's image in seventeenth and eighteenth-century Sikh texts. Pashaura Singh, *The Life and Work of Guru Arjan*, p. 233.

46. Tradition most certainly maintains such a position. See *SP* VII 4:44:28–9, p. 2413. Sarup Das Bhalla tells us that the Guru took a *chaukī* or a cushion which when elevated was understood to be a makeshift throne (chaukī also means 'guard' or 'watch-house'. The term also designates the 'mounting guard' which Mughal nobles often undertook as a demonstration of their loyalty to the emperor) along with him on a hunt (*MP* II 6:3:18, p. 428), an article which was not uncommon in Mughal hunting parties and could easily be placed within a royal tent. While Santokh Singh claims that the sixth Guru even possessed his own *naubat-khānah* (literally, 'drum-house') or 'drum ensemble' as we see here:

    The ensemble of drums played ahead [of the Guru].

    SP VII 4:43:36, p. 2410. See also Ganda Singh (ed.), *Srī Gur-Sobhā* 10:12, p. 114 for the playing of the tenth Guru's naubat during a hunt. The naubat as the symbol of kingship was, according to K.A. Nizami, 'an old Indian, as well as Persian, tradition' which included far more instruments than the kettledrum. Nizami, *Royalty in Medieval India*, p. 54.

47. Sikh tradition's Painda Khan who is also mentioned in the *Dabistān* as Payinda Khan (Isfandyar, *Dabistān*, p. 207) may be included in this list of serving nobles. J.F. Richards, 'Norms of Comportment among Imperial Mughal Officers', p. 263.

48. *Dabistān* I, p. 208:

    Guru [Hargobind] had 700 horses in his stable and 300 horsemen and 60 gunners were always in his service.

    Although such numbers suggest a court it also accords well with the Kolff's phenomenon of the 'armed peasantry' during the period of Akbar and later. Dirk H.A. Kolff, *Naukar, Rajput, and Sepoy*.

49. William Irvine, *The Later Mughals* vols 1 and 2 bound in one [Jadunath Sarkar (ed.)] (Delhi: Low Price Publications, 1995), p. 77.

50. Iqtidar Alam Khan, 'Martial and Political Culture of the Khalsa', in Reeta Grewal *et al.* (eds), *Five Centuries of Sikh Tradition: Ideology, Politics, and Culture* (Delhi: Manohar, 2005), pp. 86–7.

51. *MP* II 6:5:30, p. 443 mentions that Guru Hargobind possessed a *suet baju* or 'white hawk' which was *tat-giān sarūp* 'the form of pure knowledge'. In describing his uncle Sultan Mahmud Mirza Babur implies that as hunters aged they often gave up the rigours of the chase and made use of falcons or hawks instead. Wheeler M. Thackston (ed. and trans.), *The Baburnama: Memoirs of Babur, Prince and Emperor* (New York: Modern Library, 2002), p. 31. There may be some truth to this story as hawking was a particularly popular royal pursuit in Mandi one of the Pahari principalities within the Punjab hills just to the north of Bilaspur-Kahlur. Raja Hari Sen (d. 1637 CE), for example, a contemporary of Guru Hargobind was a well known participant in such sport as is evinced by his mention as such within the accounts of contemporary chroniclers. J. Hutchison and J. Ph. Vogel, *History of the Panjab Hill States* II (Lahore: Superintendent, Government Printing, Punjab, 1933), p. 382.

52. The version of the story to which I am referring appears in the mid to late eighteenth-century *Bansāvalī-nāmā*: *BSVN*, 6:139 ff., pp. 99–100. The other, more prominent narrative claims that it was the retainers of the Guru who were unwilling to return the emperor's Iranian hawk. *SP* VIII, pp. 2800–5. Also Macauliffe, *The Sikh Religion* IV, pp. 79–80 and J.S. Grewal, *The Sikhs of the Punjab*, p. 65. Macauliffe has a version of the Painda Khan story noted above at IV, pp. 190–3; so too Inder Singh Gill (ed.), *Gur-bilās Pātshāhī Chhevīn* 20:294 ff, p. 444. Chronicles of Shah Jahan's reign are relatively abundant in Persian, Italian, French, and Dutch. None of these refer to the sixth Guru except for the *Dabistān*.

53. *AA* I, pp. 304–5. The hawk is also a bird which is associated with Guru Gobind Singh. Although based principally upon tradition this incident nevertheless displays another facet of hunting namely that for 'armies on the move, hunting…[provided] not only fighting practice and a test of the troops' resolve under stress, but an arena for individuals to display their courage and a means of scouting information about enemy positions.' Rosalind O'Hanlon, 'Issues of Masculinity', p. 14.

54. Descriptives of the routines and appearances of the kings of both the Delhi Sultanate and the later Mughal empire are quite commonplace in the panegyric courtly literature of the period. See K.A. Nizami, *Royalty in Medieval India*, pp. 58-71. For such panegyrics within the Mughal court specifically see Muhammad Abdul Ghani, *A History of Persian Language and Literature at the Mughal Court: part III–Akbar the Great* (Allahabad: The Indian Press, Ltd., 1929). As well, we see this technique of description in courtly and devotional Brajbhasha and Hindi literatures, especially towards the male deity although similar descriptions appear of legendary male devotees. R.S. McGregor, *Hindi Literature*, p. 86. These rich descriptions may well be akin to what Kenneth Bryant terms 'verbal icons' in his study of Krishna devotion, images on which the listeners (*shrote*) are often cautioned to focus in order to visualize the divine. Kenneth Bryant,

Poems to the Child-God (Berkeley: University of California Press, 1978), pp. 72–5.
55. The appearance and daily routine of the sixth Guru finds little mention outside of Sikh tradition. Many eighteenth- and nineteenth-century Sikh texts dedicate a number of lines to such imagery. A representative passage describing the sixth Guru appears in *Mahimā Prakāsh* II 6:3:5:
    [As the Guru] reposed [on his saddle] his body [appeared] particularly marvelous, glorious, and radiant. Seeing him the royal vazir was ashamed at heart. [The Guru] was mounted on his Iraqi horse while his ornaments, jewels, and sword glittered in the light. Jahangir and his nobles all saw [him] and were astonished.
    MP II 6:3:5, p. 427. Also see Inder Singh Gill (ed.), *Srī Gur-bilās Pātshāhī Chhevīn* 5:45, p. 98; and *SP* VII 4:43–4, pp. 2407–15.
56. Inder Singh Gill (ed.), *Srī Gur-bilās Pātshāhī Chhevīn* 2:3, p. 30. Also Baba Buddha's description of the preborn Guru at 1:125–6, p. 24. The *turhī* noted here is, according to Kahn Singh a *ransinghā* which was probably a large Indian C-shaped horn (*sīng*) which we may assume was generally sounded during warfare as the prefix *ran* (battlefield) suggests (the sīng as noted by Abu'l Fazl in *AA* I, p. 53). Certainly Sikh authors would have been aware of the fact that instruments such as these were also played loudly to announce the birth of Mughal princes. Images of such heralding announcements were often the subject of Mughal painters. An example appears in Bonnie Wade, *Imaging Sound*, figure 4: 'Rejoicings at Fatehpur Sikri on the birth of Akbar's first son.'
57. Gurmeet Rai and Kavita Singh, 'Brick by Sacred Brick: Architectural Projects of Guru Arjan and Guru Hargobind', in Kavita Singh (ed.), *New Insights into Sikh Art*, 54:4 (Mumbai: Marg Publications, 2003), p. 42.
58. Rai and Singh, 'Brick by Sacred Brick', p. 43. The importance of Sri Hargobindpur between its foundation in the early seventeenth century until the nineteenth century is noted by Ganesh Das in his *Chār Bāgh-i Punjāb*. See J.S. Grewal and Indu Banga (eds and trans.), *Early Nineteenth Century Panjab: From Ganesh Das's Chār Bāgh-i-Panjāb* (Amritsar: Guru Nanak Dev University, 1975), p. 113.
59. Rai and Singh, 'Brick by Sacred Brick', p. 44. The *Dabistān* I, p. 208 may be used in support of this tradition. For example,
    A group of set persons [among the Guru] occupied themselves in trade, service, and work [on the Guru's behalf]. Whoever left his own place took refuge with him.
    Sri Hargobindpur in this context is reminiscent of 'Agra... which was very much like a huge army camp.' Kolff, *Naukar, Rajput and Sepoy*, p. 28.
60. Isfandyar, *Dabistān* I, pp. 210–11. The references to Debi Chand appear in the lengthier Aligarh manuscript of the *Dabistān* and are thus not mentioned in Rahim Rizazadah-'i Malik's edited text. Irfan Habib's translation in Grewal and Habib (ed.), *Sikh History from Persian Sources*, p. 73 does

include these. The masands mentioned here (the names within square brackets are the versions noted in Grewal and Habib) were mainly active during the period of Guru Hari Rai and so find no mention in the eleventh var of Bhai Gurdas as our theologian died before Guru Hargobind expired. The exception is Pirana the Jat who is most likely Phirana the Khahira Jat mentioned in Bhai Gurdas' var 11:14:5, *BG*, p. 184. Bidhita/Bidhia could be the famous Chhina Jat Sikh Bidhi Chand who appears in var 11:17:4, *BG*, p. 186.

61. Isfandyar, *Dabistān* I, p. 208.
62. Pashaura Singh, *The Guru Granth Sahib*, p. 54.
63. For Abdul and Natha see Kahn Singh's *MK*, pp. 69, 680.
64. Inder Singh Gill (ed.), *Srī Gur-bilās Pātshāhī Chhevīn* 6:40–77, pp. 151–3. Also *SP* VII, 4:44:37:
    Dhadhis, bhatts, virtuosoes, and minstrels all sang the Guru of the world's glory.
    And *SP* VIII 6:23, pp. 2879–80.
65. Although the Persianite term nishān generally means 'standard' or 'pennant' the nishan in question here is described in Kahn Singh's *Mahān Kosh* as a 'long kettledrum' (*lammā* naggārā) which is three hands deep. See the sixth entry for 'nishān', in *MK*, p. 702. Often it is this type of drum of which we hear in many of the battle scenes narrated within the lengthier portions of the Dasam Granth.
66. Inder Singh Gill (ed.), *Srī Gur-bilās Pātshāhī Chhevīn* 8:43, p. 151. Sikh tradition generally claims that only the tenth Guru possessed kettledrums. The history and symbolism associated with the naqqara appears in Bonnie Wade, *Imaging Sound*, p. 129–30. Wade's text contains an image of the shutri in Figure 5, titled 'Hazaras being chased by Babur's men through a ravine', Victoria and Albert Museum, IM272–1913. Sur Singh is approximately forty kilometres southwest of Amritsar.
67. Inder Singh Gill (ed.), *Srī Gur-bilās Pātshāhī Chhevīn* 8:62, p. 152. See also Macauliffe, *The Sikh Religion* IV, pp. 5–6. The Guru's magnificent appearance is also noted in *SP* VII 4:43, p. 2407 while Dhadhi Abdula's performance appears at *SP* VII 4:44, pp. 2413–14.
68. See W.E. Begley and Z.A. Desai (comp. and trans.), *Taj Mahal: The Illumined Tomb: An Anthology of Seventeenth-century Mughal and European Documentary Sources* (Seattle and London: The University of Washington Press, 1989), pp. 82–5 for an English translation of Kalim's encomium. Kalim's praise of the Peacock Throne appears in Wheeler Thackston, 'Literature', in Zeenut Zaid (ed.), *The Magnificent Mughals* (Karachi: Oxford University Press, 2002), pp. 93–4.
69. There is a hukam-nama attributed to Guru Hari Krishan but here once again we hear very little apart from basic guidelines to follow and simple requests to the sangat of Pak Patan, home of Sheikh Farid's dargah. Ganda Singh (ed.), *Hukam-nāme*, pp. 72–3.

70. Isfandyar, *Dabistān* I, p. 210.
71. The *Dabistān* seems to have mistaken Hijri 1055 for Hijri 1054 the year of the Islamic calendar during which Guru Hargobind died. For this reason it is likely that all dates dealing with Guru Hari Rai are off by one lunar year. See Irfan Habib's notes to his translation in *Sikh History from Persian Sources*, p. 83, n. 48.
72. Pashaura Singh, *The Guru Granth Sahib*, pp. 71–2. The scribe of the Jograj manuscript was one Jograj.
73. Isfandyar, *Dabistān* I, p. 210.
74. Instructive perhaps is the following statement:
    ...the *khirqa* can mean things other than simply being a symbol of the bond between a master and a disciple. It can have a transformative impact... in that it carries the master's spiritual state (as it were carrying perfume), and envelops the disciple in it, thereby helping him to attain the degree of advancement the master wants.
    Jamal J. Elias, 'The Sufi Robe (*Khirqa*) as a Vehicle of Spiritual Authority', in Stewart Gordon (ed.), *Robes and Honor*, pp. 275–89, esp. p. 276. See also his comments on p. 289, n. 34 in which the equation between the Sufi robe (khirqah) and the khil'at gifted by kings is elaborated.
75. Vir Singh (ed.), *Purātan Janam-sākhī Gurū Nānak Dev jī* (Amritsar: Khalsa Samachar, 1946), pp. 16–19. After Akal Purakh assigns Guru Nanak the task of spreading the Name we hear:
    Guru Nanak then fell to his feet [in humility] and from within the Divine Court [the True Guru] draped the robe of honour upon the [revered] Baba.
    Of course the eclectic Puratan Janam-sakhi is much later than Guru Hargobind's period but it seems likely that the story of Guru Nanak's investiture would have been a popular one by the sixth Guru's time. Background on the Puratan janam-sakhi traditions appears in W.H. McLeod, *Early Sikh Tradition: A Study of the Janam-sākhīs* (Oxford: Clarendon Press, 1980), pp. 22–30.
76. *Dabistān* I, p. 198. *MPV* sakhi 99, p. 145 and *MP* II 6:14:7, p. 499 both claim that Baba Gurditta, Guru Har Rai's father, also went hunting with the sixth Guru. Both narratives of the seventh Guru, moreover, add Guru Hari Rai's involvement in the hunt. See for example *MPV* sakhis 104, 107, 112, pp. 149, 154, 158 and *MP* II 7:4:7, 13, 14, pp. 551–2; and 7:7:4, p. 563. That Guru Hari Rai likewise made use of the symbols of royalty is also noted in the seventh chapter of Sarup Das Bhalla's *Mahimā Prakāsh*:
    [Guru Hari Rai's] unwavering mind graced the royal throne (*singhāsan*) as the imperishable devotee of the Lord reposed with the royal canopy over his head.
    MP II 7:1:5, p. 541. The zeal which the Sikhs of Guru Hari Rai around Kiratpur in particular accorded him is underscored by the inclusion of a hymn attributed to Guru Hari Rai within a manuscript copy of the Adi

Granth held by the British Library [MS OR. 2748]. On folio 746a a couplet credited to Guru Hari Rai is found which, Pashaura Singh states, shows the scribe's intention 'to have Guru Har Rai represented in the Sikh scripture.' Pashaura Singh, *The Guru Granth Sahib*, p. 212.
77. Background on the seva-panthis and this particular manuscript appears in Pashaura Singh, *The Guru Granth Sahib*, p. 76.
78. H.A. Rose, *A Glossary of the Tribes and Castes of the Punjab and North-West Frontier Province* (rpt Patiala: Language Department, Punjab, 1990), p. 685.
79. The first Sikh text to take note of this meeting is the mid-eighteenth century *Mahimā Prakāsh Vārtak*. *MPV*, sakhi 114, pp. 160–2.
80. Grewal and Habib (eds), *Sikh History From Persian Sources*, p. 94. Prince Mu'azzam's visit is also narrated in the thirteenth chapter of the *Bachitar Nātak*. See *Bachitar Nātak* 13:1, Dasam Granth, p. 71.
81. Ajit Singh Baagha, *Banur Had Orders*, p. 57. I have slightly altered Baagha's English text. By the inscription's date, however, Ram Rai and his immediate family, particularly his wife, Punjab Kaur, had been redeemed by the tenth Guru who most likely met Ram Rai in the dun when Gobind Singh was a guest of the Raja of Sirmur-Nahan at Paonta Sahib. Background in Grewal and Bal, *Guru Gobind Singh*, pp. 49–50, 72.
82. Sikh tradition seems to confuse the good nawab with his father. See for example *EoS* IV, p. 25. Sabinderjit Singh Sagar, *Hukam-namas of Guru Tegh Bahadar*, pp. 97 (Pbi), 131 (Eng.). Although Sagar claims that Khan was ranked at 4000 zat M. Athar Ali, *The Mughal Nobility*, p. 268 which produces the 1000/300 figure is most likely accurate. This was a rather modest mansab but was nevertheless improved from that of his father who is first noticed in Mughal chronicles as an *akhtahbegī* (master of the horse) around the year 1650 CE (1060 H) and last noted in 1657–8 CE (1068 H) with a rank of 700/100 and the office of the *Dāroghah-'i Qurr-khānah* (superintendant of the resthouse). M. Athar Ali, *The Apparatus of Empire: Awards of Ranks, Offices and titles to the Mughal Nobility (1574–1658)* (Delhi: Oxford University Press, 1985), pp. 257, 339. Interestingly, there is a narrative about Saif Khan and the daughter of Shah Jahan, Roshan Ara, in the *Pakhyān Charitr*. See *Pakhyān Charitr* 278, Dasam Granth, p. 1222.
83. Fauja Singh and Gurbachan Singh Talib, *Guru Tegh Bahadar*, p. 46. Saif Khan appears a number of times in traditional Sikh narratives. Some of these claim that he was so fond of the ninth Master that he eventually became a Sikh, online *SP* 12:30:28–9, 46 pp. 244, 246; and 12:31:1–2, p. 247. Also M.A. Macauliffe, *The Sikh Religion* IV, p. 373. This act of conversion highlights the heroic character of Guru Tegh Bahadar for Grewal and Bal (Grewal and Bal, *Guru Gobind Singh*, p. 44). The Guru's horse, Siri Dhar, is mentioned by name in a hukam-nama which the Guru addressed to Bhai Javehari a member of the sangat of Benares. S.S. Sagar, *Hukam-namas of Guru Tegh Bahadar*, pp. 12–13 (Pbi); p. 116 (Eng.). For

further background on Nawab Saif Khan see Kirpal Singh, 'Saif Khan and His Relations with Guru Tegh Bahadar', in *Punjab History Conference Tenth Session February 28–29, 1976 Proceedings* (Patiala: Punjabi University Press, 1976), pp. 109–14.
84. J.S. Grewal, *The Sikhs of the Punjab*, p. 70. the Guru's association with the raja was also noted in the later Persian news reports, the *akhbārāt-i darbār-i mu'allā*. See for example the report dated 25 rabī' I (24 May 1710 CE) during Bahadar Shah's fourth regnal year as it appears in Ganda Singh (ed.), *Ma'ākhiz-i Tavārīkh-i Sikhān*, p. 83. There is some controversy regarding with which raja the Guru travelled eastwards, whether Man Singh or Ram Singh. That Guru Tegh Bahadar met Raja Ram Singh in Dacca is however clear. See Ved Parkash, *The Sikh in Bihar* (Patna and New Delhi: Janaki Prakashan, 1981), pp. 52–5.
85. Wayne E. Begley and Z.A. Desai (eds), *The Shāh Jahān Nāma of 'Ināyat Khān* (Delhi: Oxford University Press, 1990), p. 304.
86. This was though a smaller rank than that of his father who was elevated to 7000/7000 by Aurangzeb for his support during the War of Succession. The numbers reflect infantry and cavalry while the words in parentheses—two-horse three-horse—indicate a particular type of mansab. Sabinderjit Singh Sagar, *Hukam-namas of Guru Tegh Bahadar*, pp. 94–5, 98–9 (Pbi), 130, 132 (Eng.) makes this claim. For the Kacchawaha Rajput courtiers see Kunwar Refaqat Ali Khan, *The Kachhwahas Under Akbar and Jahangir* (New Delhi: Kitab Pub. House, 1976) and for Ram Singh consult M. Athar Ali, *The Mughal Nobility*, pp. 177, 220. Fauja Singh and G.S. Talib, *Guru Tegh Bahadar: Martyr and Teacher* (Patiala: Punjabi University Press, 1975), pp. 41–55 presents the traditional view of the relationship between the ninth Guru and Raja Ram Singh.
87. It was Ram Singh's father Jai Singh who had eventually convinced Shivaji to enter into negotiations with Aurangzeb. James Laine, *Shivaji Hindu King in Islamic India*, pp. 26–8.
88. Fauja Singh and G.S. Talib, *Guru Tegh Bahadar*, p. 45. Some scholars claim however that Ram Singh was ordered to keep the ninth Guru under surveillance. Sagar, *Hukam-namas*, p. 42, n. 17.
89. The best account of Rajput loyalties and symbolic associations during the Mughal period remains Norman P. Zielgler, 'Some Notes on Rajput Loyalties During the Mughal Period', in J.F. Richards (ed.), *Kingship and Authority in South Asia* (Madison, Wisconsin: South Asian Studies, 1978), pp. 215–51.
90. Catherine Glynn, 'A Rājasthānī Princely Album: Rājput Patronage of Mughal-Style Painting', in *Articus Asiae* LX: 3/4 (2001), p. 229. Also John Seyller, 'For Love or Money,' pp. 13–14:
> Obliged by treaty to remain in attendance at the Mughal court, most Rajput princes had ample opportunity to become familiar with Mughal mural and miniature painting. They collected a number of examples of

120   The Darbar of the Sikh Gurus

Mughal works, and encouraged their own court painters to assimilate Mughal subjects into their local traditions.
91. Sagar, *Hukam-namas*, pp. 86–7; 126.
92. P.A. Andrews, *Felt Tents and Pavilions* II, p. 837.
93. Sagar, *Hukam-namas*, pp. 92–3 (Pbi.); p. 129 (Eng.). And so the archaic Anglicized version of *ravātī*, 'rowtee'. Henry Yule *et al.* (eds), *Hobson-Jobson* (1st edn. 1886. London: Routledge & Kegan Paul, 1969), p. 772. For the *rā'ūtī* during the period of Aurangzeb's reign see P.A. Andrews, *Felt Tents and Pavilions* II, p. 1218–19.
94. The Sikhs were certainly aware of the royal connotations associated with tents as Bhatt Kal (or Kal Shar that is, Kal the Poet) makes clear in the following shabad:

  The True Guru has pitched the tent (*khemā*) under which the four yugas have come together. He carries the lance of mystical knowledge and takes the support of the nām, the name through which the Lord's devotees are fulfilled. Through devotional worship Guru Nanak, Guru Angad and Guru Amar Das have merged into the Divine Hari. O Guru Ram Das, you alone know the essence of this raj yog.

  Bhatt Kal, *Savaīe mahale chauthe* 12, Adi Granth, p. 1398.
95. Descriptions of these items of princely tentage are taken from P.A. Andrews, *Felt Tents and Pavilions* II, pp. 1337, 1338, 1345. Also see H. Blochmann, *AA* I, pp. 47–9.
96. Andrews, *Felt Tents and Pavilions* II, pp. 1337, 1338.
97. This is the general assumption by Ved Parkash. See his *The Sikhs in Bihar*, p. 59; also, p. 144.
98. Sagar, *Hukam-namas*, pp. 90–1 (Pbi.); p. 128 (Eng.). Popular Sikh tradition often shows the ninth Guru presenting robes of honour to those who served him selflessly. See the online edition of *SP* 12:26:55, p. 217 and 12:43:26, p. 332. Also Macauliffe, *The Sikh Religion* IV, p. 342.
99. Background on khil'at appears in Stewart Gordon (ed.), *Robes of Honor: The Medieval World of Investiture* (New York: Palgrave, 2001) and Stewart Gordon (ed.), *Robes of Honour: Khil'at in Pre-Colonial and Colonial India* (New Delhi: Oxford University Press, 2003).
100. Stewart Gordon (ed.), *Robes of Honour*, p. 141.
101. Sagar, *Hukam-namas*, pp. 86–7; 126; 96–7; 131. Interestingly, the Guru requests these forty turbans just after his request for a khema. It seems likely that he may have presented these turbans within such a tent.
102. And so J.S. Grewal's claim that 'If [Guru Tegh Bahadar's] idea was to reassure the far-flung congregations...of the Guru's concern for them, he was amply successful.' Grewal, *The Sikhs of the Punjab*, p. 70.
103. *EoS* I, pp. 128–33. Macauliffe, *The Sikh Religion* IV, pp. 340–3.
104. See the online edition of *SP* 12:25–9, pp. 203–39. Here we are privy to traditions in which Guru Tegh Bahadar was very warmly received by the many sangats in the Malwa region, a number of whose members also

presented him with various offerings. For example online *SP* 12:26:29, pp. 213–14:

Afterwards groups of Sikhs had arrived and presented several offerings. The True Guru sat down, assembled his court (*dīvān*), and spoke with them all in the appropriate manner.

105. For J.S. Grewal the evidence of the hukam-namas coupled with the emphasis on fearlessness one discovers in the shabads of the ninth Master made Guru Tegh Bahadar the 'Prophet of Assurance.' See J.S. Grewal, *From Guru Nanak to Maharaja Ranjit Singh* (Amritsar: Guru Nanak Dev University Press, 1982), pp. 64–70. Although how Ram Rai eventually made his way to the Mughal court is contested, that he established his own gur-gaddī in Dehra Dun during Aurangzeb's time is not. Apparently Aurangzeb requested the raja of Garhwal to have Ram Rai reside in his territories after the execution of the ninth Guru.
106. For Sabinderjit Singh Sagar such statements support his contention that at least in the early years of Guru Tegh Bahadar's guruship these hukam-namas imply a 'crisis of guruship.' Sagar, *Hukam-namas*, p. 26.
107. Grewal and Bal, *Guru Gobind Singh*, p. 49. We are here told that although the people of the plains adjoining Kiratpur had been made Sikhs by both the sixth and seventh Gurus 'the true triumph of the Sikh faith over them came...when [Guru Tegh Bahadar] had died as a martyr.'
108. Sagar, *Hukam-namas*, p. 21.
109. Sagar, *Hukam-namas*, pp. 54–5 (Pbi); p. 110 (Eng.): *bhāī bathā tūm guru jī kā put*. Guru Hari Krishan's hukam-nama appears in Ganda Singh (ed.), *Hukam-nāme*, pp. 72–3. Guru Tegh Bahadar's hukam-nama in which Bhai Batha is elevated may be found in Sagar, *Hukam-namas*, pp. 50–1 (Pbi); p. 108 (Eng.). The lines dealing with Bhai Batha appear in the Guru's own hand rather than that of the scribe.
110. Sagar, *Hukam-namas*, p. 37.
111. Our earlier claims about hunting namely, that the presence of the Guru assured those Sikhs through whose lands he sought prey, here supports tradition's insistence on the ninth Guru's fondness for the hunt.
112. Sagar, *Hukam-namas*, p. 34.
113. Padam, *Dārbārī Ratan*, p. 248.
114. Dharampal Ashta, *The Poetry of the Dasam Granth* (New Delhi: Arun Prakashan, 1959), p. 32.
115. Grewal and Bal, *Guru Gobind Singh*, pp. 38–9, 197–8; nn. 43, 45.

4

Spirit and Structure
The Court of Guru Gobind Singh

ਸਤਿਗੁਰਿ ਮੋ ਕਉ ਦੀਆ ਉਪਦੇਸੁ । ਜੀਉ ਪਿੰਡੁ ਸਭ ਹਰਿ ਕਾ ਦੇਸੁ । ਜੋ ਕਿਛੁ ਕਰੀ ਸੁ ਤੇਰਾ ਤਾਣੁ । ਤੂੰ ਮੇਰੀ ਓਟ ਤੂੰਹੈ ਦੀਬਾਣੁ ।੧

The True Guru has divulged [these] teachings to me. My soul, body, and everything else belong to the Lord. Whatever I do is [a result of] your power. You are my refuge, you [alone] are my court (dībanu).

ਮਹਾਂ ਉਦਾਰ ਮੁਕਤਿ ਲੈ ਦੇਤਿ । ਚਹੁਦਿਸਿ ਤੇ ਕਵਿ ਤਜਾਗਿ ਨਿਕੇਤ । ਆਨਿ ਅਨੰਦ ਪੁਰਿ ਕੀਨਸਿ ਬਾਸਾ । ਸੁਤ ਬਿਤ ਆਦਿ ਪਾਇ ਸੁਖ ਰਾਸਾ ।੨

[As Guru Gobind Singh was] very generous and granted deliverance (mukti) poets from all over [India] abandoned their courts. They travelled to Anandpur to reside. Here they fathered strong sons and obtained a living and other such things the principal wealth of which was contentment.

It appears that there may be evidence suggesting the presence of at least one poet in the entourage of the ninth Guru. In a manuscript copy of a Brajbhasha translation/rendition of the well-known *Hitopadesha* (Valuable Advice) found in Patiala's Bhasha Vibhag Library in Devanagari script (ms. 404), dated sammat 1737 (1680 CE) and written by the poet Lakkhan Rai, we hear in the prologue the praises of what may be Lakkhan Rai's initial patron, Guru Tegh Bahadar. This preamble begins with allusions and thanks to the Hindu gods Vishnu and Brahma (*chaturānan*) and then to the sages Shuk (Shukdev), Vyas, and Narad (all of whom are regularly invoked in the compositions of the Dasam Granth). Lakkhan Rai then finishes the first passage with references to the ninth Master:

In this world Guru Tegh Bahadar displayed and manifest a reflection of the divine vision (*daras*).³

To which he adds, in the following line,

That person who finds [the ninth Guru's] protective shelter will be liberated from the cycle of existence (lit., 'freed of this world'). While Tegh Bahadar was Guru the treasury of his virtues was regularly sung.⁴

Whether the statements in this manuscript imply the existence of the poetic circle to which Kahn Singh Nabhawala, Dharampal Ashta, and other scholars refer is questionable. Indeed, our caution here is justified as Lakkhan Rai's translation of the *Hitopadesha* was finished five years after the ninth Guru's execution in Delhi (in *satrah sai saintīs*, states line twelve) which explains the poet's claim that he is presently *gur gobind ke dās* 'the servant of Guru Gobind'.⁵ The references to the ninth Master may then be rather indirect praise of the tenth Guru and his lineage in much the same way that we discover in the fifth chapter of the *Bachitar Nātak*, which is most likely the reason that Padam refrains from claiming that Lakkhan Rai was in fact the poet of Guru Tegh Bahadar.⁶

Such problematizing notwithstanding, that twentieth-century scholars do indeed assume the existence of a Sikh poetic circle prior to 1675 is very understandable, especially when taking into consideration the historical and cultural context in which the ninth Guru lived and in which he fostered his sangats scattered throughout India. Indeed the period of Guru Tegh Bahadar's guruship (1664–75 CE) closely corresponds to the early reign of the emperor Aurangzeb who was crowned 'Alamgir twice, first in 1658 while dealing with his eldest brother Dara Shikoh and again, in a far more elaborate ceremony, in Delhi on 12 June 1659. Their understanding of the ninth and especially the tenth Guru's darbar thus seems linked with both the history and the historiography of this emperor's reign. This has carved for Aurangzeb a special iniquitous niche in the history of India generally and that of the Sikhs in particular.

AURANGZEB AND INDO-TIMURID MUGHAL PATRONAGE

In order to understand better the reasons behind our Sikh scholars' conclusion then it is best to examine the rumoured plight of the artisans within the sixth Mughal emperor's atelier, especially those of the tasvīr-khānah. Despite news of Aurangzeb's harsh iconoclasm (as well as contemporary and later orientalist interpretations of the emperor's Islamic bent beginning with the Venetian mercenary Niccolo Manucci's hostile account),[7] an orthodox tenet for many of the Islamic religious personnel of his court who supported the new emperor's bid to power in 1657–8, 'Alamgir nevertheless retained a segment of his father's extraordinary atelier and continued most likely to personally appreciate beautiful art, although he may have avoided such 'on account of his great restraint and self-denial.'[8] The atelier's *joie de vivre*, however, may well have been profoundly muffled. Certainly members of the court (Aurangzeb included) still requested formal portraits of both the emperor and the nobility but

these were created through the successful—although increasingly mechanical—repetition of long established formulas. Images were now made for ceremonial purposes, not for pleasure.[9]

This has given rise to the view that aesthetic pleasures such as those afforded by illustrations seem to have been simply foresworn by the abstemious and self-disciplined emperor (at least for a while) and as a result, artists were no longer encouraged to be original nor to be inventive.

There seems to be some truth to this interpretation. Although it may appear to repeat what writers have been saying about Aurangzeb since Manucci first penned his self-centred narrative, the simple fact is that the number of paintings prepared within the emperor's atelier during Aurangzeb's reign dramatically declined and of these the vast majority (though not all) are of a quality seriously inferior to that created under previous Mughal emperors, especially Jahangir and Shah Jahan.[10] It is apparent that one of the only Mughal illustrations of Aurangzeb's darbar which branched out into relatively new and fresh artistic directions was painted by the artist Hashim sometime around 1658 very soon after 'Alamgir's accession to the throne, perhaps under the impression that things in the imperial atelier would be as before.[11] Such evidence no doubt fits well into the image propogated by the emperor's critics.

Rumours that such a newly artistically repressive climate existed, however, may have encouraged many of the more innovative painters to simply leave the Mughal atelier and seek a more hopeful outlet for their creative energies, looking for 'other employment [but] taking with them the styles and formulas learned at the court.'[12] Although a number of artists were patronized by lesser Mughal officials and were thus kept within the circle of the emperor's friends and loyal courtiers (and thus under the emperor's gaze), it appears that a considerable emigration of painters ensued. It is worth keeping in mind that such artistic migrations were commonplace in sixteenth- and seventeenth-century India and need not have been sparked by either conditions at court or rumours of persecution.[13] It is thanks to these movements perhaps, that a new vigour and vitality was brought to Rajput painting both in the Rajput heartland (Indian state of Rajasthan) and within the Pahari regions of the Punjab where a number of ranas and rajas traced their descent to traditional Rajput kings.[14] It seems likely too that a number of these specific artists found work in these hilly ateliers, one of whom may have eventually painted or overseen the painting of the regal portrait of Guru Gobind Singh (Fig. 1) noted in Chapter 1. While the Mughal atelier suffered a setback in this period, peripheral workshops flourished and generally 'Mughalized' styles became more prevalent away from the metropolis.

It would be about a decade after the debut of Hashim's courtly painting of the new emperor's darbar, during Aurangzeb's eleventh regnal year according to the Islamic calendar (1668–9), that Muhammad Hashim Khafi Khan (c. 1663–1734 CE) claims in his *Muntakhabullubāb* (Unadultered Selections, written between 1718–1734 CE), that a more austere tone began to dominate the Mughal court in which singers, dancers, minstrels, and artists 'of reputation in the service of the Court were made ashamed of their occupation, and were advanced to the dignities of *mansabs*.'[15] An irony here is that Khafi Khan would not have been able to write these observations were he writing during this period, for very soon afterwards Aurangzeb had dismissed his court chroniclers as well as his official historian, Muhammad Kazim, as even their histories (*tarīkh*) became understood as vanity manifest. To the emperor this represented a quality not in keeping with the pious self image he cultivated and wished to promote. Such a condemnation would not last however, for by 1684 it appears that Aurangzeb had reversed this policy when he instructed Bakhtawar Khan to pen the *Mir'at-i 'Ālam* (The World's Mirror), a general history of the world in which Aurangzeb's own history is included along with a brief section on poets including Bakhtawar Khan himself. The emperor also appointed as newswriter Ni'amat Khan whose *Wakā'i* (Battles) describes Aurangzeb's seige and conquest of Golconda.[16]

Other literary areas of Mughal courtly life are also alleged to have been similarly affected. In the atmosphere of self-discipline and self-denial described by both Khafi Khan and Aurangzeb's contemporary Bakhtawar Khan, a life of sensual and aesthetic pleasures was anything but privileged.[17] Architects (apart from those who drafted mosques), musicians, dancers, acrobats, as well as court poets and litterateurs, therefore, other than those whose areas of expertise were the strictly theological,[18] may have seen a change in their previous fortunes and followed the few of their fellow artists who did emigrate and ultimately abandon the royal darbar to search for opportunities elsewhere.

But that this emigration was prompted by persecution seems highly unlikely. Recent scholarship on Aurangzeb's attitudes towards music, for example, are studies which themselves finally bury the myth that Aurangzeb had had music buried. These studies have demonstrated how askew any such interpretations are in actuality.[19] To poets who may have chosen to leave the royal court or to those who had lost their lofty imperial positions, any such discouragement may have well seemed like persecution although as far as I know no such poet has captured or referred to in verse any such discrimination. This fact and contemporary evidence thus suggest otherwise. Indeed, musicans who self-consciously chose to stop performing were often rewarded with jagirs or generous mansabs.[20]

The same may be said for literary specialists. Aurangzeb continued to enjoy the company of literary men (and women)[21] throughout his life, particularly those nobles who were also accomplished poets such as Wuzarat Abdur Rahim whose sobriquet was Bikrami and Mukhalis Khan (d. 1701 CE), whose ghazals were well known and upon whose death Aurangzeb claimed 'I was pleased with his noble and virtuous qualities and his versatile genius.'[22] Aurangzeb himself easily possessed the best stocked library in the entire subcontinent (if not the entire Islamicate) and was quite familiar, thanks in large part to his days as a prince of the royal line, with the famous (and expensive) works on its shelves (so to speak), works that dealt with his famous ancestors and were made famous by them.[23] The new emperor was, moreover, very well educated, easily as cultured as his predecessors despite historians' claims to the contrary, proficient in both Arabic and Persian and something of a *hāfez* (one who has committed the Qu'ran to heart).[24] As a prince he spent a good amount of time studying hadiths, *fiqh* (jurisprudence) and legal cases which clearly enhanced the more pious demeanour which his later detractors made a habit of exploiting.

Such literary qualities notwithstanding, contemporaries do mention Aurangzeb's later concern with poetry itself. Both the *Ma'āsir-i 'Ālamgīrī* and the *Mir'at-i 'Ālam* claim that Aurangzeb was guided by the Quranic verse 'it is those straying into evil who follow the poets'[25] (Qu'ran 26:224) in his attitude towards poetry. Was the court thus purged of poets? After all, Khafi Khan would note some forty years later that '[Aurangzeb] abolished the custom of composing and reciting verses....'[26] But once gain such an outright, court-wide abolition seems very unlikely. If Aurangzeb did abandon poetry it was most likely a personal decision on his part not to write verse. As Bakhtawar Khan notes, '[Aurangzeb] abstains from practicing it...[and] he does not like to hear verses except those which contain a moral.'[27] This in itself suggests that certain types of poetry were very much permitted. Indeed, even Persian poets whose expertise was the satirical were still able to write poetry and find patrons amongst imperial courtiers in Aurangzeb's empire.[28]

The *Mir'at-i 'Ālam*, let us reiterate, as an official document sanctioned by the emperor carries more historical weight than either Khafi Khan or other later interpreters.[29] It was thus most likely with the Quranic admonition in mind that the emperor personally discontinued stipends earlier granted to poets and, as Khafi Khan later tells us, even eliminated the post of malikushshu'arā'.[30] Once again, however, we must approach such evidence cautiously and refrain from generalizations. The many letters which Aurangzeb wrote to his siblings prior to his accession and to his children afterwards are rife with Persian verses which he composed himself and verses written by famous Persian poets such as Hafez, Rumi, and Sa'di (as well as Arabic verses from the Qur'an and Hadith).[31] The emperor too was fond of contemporary Persian poets, especially of the famed

Mirza Bedil whose verses we discover in Aurangzeb's personal correspondance.[32] It was Aurangzeb, it appears, who granted the title Khan to the Mughal poet Mu'azzuddin Muhammad (d. 1690 CE) whose takhallus was initially 'Fitrat' and afterwards 'Muswi'. Indeed, it is by his sobriquet that Aurangzeb refers to Muswi in his communications.[33] Such actions on the emperor's part and also his regular compositions clearly demonstrate that Aurangzeb's attitude towards poetry and court poets is far more complicated than histories warrant, the vast majority of which rely on Jadunath Sarkar's monumental early twentieth-century five-volume work, the *History of Aurangzeb Based on Original Sources*.[34]

But let us keep in mind clearly that activities such as the elimination of stipends to poets represent Aurangzeb's personal proclivities, perhaps even his concern with nurturing a balanced public image of himself as a pious Muslim, and should not be confused with general Mughal state policy. Indeed, such personal actions on the emperor's part notwithstanding, not all poets did in fact leave the imperial court behind, nor did court poetry cease to be produced.[35] It seems too that rumours and news of such alleged activites, which would spread quickly throughout Aurangzeb's domains and beyond, would have curtailed the movement of non-Muslim Persian and Brajbhasha (and other regional languages) poets to the royal court.

If there was indeed such movement away from the imperial darbar for this reason, especially amongst immigrant poets of Persian, it was a stunning reversal of what had become since the time of the emperor Humayun a standard eastern Islamicate pattern—usually a one-way movement of poets and artists from India's adjoining eastern Islamicate countries along the many well-travelled highways connecting Persia and India, highways which went through Lahore, Multan, Kabul, or Qandahar. Along these many poets finally made their way to the Mughal capital.[36] Some Persian poets returned to their homes after a lengthy stay within the subcontinent while others chose to stay and live out the rest of their lives in India. A number of factors had initially enticed them to travel eastwards not the least of which may have been the later Akbari policy of *sulh-i kull* (Ar: *sulhulkul*, 'peace to all'), a welcome departure from the Safavid suspicion of religious plurality.[37] To this we may add wealth and the quest for fame. By the late-sixteenth century it was widely believed in Iran and elsewhere within the eastern Islamicate that a 'visit to India promised material comforts and an honoured position.'[38]

Although Babur was in addition to his many other talents, a man of letters, both Turki and Persian,[39] it is to Humayun, whose mother tongue was Chaghatai Turkish, that we credit the beginning of the Iranization of both the Mughal poetic and artistic darbar.[40] The reasons for such are not at all difficult to fathom. Not long after his final defeat at the hands of Sher Shah Suri at the Battle of Kanauj in 1540 CE, Humayun made his way to the Safavid court of Shah Tahmasp (1524–76 CE) in Tabriz, Persia. As the Shah's tastes were gradually becoming more orthodox and in a sense more refined he had allowed a number of Safavid court poets and painters to accompany Humayun on his return to India many years later, artists who brought along with them stylistic and literary techniques which had developed over centuries within the eastern Islamicate.[41] Treated and compensated very well for their artistic endeavours, the poets who had initially boarded the *kārvān-i hind* or the India-bound caravan may have been among the first to write back to Persia of their newfound status and modest wealth, gossip which in many ways came to establish the Mughal reputation for the respectful and handsome patronage of its poets.[42]

It was a reputation very well deserved, at least up until the mid-seventeenth century. According to Muhammad Abdul Ghani for instance, the Mughal emperors not only paid their poets well but they also doted on them and encouraged them to be as creative as they possibly could especially by pushing to their limits many of the stylistic features characteristic of the Persian ghazal genre within their own works. In regard to the techniques of *ihām* or ambiguity and homogeneity, Ghani continues,

The great incentive to this sort of production is to be found in the applausive support of the Mughal kings who encouraged its growth in India as a piece of literary skill.[43]

Such 'applausive support' should elicit little surprise as it came from a father and son, Babur and Humayun, who were accomplished poets themselves.[44] Following in their footsteps, the emperor Akbar keenly promoted social, cultural, and intellectual contacts with Iran (most likely in gratitude for the Shah's help to his father) going so far as to send envoys to the Iranian plateau to invite poets, scholars, and various other literati to take up residence at the Mughal court. Indeed, such patronage ultimately resulted in a Persian literary output within India which surpassed that of Iran itself.[45] This may perhaps have allowed the further development of what some scholars (though not all) consider the uniquely Indian variety of Persian poetry referred to by its sixteenth and seventeenth-century exponents as the *shīvah-'i tāzah* or 'Fresh Technique' but more popularly known today as the *sabk-i hindī*, the 'Indian Style'.[46]

With such a repute it seems logical that India became the desired destination of Iranian poets[47] and that positions within the royal darbar itself gradually became more and more coveted and thus more limited. It is clear that by the late sixteenth and early seventeenth centuries many Persian poets made their way to Mughal India from Iran, Khorasan, or elsewhere within the eastern Islamicate to find patrons among the Mughal nobility or to begin their careers as poets of the many smaller courts throughout the empire, hoping ultimately to further their prospects in securing an eminent position in the Mughal emperor's own darbar.[48] In some instances, these poets were encouraged to come to India by the Mughal emperor. The results of such encouragement may be judged by the number of poets at the Mughal darbar. By the 1590s, according to 'Abd al-Qadir Badauni's *Muntakhabuttavārīkh*, 168 poets received the patronage of the emperor or his nobles.[49] While Abu'l Fazl mentions 59 poets whom he had introduced to Akbar, the vast majority of these were from Persia.[50] Amongst these poets was the famed Jamaluddin Muhammad 'Urfi (1556–91 CE) whose *Dīvān* or poetic collection 'transported India and Turkey into ecstasy.'[51] Leaving Shiraz for India very soon after completing his studies 'Urfi became the darling of the court. 'The favour accorded him in court circles,' claims Jan Rypka, 'and later even with Akbar himself caused him to become disagreeably conceited.'[52]

'Urfi's career in India began by having found in Akbar's poet laureate Abu'l-Fayz Fayzi (the son of Shaikh Mubarak and brother of Abu'l Fazl 'Allami) a supportive patron.[53] This was of course the most common way to gain admittance into the court royal. Jahangir's poet laureate Muhammad Talib 'Amuli (apptd., 1618; d. 1627–8), for example, was initially introduced to the emperor by the Persian émigré and Mughal noble Ghiyasuddin Itimaduddaula, the emperor's father-in-law.[54] The history of another Mughal poet laureate allows us to observe other means by which the emperor's darbar was accessed. The career of Abu-Talib Kalim (b. circa 990/1582), the premiere poet of Shah Jahan, for example is certainly not atypical in this regard: it commenced when he moved from Hamadan in Iran to the Deccan where Kalim began his distinguished vocation as a court poet for Shah-Nawaz Khan Shirazi (d. 1611), a minister of the illustrious Ibrahim Adil Shah II of Bijapur (1580–1627).[55] From here Kalim, after a two-year interlude in his native Iran (1619–21), eventually found his way to Agra under the patronage of the Mir Jumla (Mir Muhammad-Amin Shahrastani Ruhalamin). This lasted until 1628 when Kalim finally caught the attention of those within the royal darbar of Shah Jahan. Here in the royal court as a result of his exceptional talent, he was appointed malikushshu'ārā by the Timurid emperor. Although intrigue caused him to leave the court for Kashmir before 1645 (he seems to have incurred the wrath of one of Shah Jahan's wives), he continued to participate in literary majalis and to write his Persian chronicle of Shah Jahan's reign, the *Shāh Jahān Nāmah*, until death forced him to lay down his pen in 1651.[56]

As Kalim's history cautions, not all was wealth and glory for poets in the Mughal India of Shah Jahan's later reign (1640s–50s). Kalim and numerous others for example not only had to put up with poetic competitors and rivals (which included the occasional versified attack and vilification) but also with the sycophancy of Mughal nobles and grandees, officials whom he criticizes in his baits to highlight the plight of court poets.[57] Kalim's contemporary and fellow Iranian poet in the darbar of Shah Jahan, Mirza Muhammad Ali Sa'ib (1601–78) for example, had this to say of such fawning aristocrats:

These nobodies who take pride in their ancestors are like dogs delighting themselves with bones.[58]

By Aurangzeb's period these problems and others were probably enhanced. Not only did the number of nobility increase dramatically as the emperor turned his attention to the Deccan after 1682, but even before this, by the early 1670s rumours of Aurangzeb's apparent iconoclasm and religious zeal must have made it seem as if opportunities for a glorious poetic career had all but dried up. Poetic emigration to both royal and regional Indian courts diminished to a trickle—the last Persian poet of Iranian origin who went to an Indian court was Muhammad bin Abi Talib Hazin (1692–1766/67), who arrived in Bengal in 1734 and especially disliked the Indian technique of Persian poetry as best represented by Mirza Bedil (d. 1712).[59] It seems that the fate of the Persian poets already a part of the Mughal darbar may have followed a trajectory similar to that of artists and musicians, namely the quest for fame elsewhere.[60] Contemporary Sikh tradition echoes these rumours of banishment resoundingly and with a definite Orientalist air.

Aurangzeb was a staunch Sunni Muslim. By [successive] decrees he banned all musical and poetic assemblies (*mushāire*).... In the light of such a state of affairs some singers and poets abandoned Delhi and travelled here and there to smaller royal darbars.[61]

ANANDPUR

Those smaller, peripheral darbars to which Piara Singh alludes above included the courts which had succeeded that of the glorious Bahmanid Sultanate of the fifteenth century: those of Golconda, Bijapur, and Ahmadnagar; as well as the court of Murshid Quli Khan in Bengal, the Valajah court of Chennai (Madras), and the Rajput court of Jaswant Singh (1683–1735 CE) among others.[62] Padam implies, and perhaps rightly so, that it seems rather more likely than not that we may here involve the court of Guru Tegh Bahadar. Although he says little as to why the ninth Guru's court would have enticed such poets, there are a number of reasons which would have made Anandpur-Makhowal an attractive venue.

Guru Tegh Bahadar was after all the son of Guru Hargobind who although initially cordial to Jahangir was defiant in the last decade of his life, engaging in a number of skirmishes with the emperor's minions in which he was victorious. This bold stance may have resounded with many of the poets whose services were no longer required by the emperor himself, especially those poets who were not Muslim or whose poetry was of a less religiously orthodox demeanour. If tradition is correct, Guru Tegh Bahadar himself may have also exercised what the emperor understood as rebelliousness.[63] Certainly this coupled with the ninth Master's reputation as the Guru and padishah of the respected *nānak-parastān* or Sikhs, may well have played a role in a poet's decision to relocate[64] as too the fact that Makhowal was only a short distance from the Pahari region of the Punjab, an area to which, as we have noted, many artists from the imperial atelier most likely made their way. The ateliers here were by this time justly famous for their stylistic techniques and Anandpur (which as implied in Lakkhan Rai's *Hitopadesha* may have already had a poet in residence) may well have provided an initial stepping stone for poets to the better equipped courts of Kangra and Bilaspur-Kahlur. If the subjects of late seventeenth- and early eighteenth-century Pahari art also reflected the literary tastes of Pahari patrons, then certainly any non-Muslim poets who sought sponsorship there, those whose repertoire included such subjects as the *rāg mālā*, the Ramayana, and the Mahabharata amongst many others (subjects which were generally acceptable to earlier Mughal courts) would have found an atmosphere congenial to their artistic temperaments.[65] The Pahari territory was agreeable to other interests as well as the ateliers here were in regions of the country which were not as easily accessible as others, a fact which is cited when explaining the hill rajas' often defiant attitude towards the Mughal emperor's orders.[66]

Although rather hesitant to clearly state that poets made their way to Anandpur before the ninth Guru's execution in November 1675 Padam and, indeed Sikh tradition as a whole, is quite insistent that a number of poets left the Mughal darbar for that of the tenth Guru after this date for many of the same reasons noted above and for a religious dimension which fails to appear in sources outside of the Sikh tradition which we shall shortly note. In some instances, we are told, the tenth Guru himself invited poets to join his literary darbar.[67] It is true that the names of the many poets who left the royal court are no longer generally known, perhaps because these poets and their records were forced underground by Aurangzeb's more orthodox decrees but more likely because they were simply outshone by poets such as Mirza Bedil and Nasir 'Ali Sirhindi (d. 1696 CE), creative fresh style Persian poets who composed for the darbars of lesser nobles.[68] Sikh tradition nevertheless supplies the names of many of these apparent ex-imperial poets. These are scattered throughout the late eighteenth-century *Mahimā Prakāsh Kavitā* and the *Bansāvalīnāmā* as well as the mid-nineteenth century *Sūraj Prakāsh*, and singled out in Padam's attempt to caution his Sikh readers that not all of the tenth Guru's poets were from the Punjab.

Rather, several *kavis* such as Alam, Sukhdev, Brind, Chand, Kanshi Ram, Kunvaresh [also Kuvaresh or Kuvar], Nand Ram, Nand Lal Goya and various other royal poets also together came to Anandpur from the [royal] darbar at Delhi.... The revered Guru favoured [all of his] poets with gifts and honour.[69]

What is particularly intriguing about the poets mentioned here is that all of their names save perhaps that of Alam (Per: '*ālam*) appear to be Hindu.[70] Certainly there were many Hindu poets in the courts of emperors Akbar and Jahangir, and those too in the service of Shah Jahan and other members of the Mughal nobility, especially by Dara Shikoh whose interests in Hindu cultures, Hinduisms, and Sanskrit is justly famous.[71] One such was Raja Raghunath '*Rai Rayān*' who during the twenty-third regnal year (1651–2) was granted 'the title Rai, the gift of a gold pen-case, and promoted to recordkeeper of the household lands' (*daftar dār-i khalīsah-'i tān*).[72] Another was the famed poet of Brajbhasha, Kavindracharya Sarasvati who it appears persuaded the emperor to rescind the jizya tax on Hindus, an action for which he was honoured by his mid-seventeenth century poetic contemporaries through the production of two Kavindracharya festschrifts in the mid-seventeenth century (one in Sanskrit, the other in Brajbhasha).[73] Sikh tradition's claim that such Hindu poets left the darbar of the new emperor Aurangzeb may not therefore be unwarranted although one would question the usual reasons later scholars give for their departure (that is, penury at best, persecution at the worst).[74] Nor implausible is the implication that the majority of Muslim poets in the 1660s and later in the 1670s would have rather sought employment in the courts of those nobles whose ancestors were less defiant than the Sikh Gurus after Guru Arjan.[75]

The displacement in 1658 of the Shah Jahani court—in which Hindu poets wrote alongside numerous Muslim ones—by a court far more inclined to Aurangzeb's understanding of Islamic piety and self-restraint had great potential for later Khalsa Sikh interpreters who, let us recall, wrote from the perspective of a marginalized community which invoked, resisted, and attempted in certain respects to emulate the Mughal court. Those few Hindu poets who apparently left the royal darbar (if any) thus left not for reasons of patronage or because their creativity and subject matter had been targeted by religious authorities but for fear of conversion to Islam (a moot point in regards to Alam). This was apparently not their only fear. Such interpretations of Sikh history sometimes imply and at other times explicitly state that the refusal to convert offered only one very permanent alternative, execution.[76]

We find this theme recurring time and again in both the *Sūraj Prakāsh* and the text on which Santokh Singh sometimes relied for his information, the *Mahimā Prakāsh Kavitā* of Sarup Das Bhalla.[77] In the quote at the beginning of this chapter, for example, Santokh Singh first reminds his readers and listeners that the Guru had a reputation for supporting poets and then claims that the tenth Master was able to also grant them freedom or mukti not in the cosmic sense (though the sentiments here expressed are no doubt purposefully ambiguous) but rather in a more mundane one.[78] Tradition notes that the poet Kuvar expressed such reasons for leaving the royal camp personally to the tenth Master:

"I have heard that you provide refuge to those who are homeless; that you always bestow great honour upon those hitherto disrespected; and that, indeed, to those without power you give strength (*trān*, 'protection'). Word of your beneficence (*sobhā*) has been heard around the world."

The revered Lord heard this and respectfully [beckoned the poet] to be seated. The brahman [Kuvar] then told of his own plight: "Hindus lack [the] strength (*bin bal*) [to withstand] the might of the Turks [and thus fear that] their religion (dharam) and common culture (*brindū*) will be destroyed [and that they will be] forced to convert (*melati*) [to Islam]. I left [the emperor's darbar] because of this terrible fear and came [to you] hoping to save my religion.[79]

Although the extant poetry of Kuvar himself makes no mention whatsoever of any such coercion on the emperor's part,[80] such an understanding resounds with meanings inherent within both the early Sikh narrative of Guru Tegh Bahadar's martyrdom and that of Guru Gobind Singh's divine nature. These early narratives are combined in coalition by the early eighteenth-century poet, Kavi Sainapati, and represent, assuming that Sainapati knew the tastes of his intended audience, a common Khalsa Sikh understanding of the guruships of the ninth and tenth Gurus:

O Lord, You infused the world with the [creative] energy [of the divine during] the [period of the] ninth kingdom, in the Age of Darkness. You alone are [Guru] Tegh Bahadar, [who is] the protector of the entire world (*jagg chādar sabh* lit., 'the Chador [which covers the] Whole World'). You alone are the tenth padishah Guru Gobind Singh, [you alone] have come to deliver the world [from Darkness] and you alone are the [true] Lord.[81]

Simply put, for poets who were either oppressed or who had fallen out of favour or were simply looking for a location to sell their wares, there was perhaps no safer place than the Anandpur of Guru Gobind Singh, the son of both the Hind di Chadar and the Sabh Jagg di Chadar. Once again we are here dealing principally with tradition. The source of the above statement is quite an early one (1711 CE) but it is tacitly and at times explicitly supported in the extant compositions of the tenth Guru's other poets.[82] It suggests that Guru Tegh Bahadar's posthumous reputation, that is the late seventeenth and early eighteenth-century Sikh view of his life and legacy, as for example in the *Bachitar Nātak*, doubtlessly helped legitimize Guru Gobind Singh's claim to the gur-gaddi, and would have provided some incentive for non-Muslim poets to leave Aurangzeb's court after 1675 for the refuge that was Anandpur. The irony within contemporary readings of these narratives of course is that these poets left the Mughal court for the protection of their dharam, but it was this very dharam which was simply abandoned after their arrival in Anandpur, replaced, as tradition implies, with either the Sikh or Khalsa dharam. This it seems is part of the triumphalist interpretation of Khalsa Sikh history that would very much be at the heart of later eighteenth- and nineteenth-century Khalsa Sikh literature.[83]

THE SIKH DARBAR

However such poets arrived at the tenth Guru's darbar—whether they were requested by the Guru, encouraged by fellow poets, or impelled by force of circumstance—arrive they did. Their presence and prolific output even impressed itself upon fellow members of their august fraternity. Kavi Sainapati, for example, who says little about poets and courtly life in his famous *Gur-sobhā* makes this quite clear at the end of his *Chānākā Rājnīti* (Chanakya's [a.k.a.

Kautilya or Vishnugupt] Political Maxims), also known as the *Chānākā Shāstr*:

> The poet, Sainapti by name, [refined] the *Chānākā* and translated it into the common language within the court (sabhā) of Guru Gobind [in which] the wisest (*param sujān*) of writers [reside].[84]

We can only conjecture as to when they arrived for the most part because the equivalent to the *rahīl* is very rare within the compositions of the tenth Guru's poets.[85] A rahīl is a line or more devoted to the poet's arduous journey to the patron (initially over desert terrain, a symbolic comparison to the Prophet Muhammad's Night Journey to heaven), a poetic conceit often discovered with the masnavis and ghazals of Indo-Persian poets dating back to the time of Mahmud of Ghazna and before. The only such reference I have seen is by the poet Sukhdev who relates the date of his entry to the Guru's court at the end of his *Chhand Vichār Pingal* (A Metrical Treatise on [Brajbhasha] Prosody). His was not, it seems, a passage prompted by anything apart from economic need:

> As the science of prosody was spreading throughout [northern India] (*prastār sah*) I came to the Punjab country and entered the court (lit., sabhā, 'society') of Guru Gobind. [Here] I read and was captivated by poetry. I arrived during the year 1744 according to the calendar of Rai Bikram (1687 CE). Sukhdev diligently reflected on his task and was greatly rewarded by the Guru (lit., 'obtained great wealth from the Guru').[86]

The date strongly implies that Sukhdev is not speaking here of the court at Anandpur but rather of the Guru's darbar at Paunta Sahib. Between the years 1685–8, as is well known, Guru Gobind Singh resided at Paunta on the northern banks of the Jamuna River within the territory of the Raja of Nahan, Medina Prakash as the raja's buffer between himself and the more powerful raja of Bilaspur-Kahlur, Bhim Chand. It was here that the Guru produced many of the literary works attributed to him[87] (or if traditions regarding the writing of the *Akāl Ustati* are to be trusted, it was here that they were at least begun). The darbar of his poets was first set up here, a court at which the Guru's first poets were very fruitful.

Unfortunately tradition tells us that the vast majority of these compositions written at Paunta Sahib did not survive the tumultuous history of the early eighteenth century, nor too did those produced by the Guru's poets at his court in Anandpur, nor subsequently those within his third court, the Lakkhi Jungle darbar.[88] From within those few works which are extant however, we are allowed to witness, among other things, a vignette of the court of the tenth Master—at least an image of how these poets perceived that court—beginning with a view of the centre of the court, Guru Gobind Singh himself.

Although the commemorations of the important events in the Guru's life such as his accession to the gur-gaddi, his marriage(s), the birth of his children, and the creation of the Khalsa amongst others are conspicuously absent from what remains of their translations and encomiums these poets most certainly eulogize the tenth Master himself.[89] For Piara Singh Padam, this gur-ustati literature, as he calls it, is not mere vanity of the Indo-Timurid variety he so criticizes nor is it simply the poets' attempts to ensure that they retain their positions and their employment, but rather praise for the Guru as the true liberator of humanity and as a revolutionary committed to the overthrow of tyranny.[90] We earlier became privy to such literature in the compositions of Brind and Kuvaresh, poets within the Anandpur Darbar. Another Anandpuri poet, Ani Rai, also lauds the Guru, particularly his prowess in battle:

Having selflessly served the True Guru one's whole being is thoroughly strengthened. Distress is destroyed; joy is produced and faith steels the heart. The strength of Guru Gobind Singh's sword is the power of truth. You are the true warrior in the Age of Darkness, known throughout all the nine realms which make up the entire earth.[91]

After Anandpur had been besieged and ultimately abandoned in late 1704 /early 1705 however, it seems that a number of new poets had joined the Guru in the Lakkhi Jungle forming a peripatetic darbar of sorts, perhaps reminiscent of the more itinerant courts of the emperors Babur and Humayun. The principal poet within the Lakkhi Jungle darbar was, according to Padam, one Bihari, a former head sadhu of the ecstatic (*divānā*) Udasi establishment whose compositions betray a love mysticism which is not altogether uncommon in the Sikh Lakkhi Jungle poetry of this period. In his *Mājhān Gurū Gobind Singh kīān* ([Verses in the] Majh Metre [in Honour] of Guru Gobind Singh), he states in a spirit which accords with that of both the great Sufi poets and Hindu sants and bhagats that

The Guru is Gobind. When I look [deep] within [my heart] I no longer see myself [but perceive] you [alone].[92]

Another verse claims that

The revered Lord has given his darshan to me. This is the true soap with which I have washed away all filth.[93]

One of Bihari's co-poets was the writer Adha who, it seems, remained with Guru Gobind Singh during the latter's journey to southern India to meet with the new emperor Bahadar Shah. The following glowing praises of the tenth Master discovered within the poet's *Mājhān Sassī dīān* (Verses in Majh Sassi metre) were, according to tradition, first recited in the presence of the Guru:

Gobind Singh, the heroic Guru of all Gurus has favoured [us]. Through the power of his conquering glance, through the power of his grace we have taken that favour [for ourselves]. It is said that love and purity are ours, and ours too is fame and love. No one [of us] thus lacks the gifts [imparted by the three-part formula of] nām, *dān*, and *ishnān* ([meditating upon] the Name [of God], giving charity, and [abiding in] purity). They over whom Guru Gobind watches (*sir*) lack nothing whatsoever. Petitioning in front of the sangat it is the True Guru who truly comes to one's aid. Kavi Adha says that I am a sacrifice to those who cause faith [in the Guru] to dwell within their hearts. The work of those who have faith dwelling (*vutthī*) within their heart has been done. Those who have visited (*darshan kītā*) with Guru Gobind have obtained liberation.[94]

Another poet associated with the Lakkhi Jungle period is Phattmall. Although his compositions similarly praise the tenth Master, he appears to be the only Lakkhi Jungle poet who includes a reverence for what we may assume is the early Khalsa (without naming them as such), a respect very much in line with that we discover within Sainapati's early eighteenth-century *Gur-sobhā*:

The Gurmukh has drunk the [initiatory] amrit and has become satiated while the heart (*ghat*) of the nindak, the slanderer, is empty. Greater than Phatta are those who acknowledge the Guru as they are contented (*khush-hālī*), always, for every moment of their lives.[95]

The praise of the Guru (and in some instances his disciples) in these compositions also extends to the Guru's residence and to the items which may have been in the Guru's possession especially those which were often lauded in court poetry. Such tribute is indirect praise of the Guru himself but it may nevertheless imply the tenth Guru's familiarity with the etiquette and styles of the royal darbar, an acquaintance particularly brought out within the many formulaic statements which appear either as prologues or conclusions to the translations/refinements of Sanskrit works produced by such poets to whom we have already been privy. In these works there seems to be the standard admiration of the symbols of the court. Such acclaim is very often discovered within the oeuvre of many of the poets of the Mughal darbar and other literary courts within India. In describing the splendour of the new city of Bijapur, for example, the centre of the court of the famed Ibrahim Adil Shah, the court poet (and soon after Mughal court poet) Nuruddin Zuhuri stated that

If they [ever] make an elixir of joy and pleasure they shall do so from the pure dust of Bijapur.[96]

In very much the same way the poet Hans Ram Bajpei praises the city of Anandpur in his *Karna Parab* though in a far less Islamicate way and in a style which would also run counter to descriptions we find in more Hinduized Brajbhasha courtly poetry, as it rejects the separation of castes:

This is the place where (*jahān*) the four varnas [come] from the four [directions]; it is the ashram which delights. To it has been applied the name Anandpur, the root of bliss (*ānand ko kand*).[97]

As the 'root of bliss' Anandpur was, it seems, intended to grow into a large tree. Indeed, a tree which could provide the type of refuge to which Pandit Devi Das alludes in his little known *Singh Gaū kī Kathā* (The Story of the Lion/Singh and the Cow/Poorman) prepared within the Guru's court:

Having obtained a home within Anandpur transmigration will cease to exist and the fear of death will be destroyed.[98]

Such implications doubtlessly inspired Santokh Singh to render the following and ascribe it to the poet Mangal Rai:

The bestower of joy is the revered Guru, Gobind Rai. That person who would like to [experience such] bliss should come to Anandpur.[99]

Tradition also claims that Hans Ram lauds the Guru's court at Anandpur ('where kings great and small alike come and recline their heads'),[100] especially its large number of talented poets. In one instance, Santokh Singh demonstrates, Hans Ram likens the procession of the adorned poets of the Guru's darbar to a military tattoo, cautioning the dignitaries present within the court not to fear for their lives by the clamour caused by their passing:

The thunder of drums and the boom of the kettledrums are believed to be the thundering of clouds. The symbols (lit., 'pennant') of the court shine so radiantly that the sun has gone and hidden itself [for shame]. [The sound is like] herds of elephants numbering in the thousands. [The sight] is of a dazzling body studded with precious jewels. Listening to the tumult of hooves (*nālian*) as enemies (*kor*) prepare and exert themselves gods like Indra and [great] kings are both ashamed [of their fear] in such a crisis. Hans Ram says to you who are running away [scared] be seated as this is the procession of royal poets (*kavirāj*) requested by Gobind Singh.[101]

Hans Ram himself exalts the tenth Guru's *talwār* or sword which, our poet writes, is the *sūran kī pati* the 'honour of heroes,' the 'granter of the fruits which the world desires with vigour,' and the symbol which 'always keeps the enemy in check.'[102] He continues,

Very powerful, glorious is the [true] patishah Guru Gobind Singh. Your sword (*karācholī*) itself is in the style of the wish-fulfilling tree of the gods.[103]

Such praise of the Guru's sword is also found in the *Jang-nāmā* of the tenth Guru's poet Ani Rai, dealing with the Guru's battle with Mughal forces at Anandpur:

Your sword is [that which, like Brahma,] ordains sovereignty.[104]

and

[Your sword is] The honour of heroes it [brings] joy and splendour, it is [as strong as] the elephant's tusk (*samāj āj*). Your sword is famous, it brings victory [to those oppressed] like the master of spring [brings relief from winter].[105]

The poet Mangal Rai, we are told, likewise devoted a number of lines to the uniqueness of the Guru's kettledrum, which tradition names Ranjit Nagara:[106]

The instrument [which brings] joy [to the righteous] is playing at Anandpur every day. Listening to its boom even [brave] kings lose consciousness. Residing at the fortress in Lanka Bhabhichan [hears it and] trembles in fear that a cavalryman of his brother, the many-armed Ravana, will later arrive. [Hearing it] King Bali himself loses strength and goes to hide within Patala, the netherworld.[107] This is the drum (*nishānī*) of victory, [the drum] of the court to the gateway of victory. The drum ensemble (*naubat*) of Gobind Singh, the Guru Patishah, does not give restful sleep to the wicked neither during the night nor during the day.[108]

There is nevertheless a caveat to be inserted here. Given the regular references within both the Adi Granth and the Dasam Granth to such imperial items as the kettledrum as either metaphorical symbols of the divine court or irrelevant and vain objects associated with transient earthly imperium, one may ask whether the tenth Master's poets or Santokh Singh are in fact here referring to such objects in a similar figurative spirit.[109] Although it is difficult to say whether or not actual physical items inspired our poets (rather than simply literary protocols),[110] we may state with assurance that the tenth Guru did indeed possess a number of royal trappings as these are referred to within the only writings we can ascribe to Guru Gobind Singh with any amount of certainty, his hukam-namas. It is true that in these we do not hear of canopies, whisks, and drums but all the same we observe the Guru requesting robes of honour, cloth for turbans, textiles, and for objects of a more martial character such as a sturdy battle elephant (*hacchā hāthī jangī*), numerous cavalrymen, guns, weapons, and shields.[111] Tradition adds to these accoutrements: the beautifully decorated tent gifted the Guru by Duni Chand of Kabul in 1680 which is alleged to have earned the envy of Bhim Chand, and the famous *prasādī* elephant and the massive kettledrum Ranjit Nagara, both items of which made the Guru appear as an upstart to the majority of the Pahari Rajas.[112] Tradition, as we discover within the *Mahimā Prakāsh Kavitā*, for example, also tells us of a hukam-nama sent to Bulakidas, a very pious masand of Guru Tegh Bahadar from Dacca, requesting him to make a women's litter or sedan chair (Per: *mahāfah*) out of ivory.[113] This particular hukam-nama is not included in today's standard collection (nor too is included a number of other hukam-namas, in one of which the tenth Guru requests parts of a *huqqah* or waterpipe!)[114] and may well be an exaggeration as such an ostentatious item seems very much out of character with the general tenor of those written instructions commonly considered authentic.

Although the tenth Master did possess such items (I take for granted that the sangats to whom these requests were addressed did in fact fulfil them), we must ask whether these were in fact courtly in nature, symbolic of the Guru's spiritual or even temporal sovereignty. It seems to me that the best way to begin answering this question is to start with the Guru's early life as it seems likely that the tenth Guru's understandings of courtly symbols and etiquette were gleaned from his own childhood experiences and that these experiences may well have been enhanced by the presence of poets or even ex-imperial poets.[115]

GURU GOBIND SINGH, THE TENTH PADISHAH

It is well known that during his father's lifetime the young Guru initially resided in Patna, then later in Lakhnaur, and finally in Makhowal. The special treatment given to him by Sikhs in all of these locales was only natural when one considers the significance of the young Guru's birthright.[116] Certainly the ninth Guru was highly regarded as the padishah by many Sikhs and others in Patna and elsewhere, a claim implied in both the ninth Guru's written instructions and near contemporary sources. His only son would have most likely been thought of in a similar manner and trained from an early age to ultimately assume the mantle of his father's arduous guruship. The devotion of his uncle Kirpal, for example, and the sheer joy exhibited by the sangat of Patna at his birth seem to strongly imply such conclusions.[117] After the execution of the ninth Master we may only assume that such affection for and loyalty towards the now fatherless child would have increased dramatically. Even Aurangzeb most likely recognized the significance of this event, which Sikhs have perceived as a martyrdom since the early eighteenth century, granting to Guru Hari Rai's son, Ram Rai, the territory around Dehra Dun as the emperor's hopes for having him accepted by the Sikhs as the successor guru faded.[118]

Before this execution, however, many pious accounts refer to the child Guru's training in the martial arts, a training reminiscent of both the education of epic Hindu princes such as Rama and one associated with what was known throughout the Islamicate as the *ahl-i saif* or 'men of the sword'.[119] We see the young Gobind Rai thus wrestling with his childhood friends, engaged in mock battles, and standing up fearlessly to authority, to name a few such activities.[120] This was very much the type of education which royal princes such as the young Akbar received to prepare them for the rigours of rule.[121] Tradition reflects the practices and cultural mores of the Sikh disciples responsible for the Guru's upbringing in the 1660s and 70s. Once again, one can assume that theirs was a casual familiarity with the education of Indo-Timurid princes, courtly procedures, and precedents, most likely inherited through rumours, gossip, entertainments, and other forms of oral tradition.[122]

In these same ways Sikhs of the later seventeenth century would have heard many stories regarding the rearing of Rama, Krishna, and various other great and epic figures from India's (legendary) past (*itihāsa*) and may even have been familiar with the traditional skills and disciplines which classical and popular manuals of kingship enjoined kings to cultivate.[123] With such a template composed of various and disparate elements in mind, it is not surprising that the future Guru, the son of the ninth Master, would have been raised according to numerous princely standards. The narrative section of the Chaupa Singh rahit-nama for example implies this in an attempt to focus attention upon the devoted service of the Guru's Chhibbar disciples:

[The young Gobind] learned [various skills from his Chhibbar teachers] just as Ram was taught by Vasishtha and Krishan by Sandipan, and he acquired from them a knowledge of the world in all of its many manifestations.[124]

It is likely therefore that tradition's many vignettes of the young Guru learning to wrestle and playing martial games, studiously learning Persian, Arabic, Gurmukhi, and Sanskrit; the Puranas, Shastras, Qu'ran, and classical Persian literature as well as the Sikh scripture possess a certain verisimilitude though these traditional accounts only hint at the tension that must have gone into the fashioning and self-fashioning of the Guru's subjectivity, especially since the Islamicate Mughal emperor was indeed responsible in large part for his father's execution.[125]

Like the great men of the Mughal court and the legendary heroes of India's epics, it seems that the young Guru would have been made to combine in unison the qualities of both the 'men of the sword' and the *ahl-i qalam* or 'men of the pen', or put another way the virtues of the shastrdhārī and the shāstrdhārī respectively.[126] Both contemporary Persian sources as well as later Sikh tradition for example, speak of the Guru as an accomplished archer and swordsman. Such achievements in swordsmanship may explain in part why for the tenth Guru the sword became the ultimate symbol of the Eternal Guru, the *sarab loh*, All Steel, the protector of the oppressed from the scourge of the unrighteous. If the Persian and Brajbhasha sources attributed to the tenth Guru are in anyway connected with him as I believe these are, then his training in the literary arts was also a very substantial one indeed.[127] These texts (to which we shall return) not only demonstrate a command of both Brajbhasha and Persian stylistic conventions and principles but also show a cognisance of literature, language, and symbols considered courtly within both the Islamicate and the classical Indian world (which was certainly re-energized by the Mughal emperors' patronage of Sanskrit and Brajbhasha as well as patronage from the more Sanskritized court of Shivaji Bhonsale),[128] a world which is portrayed in the Puranas, the great epics of India, and the extraordinary plays of Kalidasa.[129] Indeed, the works produced at the tenth Guru's court conform perfectly to the genres written in other contemporary Indian courts: *rītigranth*s or texts on mannerist court poetry, works on literary rhetoric, expositions in Brajbhasha on famous classical works such as the *Hitopadesha*, and the *Kokashāstra*, amongst others, as well as devotional works and popular wisdom literature to which we must also add various *nīti* compositions such as manuals on *rāj-nīti*, diplomacy or proper political conduct which often derived such maxims from popular Sanskrit animal fables refined and then retold in Brajbhasha.[130]

It is perhaps with this aspect of the Guru's training in mind that the tenth Master's court poet Chand, in his miscellaneous shloks, refers to Gobind Singh in the following fashion, signifying an addictively creative genius (*kalā-dhārī*) while, it seems to me, alluding to his court:

Guru Gobind Singh has infused the world with the [creative] energy of the Lord and made Sikhism manifest in the Age of Darkness. Shouts of victory resound throughout the three worlds while the True Guru guards the honour and self respect [of his Sikhs].[131]

To this we may add a reference in the *Krishanavtār* which could be a description of the Guru himself rather than a depiction of the Braj countryside's favourite son: *ras-bātan mai ati hī ju rasī hai* '[He is] the connoisseur (rasī) amongst all cultured men (*ras-bātan*) [who are able to discriminate between the good and the truly remarkable].'[132] Raised in such a manner (we may assume) and understood by his contemporaries as a spiritual padishah it seems quite likely then that the young Guru would have known the significance of both dimensions that were expected of him and were lauded in his poets' encomiums. A strong courtly component as well as Persianite terms which signify courtliness and comportment are also to be found within the tenth Guru's hukam-namas, although these say nothing about how courtly items were to be employed.

Let us begin by noting a very brief and undated hukam-nama in which we are introduced to one Sobha Chand. The entire order reads as follows:

[There is] One Timeless Being.
[He is known through the grace of] the True Guru.
The Guru will watch over Bhai Ram Rai and the midwife, Dai Lado.[133]
The courtier Sobha Chand has presented himself [before me] thereby ensuring my happiness and his blessing.[134]

It is not only the apparent reference to the darbārī or courtier here that is significant but also the fact that the courtier presents himself (*hazūr pahuche*) before the Guru, thus indicating the continuation of the courtly comportment which was noted in the orders of Guru Tegh Bahadar who likewise asks specific Sikhs and their sangats to present themselves before him.[135] The phrase hazūr pahuche could of course be translated simply as 'has arrived.' Hew McLeod, for example, translates the phrase *hazūri pahuchāvanā* (lit., 'ensure that it arrives in his presence') of Hukam-nama 56 in Ganda Singh's collection[136] as 'send it directly to him,'[137] a translation which is far less awkward than mine and indeed quite accurate. It nevertheless misses the semiotic potential which I believe should be explored for our purposes. The Persianite term hazūr also appears throughout the Adi Granth and is well in keeping with Christopher Shackle's ideas regarding the royal application of such Persian loan words.[138] For the Mughals, moreover, the Persianite term hazur was used in the mid to late seventeenth century to describe those great amirs who were stationed at the imperial court. According to Muhammad Saqi Musta'idd

Khan's early eighteenth-century *Ma'āsir-i 'Ālamgīrī* (Contemporary [History] of 'Alamgir) these nobles were referred to as either the *umarā'-i hazar-i rikāb*, the Amirs in the presence of the royal stirrup (i.e., household), or simply as the *umarā'-i hazar*, Amirs of the imperial presence.[139] Let us once again note that the act of 'presenting oneself' was ambiguous and could be used in both a courtly and a religious sense, especially when we take into consideration the idea of darshan, the initially Hindu concept of seeing (i.e., mystically incorporating the divine within oneself through the visible contact with the eyes) which the Mughal emperors beginning with Akbar incorporated into their daily, courtly routine, and to which the tenth Guru regularly alluded in his instructions.[140] Another example of such ambiguity appears in a hukam-nama dated 22 May 1691 (5 Jeth Sudi sammat 1747). The Guru's scribe writes:

> The Sikh who will present [contribute] rupees or gold coins in the fulfillment of this special request will ensure his place in the court of the Guru.[141]

Although these Persianite words and phrases appear within the hukam-namas of the previous Gurus these emerge far more often in the tenth Guru's written instructions implying that the tenth Guru's courtly situation was a more pronounced one, a point contemporary sources and tradition both unequivocally support.

Comportment was most likely a fundamental feature of these gatherings. The Guru it seems not only observed the comportment of his Sikhs but also comported himself in a courtly way when in the presence of the emperor. A news dispatch in the first regnal year of the emperor Bahadar Shah dated 4 August 1707 for example claims the following:

> In response to the instructions [issued by this court] Gobind, the successor of Guru Nanak (lit., 'the Nanaki') came with weapons girded (*bā yarāq amadah*) and presented himself (*malāzmat kardah*) [before the emperor]. The Guru made an offering (*nīaz gozarānīd*) of one hundred gold *ashrāfīs* (coins) and received, in return, a khil'at and a medallion studded with precious stones [as a display of the emperor's] favour (*in'ām*), and was granted permission to depart.[142]

That this meeting went well is underscored by the absolute delight with which the Guru's scribes pen these words on the first day of Katak, sammat 1764 (2 October 1707) to the sangats of both Dhaul and Khara in two separate hukam-namas. For reasons which may well have to deal with self-respect the scribes simply fail to mention the Guru's granting of the nīaz:

> With great delight [the Guru] arrived at the emperor's side and has been bestowed with (*ināmu hoī*) a robe of honour and a beautiful ornament set with jewels (*dhukdhukī jarāu*) worth 60,000 [rupees].[143]

The value of the ornament does not appear in the Persian chronicle and is most likely purposefully mentioned in the hukam-nama in order to enhance the importance of the Guru in the eyes of the emperor and demonstrate to these sangats, moreover, that things between the Sikhs and the Mughal darbar were now on a footing quite different than that during Aurangzeb's period. The robe of honour as we have so often by now seen, was in this light the mark of the new emperor's relationship with the Guru (Aurangzeb had died about seven months before these hukam-namas were dispatched), a positive relation which may well stretch back to the time of the prince's visit to the Punjab in 1696 as implied in the thirteenth chapter of the *Bachitar Nātak*. The prince's cordial relationship with the Guru is also implied within a hukam-nama dated 24 July 1698. In it Guru Gobind Singh writes in his own hand that,

> The Guru will watch over the [Sikhs in the] army of Shahzada Azim.[144]

It is therefore quite likely that the tenth Guru was on good terms with the future Bahadar Shah—tradition often claims that the two were introduced to one another through the good graces of Bhai Nand Lal—and that Guru Gobind Singh was also friendly with Prince Mu'azzam's son, Azim as implied in the hukam-nama mentioned above. This terse statement also suggests that there were indeed Sikh soldiers within the Mughal army, a claim which demonstrates that the martial codes of the Sikhs of the Khalsa were in many instances commensurate with those of the Mughals.[145]

THE DASAM GRANTH

The courtly understandings in the hukam-namas and the poetry of the tenth Guru's poets are matched by those we find in the many compositions which make up today's Dasam Granth, in both their content and their form. Certainly there is a great controversy and rightly so over virtually every aspect of this text: its origins, its authorship, the nature of certain compositions within it (whether literary or devotional), its theology, and in some cases even its contemporary divisions. A recent proposition, for example, asks if the fourteen chapters of the *Bachitar Nātak* as we find these today are a unified whole; or are these in fact a small portion of a much longer narrative, the *Bachitar Nātak Granth*, which includes the *Chandī Charitr Ukti Bilās*, the *Chandī Charitr*, the *Chaubīs Avtār*, the *Brahmā Avtār*, and *Rudr Avtār*? Certainly the word *afzū* (Per: *afzūn*, 'more') at the end of the *Bachitar Nātak*'s final chapter, section fourteen, suggesting that the text is to be continued implies the existence of further segments whether these are an extention of the *apnī kathā* story itself (the fifteenth chapter),[146] or the indication that those listening to the narrative seek extra guidance from a *kathākar* or giani (which is certainly implied).[147]

For our purposes however, many of these contentious points, especially the individual authorship of the entire text or of particular compositions within it are not altogether important. Indeed, the existence of numerous pennames or poetic signatures, ta<u>kh</u>allus in Persian or *chhāp* (lit., 'impression') in Brajbhasha, within the lengthier compositions of the Dasam Granth (the *Chaubīs Avtār* and the *Pakhyān Charitr*), the most popular of which is Kavi Shyam followed by Kal Ram, and in one instance Chhabi;[148] the appearance of scribes allegedly writing on behalf of the tenth Guru;[149] and the presence of the code phrase *srī mukhvāk pātishāhī dasvīn*, 'uttered from the mouth of the tenth lord, the [true] king'[150] (which also suggests busy scribes diligently copying the Guru's words)[151] make it difficult to allocate all of these compositions to a single poet. There is simply not enough evidence at our disposal to make conclusive statements about either individual authorship or the history of its compilation.[152]

Collective authorship is far easier to assign, however, as many of its compositions are very similar in style, format, and spirit to those we discover in other late sixteenth-, seventeenth-, and eighteenth-century courts such as the darbars at Jodhpur, Amber/Jaipur, Kishengarh, the Bundela kingdom at Orcha, Gwalior, and Pune, to name a few where court poets wrote predominantly in Brajbhasha.[153]

Put simply, the striking similarities which the compositions of the Dasam Granth bear with the courtly literary and poetic forms employed by such contemporary darbars reveals to my mind the courtly nature of the Sikh works in the Dasam Granth.[154] The fact that we find dates and in some cases, references to the places at which the work was completed mentioned within the text, suggests that the court in question is that of the tenth Guru. The ending of *Rāmavtār*, a concluding passage commonly found in Brajbhasha courtly literature, may be cited as example:

During the year sammat 1755 [1698 CE] on the first day of the dark half of the month of Asharh (*hār*) this granth was finished through Your grace and with great pleasure. Please improve upon any errors within it. This story (kathā) of Raghunath (Rama) was completed through the Lord's grace at the foot of a high mountain down from where flows the Sutlej River.[155]

The predominant genre in the Dasam Granth is easily the charitr, which accounts for more than three quarters of the text. This format is a style of narrative very common to courtly Brajbhasha since the early seventeenth century which was adopted from the much older Sanskrit *charitra* (lit., 'deeds').[156] Well before the seventeenth century charit was known as an 'expressive' style of Indic narrative and/or inscriptional discourse, a format much like the Sanskrit *mahākāvya*, used to narrate the biographies of kings and their kingly deeds that was regularly employed within Indian courts and beyond in the vast region which Sheldon Pollock has identified as 'the Sanskrit cosmopolis' since the early Indic period of Indian history (*c.* 300–*c.* 1300 CE) beginning just before the dawn of the Gupta imperium.[157] There was, Pollock shows, a strong connection between the literary will and the political will during this period, in what he calls a 'poetry of politics', a 'politics of aesthetic power' which was etched into the very form of these narratives.[158] These did far more than relate the mere fanciful stories which many contemporary scholars alone extract from them. As mahakavya and charit were the dominant literary genres, these were also the vehicles through which history was communicated and recorded, much like prose is the dominant literary genre in which western history is recorded.[159] In other words, these poetic forms were adopted by traditional pandits who wrote the history of their rulers.

The historical character of this style of writing seems to have survived despite Sanskrit's eventual demise by the end of the Indic period, supplanted as it was by more 'cosmopolitan vernaculars' such as Tamil and Kannada, Brajbhasha, and Bengali.[160] In southern India after 1600 CE, for example, the Telugu version of charitr, *charitramu*, was used in very much the same way: to designate 'history' as a 'story in the past' without the built-in bias for 'fact' and 'truth' within post-Renaissance, positivistic notions of history.[161] Indeed, the blurring of lines that we see between history and literature in India is evident in the fact that both the Ramayana and the Mahabharata are commonly described as itihās, the contemporary Hindi and Punjabi word for history.[162]

That the charitr format was employed with this same emphasis on biography and history is clear in texts such as the *Bachitar Nātak*. In this wonderful drama (which despite the title is not presented as a nātak or drama in the traditional sense but rather in a more charitr-like style), we hear the history of Guru Gobind Singh set within the much more cosmological scale of the battle between dharma and tyranny, a narrative which is symmetrical to those of Chandi, Ram, and Krishan as found in the Dasam Granth.[163] These similarities also extend to various tropes, styles, poetics, descriptions, etc. in other Dasam Granth charitrs. In the *Krishan Charit* (or *Krishanavtār*) for example we discover the standard *phalashruti* passage narrating the benefits one accrues from hearing or reading the preceding narrative (a trend which Sikh literature continues well into the late nineteenth century).[164] We also find conventional descriptions of the seasons (*shadrituvarnanam*);[165] time-honoured taxonomies of heroes and heroines (*nāyak-nāyikā bhed*); of the love between Radha and Krishna reminiscent of Jayadeva's *Gītgovind* (12th century);[166] the standard 'head to toe' descriptions of heroines (*shikha-nakha*);[167] and the reiteration of such time-honoured motifs such as the 'waterplay' of lovers (*jala krida*)[168] and their flower-strewn bed (*pushpasayya*), to name but a few.[169] These conventional motifs abound in Brajbhasha courtly literature as too do the traditional classifications of certain female characters found in certain charitrs of the *Pakhyān Charit*, demonstrating a keen familiarity with the standard rītigranths (systems book) of the period.[170]

The Dasam Granth also follows its courtly Brajbhasha predecessors in that it too possesses an intertextual resonance with the greater corpus of classical Sanskrit literature. The tapping into Sanskrit textual authority for example appears throughout the three compositions in honour of the goddess Chandi, especially the references to the Markandeya Purana in which we discover the *Devī-mahātmya* as the source for many of these Dasam Granth goddess narratives.[171] The style of the *Pakhyān Charitr*, furthermore, of which we are reminded at the end of every one of the 404 narratives and, also certain passages within both the *Rāmavtār* and the *Krishanavtār*, as well as the *Giān Prabodh* adopt a *samvād* or 'dialogue' format which connects these compositions intertextually to the Bhagavad-Gita, the famous Indic-period Hindu text in which the minister of King Dhritarashtra, Sanjaya, narrates to his Lord the events which took place on the battlefield of Kurukshetra between the Pandava and Kaurava armies.[172] The point to be made by such references, I believe, is not the author's indirect glorification of the Sanskrit 'original' used to buttress the existence of what the author(s) of the *Krishan Charitr* refer(s) to as this new vernacular 'improvement' (*sudhār*) [upon the Bhagavata Purana] but rather, in much the same way we note in earlier Brajbhasha literature, the displacement of Sanskrit's status (and perhaps by implication the status of the Hindu tradition) with this new Brajbhasha, indeed Sikh, work. It is in the end an improvement, a reformulation (sudhār).[173] This is perhaps why there is a very noticeable difference between the Brajbhasha compositions of the Guru's court and works of other Brajbhasha courts, their correspondence in other matters and styles notwithstanding.

It is very likely, based on the earliest extant manuscripts of the Dasam Granth and those of the tenth Guru's poets, that the vast majority of these Sikh courtly compositions were written not in the script fashioned 'in the city of the gods', Devanagari (though some were), but rather in the same script in which the Adi Granth was written, Gurmukhi, the script which came from the Guru himself as the name implies.[174] Although both scripts have names which suggest a divine origin, the Gurmukhi script was it seems uniquely associated with the Sikh Gurus since at least the completion of the Goindwal Pothis in the late sixteenth century. It may well be true therefore that its use thus verified 'an emphatic rejection of the superiority of Devnagari [sic] and Persian scripts...and the hegemonic authority they represented in the scholarly and religious circles of that time', a point which may also reinforce its appearance in the Dasam Granth compositions.[175] With this in mind therefore, portions of the Dasam Granth also draw upon the authority of bani as found in the Adi Granth. This strikes me as only logical since the court of Guru Gobind Singh was the inheritor of this bani and that there was perhaps no person alive in the late seventeenth century as conversant with such bani as Guru Gobind Singh, a point which Sikh tradition affirms in earnest. Although there are direct allusions to the Sikh Gurus, the most popular of which is *Bachitar Nātak* 5:4–16, the majority of these references are mainly oblique.[176] In one instance, we find allusions to the works of Guru Nanak: the *Jāp* of Guru Gobind Singh, for example, most likely provides a link to Guru Nanak's *Japu*. Such intertextual associations also appear in more subtle ways. Compare for example a passage from one of the lengthier narratives in the *Pakhyān Charitr* to Kabir's eighty-first shlok as found in the Bhagat Bani. In this the heroine of Charitr 266, Sri Rann Khambkala, confronts her brahman teacher with the following words after she observes him venerating the *shālgrām* or stone form of Lord Vishnu:

If all the continents (*dīp*) are transformed into paper and all the seven seas changed into ink; if all the world's vegetation is cut down to make writing instruments; if Saraswati, the goddess of speech herself was to speak (*baktā kari kai*); and if all beings wrote throughout all the various ages together (*sāmthi*) [still the Lord could not be obtained]. How therefore can the Lord who is not obtained be set in stones?[177]

Kabir's shlok follows:

O Kabir, if I could change the seven seas into ink, transform all the world's vegetation into pens and the very earth itself into paper even then I would be unable to write [enough] in praise of the Lord.[178]

Interestingly the disparate compositions of the Dasam Granth also refer to one another, in one instance clearly stating that the full story [of Dasaratha and Kaikeyi] may be read within another of the Dasam Granth's works.[179] Such intercompositional, intra-textual echoes may be modelled on the compositions of the Adi Granth which reference some of the shabads of Guru Nanak within that same text, a very significant point of which we shall make full use shortly.[180] Indeed, such echoes would most likely have been familiar to all those Sikhs engaging with this material, a fact which bring up another feature of this text that also accords with courtly Brajbhasha poetry.

It is worth noting that as courtly poetry one of the fundamental dimensions of both the compositions of the Dasam Granth and the works of the Guru's poets was their performative nature. Most of these works were prepared in order to fulfil the needs of seventeenth- and eighteenth-century Sikhs, authors, patrons, and listeners alike. As this was principally a non-literate society it is instructive to remember that these compositions were not merely composed to be read but were meant to be recited, sometimes sung, acted out, and in some cases danced.[181] These courtly productions were thus very much like earlier Arabic and Persian court poetry as these were of an essentially public nature.[182] It is indeed difficult for contemporary readers to recall this fact particularly because the author(s) of the Dasam Granth text regularly vocalize their fears of making the granth too bulky. Although this anxiety may have everything to do with simple locomotion it nevertheless implies a partiality towards reading.[183]

This is a bias we also find in the existence of manuscripts such as the diminutive *tarkash kī pothī* copy of the *Pakhyān Charitr* at Panjab University, Chandigarh.[184] While eighteenth- and nineteenth-century Sikh traditions imply the performative nature of these compositions (although they do not exclude the fact that these were also read), one still sees today a dramatic character in such Sikh activities as *kīrtan* (collective devotional singing), *kathā* (homily recitation), and the musical recitals by dhadhi jathas (which are in many ways like the charitrs of the Dasam Granth as these fit the characters of their repertoire into time-honoured literary and musical conventions). The very structure of these compositions, that is their metrical devices, phono-aesthetic indicators, changing tenses of verbs, and structured gaps and silences, among other features likewise implies the same. All these provided contemporary Sikhs with recognizable registers through which they would filter all the information received, allowing them to effortlessly navigate its many textures to process what was fact and what was fancy.[185]

In his celebrated analysis of the Dasam Granth, Dharmpal Ashta very much implies the performative character of certain components of the Dasam Granth. Although he reflects solely upon the verses and measures within the *Chandī Charitr* the following statements may be expanded to include the more narrative, lengthier portions of the Dasam Granth:

The rhythm of the verse, the use of alliteration and the diction, all combined together produce a music, which is played in accompaniment with the twanging of arrows, the clashing of swords, the beating of drums, the blowing of conches and the shouts of war cries. The verbal music chiefly employed the devices of alliteration and onomatopoeia seems to reproduce the actual action which this verse sets out to echo. The galloping verse, the best of accented sounds and the varying pause reproduce the speed of action and the hurry of movement in actual fighting.[186]

As the vast majority of the charitr compositions within the Dasam Granth thus appear to be literary/performative texts, it is very likely that these were not meant to be understood in the same way as the Adi Granth (which as any of us who have sat in on a kīrtan performance can verify also occupies a performative dimension), nor were these charitrs meant to be historical in the modern sense. As with most pre-modern Brajbhasha charitrs, these texts occupy a realm in which multiple truths can exist eschewing clear-cut interpretations as well as the outstanding realities of contemporary histories. Within the *Pakhyān Charitr* for example, we hear glowing praises of the Mughal emperors. Certainly one can understand such testaments regarding Akbar who graciously met with Guru Arjan in 1598, but few words can convey our surprise at the praise we also hear of Jahangir,[187] Shah Jahan, and even Aurangzeb, the man responsible for the execution of the tenth Guru's father, Guru Tegh Bahadar: Charitr 195 for example states in no unequivocal terms *dhani dhani Aurang shāh*, 'great is the glory of the emperor Aurangzeb!'[188]

Such a fanciful charitr may suggest the fact that by the seventeenth century Mughal rule had become customary to the point that it was comprehensible within Sikh notions of dharma. Although it may also point to the Mughalization of the Sikh court in the same way as the painting of Guru Gobind Singh we discussed in Chapter 1,[189] it may just be that the many charitrs in this portion of the Dasam Granth critique those aspects of courtly life outside of the Sikh court. Indeed, the setting of these charitrs is often courtly and the environment in which these were recited was most certainly so. The contrast between the court of the Guru and that of the Mughal emperors therefore would have been most likely recognized. And so although there is the rare charitr which takes on a theological urgency (Charitrs 262, 373, and 404: 376–401 for example)[190] for the most part these compositions generally seem to be entertaining and moralistic narratives aimed at satirizing many of the men and women who occupied lofty positions of political power while simultaneously providing valuable lessons about the cultivation of immoral and in some cases moral behaviour. There is therefore a clearly ethical dimension to these tales. These narratives, including the many charitrs of a more lascivious and scatological character, moreover, follow styles, forms, and tropes which too date back to the very courts of classical India and smack of the advice and indeed the humour we discover in texts such as the *Hitopadesha*, the *Kāmasūtra*, and the *Panchatantra*.[191] As such there is no need for certain compositions within the Dasam Granth to conform to the truth of the Adi Granth, as these are charitrs. Charitrs, in particular these, are of a different nature altogether, a fact with which contemporary readers and listeners were readily familiar. This is perhaps why the author of the *Rāmavtār* can on the one hand speak of Lord Rama in terms which evoke descriptions of the True Guru in the Adi Granth (verses 706–7), and yet a number of lines afterwards remind us that Rama himself was mortal and thus subject to the 'drum of death'.[192]

It seems in this light therefore that the oft-repeated dialogue which is found in Kesar Singh Chhibbar's mid to late eighteenth-century *Bansāvalī-nāmā* between the Guru and his disciples regarding the nature of the Dasam Granth far better reflects the spirit in which seventeenth and eighteenth-century Sikhs understood these works than recent interpretations on the nature of the text:

In the year sammat 1755 [1698 CE] a number of Sikhs came forward and requested [the following]: 'O Nourisher of the Poor! We ask that you ought to bring together as one both [the Adi Granth] and [your own] granth into a single volume.'

The Guru replied, 'The Adi Granth alone is the Guru. This [granth] of ours is just play (*khed*) and [although] it stirs us [at the very core of our] beings it [must nevertheless] remain separate.'[193]

This dimension of playfulness is quite common in Sikh understandings of the divine, a similarity to the Krishanite theology of *līla* or the divine sport or play which on the one hand suggests Krishna's love-playing with the Gopis in Vrndavana and on the other alludes to the sport through which the universe was brought into being and which will ultimately bring it to its end.[194] As such this ambiguous idea of play is found reiterated within the *Krishanavtār* (where it rightfully belongs) and within other Dasam Granth works.[195] The manuscript evidence likewise supports this idea. The eighteenth-century *Sākhī Bhāī Nand Lāl jī kī* for example claims:

The True Guru is both constant and endless who sports for the sake of the world.[196]

Chhibbar's idea of play here is no doubt a two-way experience which involves both the speaker/performer/narrator and the audience, the latter as it were becoming a part of the play. Such understandings may well have been taken for granted by earlier Sikhs who would have confronted and very likely engaged with many of the Dasam Granth compositions as an audience in an open setting. A public reading, narration, or performance of such compositions would have rendered seventeenth- and eighteenth-century Sikhs a far richer, multi-textured sensory experience, allowing them to participate in the glory of the tenth Guru and indeed in the glory of the divine especially when we heed the organic unity of the *Bachitar Nātak*, a cosmic drama meant to be holistic, wonderous, edifying, and inspiring; a fundamental portion of which played itself out within the lifetimes of many of those present.

Here it is instructive to remember that for Sikh listeners/participants of this period there was no question as to the identity of the author of these compositions. Such performances thus allowed Sikhs to play out, or to become a part of the play of the Guru's grandeur. Kesar Singh Chhibbar's passing metaphor of churning and transformation (*man manth*, also suggestive of the Krishnaite experience in the young Krishna's playful capacity as the *makhan chor*, the butter thief), perhaps refers to the oft-repeated Hindu story of the churning of the ocean out of which the universe sprang forth. It is thus an apt reference in this context of the poetic transformation (leading it seems to a mystical change) believed to be inherent in the rasas, especially the heroic rasa regularly employed in the Dasam Granth compositions, a point we often hear when it concerns the ability of gur-bānī as found in the Adi Granth to transform people's hearts and lives.[197] Although the written word is privileged by Sikhs all over the world, particularly by those living in the diaspora who have been detached from what they perceive as their homeland, there are still vast communities of Sikhs within the Punjab for whom the spoken word is still predominant. For both, these and other Sikhs such experiences persist in contemporary versions of performance poetry such as dhādhī saṅgīt and kīrtan.[198]

COURTLY REFERENCES WITHIN THE DASAM GRANTH

Now that we have set the Dasam Granth within the courtly culture of performed poetry let us briefly turn to its allusions to the court and courtly items. In the three compositions dedicated to the heroic deeds of the goddess Chandi and certain anecdotes related in the *Pakhyān Charitr*, as well as in the two lengthiest narratives of the *Chaubīs Avatār*, the first detailing the life of Rama, the second that of Krishna, we see the court generally as well as the courts of King Dasaratha, Bharata, and of Rama himself with all of their associated finery.[199] To these we add descriptions of Raja Kans' court in the *Krishanavtār* in which we find numerous courtiers and imperial symbols as well as bards and poets receiving gifts and rewards for their compositions,[200] and also the delightful (if not conventional) description of the darbar of Raja Aj whose story is told by the Vyasa incarnation of the god Brahma (Vyasa is Brahma's fifth avatar) in the *Brahmā Avtār*.[201] For the poetic author(s) of these narratives and others attributed to the tenth Master, the sovereignty of these kings and others is often reduced to the courtly items in their possession through synecdoche. The authors' constant use of the term chhatr 'canopy' or in some cases derivatives such as chhatrdhārik and chhatrdhārī, both of which mean 'the one over whom the canopy has been spread' indicate this.[202] Perhaps one of the most important courtly descriptions for our purposes here occurs not in the *Chaubīs Avatār* but rather in a far shorter text, the two-part *Giān Prabodh* (Guide to the Knowledge of Liberation), which supplies in its first segment grand exaltations of the divine and in its second, dialogues about the nature of the world illustrated with legends from the Mahabharata, in which there is an extended and anachronistic description of the court of Ajai Singh, a successor to Yudhishthira the eldest of the Pandavas, which seems more like the contemporary courts, both imperial and sub-imperial, with which the tenth Master was most likely familiar. In this darbar we find brahmans discoursing about the Vedas, the Puranas, the six systems of classical Hindu philosophy, and the various styles or ritis of performance poetry, and alongside them we have scholars studying Greek, Arabic, and Persian; scrutinizing both the Puranas, the Qu'ran, and other Semitic scriptures (*kateb*). This is not just a literary darbar however, for we also discover the study of the martial arts, of weaponmaking, and of dance and music as well. It ends with the following verse in the well-worn *Bhujang Prayāt* poetic measure:

[Here in this court] there is the study of all scripts (*achhr*) and of the languages (bānī) of all countries. [Here in this court] every region's way of worshipping the divine, all of these, are understood as equally excellent (*pradhānī*).[203]

This final description may indeed have been what the Guru himself intended as the foundation of his own court, a theme of inclusion and universality we discover reiterated often enough within the noncharitr, 'theological' texts of the Dasam Granth such as for example the *Akāl Ustati* and *Shabad Hazare*. It is this, I would like to conjecture, that is the underlying rationality of the Guru's court, a courtly ethos which was both encouraged and spread through the performance of such poetry perhaps forming but most certainly sustaining what Daud Ali in a different courtly context refers to as the 'interpretive community.'[204]

There is little doubt, given the amount of evidence we have mustered at this point, that in many ways the court of Guru Gobind Singh was based in part upon the same mechanically functional foundations as both the imperial and sub-imperial courts of the late seventeenth- and early eighteenth-century Mughal empire namely power, legitimacy, authority, and (perhaps) competitiveness.[205] Not only do we infer so from the accounts of Persian chroniclers and newsreporters but it seems that the very compositions of the Dasam Granth may well hint at such mechanist functions as there are many charitrs included whose basis were the many folk tales known and recited around both Anandpur and within the regions served by the courts of the Pahari Rajas.[206] I would be inclined to think moreover that the selection of certain metres, and resonances to more classical literature, also reflected attempts to garner some type of legitimacy through familiarity from the peoples of the surrounding areas.

Although the tenth Guru did not confront the same type of detraction from relatives as did the previous Sikh Gurus,[207] he nevertheless had to contend with the pretensions and ambitions of powerful and independent Pahari Rajas such as Medina Prakash of Sirmur and Fateh Shah of Garhwal, and the preeminent Bhim Chand of Kahlur-Bilaspur who at one point so preoccupied the Sikh master of Anandpur that the ninth and tenth chapters of the *Bachitar Nātak* mention him specifically.[208] There was also the constant threat of Mughal incursion especially since the emperor's relations with the adjoining hills was a tempestuous one. This threat for example, is almost palpable in the exhortation and the clear sense of urgency that we find in the tenth Guru's hukam-nama dated 2 August 1696 just a few months before Prince Mu'azzam arrived within his territory in order to censure the rajas of the hills.[209]

A fine literary court most certainly presented an image of the Guru and his Sikhs as refined, cultured, and knowledgeable in the functions and etiquettes of the state: a cognisance of Mughal courtly etiquette which allowed the Guru and his closest Sikhs to deal with various provincial administrators and great Mughal generals, as well as with the Pahari Rajas themselves. Its more martial component, especially after 1699 must have further encouraged this perception. It may have been such a coterie which initially prompted Medina Prakash to invite the young Guru and his uncle to set up their darbar within Paunta Sahib. The tenth Guru's diplomacy while residing here shown through his efforts to breach the separation between the rajas of Sirmur and Garhwal demonstrates how intimately embroiled he was with the Pahari kingdoms and that of the Mughals.[210]

As such one may contend that in many ways it was the structures and norms of this state, of which the court was a powerful if not the most powerful component, which he emulated, adopted, and adapted in order to negotiate with it and, at certain points in time, to defy it. Indeed, such a contention adds weight to the belief that the *Zafarnāmah* was actually written by the tenth Guru. This text certainly appropriates the very Persianite norms and standards commonly expected within Indo-Timurid literary culture and criticizes the emperor through Islamicate standards of *izzat*, honour and self-respect, which were very well known to all cultured gentlemen of the Indo-Timurid court.[211] But these were nevertheless cultivated standards which only partially explain the function and the nature of the Guru's court.[212] For its other less mechanist foundations let us once again take a page from the *Bachitar Nātak*.

The passage in question begins the eighth section describing Guru Gobind Singh's journey and residence in Paunta within the territory of Garhwal. It likewise demonstrates the adoption of Islamicate standards:

> When rule became my lot I spread dharma to the best of my ability. I hunted many different types of animals within the forest, killing bears, antelopes, and elks. I left my home territory and made my way to Paunta. Here, on the banks of the Kalindri (Yamuna) River I saw various spectacles (*tamāshā*). There too I hunted and killed lions, antelopes, and bears of many varieties. The king, Fateh Shah, was angered and attacked me without provocation.[213]

The reference to hunting for example once again suggests the courtly atmosphere we witnessed in our discussion regarding the Guru's grandfather, Guru Hargobind. Hunting with all of its implied meanings by no means suggests a carefree life, a fact which both Grewal and Bal mentioned in their seminal text,[214] as it demonstrated the recognition of etiquettes and displays of power which were commonly understood amongst Mughal courtiers.

There is a feature of this passage which is not Islamicate in tenor however, namely the implicit equation between rule and the spread of dharma (though justice which is also included within the semantic range of the Sanskrit term dharma was very much a part of Islamicate rule).[215] Of course ancient Indian discussions of kings make this the king's principal prerogative, underscored by the king's implied divinity, a point to which our *Bachitar Nātak* poet most likely alludes, though with the caveat that the Guru is by no means to be understood as the divine itself.[216] Islamicate texts on rule take a number of approaches in this regard, none of which presents the king as divine in any way as this is tantamount to *shirk*. In one such approach, that which highlights monarchical absolutism, it is royal justice, not the divine, which binds together the moral, political, and economic basis of society.[217]

For Guru Gobind Singh the single source of dharma was the immortal being from whom dharma ultimately emanates, Akal Purakh. As such the Adi Granth, which allows human beings to understand the grandeur of Akal Purakh would have been the best available source for dharma. It seems very likely therefore, as tradition often claims, that the Guru reflected upon this text, its verses and its poetry as he 'established his rule' and his court.

We have already mentioned the tenth Guru's intimate familiarity with the Adi Granth. Concerned as he was with his inheritance, a concern no doubt enhanced by the manner of his father's death and which occurs not only within his poetry but within that of his poets, this should elicit little surprise. That the Guru therefore drew much of his inspiration from this text is something we may take for granted. The numerous references to the divine court, especially within the bani of Guru Arjan may be instructive in this regard. We began this long chapter with a shabad from the fifth Master's bani. Let us for the sake of convenience, reproduce it below:

The True Guru has divulged [these] teachings to me. My soul, body, and everything else belong to the Lord. Whatever I do is [a result of] your power. You are my refuge, you [alone] are my court (dibanu).[218]

The Lord alone is the court according to Guru Arjan, something with which Guru Gobind Singh doubtlessly agreed. In the light of the Guru's familiarity with the standards and etiquettes of the Islamicate court and his intimacy with the content of the Adi Granth (and his legacy as the inheritor of the renown of the Sikh Gurus) it seems very likely to me that such a shabad and the many others which refer to the divine court would have provided a powerful source of deliberation. Guru Gobind Singh's court had a purpose, a point which Sikh tradition rarely acknowledges, outside of falling upon the mechanist functions to which we have regularly alluded. With these shabads in mind it is valid to conjecture that the Guru's intentions in the formation of his literary darbar was to translate into flesh, blood, and indeed sound the divine court of which we regularly hear in the primary Sikh sacred text, an attempt to emulate on earth the divine court which radiating outwards through its performances or kirtan allowed all those present to participate in the play of the divine.[219]

This provided Guru Gobind Singh a powerful incentive to surround himself with devotees, poets, and bards.

This was not an attempt to deify the court of the tenth Guru but rather to adapt the divine court to worldly conditions as a way of further communicating the message of liberation conveyed within the Adi Granth. In other words, the tenth Guru's court was on the one hand Guru Gobind Singh's attempt to manifest the idea of the Adi Granth as an aid to secure liberation, while on the other the inclusion of poets whose expertise was not devotional poetry demonstrates his cognisance of those mechanist functions to which we have often made reference. And this may also help explain why an author as prolific as Guru Gobind Singh would have stopped short of adding his compositions to this text although it seems likely that he chose not to include his own work out of humility, a point which Kesar Singh Chhibbar implies as we noted above. Whatever the explanation it seems that by this time the Adi Granth was considered a 'closed canon.'

It seems to me that it was not only the structure of the Adi Granth's poetry which inspired the Guru but also the poetry of its structure. Surely Guru Gobind Singh was quite familiar with the text's arrangement. Tradition certainly underlines this point although it is incorrect in its claim that he was also responsible for modifying its structure with the inclusion of his father's bani since there do exist manuscript copies of the scripture which appear just after the ninth Guru's execution with his hymns included.[220] It seems likely that the tenth Guru may have recognized, upon close examination of the Adi Granth, an inherent structure which went beyond the powerful rag structure which was so obvious after the 1680s.[221] This secondary structure is one which corresponds in many ways to the structure of royal poetic courts and precedents. That this was purposefully put into place by Guru Arjan is beyond the scope of this discussion though the fifth Master who often refers to the divine court in his hymns may well have had this partially in mind as he enhanced the structure of the text and chose the hymns to be included. His awareness of courtly precedent has already been noted in both his inclusion of the *Bhattān de savaīe* and the strongly Brajbhasha character of his poetry, notwithstanding his strong critique of the outward displays of such courts.[222]

At a basic level, the structure of the Adi Granth revolves around the authority and hymns of Guru Nanak, whom the earliest Sikhs considered the supreme spiritual padishah. This is seen particularly in the appropriation of the sobriquet Nanak by all of the Gurus whose hymns are included within the text. Later scribes and copyists would further underscore this authority in their adoption of the designation *mahala* to indicate the successors of Guru Nanak (the earliest manuscripts do not regularly employ the mahala indicator).[223] The Adi Granth's structure may thus be likened to a society of poets surrounding Guru Nanak, the first Guru and founder of the Sikh tradition, regularly discoursing upon a lone subject, a solitary poetic utterance.

This point is made particularly clear in the hymns of Guru Amar Das which regularly echo or 'respond to' those of Guru Nanak in a style that is reminiscent of the Islamicate majalis, drawing authority from the first Guru in ways similar to those of Persian poets who draw upon the authority of such figures as Rudaki, Rumi, Hafez, Sa'di, and Baba Fighani in their compositions forming in many instances 'poetic conversations' and fashioning a virtual literary culture.[224] As the Adi Granth includes, alongside the hymns of the aforementioned bhatts the more significant works attributed to the bhagats, often poets who were not Sikh but rather Hindu or Muslim, this may have provided the tenth Guru with a blueprint for his own court which, as we noted, earlier tradition claims was home to many ex-imperial Hindu poets who made their way to Anandpur.

The idea of the Adi Granth providing a structural blueprint for the Sikh darbar is a point which may account for the relative popularity of the *Prem Abodh* (Love Indiscriminate), a performative hagiography which contains the stories of sixteen bhagats, many of whose hymns find a home in the Adi Granth, associated with the court of the tenth Master.[225] Although the work is generally attributed to the tenth Master, there are scholars who posit as its author one Keval Das while others claim one Hari Das as its author (not to be confused with the founder of the Niranjani sect).[226] Although Keval Das is noted in neither Piara Singh Padam's nor in Harmahendra Sinha Bedi's compendiums of court poets, Hari Das most certainly is and may have been one of the ex-imperial poets earlier mentioned.[227] It is now to one of Hari Das's fellow ex-imperial poet to whom we shall turn in the attempt to supplement and end our discussion.

Notes

1. Guru Arjan, *Rāg āsā* (2)5, Adi Granth, p. 371.
2. Online edition of *Sūraj Prakāsh* 5:51:3, p. 482.
3. Bhasha Vibhag Library, Devanagari ms. 404, line 1 as noted in Padam, *Darbārī Ratan*, p. 93. Gurmukhi manuscripts of the *Hitopadesha* attributed to another of the tenth Guru's poets, Tansukh Lahauri are found in the Sikh Research Library of Khalsa College: mss. SHR 1583, 2209.
4. Ms. 404, line 2, Padam, *Darbārī Ratan*, p. 93.
5. Ms. 404, lines 3 and 12 respectively, Padam, *Darbārī Ratan*, p. 93. Also see p. 92.
6. Padam notes (pp. 92–3) that both Lakkhan Rai and his brother Bhojraj became Sikhs during the ninth Master's time but that they regularly performed *kalamī sevā*, 'pen service' within the darbar of the tenth Guru. The tenth Guru's poet, Kunvaresh also draws out Guru Gobind Singh's lineage in a *Bachitar Nātak*-like passage in the poet's *Dronā Parab* as too does the poet Chand the Goldsmith in his shabads and shaloks. Padam, *Darbārī Ratan*, pp. 139–40; 148–9.
7. Niccolao Manucci, *Storia da Mogor; or Mughal India, 1653–1708* 4 volumes [William J. Irvine (trans.)] (London: J. Murray, 1907–9).
8. See Elliot and Dowson (eds), *The History of India as Told by its Own Historians* VII (Delhi: Low Price Publications, 2001), p. 158. Simply put, if Aurangzeb was as iconoclastic as his later image in Indian historiography warrants it is almost certain that he would have had destroyed the vast collection of painted albums in his care, many of which are today scattered throughout the world's museums and amongst private owners.
9. Milo C. Beach, *Mughal and Rajput Painting*, p. 173.
10. Beach, *Mughal and Rajput Painting* among many others.
11. Beach, *Mughal and Rajput Painting*, figure 117, p. 155. A stunning colour reproduction of this painting appears in Stuart Cary Welch, *Imperial Mughal Painting*, plate 37, p. 113. One should discount Welch's commentary on page 114 as this manifests the same old tired interpretation of the emperor's reign.
12. Beach, *Mughal and Rajput Painting*, p. 173. The same seems to have happened to Mughal court musicians. Katherine Butler Brown, 'The Social Liminality of Musicians: Case Studies from Mughal India and Beyond', in *Twentieth-century Music* 3:1 (2007), pp. 13–49, esp. pp. 26 ff.
13. Pietro della Valle, *The Pilgrim: The Travels of Pietro della Valle* [George Bull (trans.)] (London: Hutchinson, 1989) as noted in Katherine Brown, 'Did Aurangzeb Ban Music? Questions for the Historiography of His Reign', *Modern Asian Studies* 41:1 (2007), pp. 77–121, esp. p. 93.
14. It should be noted as well that it was not only during the period of Aurangzeb that court painters probably left the Mughal atelier. Apart from the fact that poetic and artistic movement from court ot court was not uncommon we also

have evidence from the reign of Jahangir. Bonnie Wade notes for example that Jahangir himself restricted the number of painters in his court even before the death of his father in 1604 to only those poets whom he considered to be masters, an act which led to an artistic exodus to sub-imperial courts which in turn saw the rise of the Mughalized style for which some eighteenth-century Pahari art is known. Bonnie Wade, *Imaging Sound*, pp. 162–3.

15. I was alerted to this quotation by Milo C. Beech, *Mughal and Rajput Painting*, p. 172. Beech, however, omits the final statement regarding mansabs. See Elliot and Dowson (eds), *The History of India as Told by its Own Historians* VII, p. 283 and Anees Jahan Syed (trans.), *Aurangzeb in Muntakhab-al Lubab* (Bombay: Somaiya Publications Pvt. Ltd., 1977), p. 245. This seems to me an important omission as its absence casts a much darker intent on the person of the emperor, implying that these artists and musicians were forced to leave the court under duress and perhaps face sheer impoverishment. Recent research has shown in effect how exaggerated such implications and indeed claims are. François Delvoye for example has questioned Khafi Khan's purpose in penning this specific date as the good Khan was antagonistic towards the emperor. He believes that it occurred far later. François Nalini Delvoye, 'Indo-Persian Literature on Art-Music: Some Historical and Technical Aspects,' in Delvoye (ed.), *Confluence of Cultures* (New Delhi: Manohar, 1994). Delvoye's conclusions and so too Beech's in this regard are somewhat tempered in Katherine Brown's works on music in later Indo-Timurid Mughal India. See her insightful article, 'Did Aurangzeb Ban Music?', pp. 77–121 which likewise questions the misuse of Khafi Khan (p. 88 of her article in particular) and her 'Reading Indian Music: the Interpretation of Seventeenth-century European Travel Writing in the (Re)Construction of Indian Music History', in the *British Journal of Ethnomusicology* 9:2 (2000), p. 19. See also Bonnie Wade's *Imaging Sound*, pp. 185–7 which reproduces the more standard interpretation of music during Aurangzeb's reign. It seems clear that in all three areas (music, art, and poetry/literature) Aurangzeb's reputation for iconoclasm is far worse than contemporary sources warrant. Unfortunately neither the poetry nor the painting of Aurangzeb's reign nor his actual attitudes (both private and public) towards these have been thoroughly examined.

16. For the *Mir'at-i 'Ālam* see Elliot and Dowson, *The History of India as Told by its Own Historians* VII, pp. 145–65. For a brief history of Ni'amat Khan who because of his satires fell out of the emperor's favour see the same volume of Elliot and Dowson, pp. 200–1. Also Anees Jahan Syed (trans.), *Aurangzeb in Muntakhab-al Lubab*, pp. 348–9 including note 19.

17. See Elliot and Dowson (eds), *The History of India as Told by its Own Historians* VII, p. 158.

18. During Aurangzeb's first and only visit to Kashmir in 1662, for example, the emperor did not receive nor reward any of the area's court poets choosing

Spirit and Structure 167

to honour in their place 'scholars, shaikhs, and theologians.' G.L. Tikku, *Persian Poetry in Kashmir 1339–1846* (Berkeley: University of California Press, 1971), p. 85. As we Earlier noted Aurangzeb's dislike of music became legendary already by the mid-eighteenth century thanks in large part to Khafi Khan. The famous story which first appears in the *Miratulkhiyāl* and is retold in the *Muntakhab-al Lubab* tells of a mock funeral held by the musicians of the city for their instruments. No doubt this story is apocryphal as Katherine Brown makes clear in her 'Did Aurangzeb Ban Music?'

19. Katherine Brown, 'If Music be the Food of Love: Masculinity and Eroticism in the Mughal *mefil*', in Francesca Orsini (ed.), *Love in South Asia: A Cultural History* (Cambridge: Cambridge University Press, 2006), pp. 66–8 and her 'Did Aurangzeb Ban Music?'

20. Brown's 'Did Aurangzeb Ban Music?' p. 100 discusses just such a jagir granted 'of ten *bighas* of fallow but cultivateble land' in Batala, Punjab was assigned to one Ilah-Dad 'on account of his giving up music as a means of earning...'

21. It is certainly possible that Aurangzeb would have been aware of his daughter Zebunnisa's poetry. Magan Lal and Jessie Duncan Westbrook (trans.), *The Diwan of Zeb-un-Nissa: the First Fifty Ghazals* (New York: Dutton, 1913).

22. Jamshid H. Bilimoria (trans.), *Ruka'at-i-Alamgiri or Letters of Aurangzebe [with Historical and Explanatory Notes]* (London: Luzac & Co., 1908), letters 149 and 156, pp. 142, 149 (n. 1). Aurangzeb appointed Abdur Rahim Khan governor of Bijapur and Malwa. For the Mukhlis Khan here noted, son of Saf Shikan Khan see Jadunath Sarkar (trans.), *Maāsir-i-'Ālamgiri*, p. 261.

23. Indeed, Aurangzeb's seal may be seen on a number of imperial manuscripts. Michael Brand and Glenn Lowry, *Akbar's India: Art from the Mughal City of Victory*, p. 90. As a prince the young Aurangzeb most likely read and was read a number of such famous works. Note for example Shah Jahan's words as he penned them on the flyleaf of the circa 1440 manuscript of Sharafuddin Yazdi's *Zafar-nāmah* (not to be confused with the work of the same title attributed to Guru Gobind Singh) detailing the exploits of Amir Timur:

> This noble *Zafarnama*, which is one of the marvels of the age, has been deposited in the private library of this suppliant at the court of God, on the 25th day of the month of Bahman, corresponding to the 6th day of the month Jumada II, in the year 1037 of the Hijra (12 February 1628), which is the date of my blessed accession; and because of its exceedingly fine character it shall always remain in my presence and shall frequently be read.

The English translation of this quote appears in Brand and Lowry, *Akbar's India*, pp. 150–1. Aurangzeb's early interest in Muslim literature is noted in Jadunath Sarkar, *History of Aurangzeb Based on Original Sources* vols. I and II (second edition, Calcutta: M.C. Sarkar & Sons, 1925), p. 4. It is

168 The Darbar of the Sikh Gurus

thus likely that the young prince would have often heard passages from this history of Timur. In fact Khafi Khan likens a wound which Aurangzeb had received while leaving toilet to the wound which ultimately made Timur lame. Khafi Khan notes,

> The emperor who was in the latrine, thought that the enemy had made a surprise attack on the army. As he suddenly rose in perplexity, his foot slipped and he received an injury which could not be cured for the rest of his life, causing lameness; thus the defect of the Sahib Qiran reappeared.

S. Moinul Haq (ed.), *Khafi Khan's History of Alamgir* (Karachi: Pakistan Historical Society, 1975), p. 469.

24. There is also evidence to suggest that Aurangzeb knew Sanskrit. Jamshid H. Bilimoria (trans.), *Ruka'at-i-Alamgiri*, letter 9, p. 12.
25. Elliot and Dowson (eds), *The History of India as Told by its Own Historians* VII, p. 162 and Jadunath Sarkar (trans.), *Maāsir-i 'Alamgiri: A History of the Emperor Aurangzib-'Alamgir (reign 1658–1707 AD) of Sāqi Must'ad Khan* (Calcutta: Royal Asiatic Society of Bengal, 1947), p. 318. For sixteenth-century Timurid concerns about the Qur'an's and the sunna's negative attitude towards poetry see the interesting discussion in Maria Eva Subtelny, 'The Poetic Circle at the Court of the Timurid, Sultan Husain Baiqara, and its Political Significance.' (Unpublished PhD thesis, Department of Near Eastern Languages and Civilizations, Harvard University, 1978), pp. 63–5.
26. Anees Jahan Syed (trans.), *Aurangzeb in Muntakhab-al Lubab*, p. 247.
27. Elliot and Dowson (eds), *The History of India as Told by its Own Historians* VII, p. 162 also Sarkar (trans.), *Maāsir*, p. 318:

> [Aurangzeb] did not incline to the hearing of useless poetry. How then could he be expected to listen to adulatory verses? But poems breathing moral advice (he liked).

28. A petition sent by Aurangzeb's *khān-i sāmān* Kamgar Khan asks the emperor to punish Ni'amat Khan for a satire he wrote against the khan's marriage. See Jadunath Sarkar (trans.), *Anecdotes Of Aurangzib (English Translation of Ahkam-i-Alamgiri ascribed to Hamid-ud-din Khan Bahadur) with A Life of Aurangzib and Historical Notes* (Calcutta: M.C. Sarkar and Sons, 1925), pp. 117–18.
29. Obviously this clearly contests the obstinate claim that Aurangzeb had continued to prohibit the writing of historical chronicles of his rule. I would like to single out Brown's claim that Musta'idd Khan's work, based in part on the work of his master Bakhtawar Khan, 'represent[s] Aurangzeb's official stance on music [and in our case, by extension, poetry and literature].' Brown, 'Did Aurangzeb Ban Music?', p. 101.
30. Syed (trans.), *Aurangzeb in Muntakhab-al Lubab*, pp. 246–7. Such statements as Bakhtawar Khan's do suggest that works with morals such as for example Sa'di's *Bustan,* the *Dīvān-i Hāfez,* the works of Jalaluddin

Rumi, and even those of contemporary poets would have still been widely read. Even in regard to the Quranic ayat we must temper contemporary interpretations. Aurangzeb was not so rigid as to uncritically accept any verse of the Qur'an at face value as the numerous letters between himself and his father while the latter was in captivity make clear. Indeed, Aurangzeb was easily able to supply Shah Jahan with different interpretations to the ayats which the imprisoned emperor had sent his son to critique what Shah Jahan felt was Aurangzeb's treachery. See the third letter in Jonathon Scott's translated collection of 1800 CE. Jonathan Scott (trans.), *Tales, Anecdotes, and Letters. Translated from the Arabic and Persian* (Shrewsbury: J. and W. Eddowes for T. Cadell and W. Davies, London, 1800), pp. 370–3.

31. Across the sheet of a letter sent to Aurangzeb detailing the activities of his grandson Prince Bidar Bakht Aurangzeb wrote a passage from a ghazal of Hafez Shirazi. As well in a letter to his son Aurangzeb includes verses by both Rumi and Sa'di. The first appears in Jadunath Sarkar (trans.), *Anecdotes Of Aurangzib*, p. 75. The second, in which Rumi is referred to as 'the Spritual Leader' (*maulānā*) and Sa'di noted by name is Jamshid H. Bilimoria (trans.), *Ruka'at-i-Alamgiri*, letters no. 45, 54, 176 pp. 47, 55–7, 170. See also letters 112, 154, pp. 111, 147–8.

32. Bilimoria (trans.), *Ruka'at-i-Alamgiri*, letters no. 98, 178, pp. 100, 172. Aurangzeb also writes a bait of the poet 'Nakhashaby' in letter 179, p. 164.

33. Aurangzeb actually calls him Muswi Khan in a letter written to his son in which he expresses satisfaction at having appointed Muswi the chief paymaster on his son's advice. The emperor notes Muswi's physical appearance and then advises his son to judge his character fairly. Bilimoria (trans.), *Ruka'at-i-Alamgiri*, letter 62, pp. 62–3. M. Athar Ali, *The Mughal Nobility Under Aurangzeb*, p. 247 mentions Muswi (noble 317) as an Iranian emigre with a rank of 2000/400.

34. Jadunath Sarkar, *History of Aurangzeb Based on Original Sources* 5 vols (second edition, Calcutta: M.C. Sarkar & Sons, 1928, 1930).

35. One munshi cum poet who did indeed leave the emperor's court for a south Indian one was Jaswant Rai. V. Narayana Rao, David Shulman and Sanjay Subrahmanyam, *Textures of Time: Writing History in South India 1600–1800* (New York: Other Press, 2003), pp. 193–4. Here they also note the number of munshis who left southwards with the great nobles. One such courtier who did remain with the emperor's court, however, was the very famous Hindu Persian scholar and poet, Dara Shikoh's *mīr munshī* Chandar Bhan Brahman. The extent of his expertise may be judged by the fact that Brahman, a Hindu, tutored Muslims in both Arabic and Persian. Brahman's work *Guldastah* (The Bouquet) describes the liveliness and splendour of Shah Jahan's court. Jan Marek, 'Persian Literature in India', in Jan Rypka, *History of Iranian Literature*, pp. 727–8. Aurangzeb's daughter, Zebunnisa, an accomplished poet as well remained and prepared a dīvān under the

170 The Darbar of the Sikh Gurus

penname *Makhfī* or the 'Hidden One'. Also Brown's comments about Muhammad Akram Ghanimat's popular masnavi written in 1685. Brown, 'Did Aurangzeb Ban Music?', p. 103 and too the fact that the poet Ni'amat Khan whose sobriqeut was 'Ali continued to write satirical poetry.

36. Royal highways are noted in Chetan Singh, *Region and Empire: Panjab in the Seventeenth Century* (Delhi: Oxford University Press, 1991), pp. 204–55.

37. Akbar's well-known attitude towards religions and religious plurality contributed famously to his image in both contemporary Jain literature and Hindu Brajbhasha literature. Indeed, in the famous *Chaurāsī Vaishnavan kī Vārtā* (Stories of 84 Vaishnav Saints: circa early 17th century) the author Gokulnath (commentary by Hariray) claims the following of Akbar in the Bhagat Surdas narrative:

> The Emperor Akbar possessed the power of discrimination. How was this possible [in a Muslim]? Through a ritual fault he was born into this community led astray (*malechchha*). In his previous life he had been a celibate Vedic student [devoted to] the young Krishna, Bālamukanda. One day he was drinking milk without having [first] filtered it. In it there was a cow's hair [which] went into his stomach [after it had been drunk]. Through this religious offence he became a Muslim (malechchha) [in this present life].

The Brajbhasha text appears in Dwarakadas Parikh (ed.), *Go. Shrī Hari Rāy jī Pranīt Chaurāsī Vaishnavan kī Vartā [Tīn Janam kī Līlā Bhāvanā Vālī]* (Mathura: Shri Bajrang Pustakalay, 1959–60), p. 394. For similar, Jain appreciations of the emperor see Shirin Mehta, 'Akbar as Reflected in the Contemporary Jain Literature in Gujarat', in Iqtidar Alam Khan (ed.), *Akbar and His Age* (New Delhi: Northern Book Centre, 1999), pp. 223–30.

38. Muzaffar Alam, 'Persian in Precolonial Hindustan', p. 160. The same held true for painters and calligraphists. According to Priscilla Soucek, for example, a few artists

> ...came in response to invitations from the Mughal rulers, but most, including Mir Muhammad Baqir...appear to have come seeking their own fortune.

Priscilla P. Soucek, 'Persian Artists in Mughal India: Influences and Transformations', in *Muqarnas* 4 (1987), pp. 166–81 esp. p. 166.

39. Stephen Dale, 'Steppe Humanism: The Autobiographical Writings of Zahir al-Din Muhammad Babur, 1483–1530', in *International Journal of Middle East Studies* 22 (1990), pp. 37–58; and his 'The Poetry and Autobiography of the *Bābur-nāma*', in *Journal of Asian Studies* 55:3 (1996), pp. 635–64.

40. Iranization was further embraced by the emperor Akbar whose finance minister Todar Mal declared Persian the official language of the Mughal court in 1582. See Muzaffar Alam, 'The Pursuit of Persian: Language in Mughal Politics', in *Modern Asian Studies* 32, 2 (1998), pp. 317–49. The trend continued during the period of Jahangir, especially after his favourite

wife, Nur Jahan, had been informally given the reigns of power in the early 1620s. Thanks to Nur Jahan and her family, her father Ghiyasuddin Itimaduddaula and her brother Asaf Khan a large number of Iranian poets, scribes, and scholars made their way to the Mughal court ensuring that the Turkic languages and cultures which had so influenced both Babur and Humayun were forever marginalized. See Wheeler Thackston, 'The Poetry of Abu-Talib Kalim Persian Poet-Laureate of Shahjahan Mughal Emperor of India (Harvard University, Dept. of Near Eastern Languages and Civilizations, 1974), pp. 9–10.

41. That Shah Tahmasp, a staunch Shi'i Muslim, disregarded poets and poetry is simply incorrect. The presence of a number of court poets— famous panegyrists such as Vahshi and Muhtasham for example—puts such claims to rest. Wheeler M. Thackston, *A Millennium of Classical Persian Poetry* (Bethesda, Maryland: Ibex Publishers, 2000), pp. 78–82. Also Ehsan Yarshater, 'The Indian Style: Progress or Decline?', in E. Yarshater (ed.), *Persian Literature* (New York: Columbia University Press, 1988), pp. 249–88.

42. A list of poets within Humayun's darbar is noted in 'Ali Quli Walih Daghistani's *Riyāzushshu'arā* [Gardens of Poets] as noted in Muhammad Abdul Ghani, *A History of Persian Language and Literature at the Mughal Court: with a brief survey of the growth of Urdu [Babur to Akbar] volume 2, Humayun* (Allahabad: the Indian Press, Ltd., 1930), p. 36, n. 1. The emigration of poets from Iran to India during the Safavid era is documented in Ahmad Gulchin-i Ma'ani, *Kārvān-i Hind: dar ahvāl va āsār-i shā'irān-i 'asr-i Safavī keh beh Hindūstān raftan and* 2 vols. (Mashhad: Astan-i Quds-i Razavi, 1369/1990–1). See also Yar Muhammad Khan, *Iranian Influence in Mughal India* (Lahore, 1978) and P.N. Chopra, *Life and Letters Under the Mughals* (New Delhi: Ashajanak Publications, 1976), pp. 315–80.

43. Ghani, *Persian Language and Literature at the Mughal Court*, p. 64. The encouragement of *ihām* may stem from the belief that this particular stylistic device was developed by the Indo-Persian poet Amir Khusrau... at least according to Khusrau himself.

44. Humayun wrote a Persian rather than a Turki Dīvān under the penname 'Humayun' which comprised 211 highly lyrical verses. Ibid., p. 10. Selections of Humayun's ghazals appears on pages 10–14; rubaiyat on pp. 14–18; and a masnavi on pp. 18-20. For a general history of Humayun consult his sister's memoirs, Annette S. Beveridge (ed. and trans.), *The History of Humāyūn: Humāyūn-Nāmā by Gul Badan Begum* (New Delhi: Low Price Publications, 1994), pp. 83–201. Persian version appears on Persian pagination pp. 2–91.

45. Note for example the words of Annemarie Schimmel: '...in fact, the [Indian] Subcontinent produced more Persian works than Iran proper.' See her *As Through a Veil: Mystical Poetry in Islam* (New York: Columbia University Press, 1982), p. 55. There was a backdrop to this promotion as

172 The Darbar of the Sikh Gurus

Muzaffar Alam points out in which the Mughals felt culturally inferior to the Iranians and as a consequence devoted far more energy to the production of Persian translations of Turkish and Arabic texts as well as (and more importantly) to Persian dictionaries and lexicons which attempted to reinject the Persian of India with elements drawn principally from Iran. Muzaffar Alam, 'The Culture and Politics of Persian in Precolonial Hindustan,' pp. 131–98.

46. This style of poetry is also known as *tāzā-gū*, *tāzā-guftār*, or *tāzah-gū'ī* 'speaking the fresh', 'newspeak', etc. by contemporary Persian writers. However, it has been known as the *sabk-i-hindī* or the *isti'māl-i hind* only since the nineteenth century. Background on sabk-i hindi appears in Shamsur Rahman Faruqi's lengthy article 'A Stranger in the City: The Poetics of *Sabk-e Hindi*', in Naqi Husain Jafri (ed.), *Critical Theory: Perspectives From Asia* (New Delhi: Creative Books, 2004), pp. 180–285. I would like to thank Dr Faruqi for bringing this article to my attention. For the cultural and political ramifications of sabk-i hindi and an origin which well predates the Mughal court see Muzaffar Alam, 'The Culture and Politics of Persian in Precolonial Hindustan.'

47. By the sixteenth century it should be noted other areas outside of Iran such as Ottoman Rum and *Māvarā'annahr* were gradually displacing Persian as the court language par excellence with Turkish. Such a change may have curtailed any possible employment for Iranian poets making India seem even more attractive.

48. The existence of Mughal nobles who were not only themselves poets but also patronized Persian poets in a smaller darbar of their own are very well known. Amongst others we may cite Abu'l-Fayz Fayzi; Bayram Khan-i Khanan; and the latter's son Abdurrahim Khan-i Khanan who alone was responsible for patronizing over 100 poets and thirty one scholars [C.R. Naik, *Abu'r-Rahim Khān-i Khānān and His Literary Circle* (Ahmedabad: Gujarat University Press, 1966)]. (Abdurrahim also possessed his own flourishing atelier (Mahfuzul Haq, 'The Khan Khanan and His Painters, Illuminators, and Calligraphists', in *Islamic Culture* 5 (1931), pp. 627–9.) According to the early twentieth-century Urdu literary critic Shibli Nu'mani, for example,
...a newcomer would first be patronized by a junior officer, who upon discovering his merit would recommend him to a higher official, who in turn would present the find to the emperor.
Shibli Nu'mani, *Shi'rul'ajam* [trans. Fakhr-i Da'i] (2nd edn., Tehran: Ibn Sina, 1956–61), volume III, p. 4 as noted in G.L. Tikku, *Persian Poetry in Kashmir 1339–1846* (Berkeley: University of California Press, 1971), p. 91.

49. These poets are listed by name in Badauni's *Muntakhabuttavārīkh* volume 3 [edited by Ahmad Ali and Nassau Less] (Calcutta: Bibliotheca India, 1869), pp. 171–288. See also Aziz Ahmad, 'Safavid Poets and India', in *Iran* 14 (1976), pp. 17–32.

Spirit and Structure 173

50. *AA* I, pp. 617–80. Persian artists were also invited and were a part of Akbar and Jahangir's *tasvīr-khānah*. See Priscilla Soucek, 'Persian Artists in Mughal India.'
51. Jan Rypka, *History of Iranian Literature* (Dordrecht: D. Reidel Publishing Company, 1968), p. 299.
52. Rypka, *History of Iranian Literature*, p. 299. Also *AA* I, p. 629. A brief biography of 'Urfi with samples of his Persian poetry appears in Ahmad Gulchin Ma'ani, *Kārvān-i Hind* II, pp. 872–90 and in Muhammad Abdul Ghani, *A History of Persian Language and Literature at the Mughal Court: with a brief survey of the growth of Urdu [Babur to Akbar]* volume 3, Akbar (Allahabad: the Indian Press, Ltd., 1930), pp. 103–80.
53. Fayzi was not Akbar's first poet laureate, but his third. The first was Ghazali of Mashhad (Iran) who died in 1572 CE while the second was Khwaja Husain Sina (d. 1581).
54. Ahmad Gulchin Ma'ani, *Kārvān-i Hind* I, pp. 758–83.
55. For background on the Bijapur court of Adil Shah II see Richard Maxwell Eaton, *Sufis of Bijapur 1300–1700* (Princeton: Princeton University Press, 1978), pp. 70–5.
56. This truncated biography of Kalim is extracted from Wheeler M. Thackston, 'The Poetry of Abu-Talib Kalim Persian Poet-Laureate of Shahjahan Mughal Emperor of India' (Harvard University, Dept. of Near Eastern Languages and Civilizations, 1974), pp. 19ff. Also G.L. Tikku, *Persian Poetry in Kashmir 1339–1846* (Berkeley: University of California Press, 1971), pp. 85, 87 and Ma'ani, *Kārvān-i Hind* II, pp. 1175–87. While Kalim stayed in India some of his contemporaries did not. The poet Muhammad Ali Sa'ib (1601–78) for example born and raised in Isfahan travelled twice to Shah Jahan's India before he finally became the poet laureate of Shah Abbas II. Ma'ani, *Kārvān-i Hind* I, pp. 700–12 and W.M. Thackston (ed.), *A Millennium of Classical Persian Poetry*, p. 87.
57. For example:
    Because of the deprivation of artists I am surprised that the bones do not stick in the Huma bird's throat!
    Thackston's translation. See his 'The Poetry of Abu-Talib Kalim', p. 118.
58. Wheeler Thackston, 'Literature', in Zeenut Ziad (ed.), *The Magnificent Mughals* (Karachi: Oxford University Press, 2002), p. 101. Translation is very slightly adapted from Thackston's. For Sa'ib see Edward G. Browne, *A History of Persian Literature in Modern Times (AD 1500–1924)* (Cambridge: Cambridge University Press, 1924), pp. 265–76.
59. Although it was Hazin who was regarded as the most distinguished poet who gathered to honour Mirza Bedil on his *'urs* or day of commemoration. Blake, *Shahjahanabad*, p. 156. Further background appears in Ma'ani, *Kārvān-i Hind* I, pp. 314–21. I base the decreasing number of poets principally upon Ma'ani, *Kārvān-i Hind* I, p. vi which notes the number of poets who had left Iran during the period of the Indian *tīmūriyān*. While Akbar

174 The Darbar of the Sikh Gurus

saw 259 poets in total emigrate (to both his court and those of Ahmadnagar, Golconda, and Bijapur), Jahangir 173, and Shah Jahan 114 Aurangzeb only managed to receive 66. This was a dramatic decrease when we consider that both Jahangir and Shah Jahan's combined rules (1605–57 CE) lasted only three years longer than Aurangzeb's individual reign (1658–1707). Telling too is the fact that Aurangzeb's successors between 1707–48 saw only eight poets move to the subcontinent in total the last of whom did so in 1734. Also see Jan Rypka, *History of Iranian Literature*, pp. 308–9.
60. Jan Marek, 'Persian Literature in India', in Jan Rypka, *History of Iranian Literature*, pp. 729–31. It is likely that Mughal nobles close to the emperor continued to patronize poets and that poets attached to disgraced nobles such as Aurangzeb's son, Prince Akbar who had rebelled against his father and the latter's orthodoxy and had himself crowned emperor in 1681, would have followed their patrons into exile. Khafi Khan's *Muntakhab-al Lubab* tells us in regard to Prince Akbar that 'not more than three or four hundred men remained with him.' Elliot and Dowson (eds), *The History of India as told by Its Own Historians: The Muhammadan Period* (Delhi: Low Price Publications, 2001), p. 308. Tracing the movements of many such poets in either of these scenarios would be difficult. Indeed, the history of Mughal poets during Aurangzeb's period has yet to be written.
61. Padam, *Darbārī Ratan*, p. 34.
62. Padam also mentions the poets Chintamani, Bihari, Matiram, Dev, and Kulpati Mishar. *Darbārī Ratan*, p. 35. Once again these are all Hindu names. Also see Jan Marek, 'Persian Literature in India', in Jan Rypka, *History of Iranian Literature*, pp. 730–1.
63. Of course I am in no way here alluding to the statements we discover in Muhammad Latif's *History of the Panjáb: From the Remotest Antiquity to the Present Time* (New Delhi: Kalyani Publications, 1989), p. 259: 'From a devout *Udási*... in Bengal, the Guru seems to have turned out a regular freebooter on his return to the Panjab', but rather have in mind Grewal's understandings which portray Tegh Bahadar's simple acceptance of the guruship as an act designed to defy the emperor's desire to choose the successor guru. See J.S. Grewal, 'The Prophet of Assurance', in his *From Guru Nanak to Maharaja Ranjit Singh* (Amritsar: Guru Nanak Dev University Press, 1982), pp. 64–70.
64. That the followers of Guru Nanak and the first Guru himself were respected in the late seventeenth and early eighteenth centuries is noted for example in Muhammad Qasim Lahori's *'Ibrat-nāmah* (1722 CE):
> [Guru Nanak's] garment was Truth, the foundation [of which was woven by] his insight into divine matters. He was adorned with all forms of [spiritual] perfections.

S.H. Askari, 'Baba Nanak in Persian Sources,' in the *Journal of Sikh Studies* II:2 (Aug., 1975), pp. 112–16. The Persian text appears on p. 115. See also Gurbux Singh Bhatia, 'Persian Writings on Guru Nanak,' in *Punjab*

Spirit and Structure 175

History Conference Fifth Session (March 8–10, 1970) Proceedings (Patiala: Punjabi University Press, 1971), pp. 52–61.
65. W.G. Archer, *Indian Paintings from the Punjab Hills: A Survey and History of Pahari Miniature Painting* I (Delhi: Oxford University Press, 1973) and Roy C. Craven, Jr., 'The Reign of Raja Dalip Singh (1695–1741) and the Siege of Lanka Series of Guler', in *Mārg: Ramayana: Paintings from the Hills* (September 1990), pp. 4–56. That these subjects were acceptable to earlier emperors is brought out by the many 'Hindu-themed' Indo-Timurid manuscripts still extant. A representative text would be the Persian translation of the Sanskrit Mahabharata known as the *Razm-nāmah* or 'Book of Battles.'
66. Grewal and Bal, *Guru Gobind Singh*, pp. 9 ff.
67. According to Sikh tradition some of these poets included Mangal, Keshav Das, Amrit Rai and Sadama. Grewal and Bal, *Guru Gobind Singh*, pp. 100, 223 (n. 79). References to these poets appear in Padam's *Darbārī Ratan*, pp. 122–9, 129–34, 205.
68. One may assume that although poets were not chased out of the darbar as Sikh tradition often implies, they were urged to follow Islamicate forms well established and discouraged from creating afresh. The situation was probably very much like that we saw for painters and indeed for musicians in which creativity was stifled and tired, old conventions more strictly encouraged. In this atmosphere it may well be that standard poets became more attuned to diverging styles such as the shīvah-'i tāzah. I would however be very hesititant to apply Browne's statements regarding the Persian poetry of the eighteenth century to the general situation in northern India a decade or so after Aurangzeb's ascension to the throne despite the emperor's more pious inclinations: 'From the literary point of view this century [the eighteenth] is perhaps the most barren in the whole history of Persian...' Edward G. Browne, *A History of Persian Literature in Modern Times* (AD 1500–1924) (Cambridge: Cambridge University Press, 1924), p. 277. What for Browne is 'barren' is most certainly innovative for those connoisseurs of the eighteenth-century sabk-i hindi poetry especially by Mirza Bedil or poets of more regional dialects.
69. Padam, *Darbārī Ratan*, p. 27. Brief references to the previously imperial poets here noted appear scattered throughout the portion of the *Sūraj Prakāsh* dealing with the Guru's darbar, especially 5:24 and 5:51–2.
70. Even this conjecture must be qualified as according to Padam, *Darbārī Ratan*, p. 173,

> [Alam] was [initially] a brahman, but having fallen in love with some dyer woman named Shekh [*sic*] he had become a Muslim.

Further background appears in Harmahendr Singh Bedi, *Gurmukhī Lipi men*, p. 252. Also definition 5 of '*Ālam*', in *MK*, pp. 105–6. Both texts mention the uncertain identity of Alam, who is also said to have been a poet in Akbar's entourage, although it is clear that he was previously in the employ of Prince Mu'azzam. A more thorough account of Alam appears in

Bharat Bhushan Chaudhari's *Ālam aur unkā Kāvya* [Alam and His Poetry] (Delhi: Sahitya, 1976).
71. In his famous *Sirr-i Akbar* ('The Great Secret' or 'The Secret of Akbar') Dara Shikoh himself mentions the many Sanskrit and Hindu scholars with whom he was associated without actually naming them. Bikrama Jit Hasrat, *Dārā Shikūh: Life and Works* (2nd revised ed., Delhi: Munshiram Manoharlal Publishers, 1982), p. 213. Also Piara Singh Padam, *Darbārī Ratan*, p. 34 who mentions Shah Jahan's Hindi poets Sundar Das and Chintamani and the darbar's famous Sanskrit scholar Panditraj Jagannatha [Misra]. These men 'amongst the courtly jewels [of Shah Jahan]' we are told, 'had written the [Sanskrit] text *Īshvaro va Dilīshvaro va* [Either the Lord (of the World) or the Lord of Delhi] in order to welcome the emperor.' This line is part of a lengthier Sanskrit shloka attributed to Jagannath alone which was widely circulated during the periods of Jahangir and Shah Jahan underscoring the poets' lofty expectations upon entering the court of the Mughal emperor. The entire couplet claims:

[My] desires can be fulfilled by either the lord of Delhi or the lord of the world. What is an abundant gift for other kings will merely supply me vegetables or just the salt to flavour them.

The translation belongs to Sumit Guha, 'Transitions and Translations', p. 29. Padam also tells us of the tenth Guru's poet Prahilad Rai who may have been one of the 'wise pandits' who helped Dara Shikoh translate the fifty Upanishads which formed the content of his *Sirr-i Akbar*. *Darbārī Ratan*, pp. 115–16. Also see Aziz Ahmad, *Studies in Islamic Culture in the Indian Environment* (Oxford: Clarendon, 1964), pp. 221–2. The many Hindi and Brajbhasha poets in the darbars of Akbar and Jahangir are briefly noted in R.S. McGregor, *Hindi Literature*, pp. 118–32.
72. Blake, *Shahjahanabad*, p. 133. Also M. Athar Ali, *The Apparatus of Empire: Awards of Ranks, Offices and Titles to the Mughal Nobility (1574–1658)* (Delhi: Oxford University Press, 1985), p. 268.
73. As noted in Allison Busch, 'The Anxiety of Innovation', p. 57, n. 13.
74. Bakhtawar Khan claims in his *Mir'at-i 'Ālam* that

Hindu writers have been entirely excluded from holding public offices, and all the worshipping places of the infidels and the great temples of these infamous people have been thrown down and destroyed in a manner which excites astonishment at the successful completion of so difficult a task.

See Elliot and Dowson (ed.), *The History of India as Told by its Own Historians* VII, p. 159. This implies that amongst these Hindu writers were included poets and litterateurs though not all Hindu writers left the court. Certainly Bakhtawar Khan here exaggerates in order to demonstrate the extraordinary piety of Aurangzeb. The reality is quite different though as Catherine Asher has clearly demonstrated in regard to Mughal architecture. Catherine Asher, *Architecture of Mughal India*, pp. 254–5. Incidentally, it is likely that one of the reasons for the continuing belief in Aurangzeb's iconoclasm and anti-Hindu stance may be attributed to the selective nature of Elliot and Dowson's collections. Background appears in Barbara Metcalf, 'Too Little and Too Much: Reflections on Muslims in the History of India', in *Journal of Asian Studies* 54:4 (1995), pp. 951–67.

75. The implication is noted in Padam's discussion of the poet Sukhdev. In discussing the arrival of poets from their previous courts to that of the Guru he claims that

> It is only natural to doubt that scholars who lived within the royal courts of such governors [as Fazil Ali Khan who were very sympathetic to Hindu poets] and sang of their virtues would have arrived at the side of a revolutionary guru who opposed the Mughal empire like Guru Gobind Singh. For what reasons did they come? It is very difficult to give a definite answer, but it is not incorrect to conjecture that they were simply unsatisfied with matters as they were during their time of service with the nawabs and thus simply abandoned Delhi to have made their way to the Guru.

Padam, *Darbārī Ratan*, p. 162. Aurangzeb's governor, Fazil Ali Khan was a patron of the Hindu poets Jai Dev and Nathand and of the prosodist Sukhdas Misra. Also we find the existence of the Persian work on Brajbhasha and Hindu 'good-living' called *Tuhfatulhind* (India's Rarity) written by Mirza Khan (Muhammad ibn Fakhruddin Muhammad, c. 1676) for one of Aurangzeb's sons. See Aziz Ahmad, *Studies in Islamic Culture in the Indian Environment* (Oxford: Clarendon Press, 1964), p. 222. A translation of the *Tuhfat* may be found as M. Ziauddin (trans.), *A Grammar of the Braj Bhakha by Mīrzā Khān (1676 AD) The Persian Text critically edited from original MSS. with an Introduction, Translation and Notes together with the contents of the Tuhfatu-l-Hind* (Calcutta: Visva-Bharati Book Shop, 1935).

76. In some Sikh accounts the implication is that Aurangzeb ejected these non-Muslim poets with the same enthusiasm through which he ultimately sought the throne of his father, executing in this pursuit all those relatives and their followers who barred his progress. This does seem very unlikely as a number of Hindus retained their positions within the imperial darbar. That European and Indian Orientalist scholars have embraced this interpretation of Aurangzeb's character has given it a tenacity which scholars still confront.

77. *MP* II, 10:4–6, pp. 766–78. Here I specifically have in mind the rather lengthy narrative dealing with Bhai Nand Lal Goya. See Chapter 5.

78. Again this may not be mere hyperbole on Santokh Singh's part as even the tenth Guru's poets themselves made such sentiments clear. Hans Ram for example while lauding the personality of the Guru in the introduction to his *Karna Parab* claims (perhaps ambiguously since Gobind is also a word for Akal Purakh) that

> Liberation is obtained at the feet of [Guru] Gobind.

178 The Darbar of the Sikh Gurus

Padam, *Dārbārī Ratan*, p. 136. Also note the compositions of the 'Lakkhi Jungle' poets to which we shall refer momentarily.
79. *Sūraj Prakāsh* online edition 2:50:10–11, p. 380. Also see 2:50:6 (p. 379) at which point Kuvar claims:
It was Aurangzeb's intention to convert us all to Islam (lit., 'to make [us] Turks').
A line we find in Ani Rai's *Jang-nāmā* also suggests this:
Hindus were converted into Muslims and temples were daily razed to the ground.
Jang-nāmā Srī Gurū Gobind Singh jī kā 7 in Ashok (ed.), *Prāchīn Vārān te Jangnāme*, p. 18.
80. Samples may be found in Padam, *Dārbārī Ratan*, pp. 139–43. A passage from Hans Ram's *Karna Parab* which has wording similar to the one from Santokh Singh appears on page 135. One line, for example, claims that
True is the Guru who is Gobind [Singh?]! [He is the] support of the supportless.
81. Ganda Singh (ed.), *Srī Gur-Sobhā* 2:5, p. 68. The reiteration of the term *tuhī* is reminiscent of the *Akāl Ustati's* famous repetition of the word which makes up lines 69–70. Dasam Granth, pp. 16–17.
82. The tenth Guru's court poets, especially in compositions praising the tenth Master, appropriate similar language to describe Guru Gobind Singh. See for example the vār attributed to one Gurdas Singh (or Bhai Gurdas 'the second') and a savaīā of Hir Bhatt. Padam, *Darbārī Ratan*, pp. 189–91, 202. Also the third chaupai of the reinterpretation of Lakkhan Rai's *Hitopadesha* by the Guru's poet Tansukh Lahauri titled *Rājnīti Granth* (Political Exposition):
Blessed is the heart of that person who focuses attention upon the Guru's feet. In both this world and the next he obtains the highest knowledge of emancipation. The Guru is the highest Lord, the Guru is Gobind, the merciful Guru who destroys both pain and affliction (*dukh dund*). It is through the Guru that all treasure is found. It is through the Guru that the highest knowledge of liberation is discovered. It is through the Guru that transmigration is restrained and through the Guru's mercy that all joy is found. Blessings all come from the Guru. Fix your attention upon the Guru.
Padam, *Darbārī Ratan*, p. 98. There are many more examples of such encomiums.
83. Let us qualify here as the term Khalsa indicated an order which was far more fluid and inclusive than today's Sikh Khalsa. Moreover, such 'conversion' would have been a far more simple affair in the late seventeenth century than in the late nineteenth. It would have required very little effort to incorporate a reverence for the Sikhs Gurus, Sikh writings, and various Sikh religious personnel into the religious sentiments of such Hindu poets since boundaries between the Hindu and Sikh traditions were

exceptionally porous, an absorbency no doubt exacerbated by the seventeenth-century appropriation of Brajbhasha, a language intimately connected with Hindu courts and devotion to Krishna. Sikh and later Khalsa Sikh praxis was as a result very much situated within a shared 'Hindu' mystical universe (I should point out that this does in no way necessarily indicate that Sikhs were or are Hindus), a point which any careful reading of the Dasam Granth or the poetry of the tenth Master's court poets will substantiate. For a historical analysis of Sikh/Khalsa Sikh 'conversion' see my 'Conversion and Sikh Tradition', in Rowena Robinson *et al.* (eds), *Religious Conversion in India: Modes, Motivations, Meanings* (New Delhi: Oxford University Press, 2003), pp. 149–80. For Khalsa Sikh praxis during the early eighteenth century see Jeevan Deol, 'Eighteenth Century Khalsa Identity: Discourse, Praxis and Narrative', in Christopher Shackle *et al.* (eds), *Sikh Religion, Culture and Ethnicity* (London: Curzon, 2001), pp. 25–46.

84. Khalsa College ms. 2988B, folio 17b. Also see Padam, *Darbārī Ratan*, p. 101. In his *Sukhsain Granth* Sainapati mentions a few of the darbar's poets by name, one of whom was Sainapati's own teacher Pandit Devi Das who was apparently a Chhibbar brahman. In fact, Padam claims, that Sainapati's *Chānākā Rājnīti* often appears coupled with Devi Das' *Rājnīti krit Devī Dās* in the manuscript record. *Darbārī Ratan*, p. 89; also p. 102. Furthermore, Padam also mentions Sainapati's post-Anandpur works (p. 101) as too does Harmahendr Sinha Bedi's *Gurmukhī Lipi*, pp. 258–9. The latter, however, does not include the *Chānākā Rājnīti*.

85. Julie Scott Meisami, *Medieval Persian Court Poetry*, p. 52. There are also similar journey poems in Brajbhasha and references to journeys in Sanskrit courtly literature as well. For Brajbhasha see the sixth canto of Jayarama's *Radhamadhvavilasachampu* as noted in Sunit Guha, 'Transitions and Translations', p. 27.

86. *Chhand Vichār Pingal*, ms. 168 Khalsa College Library as noted in Padam, *Darbārī Ratan*, p. 162. For another of Sukhdev's works see ms. SHR 2247 which is a 1914 CE transcription of Sukhdev's *Adhiyātam Prakāsh* (The Manifestation of the Supreme Spirit) dated to 1698 CE.

87. We also discover dates of completion within certain Dasam Granth compositions. See for example *Krishanavtār* 755, 983, Dasam Granth, pp. 354, 383. The two passages here indicate that the author(s) did not write the text all at once and that they may not have even written in a linear fashion as it appears that the second reference above though written first follows the other in sequence.

88. According to Padam a number of poets came to the Guru's court during the time he spend in the Lakkhi Jungle amongst whom are included Bihari, Lal Das Khiali, and Adha. Padam, *Darbārī Ratan*, pp. 232–46.

89. Perhaps the nearest work to a commemorative encomium we find is a photocopy of an undated manuscript of 234 lines ascribed to the tenth Guru's

180   The Darbar of the Sikh Gurus

poet Kankan titled *Das Gur Kathā* (The Story of the Ten Gurus). Khalsa College SHR 1797A. The original is a manuscript held in the Punjab Public Library in Lahore, Pakistan (accession number 1797). The conclusion of the work describes the tenth Master's investiture as Guru and the creation of the Khalsa. Incidentally, this poet is not listed in Padam's *Darbārī Ratan*.
90. Padam, *Darbārī Ratan*, p. 37.
91. *Jang-nāmā Srī Gurū Gobind Singh jī kā* 61 in Shamsher Singh Ashok (ed.), *Prāchīn Vārān te Jangnāme*, p. 31.
92. Padam, *Darbārī Ratan*, p. 232. Note the use of the more familiar and intimate *tum*, 'you'.
93. Padam, *Darbārī Ratan*, p. 236.
94. Ibid., pp. 240–1.
95. There is a nice double entendre here as the term *ghat* (also a 'large water jug') can mean 'diminish' and even 'inferior' as well. Padam, *Darbārī Ratan*, p. 243.
96. Muhammad Abdul Ghani, *A History of Persian Language* III, pp. 197–8.
97. According to Padam, for example the court poet Hans Ram Bajpei thought that

Anandpur was the city in which the Guru and tenth Lord regularly displayed these splendours. The poet Hans Ram simply could not be restrained from praising this celestial city.

Padam, *Darbārī Ratan*, p. 137. Describing the splendours and perfections of the raja's city was as I imply also a common theme in seventeenth-century Brajbhasha poetry. See Allison Busch, 'Literary Responses to Mughal Imperium', pp. 43–4.
98. *Singh Gaū kī Kathā* 48 as noted in Padam, *Darbārī Ratan*, p. 90. Padam mentions that he possesses two copies of this particular hand-written manuscript.
99. Online *SP* 5:52:14, p. 502.
100. The words are Padam's own. Padam, *Darbārī Ratan*, p. 138.
101. Online *SP* 5:51:28, p. 494 and Padam, *Darbārī Ratan*, p. 135. For Padam this passage explicitly notes that that the Guru 'had gifted to poets elephants, horses, and several other expensive things and ornaments' (*kavīān nūn hāthī ghore ate hor kīmatı vastān bhūshān dā dān ditā giā*) though the passage belongs to the mid nineteenth century and not the late seventeenth as he implies. Compare this praise with one similar which appears in *rasāval chhand* mode in the *Bachitar Nātak* 1:20–3, Dasam Granth, p. 40.
102. Padam, *Darbārī Ratan*, p. 135:

sūran kī pati ati jānat jahān jān ko tān ko phal det sadā ari par jīt hai
103. Padam, *Darbārī Ratan*, pp. 135–6.
104. *Jang-nāmā Srī Gurū Gobind Singh jī kā* 4 in Shamsher Singh Ashok (ed.), *Prāchīn Vārān te Jangnāme*, p. 17.
105. *Jang-nāmā Srī Gurū Gobind Singh jī kā* 5 in Ashok (ed.), *Prāchīn Vārān te Jangnāme*, p. 18. Also see savaiyyā 29, p. 23:

The might of Guru Gobind Singh's sword is that which buoys the spirits [of those] on the battlefield.

106. Perhaps the earliest reference to the name of the Guru's kettledrum appears in an anonymous work written apparently sometime in the early eighteenth century, the *Bherā Srī Gobind Singh jī kā*. Within the fourth canto we hear that the True Guru shouted that the 'Ranjit' be struck. *Bherā Srī Gobind Singh jī kā* 4 in Shamsher Singh Ashok (ed.), *Prāchīn Vārān te Jangnāme*, p. 34. Also see a reference to the Battle of Bhangani in the *Karakhe Pātshāh Dasven ke* (Commemorations of the Tenth Guru's Deeds) attributed to Sainapati:
    The chief of [that] country stood firm, battling on the battlefield. The horse-mounted drum (nishān) Ranjit (Victory in Battle) had come.
    Padam, *Darbārī Ratan*, p. 106.
107. This King Bali, the son of Virochan and grandson of Prahilad, is the raja who was asked for a small parcel of land by the disguised Vamana incarnation of Vishnu. Having been told he could take as much land as could be covered by three steps the dwarf Vishnu grew in size until his three strides covered the known universe. In some versions of the tale King Bali is given sovereignty over Patala as a boon for having agreed to allow Vamana to step on his head, a sign of humility. See the fifth definition of 'Bali' in *MK*, p. 844. The Bhabhichan here is Vibhishan, the brother of Ravana and devotee of Rama who appears throughout the fifth book of the *Ramcharitmānas*, the *Sundarkānd*.
108. Online *SP* 5:52:8–9, pp. 498–9 and Padam, *Darbārī Ratan*, pp. 131–2. For more on the frightening sound of kettledrums, especially on the battlefield see *Giān Prabodh* 183, Dasam Granth, p. 143:
    The kshatriya warriors fell dead on the battlefield. The terrifying sound of drums and kettledrums filled the air.
109. For example, Guru Nanak's *Āsā ashtapadīān* 1(12), Adi Granth, p. 417 notes the evanescent character of such royal paraphernalia:
    Where is the hunt (literally, *khel* 'sport'), the stables, and the horses? Where are the kettledrums (*bherī*) and the military trumpets (*shahnāī*; Per: *shāh-nāy*)? Where are those warriors and chariots immersed in the fray? Where are those scarlet robes? Where are those rings and the lovely faces [of the women of the court]? These are nowhere to be seen [after death]. This entire world is Yours, [You alone are] the Lord.
    Also see Guru Nanak, *Sārang kī vār* 2:17, p. 1244. Representative of the ephemeral nature of such items as noted in the Dasam Granth is *Akāl Ustati* 23, Dasam Granth, pp. 13–14.
110. We should briefly note here that the literary context of these narratives and encomiums followed strict sets of rules and procedures and as such images of the Guru, the hero, the king and various others were very often if not always modified in order to better cultivate certain moods and sentiments (rasas) or to emphasize the ideal traits of heroines, heroes, and kings.

182   The Darbar of the Sikh Gurus

Background in Allison Busch, 'Literary Responses to the Mughal Imperium', p. 33.
111. Hukam-namas 35, 37, 50, 55, amongst many others. See Ganda Singh (ed.), *Hukamnāme*, pp. 131, 135, 161, 171.
112. The so-called prasādī (offering) elephant which was gifted to the Guru by the Raja of Assam was able to fan the Guru and wash his feet with its trunk according to tradition (online edition *SP* 1:23:16–20, p. 185). The beautiful tent from Kabul is mentioned at online *SP* 1:20, pp. 164–7. At one point in the account we are told that the tent served as the canopy under which a poetic gathering was held. For example, at 1:20:25–6, p. 167 we hear that

After about three hours the carpets (Per: *fara<u>sh</u>*) were spread which were brought along with the tent. A poetic assembly (divān) was [then] brought together [under the tent] while court was held. The glorious and benevolent Guru was seated [within]. The Sikh sangat and a group of masands [were also present]. The rababis sang the blissful shabads [from the scripture].

Santokh Singh devotes a considerable amount of time to the famous kettledrum and how this figured in the relationship between Guru Gobind Singh and Raja Bhim Chand. He also refers to Bhim Chand's desire to secure both the prasadi elephant and the beautiful tent. Online edition of *SP* 1: 24–6, pp. 191–211 and 1:29, pp. 226–32. An abridged version of this narrative appears in M.A. Macauliffe, *The Sikh Religion* V, pp. 4–6.
113. *MP* II 10:217–20, pp. 755–6.
114. Ved Parkash, *The Sikh in Bihar*, p. 137. As Ved Parkash does not supply a facsimile or transliteration of this hukam-nama it is difficult to determine its authenticity. For other hukam-namas which are not included in Ganda Singh's collection see Balwant Singh Dhillon, 'Some Unknown Hukam-namas of Guru Gobind Singh', and Madananjit Kaur's perceptive, 'A Study of the Hukam-namas as Source Material for the History of the Sikh Gurus', both of which appear in *Punjab History Conference Thirteenth Session March 2–4, 1979 Proceedings* (Patiala: Punjabi University, 1980), pp. 103–9; 110–16.
115. Grewal and Bal, *Guru Gobind Singh*, pp. 52–3.
116. A traditional account of the Guru's early life is given in ibid, pp. 33 ff.
117. In a hukam-nama written in by Guru Tegh Bahadar we hear of the great rejoicing in Patna at the birth of the future tenth Guru. Hukam-nama 24, S.S. Sagar, *Hukam-namas of Guru Tegh Bahadar*, pp. 90–1.
118. Grewal and Bal, *Guru Gobind Singh*, pp. 49–50.
119. For example note the sixtieth couplet of the *Rāmavtār*:

[Rama] was given a well-rounded, refined education in both weapons (shastr) and literatures (shāstr). The prince, Rama, absorbed all such learning in as short a time as eight days.

Rāmavtār 60, Dasam Granth, p. 193. That Sikhs were familiar with the great epics of India is a certainty. The description of the ahl-i saif appears

Spirit and Structure 183

in G.M. Wickens (trans.), *The Nasirean Ethics* (London: George Allen and Unwin Ltd., 1964), p. 230.
120. Online edition of *SP* 12:21, pp. 175–82.
121. Abu'l Fazl refers us to an incident in which the two-year old Akbar wrestles his cousin Ibrahim for a naqqara, the symbol of power and prestige. H. Beveridge (ed. and trans.), *The Akbar Nama of Abu-L-Fazl* I and II, pp. 455–6. A beautiful seventeenth-century painting of the scene is found in the Bodleian Library, Oxford and is reproduced as Figure 15 in Bonnie Wade, *Imaging Sound*.
122. Certainly the royal Indo-Timurid courts of Akbar, Jahangir, Shah Jahan, and even on occasion Aurangzeb were often the context of a number of the narratives we discover within the Dasam Granth, especially within its lengthiest portion, the *Pakhyān Charitr*. Although the charitrs here are attributed to the Guru and may not have been known in the form we discover within the Dasam Granth many of the stories on which these were based would nevertheless have been circulating during the Guru's childhood in numerous formats. Some examples within the Dasam Granth of such Mughal court settings appear as *Pakhyān Charit* 39, 48, 82, 121, 155, 185, 195, 278, and 389, Dasam Granth, pp. 864–5; 870–2; 916–18; 987; 1042; 1078–9; 1085–7; 1222; 1343–4 respectively.
123. Classical descriptions of the skills enjoined for kings appear in Indic-period manuals of kingship such as the *Arthashāstra* of Kautilya and the *Manusmriti*. Wendy Doniger and Brian K. Smith (ed. and trans.), *The Laws of Manu* 7:43; 87–98 (New Delhi: Penguin Books, 1991), pp. 133, 137–8 and L.N. Rangarajan (ed. and trans.), *Kautilya: Arthashastra* 3:1 (New Delhi: Penguin Books, 1992), pp. 142–3. See also the relatively lengthy, Adi Granth-esque *Pakhyān Charit* 266:6–8, Dasam Granth, p. 1198.
124. *CSRn* 158, pp. 79; (English translation p. 167). My translation is only slightly modified from McLeod's.
125. *BSVN* 10:6–10, p. 125. Grewal and Bal, *Guru Gobind Singh*, pp. 37–9.
126. See Stephen Blake, *Shahjahanabad*, p. 147.
127. The sheer breathlessness with which the author deploys terms compounded of both Persianite and Sanskritic elements in such compositions as the *Jāpu* and the *Akāl Ustati* suggests the Guru's intimate familiarity with the Brajbhasha rīti literature, perhaps even with the most famous works of the lot, the *Rasikpriyā* and the *Kaviyapriyā* of Keshavdas (Handbook for Connoisieurs and Handbook for Poets respectively). Background on these texts appears in Allison Busch, 'Literary Responses to the Mughal Imperium: The Historical Poems of Keśavdās', in *South Asia Research* 25:1 (2005), p. 32 and her 'The Anxiety of Innovation', esp. p. 55.
128. M. Athar Ali, 'Translation of Sanskrit Works at Akbar's Court', in Iqtidar Alam Khan (ed.), *Akbar and His Age* (New Delhi: Northern Book Centre, 1999), pp. 171–80. For Shivaji's patronage see Krishna Divakar, *Bhonsla Rāj-darbār ke Hindī Kavi* (Varanasi: Nagari Pracharini Sabha, 1969). As

184　The Darbar of the Sikh Gurus

we know clearly there were a small number of men within the court of Akbar who were intimately familiar with both symbolic universes the most famous of whom was Abdurrahim Khan-i Khanan whose penname was Rahim, both an accomplished poet of Persian and Brajbhasha.
129. See Barbara Stoler Miller (ed.), *Theatre of Memory: the Plays of Kālidāsa* (New York: Columbia University Press, 1984). See also Jeevan S. Deol, 'Eighteenth Century Khalsa Identity', pp. 25–46.
130. A readily available example is Lallulal's *Rājnīti* seven maxims of which are reproduced in Rupert Snell's *The Hindi Classical Tradition*, pp. 65–70. Many of these are derived from the *Hitopadesha*. Also see Devi Das' *Rājnīti* which was written prior to his arrival at Guru Gobind Singh's court (Padam, *Darbārī Ratan*, pp. 91–2). A list of the various works alleged to have been produced by the poets of the Guru's court appear in H.S. Bedi's *Gurmukhī Lipi*, pp. 242–7 and are mentioned throughout Piara Singh Padam's *Darbārī Ratan*. For the similar literature of other Brajbhasha courts the basic text remains Ronald Stuart McGregor, *Hindi Literature from its Beginnings to the Nineteenth Century*.
131. Padam, *Darbārī Ratan*, p. 149. The term *kalā* strongly connotes artistry amongst other things.
132. *Krishanavtār* 584, Dasam Granth, p. 330. One who appreciates such poetry is often called the rasik in Brajbhasha poetry. The term is derived from Sanskrit and refers to the connoisseur of ras, the poetic sentiments. Incidentally, the term rasī also implies one devoted to Krishna (although it also appears in poetry associated with Rama). I have glossed it as I do in the light of Rosalind O'Hanlon claims that the elite courtiers within the Mughal darbar were trained from an early age to distinguish between the mediocre and the superb in poetry, art, and various other arenas. Rosalind O'Hanlon, 'Issues of Masculinity,' p. 6.
133. It may be that this midwife, the only woman mentioned in the hukam-namas of the tenth Master found in Ganda Singh's collection, was the nurse who had helped deliver the infant Gobind into this world. In fact she may well be one of the nursemaids (*dāīan*) referenced in the seventh chapter of the *Bachitar Nātak*. See *Bachitar Nātak* 7:2, Dasam Granth, p. 59. Rajindar Singh, 'Historical Accounts of the Childhood Days of Guru Gobind Singh', in *Punjab History Conference Eight Session December 15–16, 1973 Proceedings* (Patiala: Punjabi University Press, 1974), pp. 41–8, esp. p. 43. According to Piara Singh Padam the Ram Rai here mentioned is the same Ram Rai whose name appears in a note found within a bir which lays in Patna. He thus concludes that Ram Rai was a scribe or munshi in the court of the tenth Guru. Padam, *Dārbārī Ratan*, p. 254.
134. Hukam-nama 39, Ganda Singh (ed.), *Hukamnāme*, pp. 138–9. An alternate reading follows: 'Sobha Chand has presented himself within the court.'
135. For example Hukam-nama 25, Ganda Singh (ed.), *Hukamnāme*, pp. 110–11. I single this one out because it adds a nuance to the discussion:

Spirit and Structure 185

Bhai Batha...come with the sangat and present [yourselves] before the Guru for darshan...

Certainly the idea of darshan has its origins within earlier Hindu traditions where it continues to be observed to this day. The Mughal emperors from Akbar to Shah Jahan had, however, adapted this practice to suit their imperial needs, presenting themselves to their subjects on a daily basis (at least in theory) on a specially designed balcony (*jharokhā*) to in part improve a subject's access to the justice manifest within the emperor's person. That the Sikhs were aware of such practices is clear from both *Srī Gur-sobhā* 16:37, p. 157 and *Pakhyān Charitr* 195, Dasam Granth, p. 1087. Here we are told:

The Emperor [Aurangzeb] crossed over to the balcony viewing window (jharokhā) and observed their trickeries (charitr).

It is possible that this charitr was told much earlier as by the tenth Guru's third birthday in 1669, the eleventh regnal year, Aurangzeb did away with the practice of appearing in the jharokha (1669)—although the notion of darshan is not present within this charitr. Richards, *The Mughal Empire*, p. 172.

136. Ganda Singh (ed.), *Hukamnāme*, p. 173.
137. W.H. McLeod, *Sikhs of the Khalsa*, p. 37.
138. Christopher Shackle, 'Approaches to the Persian Loans in the *Ādi Granth*', in the *Bulletin of the School of Oriental and African Studies* 4:1 (1978), pp. 85–6. In fact within the Adi Granth the term hazūr is often used in conjunction with the word *sadā* or 'always' implying that the Lord is always presenting him/her/it/self within the divine court underscoring the belief in the eternal Guru's immanence (*sarab viāpak*). See for example Guru Arjan's *Āsā rāg* 4:4:139, Adi Granth, p. 406:

The cultivation of devotion destroys both doubt and fear. May Nanak always abide in your presence.

139. As noted in Blake's *Shahjahanabad*, p. 87.
140. For example hukam-nama 37, *Hukamnāme*, p. 135:

The Sikh who comes for darshan: his feet will obtain a place [to stand in the Guru's court].

The same formula is reiterated after the formation of the Khalsa in 1699. In hukam-nama 59 of Ganda Singh's collection, Hukamnāme, p. 179, dated 1702:

Come for darshan with five weapons girded. All shall be blessed.

141. Hukam-nama 40, *Hukamnāme*, pp. 140–1.
142. Ganda Singh (ed.), *Ma'ākhiz-i Tavārīkh-i Sikhān*, p. 82. William Irvine claims that this meeting and exchange of gifts took place on 2 August 1707 as noted in the *Bahādar Shāh Nāmah*. William Irvine, *The Later Mughals* vols 1 and 2 bound in one [Jadunath Sarkar (ed.)] (Delhi: Low Price Publications, 1995), p. 90.
143. Hukam-nama 63, *Hukamnāme*, p. 186–7.

144. Prince Muhammad Azimuddin later known as Azimushshan was the son of Prince Mu'azzam later Bahadar Shah. He was the Viceroy of Bengal in 1697 after which he was confirmed with the Subadari of Bihar in 1703.
145. Again, I am here reminded of Dirk Kolff's work on the military labour market in Indo-Islamic and Indo-Anglian India. See his *Naukar, Rajput, and Sepoy* and, as well, Stewart Gordon, 'Zones of Military Entrepreneurship in India', in Gordon's *Marathas, Marauders and State Formation* (Delhi: Oxford University Press, 1994), pp. 182–208.
146. Since the late nineteenth century the only portion of the *Bachitar Nātak* which is believed to have been prepared by Guru Gobind Singh is the *apnī kathā* segment which begins the sixth chapter. These issues are discussed in Robin Rinehart, 'Strategies for Interpreting the Dasam Granth', in Pashaura Singh *et al.* (eds), *Sikhism and History* (Delhi: Oxford University Press, 2004), pp. 135–50 and Jeevan S. Deol, 'Eighteenth Century Khalsa Identity', pp. 25–46, esp. pp. 32–3 which discusses the 'intended unity' of the *Bachitar Nātak*.
147. And so the term afzū may reinforce what seems to be the 'performative nature' of certain Dasam Granth compositions, a point I will discuss further on. For this interactive facet of contemporary *Ramcharitmānas* katha see Philip Lutegendorf's *The Life of a Text*, p. 132, n. 46.
148. The poet Shyam is regularly noted in the *Chaubīs Avtār* and the *Pakhyān Charitr*. Ram also appears in the latter. The poet Chhabi is noted in *Pakhyān Charitr* 310:2, Dasam Granth, p. 1265.
149. The *Akāl Ustati* begins with just such a reference:
    [This is] a copy of the original prepared by [he who sits on] the tenth throne, the tenth true king.... The statements which follow were prepared by a scribe of the tenth king. Through your grace...
    Akāl Ustati 1, Dasam Granth, p. 11.
150. See the preambles to the *Jāpu*, the *Bachitar Nātak*, and the Thirty Three *Swaiyyās*, Dasam Granth, pp. 1, 39, 712.
151. Gurinder Singh Mann has recently suggested that the term mukhvāk in these instances is more likely to be understood as an analogue to the Persian mukhātib (i.e., a second speaker or one who addresses another) further buttressing the presence of diligent scribes. If this is the case the passage should then read, 'addressed to the the tenth Lord, the true king.' This Persian analogy is certainly questionable. I would like to thank J.S. Hawley for sharing this information with me.
152. Although (as I imply above) I would strongly agree with both Dharampal Ashta and Jeevan Deol's statements about the organic unity of the *Bachitar Nātak* compositions. See Ashta, *Poetry of the Dasam Granth*, p. 130 and Deol, 'Eighteenth Century Khalsa Identity', p. 32–3.
153. Allison Busch, 'The Courtly Vernacular: The Transformation of Braj Literary Culture, 1585–1675' (PhD dissertation, University of Chicago, 2002) and R.S. McGregor, *The Language of Indrajit of Orcha: A Study of*

Spirit and Structure 187

Early Braj Bhāshā Prose (Cambridge: Cambridge University Press, 1968), pp. 6–7. A different emphasis in a similar type of Brajbhasha literature is Monika Thiel-Horstmann, *Crossing the Ocean of Existence: Braj Bhāshā Religious Poetry from Rajasthan: A Reader* (Weisbaden: Otto Harrassowitz, 1983) which focusses upon the poetry of the Dadupanthis. Perhaps the most famous of the Brajbhasha poets was Bihari (not the Bihari in the tenth Master's jungle court), master of the *dohā* couplet whose poetry is distinguished as *gāgar mem sāgar*, 'ocean in a pitcher'. Bihari's patron was the famous Jai Singh of Amber. Brief accounts of such Brajbhasha poets may be seen in Rupert Snell, *The Hindi Classical Tradition*, pp. 29–47. For Bihari see R.S. McGregor, *Hindi Literature*, pp. 173–4. For other Brajbhasha poets see Charles S.J. White, *The Caurāsī Pad of Shri Hit Harivamsh: Introduction, Translation, Notes, and edited Braj Bhāshā text* (Honolulu: University of Hawaii Press, 1977).

154. All of the poetry found within the Dasam Granth, implies Harmahendr Singh Bedi, should be understood as 'courtly.' See his *Gurmukhī Lipi*, pp. 221–43.

155. *Rāmavtār* 860–1, Dasam Granth, p. 254. Dharmpal Ashta claims that this location is Naina Devi. Ashta, *Poetry of Dasam Granth*, p. 66. For other dates and places of completion see *Krishanavtār* 2490 and *Pakhyān Charitr* 404:405, Dasam Granth, pp. 570, 1388.

156. Allison Busch, Literary Responses to Mughal Imperium', pp. 37–8.

157. Sheldon Pollock, 'The Sanskrit Cosmopolis, 300–1300 CE: Transculturation, Vernacularization, and the Question of Ideology', in Jan E.M. Houben (ed.), *Ideology and Status of Sanskrit: Contributions to the History of the Sanskrit Language* (Leiden: E.J. Brill, 1996), pp. 197–248 describes in part the Sanskrit mahakavya as an expression of the political will. Also noted is itihāsa, the uniquely premodern Indian understanding of 'history' which blurs the line between positivistic history and literature. Pollock's essays and further thoughts regarding the Sanskrit Cosmopolis, its literature and history within the various royal courts scattered throughout its vast neighbourhood is found in his *The Language of the Gods in the World of Men: Sanskrit, Culture, and Power in Premodern India* (Berkeley: University of California Press, 2006), chapters 3–4. For a famous Sanskrit charitr itself see the eighth-century *Dashā Kumāra Charitam* of the Pallava court poet Dandin. A.N.D. Haksar (trans.), *Dandin Tales of The Ten Princes (Dasa Kumāra Charitam)* (New Delhi: Penguin Books, 1994). Background on charitra and mahakavya appear in Allison Busch, 'Literary Reponses to Mughal Imperium', p. 34. Background on Sanskrit charitr and mahakavya appears in M. Krishna Machariar, *History of Classical Sanskrit Literature* (New Delhi: Motilal Banarsidass, 1970), pp. 79–308l. Dharmpal Ashta notes the difference between certain compositions of the Dasam Granth, especially the *Chaubīs Avatār* and mahakavya in his *Poetry of the Dasam Granth*, pp. 112–13.

188 The Darbar of the Sikh Gurus

158. Pollock, 'The Sanskrit Cosmopolis,' pp. 198–9. For a brief history of Sanskrit courtly literature see Daniel Ingalls (ed. and trans.), *An Anthology of Sanskrit Court Poetry Vidyākura's* Subhāshitaratnakosha (Cambridge, Mass.: Harvard University Press, 1965), esp. pp. 1–29.
159. I here follow the insightful work of Velcheru Narayana Rao, David Shulman, and Sanjay Subramanyam, *Textures of Time: Writing History in South India 1600-1800* (New York: Other Press, 2003), p. 4. For the intimate connection between literary styles and history one need consult Hayden White, *The Content of the Form: Narrative Discourse and Historical Representation* (Paperback edition, Baltimore: John Hopkins University Press, 1992).
160. Sheldon Pollock, 'Cosmopolitan and Vernacular in History', in *Public Culture* 12:3 (2000), pp. 591–625 and his 'The Cosmopolitan Vernacular', in the *Journal of Asian Studies* 57 (1998), pp. 6–37. Also R.S. McGregor, *Hindi Literature*, p. 35 for Brajbhasha.
161. Rao, Shulman, and Subramanyam, *Textures of Time*, p. 21.
162. Busch, 'Literary Responses', p. 34. The Sanskrit terms itihāsa is literally defined as 'so indeed it was' favouring in many ways oral transmission. Monier-Williams, *A Sanskrit-English Dictionary* (Delhi: Motilal Banarsidass, 1990), p. 165.
163. Grewal and Bal, *Guru Gobind Singh*, pp. 74–6. Deol, 'Eighteenth Century', p. 33. The tenth Guru's spiritual and paternal lineage is also traced to the god Rama himself a mythic origin aimed to further buttress the lineage of the Sikh Gurus, a technique exhibited elsewhere within the seventeenth-century subcontinent.
164. There are many of these. See *Krishanavtār* 750, Dasam Granth, p. 353. Others appear at *Vār Srī Bhagautī jī kī* 55 and *Pakhyān Charit* 404: 20, 23, 403–5, Dasam Granth, pp. 127, 1360–1, 1377.
165. See for example the two *bārahmāh* or encomiums of the twelve months which comprise *Krishanavtār* 867–79, 914–25, Dasam Granth, pp. 369–71; 376–8.
166. This is the mainly topic of the second and third parts of the *Krishanavtār*. *Krishanavtār* 441–756; 757–1028. For the *Gītagovind*, see Barbara Stoller Miller (ed. and trans.), *The Gītagovinda of Jayadeva: Love Song of the Dark Lord* (New Delhi: Motilal Banarsidass, 1984).
167. For example *Krishanavtār* 190, Dasam Granth, pp. 276–7.
168. *Krishanavtār* 751–4, Dasam Granth, pp. 353–4.
169. *Krishanavtār* 671, Dasam Granth, p. 342. Background on such conventions appears in Allison Busch, 'The Anxiety of Innovation', p. 48. For the theory of poetics in India see Edwin Gerow, *Indian Poetics* (Weisbaden: Otto Harrassowitz, 1977). Moreover, for one poet's (Keshav Das) technique in appropriating poetic norms from Sanskrit into Brajbhasha, see G.H. Schokker, 'Keshavadasa's Method of Basing Braj Krishna-lyrics on the Sanskrit Tradition of Literary Aesthetics', in Monika Thiel-Horstmann

Spirit and Structure 189

(ed.), *Bhakti in Current Research 1979–1982* (Berlin: Dietrich Reimer Verlag, 1983), pp. 307–24.
170. R.S. McGregor, *Hindi Literature*, pp. 31–2. The majority of these classifications appear in the *Pakhyān Charitr*. For one classical type, the 'anxious' heroine (*nayika*), see the tale of Rani Bir Kala. *Pakhyān Charitr* 170:6–9, Dasam Granth, pp. 1062–3.
171. At the end of *Chandī Charitr Ukti Bilās* 1, Dasam Granth, p. 75 for example we find:
Here is completed the first segment of the *Chandī Charitr Ukti Bilās* [as rendered] from the Markanadeya Purana dealing with the restraining of the demons Madhu and Kaitabh.
I am very much aware of the perceptive statements in Grewal and Bal, *Guru Gobind Singh*, pp. 60–1 which highlight the difference between these Dasam Granth goddess narratives and those found in the Markandeya Purana. Generally, I agree with their claims but with the addendum that such difference demonstrates a freshness of perspective which was common amongst poets of courtly Brajbhasha. Indeed, as Grewal and Bal imply, neither the Guru nor his poets can be accused of mere mimicry. See Allison Busch, 'The Anxiety of Innovation', pp. 45–59, esp. p. 51 which claims, in a different context that such texts were 'both new and not new in complex ways.'
172. We should note that within the *Krishanavtār* direct speech is not indicated by the Sanskrit word *uvācha* '[someone] said' often found in the Gita, but rather the Brajbhasha equivalent, *bāch*. The dialogue in the *Giān Prabodh* which begins at line 126 occurs between the embodied soul (*jīvātma*) and the Supreme Soul (*Paramātma*). In regard to the *Pakhyān Charitr*, the passage following provides the standard ending of each charitr. There is some variation within these depending in many instances upon whether the charitr deals with the deceptions, trickeries, or immoral actions of men (purakh) or of women (triā). This particular ending is from the relatively lengthy Charitr 81 dealing with the wife of Raja Siroman Singh, Drig Dhanya. *Pakhyān Charitr* 81, Dasam Granth, pp. 908–16.
Completed here with truth and blessings (*samāpatmasatu shubhamasatu*) is the eighty first charitr of the [segment of the] revered *Pakhyān Charitr* which relates the narratives of women (triyā charitr) as a dialogue (*sambād*) between the minister (*mantrī*) and his king (*bhūp*).
For such allusions within the *Bachitar Nātak*, see Jeevan Deol's comparison in his 'Eighteenth Century Khalsa Identity,' p. 33. Of course all this is not to mention the fact that many of the charitrs in the *Pakhyān Charitr* draw upon the Sanskrit stories of the Mahabharata, the Ramayana, the Puranas, and so on.
173. See *Krishanavtār* 755, Dasam Granth, p. 354:
This portion (kathā) [of the Krishanavtār] was improved (sudhār) in the year sammat 1745 (1688 CE). Please excuse any errors wherever these may appear. Poets may still improve upon the whole of it.

190 The Darbar of the Sikh Gurus

and *Krishanavtār* 983, Dasam Granth, p. 383:
This granth was improved after writing on Wednesday during the light half of the month of Sawan sammat 1744 (1687 CE) in the town of Paunta.

This trope of refinement which regularly appears in the Dasam Granth is common in the work of courtly Brajbhasha poets and has been examined in the scholarship of Allison Busch. Note for example, her claim that such 'improvement' demonstrated 'the usurping of Sanskrit cultural space by the suggestion that a *bhasha*...[Bhagavata Purana] can take [the Sanskrit composition's] place.' Allison Busch, 'The Anxiety of Innovation', p. 48; also see Schokker, 'Keshavadasa's Method,' pp. 307, 324. My understanding differs slightly since Busch takes into account Brajbhasha works produced almost a century before the *Krishanavtār*, as poets of the language were beginning to gain their courtly footing so to speak. The Guru is here emphasizing what I think, is his belief (which appears elsewhere in the Dasam Granth) that the divine may be venerated in any human language, a belief brought out sharply by the last humble exhortation to others to 'improve' upon it, which given the context may well indicate translation into another language perhaps a point required to be made in light of the fact that Brajbhasha was very intimately associated with the worship of Krishna (Rupert Snell, *The Hindi Classical Tradition*, pp. 30–2). Busch also elaborates upon this common Brajbhasha trope, the poet's expression of humility, a corollary in this case to the idea of improvement. This I believe was a moralistic value totally in accord with its emphasis within the Adi Granth, which the tenth Guru self-consciously cultivated, an important fact which is often left unsaid in traditional Sikh histories of this period. Indeed, I would argue that his choice not to include his own writings within the Adi Granth is indicative of the tenth Guru's fundamental regard for humility. Busch, 'The Anxiety of Innovation', pp. 50–3.

174. For early manuscripts of the Dasam Granth see Rattan Singh Jaggi, *Dasam Granth dā Kartrtva* [Authorship of the Dasam Granth] (New Delhi: Punjabi Sahit Sabha, 1966).
175. Pashaura Singh, *The Guru Granth Sahib*, p. 17.
176. *Bachitar Nātak* 5:4–16, Dasam Granth, pp. 53–4. Also *Vār Srī Bagautī jī kī* 1, Dasam Granth, p. 119.
177. *Pakhyān Charitr* 266:14, Dasam Granth, p. 1200.
178. Kabir, *shlok* 81, Adi Granth, p. 1368. Echoes of this hymn may be heard in Guru Nanak's *Sirī rāg* 4(2), Adi Granth, p. 15:
O Nanak, if I possessed heaps of paper in the hundreds of thousands and continually recorded and studied the Lord's love being performed; if ink was in limitless supply and my pen wrote with the speed of the wind; still would I be unable to estimate your true value. How can I ever describe [the glory of] your Name?

Spirit and Structure 191

This passage also appears just slightly modified as *Bachitar Nātak* I:101, Dasam Granth, p. 46

179. The second point is noted in *Rāmavtār* 17, Dasam Granth, p. 189: King [Dasaratha] was pleased and bestowed two other boons. He had no misgivings whatsoever. How the king helped the king of the gods become victorious has been told in both the [*Hanuman*] *Nātak* and the [*Pakhyān*] *Charitr*.

The identity of the Natak so mentioned seems quite logical and belongs to Randhir Singh's editorial notes in Randhir Singh (ed.), *Shabadārath Dasam Granth Sāhib (pothī pahilī)* (Patiala: Punjabi University Publication Bureau, 1985), p. 216, n. 25. Apparently, Dharmpal Ashta mentions, Guru Gobind Singh kept a copy of the *Hanuman Nātak* within his *gatrā* or baldric (Ashta, *Poetry of Dasam Granth*, p. 34.) The same author too notes the fact that there is a line in the Dasam Granth which is echoed or reproduced in four different works: *Akāl Ustati* 93; *Bachitar Nātak* 1:14; *Giān Prabodh* 6; and *Pakhyān Charitr* 266:87; Dasam Granth, pp. 20, 40, 128, 1207. (Ashta, *Poetry of Dasam Granth*, pp. 21–2). Such echoes are not uncommon. Indeed the last line of what is perhaps the most famous passage in the entire compendium, *Chandī Charitr Ukti Bilās* 231, Dasam Granth, p. 99 known today as Guru Gobind Singh's Prayer also appears at *Krishanavtār* 2489, Dasam, Granth, p. 570. I should note that Ashta points to such reproductions in order to support his thesis that these different works are all those of a single poet, a position with which I disagree. All this suggests is that the authors of one work may have been familiar with the words or the works of other poets.

180. I will expand upon a theme we find in Pashaura Singh, *The Guru Granth Sahib*, pp. 157–61.

181. All this suggests that at the very least Guru Gobind Singh was aware of the existence of these many works and gave their authors his approval. At the most, however (assuming that the tenth Master was not the actual author of these verses), it seems that the poets would have within reason tailored their compositions to reflect both the general and newer literary trends of the period and the tastes of their patron. The tenth Guru then may not have authored these texts, but it is likely that he did authorize them. If this is indeed the case then it is perhaps appropriate to opine that the tenth Guru may have incorporated these works into the text in a way which mirrors Guru Arjan's inclusion of the Bhagat Bani into the Adi Granth. For musical measures of Brajbhasha connected with dance see Rupert Snell, 'Metrical Forms in Braj Bhāshā Verse: The *Caurāsī pada* in Performance', in Monika Thiel-Horstmann (ed.), *Bhakti in Current Research 1979–1982* (Berlin: Dietrich Reimer Verlag, 1983), pp. 353–83. It is worth noting that ragas which are often used in dance such as *sār* are absent from today's Dasam Granth which may have to do with the nature of dance and dancers in Indo-

192 The Darbar of the Sikh Gurus

Persian courtly culture. For understandings of dance with which the tenth Guru was most likely familiar see Katherine Brown, 'Masculinity and Eroticism in the Mughal *mehfil*', pp. 74–5. It is worth recalling that Brajbhasha could be read ambiguously as describing both the love of the divine and a lover's mundane affection for the beloved. The true rasika however would easily see through such ambiguities. Francesca Orsini, 'Introduction', in Francesca Orsini (ed.), *Love in South Asia: A Cultural History*, p. 27.
182. Meisami, *Medieval Persian Court Poetry*, p. 8, n. 18 commenting upon M.M. Badawi, 'From Primary to Secondary Qasīdas: Thoughts on the Development of Classical Arabic Poetry', in the *Journal of Arabic Literature* 9 (1980), pp. 1–31.
183. Statements to this effect appear constantly within the Dasam Granth. Representative examples appear at *Rāmavtār* 698, 832; *Naravtār* 4; *Pakhyān Charitr* 404:20, 23, 247, Dasam Granth, pp. 243, 252, 570, 1360, 1361, 1377. The bulk of the text was of paramount concern in the eighteenth century as Sikhs, Khalsa Sikhs in particular, were generally forced to be rather mobile.
184. The manuscript of the *Pakhyān Charitr* noted above is Panjab University, Chandigarh ms. 783. Its colophon claims that it is *tarkash kī pothī* (quiver pothi). The text came to my attention in J.S. Deol's 'Eighteenth Century Khalsa Identity', p. 31.
185. Also see for the performative nature of the *Rāmcharitramānas*, Philip Lutgendorf, *The Life of a Text: Performing the* Rāmcaritmānas *of Tulsidas* (Berkeley: University of California Press, 1991). Also Rao, Shulman, and Subramanyam, *Textures of Time*, p. 5: 'Readers or listeners at home in a culture have a natural sensitivity to texture. They know when the past is being treated in a factual manner. Signals and markers of many subtle kinds and qualities abound in every text…' Certain traditions associated with Guru Gobind Singh also claim that the Guru was quite skilled in playing among other instruments the *mrdang* the hand drums all of which were used in such performances. See Gopal Singh, *A History of the Sikh People* (New Delhi: World Sikh University Press, 1979), p. 263. For mrdangs associated with dance see Bonnie Wade, *Imaging Sound*, p. 90.
186. Dharmpal Ashta, *The Poetry of the Dasam Granth*, pp. 54–6; 132. The latter notes for example:
   Tradition says that the *Chandi di Var* came to be recited later on in diwans or special congregations after the custom of the Guru's own court.
187. Who is likewise lauded in The *Mahimā Prakāsh* of Sarup Das Bhalla. See *MP* II, chapter 5. Also Pashaura Singh, *Life and Work of Guru Arjan*, p. 77.
188. Incidentally the context of this certain charitr is not satirical or ironic. *Pakhyān Charitr* 195:21, Dasam Granth, p. 1087. This is not the only such praise of Aurangzeb we find in the Dasam Granth. There is indirect praise of Indo-Timurid rule (and thus of Aurangzeb) in the *Bachitar Nātak* [13:9, Dasam Granth, p. 71] as well as a number of baits which speak of the

emperor in a very positive light in the *Zafar-nāmah* [baits 89–94, Dasam Granth, p. 1393] although to be sure in this last example the positive light is later extinguished by negative references.
189. I draw here upon Allison Busch's 'Literary Responses to Mughal Imperium', which examines the historical dimensions of Brajbhasha courtly literature: Such shows, she claims, that 'Mughal rule had become fully routinized and was entirely comprehensible within the traditional Sanskritic[/Brajbhashic] episteme of Hindu dharma and kinghip' (p. 47).
190. *Pakhyān Charitr* 262, 373, 404:376–401, Dasam Granth, pp. 1200, 1328–30; 1386–8. The final reference is popularly known as the *Benatī Chaupaī* (supplication in the four-stanza metre) and is included in the liturgical *sodhar rahirās*, the evening prayer. See W.H. McLeod (ed. and trans.), *Textual Sources for the Study of Sikhism* (Manchester: Manchester University Press, 1984), pp. 99–100.
191. See particularly the chapter entitled, 'The Laughter of Kali', in Lee Seigel, *Laughing Matters: Comic Tradition in India* (New Delhi: Motilal Banarsidass, 1987), pp. 94–186. With only slight modifications we are able to read many of the erotic tales of the *Pakhyān Chairtr* with Seigel's comments about Sanskrit satire well in mind (p. 101):
...there are two kinds of erotic satire in Sanskrit literature: one is good humored and gentle as it laughs without condemnation at lovers, at their affectations as folly; the other is bad tempered and acerbic as it laughs scornfully and cynically at lovers, at their affectations as vice.
192. And so compare *Rāmavtār* 706–7, Dasam Granth, p. 244:
He is the Lord, unborn. Invincible and beyond birth, he absorbs all things into himself (*atā*), never takes, and is unconquerable.
with *Rāmavtār* 834–5, Dasam Granth, p. 252:
Rama ruled over Audh-pur (Ayodhya) for ten thousand and ten years. And then death approached (*niarāī*). Even over the head of Raghubar (Rama) the drum of death (*mrit tank*) was sounded. I bow before the mighty Kal (i.e. Akal Purakh) which conquers all and has all within its control. It beats its drum over everyone's head. Neither kings nor beggars have the ability to conquer it.
Also see *Rāmavtār* 863–4, Dasam Granth, p. 254 the last two stanzas which firmly punctuate this latter line of thought.
193. *BSVN* 10:389, p. 161.
194. David R. Kinsley, *The Divine Player: A Study of Krsna Līlā* (Delhi: Motilal Banarsidass, 1979). Particularly intriguing in the context of the Dasam Granth are Kinsley's ideas regarding the act of combat as a form of divine play (pp. 49–55). Alf Hiltebeitel's interpretation differs slightly but with the same ultimate effect in that he sees the combat in which Krishna is involved as a grand sacrifice (also in some cases understood as līlā). Alf Hiltebeitel, *The Ritual of Battle: Krishna in the Mahābhārata* (Albany: State University of New York Press, 1990).

194   The Darbar of the Sikh Gurus

195. *Krishanavtār* 395, Dasam Granth, p. 305. The divine and play is alluded to in *Jāp* 81, Dasam Granth, p. 5:
    You are one image visible in many, manifest in any number of forms. After the wondrous play of creation and destruction marked by the end of this play all such forms again merge into the one.
    We also find such understandings within the Adi Granth. Guru Arjan notes in his *Bāvan Akhrī* (Guru Arjan, *Gaurī Bāvan Akhrī* 1(1), Adi Granth, p. 250) for example that
    O Nanak, his wondrous sport cannot be fathomed.
    Līlā is also used in both the Adi Granth and Dasam Granth in other senses: a theatrical performance, a participatory performance (*Rāmlīlā* for example), sacrifice, and for a narrative. The works of the Guru's court poets likewise use līlā and khel/khed in similar ways. See Sainapati's *Gur-sobhā* 2:7 and 2:8. In the latter we are told that after the Guru went to Paunta:
    There [at Paunta Sahib the Guru] engaged in many varieties of sport.
    Ganda Singh (ed.), *Srī Gur-sobhā* 2:8, p. 69. As we will note this passage references *Bachitar Nātak* 8:1–3, Dasam Granth, p. 60.
196. Ms. 91 (s), Guru Nanak Dev University Library, folio 163b.
197. For the rasas and transformation see Edwin Gerow, *Indian Poetics*, pp. 250–1. I believe his statements in this regard are worth quoting:
    ...the expressive goal...of verbal art is often not the same thing as the expressive content of the words and sentences employed. In effect, the meticulous analyses of poetic utterance and poetic imagination that were the business of the *alamkāra* school seemed to come to precisely this conclusion: insofar as utterance can be considered 'poetic', ... it must involve, as an essential element, some such detour in the usual or normal apprehension process—a *vakrokti*: an understanding that the refined mind grasps as a result of the word heard or read, but not directly by means of it.
    Also see Susan Schwartz, *Rasa: Performing the Divine in India* (New York: Columbia University Press, 2004), pp. 1–20.
198. The disturbances of the 1980s and 1990s in the Punjab saw a number of Punjabi militants transformed through dhadhi sangit. Here we have works which clearly fit the paradigm put forward by Schulman *et al.*, *Textures of Time*. For dhadhis and the Punjab crisis of the late 1980s and early 1990s see Joyce Pettigrew, 'Songs of the Sikh Resistance Movement', in *Asian Music* (Fall/Winter 1991–2). The aim of the Javaddi Taksal just on the outskirts of Ludhiana is to preserve and perform the classical styles of kirtan.
199. See *Pakhyān Charitr* 25:9, Dasam Granth, p. 848 in which the rani Prem Kumari patronizes Muslim minstrels (*dom*), bhatts, and dhadhis. Also *Rāmavtār* 42, Dasam Granth, p. 191 offers a description of King Dasaratha's court in the context of the performance of the kingly ritual, the *rājasūya*:
    [The king] summoned the rulers (*naresh*) of many countries. Many brahmans who all donned different apparel (i.e., belonged to different

Spirit and Structure 195

sampradayas) also arrived. The king [first] honoured them all within his court (dīvān) in [the] different ways [prescribed by courtly precedent] and then the ritual of kingship began.

Further descriptions appear at *Rāmavtār* 175–6, Dasam Granth, pp. 201–2. Also described is the court of Ravana at *Rāmavtār* 377, Dasam Granth, p. 219.

200. *Krishanavtār* 21, Dasam Granth, pp. 256–7 claims that on the occasion of the marriage of Vasudeva to Devaki:

Bards, artists, and singers all received rewards for singing many songs of praise [in their] honour (jasu).

Also *Pakhyān Charitr* 84:1, Dasam Granth, p. 919:

In kingdom of Maharashtra [lived] its king [known as] the Protector of the Great State. To both poets and talented men he generously (*bhāv*) distributed wealth (*darbu*).

201. The description of Raja Aj's court and kingdom is Vyasa's eighth narrative regarding the great kings of the world (the others are Manu, Prithu, Sagar, Benu, Mandhata, Dalip, and Raghu). See the *Panchmo [A]vtār Brahmā Biās Rājā Aj* 8–42, Dasam Granth, pp. 627–9. Also *Bachitar Nātak* 2:20, Dasam Granth, p. 48.

202. Such use permeates the Dasam Granth. See *Akāl Ustati* 253; *Bachitar Nātak* 1:42; *Vār Srī Bhagautī jī kī* 3; *Giān Prabodh* 42, and *Pakhyān Charitr* 297:92, Dasam Granth, pp. 35, 42, 119, 132, and 1251 amongst many others. *Akāl Ustati* 119, Dasam Granth, p. 22 may be given here by way of example:

[You are] sometimes [present] in the youth dressed in fine skins and sometimes in [the king who] sits under a canopy (chhatrdhāri).

203. *Giān Prabodh* 283, Dasam Granth, p. 151.

204. Daud Ali, *Courtly Culture and Political Life in Early Medieval India* (Cambridge: Cambridge University Press, 2004), pp. 18–19.

205. The competitiveness of fifteenth and sixteenth-century Timurid courts is the topic of Maria Subtelny's, 'The Poetic Circle at the Court of the Timurid'.

206. For example we hear specific references to the stories of Mirza Sahiban (charitr 129), Nala Damayanti (charitr 157), and Hir Ranjha (charitr 309) amongst others. See Dharampal Ashta, *The Poetry of the Dasam Granth*, pp. 150–2, 223.

207. It seems that Guru Gobind Singh very quickly patched things up between himself and the still living Ram Rai who resided only 30 miles away from Paunta Sahib. Grewal and Bal, *Guru Gobind Singh*, p. 72.

208. *Bachitar Nātak* 9, 11:8, Dasam Granth, pp. 62–4; 66. Courtly poetry, especially the many vārs and jang-nāmās of the Guru's darbar, also reference Bhim Chand. See the anonymous *Vār Srī Gurū Gobind Singh jī kī Arthāt Jang-nāmā Bhangānī* 17 in Shamsher Singh Ashok (ed.), *Prāchīn Vārān te Jangnāme*, p. 8.

209. In his own hand the tenth Guru writes:

Take a horserider and come, most certainly come and on you will fall our profound thanks (*bhārī mehrvangi*).

While his scribe emphasizes the request a few lines down:
Come promptly into our presence. My house is yours. Quickly (*sitabi*) read this request and come.
Ganda Singh (ed.), *Hukamnāme*, pp. 146–7.
210. Grewal and Bal, *Guru Gobind Singh*, p. 71.
211. Gurbachan Singh Talib, after Indubhusan Bannerjee, notes that this text does not follow the general styles and tones of Mughal diplomatic correspondence. As such, he continues, it is unlikely that it was actually sent to and received by Aurangzeb as strong Sikh traditions claim over and again. Gurbachan Singh Talib, 'The Zafar-Namah', in Prakash Singh (ed.), *The Saint Warrior Guru Gobind Singh* (Amritsar: Khalsa College, 1967), pp. 33–8, and Indubhusan Bannerjee, *Evolution of the Khalsa* II (3rd edn., Calcutta: AMC, 1972), p. 143. I would disagree on this point for the simple reason that the format and tone of the *Zafar-nāmah* are exactly what would have made the missive stand out from ordinary correspondence. We first hear of the Guru's petition to Aurangzeb in Sainapati's *Gur-sobhā* 13:10–51, pp. 133–40 who simply refers to it as a letter (*likhā*). Here it is entrusted to one Bhai Daya Singh alone who spends many months carrying it to the emperor (Bhai Dharam Singh who is meant to have accompanied him after he had reached Agra is not introduced into the narrative until the early nineteenth century, first appearing it seems in sakhi 28 of the *Sau Sakhian*: G.S. Naiar (ed.), *Gur-ratan Māl: Sau Sākhī*, pp. 42–3). It is not known whether this is the work we today know as the *Zafar-nāmah*. The next Sikh text to mention this petition is the *MPV* of the 1740s which does in fact refer to it as the *Zafar-nāmah* and ascribes to it a magical function as we note in the allusion below:

[The young Guru] then commanded the Khalsa, 'Go, battle the Turks and slay them.' The Khalsa then replied, 'O true king, the emperor has along with the Turk [footsoldiers themselves] ten lakhs of cavalry. We will however obey your order.' The Guru replied, 'Good, assistance will come in this way: a letter [will be] written to the [emperor of the] Turks [which when read] will kill him.' The Khalsa then said, 'O true king, if the emperor will be die in this way tremendous praise will ensue.' The Guru Baba then wrote the letter and titled it *Zafar-nāmā*, the Epistle of Victory.

This may seem conclusive proof but it is not. Although the first few lines of Bhalla's text of the *Zafar-nāmah* (pp. 177–8) capture the spirit of those in today's version our author claims that the text has both *rubā'iyāt* and other verses which he 'accurately reproduces'—and indeed he does supply a Persian *rubā'ī* from it. Unfortunately today's version of the text is made up of baits alone. *MPV* 126, pp. 177–81. The *MP* II 26, pp. 886-90 also mentions the Guru's '*arz da<u>sh</u>t* but titles it the *Shauq-nāmā* (Text of Wants):

The True Guru told Daya Singh that he must go to the emperor: 'Please take give him my formal appeal (shauq-nāmā) and return with an answer.'

Sarup Das Bhalla's account likewise has the emperor die very soon after reading the text though he claims this is principally because of remorse for his past misdeeds (*MP* II 26:25, p. 890):

The emperor felt a terrible remorse.

Kesar Singh Chhibbar's version, *BSVN* 10:587–604, pp. 180–2, in which Bhai Daya Singh in order to get the Guru's petition to Aurangzeb disguises himself as a Hajji carrying a Qur'an, also notes that Aurangzeb dies forty days after he reads the *Zafar-nāmah* and speaks to Daya Singh (line 604).

212. The Guru's inclusion of poets and litterateurs who prepared pingals and various other texts dealing with 'grammaticality' in Brajbhasha (no such were written in Persian in the Guru's darbar) may reflect the same discursive features of language and power, that is to say similar mechanist foundations, as noted in Pollock's study of kings, language, and power in the Sanskrit Cosmopolis. See Sheldon Pollock, *The Language of the Gods in the World of Men*, pp. 165–6 esp. (though with the obvious caveat that Brajbhasha learning did not become 'an essential component of power' as did Sanskrit).

213. *Bachitar Nātak* 8:1–3, Dasam Granth, p. 60.
214. Grewal and Bal, *Guru Gobind Singh*, p. 71.
215. Ann Lambton, 'Justice in the Medieval Persian Theory of Kingship', in *Studia Islamica* 17 (1962), pp. 91–119; see also Linda Darling, 'Middle Eastern Advice for Indian Muslim Rulers', pp. 3–19.
216. *Bachitar Nātak* 6:32, Dasam Granth, p. 57. For kingship in Hindu traditions see Doniger and Smith (eds. and trans.), *The Laws of Manu* 7, pp. 128–51 and C.J. Fuller, *The Camphor Flame: Popular Hinduism and Society in India* (Princeton: Princeton University Press, 1992), pp. 102–27.
217. Ann K.S. Lambton, *State and Government in Medieval Islam* (New York: Oxford University Press, 1981) and Richard Eaton, *The Rise of Islam and the Bengal Frontier, 1204–1760* (Delhi: Oxford University Press, 1994), p. 30.
218. Guru Arjan, *Rāg āsā* 2(5), Adi Granth, p. 371.
219. The role of kirtan in the Sikh tradition is a particularly important one in communicating the divine message. Gurinder Singh Mann, *The Making of Sikh Scripture*, pp. 87–8.
220. Pashaura Singh, *The Guru Granth Sahib*, p. 222. Although it is likely that scribes and devotees surrounding the young Guru may have requested his permission to do such.
221. According to Gurinder Singh Mann the final rag structure of the current Adi Granth was firmly in place by the 1680s. Mann, *The Making of Sikh Scripture*, p. 86. The Rag organization of the Adi Granth is the subject of chapter four of Pashaura Singh, *The Guru Granth Sahib*, pp. 50.
222. Guru Arjan, *Gaurī Guārerī* 2–3(81), Adi Granth, p. 179.
223. Pashaura Singh, *The Guru Granth Sahib*, pp. 103–4.

224. For Guru Amar Das modelling his hymns upon those of Guru Nanak see Pashaura Singh, *The Guru Granth Sahib*, pp. 157–61. Note particularly the comments on page 126:

...Guru Nanak's successors drew inspiration from his bani and added their own compositions to the evolving corpus of Sikh scriptural tradition. Thus they reinterpreted the message of Guru Nanak in new contexts and laid the foundation for its living survival.

Guru Nanak one may argue also involved himself in poetic conversations which Guru Arjan retained for posterity in the Adi Granth. See, for example, the first Master's comments upon the bani of Shaikh Farid as noted in Pashaura Singh, *The Bhagats of the Guru Granth Sahib: Sikh Self-definition and the Bhagat Bani* (New Delhi: Oxford University Press, 2003), pp. 54, 58. For the Timurid example of poetic conversations between present poets and past masters and amongst contemporary poets as well, see Paul E. Losensky, *Welcoming Fighānī: Imitations and Poetic Individuality in the Safavid-Mughal Ghazal* (Costa Mesa: Mazda Publishers, 1998).

225. Padam, *Darbārī Ratan*, pp. 179 ff. Also see John Stratton Hawley's 'Mirabai at the Court of Guru Gobind Singh.' Typescript of a paper presented at the conference of the European Association of South Asian Studies, Leiden, June 2006. I would like to thank Professor Hawley for sharing his paper with me. Poets within the *Prem Abodh* whose hymns are also included within the Adi Granth are Kabir, Dhanna, Trilochan, Namdev, Jaidev, Ravidas, Pipa, Sain, and Sadhana. Poets not included within the Sikh scripture are Mira Bai, Karam Bai, Balmik, Sudhev, Badhak, Dhruhi, and Prahlad. Two late seventeenth-century manuscript copies of the *Prem Abodh* are ms. 810 at the Guru Nanak Dev University Library and ms. 1737 within the research library at Khalsa College. For the bhagats of the Adi Granth see Pashaura Singh, *The Bhagats of the Guru Granth Sahib*.

226. Piara Singh Padam notes that those who claim that Guru Gobind Singh wrote this text are simply incorrect. Rather, he states, in sammat 1750 (1693 CE) that Hari Das wrote the *Prem Abodh*

in which the beloved stories of sixteen bhagats are presented. For this reason alone the text is called *Parchīān Bhagatān kīān* (Stories of the Saints) and also thought of [by this title].

Padam, *Darbārī Ratan*, p. 179. After having taken initiation into the Khalsa Padam continues, Bhai Hari Das was killed at Chamkaur.

227. Devinder Singh Usahan, *Prem Abodh Pothī* as noted in Hawley, 'Mirabai,' pp. 6–7.

5

In the Tenth Master's Court
Bhai Nand Lal Goya[1]

ਨੰਦ ਲਾਲ ਜੀ ਸਭ ਸਿਖਨ ਮੈ ਚੰਦ ।[2]

For all the Sikhs Nand Lal [shines like] the moon.

We have thus far referred to the compositions of a number of poets within the Guru's darbar, including those that are included in today's Dasam Granth. One would assume that some of this poetry, particularly those compositions which are commensurate with the theology of the Adi Granth and which eulogize the tenth Guru and his court, would be generally acceptable to the Sikh Panth at large. Yet, apart from certain portions of the Dasam Granth none of this poetry is well known or even recited.

Perhaps this state of affairs may be explained by noting both the scattered nature of the compositions of the Guru's courtly jewels and the controversial nature of at least some of their selections. These contentious collections, particularly the 'reformulations' of the great epics are, like the charitr portions of the Dasam Granth, often regarded as Hindu by Sikhs today. Indeed, as we have noted many of the praises of the tenth Guru, apart from those written by the poets of the 'Lakkhi Jungle Darbar,' often occur at the beginning or the end of such refinements into Brajbhasha of the Sanskrit original. It appears, moreover, that there is at least one instance when a poet of the tenth Master's darbar has included sustained praise of a Hindu bhagat whose poetry was expunged from the Adi Granth apparently by Guru Arjan himself.[3] This is the Rajasthani princess Mira Bai, whose atypical hagiography is included in Khalsa College manuscript ms. 1737A which is a 1693 manuscript copy of the *Prem Abodh* wrongly attributed to Guru Gobind Singh.[4] Whatever the case for this neglect may be, it is ironic that the best known of this courtly poetry is that of a poet whom we have yet to seriously discuss, Bhai Nand Lal Goya.

The irony lies not in the absence of discussion but rather in the fact that although best known, these compositions are by no means the best understood. What makes this Sikh poetry especially conspicuous is the fact that it is not in Brajbhasha, the *lingua franca* of the seventeenth and eighteenth-century Punjab. It is, surprisingly, in classical Persian. Since it is in classical Persian it tends not to manifest that sentiment for which the poetry of the Guru's darbar is today best known, vīra-ras. Yet it became popular by the early to mid-eighteenth century, despite the poetry's general incoherence to contemporary Sikhs. Unlike any of the Guru's other courtly poets, Nand Lal's name not only appears regularly throughout the Sikh records of this period and beyond, at times emerging in singular contexts with which one would not necessarily associate the name of a poet of the tenth Master,[5] but eighteenth- and nineteenth-century manuscripts of what would become his two most famous compositions abound with some frequency. As a result therefore, as early as the mid-nineteenth century (and perhaps earlier) we hear of his poetry as bani, sacred utterance, a very rare distinction in the Sikh tradition (unique when we consider the language in which it is written) which today is shared by the poetry of only one other Sikh, the disciple and amanuensis of Guru Arjan, Bhai Gurdas Bhalla whose Punjabi vars are often referred to as the key to the Guru Granth Sahib.[6]

Although there are the stray references to the poetry of Nand Lal's fellow poets as bani[7] perhaps suggesting a similar status, Nand Lal's works are the only ones to have been formally designated as such by the mid-twentieth century Sikh authorities who prepared the contemporary Khalsa Sikh Code of Conduct, the *Sikh Rahit Maryādā*. Why this poetry was selected as sacrosanct, as it was not readily intelligible to the majority of Sikhs (as is still the case today) is an intriguing puzzle. For the Sikh scholars of the SGPC who drafted the code of conduct, the selection may have simply been due to the *pra-shāsti*-like or eulogizing quality of Nand Lal's poetry whose praise of the tenth Master, especially in the tenth chapter of his *Ganj-nāmah*, soars to dizzying heights but if this was the case why did they then pass over the easily understood poetry of poets such as Alam or Ani Rai which likewise praises the tenth Master and Akal Purakh? We shall, as the final section of this chapter, suggest potential answers to this riddle. In the meantime, let us turn our attention to the traditions, writings, and narratives of this most esteemed Indo-Persian poet of the tenth Guru. An examination of these sheds an even brighter light on both the darbar of Guru Gobind Singh and upon the tenth Master himself.

THE INTERROGATOR

Let us begin this record not with the narrative of Nand Lal's life which is first formally enunciated as far as I know in the late eighteenth-century *Mahimā Prakāsh Kavita* of Sarup Das Bhalla and to which we shall turn momentarily, but with the sheer number of eighteenth and early to mid-nineteenth century manuscripts, the earliest of which we can date to 1719 CE, in which Nand Lal emerges as a figure of reverence and veneration.[8] In many of these, our poet appears as the same kind of jack-of-all-trades as we shall notice in the contemporary narratives of his life. While in these more itihāsik sources, which include late nineteenth- and early twentieth-century texts which draw upon both the gur-bilas and bansavali literature as well as the testimony of Nand Lal's early twentieth-century descendants, Nand Lal is shown as scribe, poet, soldier, deputy governor, puzzle solver, emissary, Quranic scholar, and finally Sikh devotee par excellence, in other texts we discover Nand Lal constantly questioning the tenth Guru about certain facets of the universe and of Sikh discipline and belief as in the many versions of the three rahit-namas attributed to him and in the *Gurpādhantī* noted above.[9] In others he is conversing with the tenth Master about subjects as wide-ranging as the Bhagavad-Gita,[10] magical and curative hymns from the Adi Granth, and the benefits accrued from 'broken' (literally, 'ordinary' or *sādhāran*) and unbroken (*akhand*) readings (*pāth*) of the text;[11] we also find the two discussing the nature of the Kaliyug, the Age of Darkness. Let us reproduce the opening of this conversation about the ultimate age of degeneracy as representative of such texts in which we find a questioning Nand Lal. Nand Lal typically begins by invoking the majesty of the Guru,

O true King, you are the Lord of the three realms who sees the past and knows the future and the present. O True King please [tell us] as follows what will be the pattern of living (*vartārā*) [during the Age of Degeneracy]?

to which Guru Gobind Singh responds:

O Bhai Nand Lal ji, the standard of conduct which [is generally observed] during the Kaliyug cannot be explained completely I will [therefore] offer a summary. This [summary] will be dictated as follows: In this period fathers and sons and sons and fathers together will oppose each other. So too will wives and husbands and husbands and wives, and brother and brother. All of these relatives will plot against one another. Their desires will be profoundly changed to greed for money. And for the sake of [fulfilling such] desires people will regularly perform sinful acts [in the Kaliyug]. And other sins too such as those of lust will increase [dramatically]. For the sake of such desires pride (*dimbhu*) will know no limits. Such pride will regularly culminate in people who will call themselves gurus. They will tell many falsehoods and so too engage in pointless discussions [which distract and lead one astray].[12]

The discussion of the Kaliyug continues with regard to the false gurus and their grandiose statements and then takes us into a conversation about the style of true devotion and the nature of the genuine devotee (*shakta*).

This theme of true as opposed to false devotion is predominant in Nand Lal's manuscript record under discussion and indeed is also the subject of a number of his Persian baits.[13] In what appears to be a lengthy rahit-nama titled *Sākhī Bhāī Nand lāl jī* and which is found in manuscript 91 at Guru Nanak Dev University the tenth Guru and Nand Lal initially discuss the nature of true devotion:

Know that the Sikh is the *paramhans* (supreme ascetic) who takes refuge with the True Guru. Nand Lal ji know that true joy (*rat*) [is found both in] the nām and at the feet of the Guru. Apart from the Guru know that [all] others and the world is both delusion and deceit [and both should thus be] abandoned. Truth, contentment and bliss are found by lovingly attaching oneself to the feet of the Guru. Nand Lal the Name, just like the feet of the True Guru, brings joy and removes both delusion and doubt [from the entire world]. Know that the True Guru is true. They love him who centre the heart in the lotus feet of the Guru and fix it there. Having seen the True Guru, the pure

Brahman, the concern for loving devotion becomes evident within the heart and he is perfected from the heart. He becomes *jivan-mukt* and plays in the world seeing that the difference between the lotus and the water is simply *māyā* [or cosmic delusion] once again.[14]

We discover more such in eighteenth- and nineteenth-century Sikh works, for example, those in which Nand Lal appears as the Guru's emissary sent to deal with the questions and concerns of brahmans irate at the creation of the Khalsa. Sakhi 161 of the nineteenth-century *Sikhān dī Bhagat-mālā* (The Devotee Garland of the Sikhs) attributed to Bhai Mani Singh for example addresses the concerns of these brahmans and includes within this discussion the Sikh vision of the true brahman:

Bhai Nand Lal replied, 'The [true] brahman will be one who possesses contentment, spiritual knowledge, and a virtuous nature. It is this type of brahman who is worthy of worship. It is said [by Guru Nanak in the Adi Granth] that "He is the type of brahman who tears away the fetters and achieves liberation: this brahman is precious." It is [further] claimed that, "Having torn away the bonds and procured salvation this brahman is worthy of veneration." He is the one who takes the knife of knowledge and rips through the restraints of ignorance. He is indeed worthy of admiration. One must venerate and bequeath to this brahman food (*an*), water (*jal*), and clothing (*bastr*). Only such a brahman has the right to be worshipped.[15]

Here it appears that Nand Lal often employs the very same reasoning that we find the Gurus utilizing in the Adi Granth and within the eighteenth-century rahit-namas. We will note this again in sakhi 163 which includes a discussion regarding the fourfold classifications of varna and ashrama or caste and the stages of life, which once again touches upon the notions of the counterfeit versus the genuine:

The brahmans then questioned [Nand Lal]. 'There are four varnas just as it says in the Puranas. There are also four stages of life. Do the Sikhs also possess a varnashrama classification or not?'

[Bhai Nand Lal] replied, 'In living a married life [Sikhs] possess all of the varnas and ashramas. But in reality (*vastav*) they possess neither varnas nor ashramas.'

After he so explained they spoke, 'Tell us then: if there is a varnashrama [amongst the Sikhs] how is it followed and how is it not followed?'

Bhai Nand Lal said, 'He is a [true] Brahman who practices [meditating upon] the shabad throughout the eight watches of the day. He is a [true]

Khshatriya who picks up the sword and other weapons. He is a [true] Vaishya who tills the land (*bapar kheti* 'engage in agriculture'). And he [alone] is [truly] Shudra who opposes and slanders others. These are the four varnas.'

[He continued,] 'How [you ask] are the four ashramas observed? He is a [true] brahmacharya who contemplates the shabad and eats little. He is a [true] householder who serves the Sikhs of a household selflessly along with his wife and sons. He who performs penances is a [true] forest dweller. And he who possesses mystical knowledge is a [true] world renouncer.'[16]

The style of narrative here is indeed quite reminiscent of the hymns of Guru Nanak in which the first Guru contrasts the physical with the sentiment it is meant to manifest (i.e., *mihr masīti sidaku musālā haqqu halālu korānu* 'make mercy your mosque, faith your prayer mat, and righteousness your Qur'an')[17] and the vars of Bhai Gurdas, and may play upon a symmetry between the first Guru and Nand Lal which often occurs in retellings of the standard Nand Lal narrative, beginning in the late eighteenth century. Nand Lal it seems is progressing well beyond his capacity as a mere poet of the tenth Guru's darbar into a truly remarkable Sikh devotee; into a true and sincere representative of the tenth Guru's darbar. Indeed, in one nineteenth-century text Nand Lal assumes the intimate position of the Guru's courtly boon companion.

In another of the many conversations held between the poet and his master, recorded in what appears to be a mid to late eighteenth-century manuscript copy of the *Prashan-uttar* (Question and Answer) attributed to our poet, Nand Lal asks the Guru about the forms in which the pious Sikh will be able to perceive the Guru after the tenth Guru has died.[18] This is, to be sure a conversation we also find in the many printed editions of the *Prashan-uttar* text[19] but our copy is it seems unique in that it contains a variant reading which is particularly significant in the context of the Guru's poetic darbar. We pick up the conversation just after Nand Lal and the Guru have discussed the nature of the true devotee as opposed to the false one (*sachīā aru jhuthīā shaktā*):

'O true king everything is complete, [fashioned] from your own being. He who is without the True Guru cannot obtain such a place [by your side]. But, O true king, of such a kind are your Sikhs with firm faith that they are those rare persons (*virale*) who are cognisant of your [true] form. To which ever direction they turn their faces they recognise you. What is it they see and [who do they] serve selflessly (*tahal sevā*)?'

'O Bhai Nand Lal ji, listen [attentively] to the response to your enquiry. From the statement it is clear that he who is without the True Guru is not awakened. Where is that place where the Wonderful Lord is not? The True Guru is indeed seen residing everywhere, completely. Therefore turn towards this direction and hear the answer to your [first] query. He who turns his face [towards me] may see and understand me to reside in four places: The first is within the pages of the Granth Sahib ji; the second is within the true court (*darbār jī*); the third is within the Guru Khalsa; and finally the fourth is within Sri Bhagauti ji, the all-steel sword. A loyal Sikh who is firm in his faith and who is a disciple of the House of the Wonderful Guru (*vahigurū*) will not acknowledge any other person claiming himself to be Guru apart from these [four mentioned above].'[20]

Not only is the Guru Granth/Guru Khalsa doctrine enunciated and the importance of the sword clearly brought forth in a way reminiscent of the opening chapter of the *Bachitar Nātak*, but the equation between the Guru himself and the Guru's darbar is also made here, supporting our earlier contention that Guru Gobind Singh attempted, in crafting and bringing together his poetic darbar, to realize the grandeur of the Adi Granth which is also mystically the Guru's visible form. Indeed, if this list represents a hierarchy then for the author of manuscript 684, the Guru Darbar occupies a more prominent place than the Guru Khalsa.

Of course the term darbar here could be a metaphorical reference to either a Sikh dharamsala or gurdwara or indeed to the Guru Granth Sahib itself or any place that the scripture is kept,[21] but since the tenth Master addresses this response to a poet of that particular darbar, easily the most well known poet by the time this manuscript was prepared, it is likely that the reference is in fact to the collection of poets and scholars who surrounded Guru Gobind Singh. It appears therefore that there were some Sikhs during the eighteenth century who understood the Guru's court to manifest that same spirit which was believed to inhabit the Guru Granth Sahib: hearing the poetry produced here therefore may have been believed to possess that very same transformative character noted in the Adi Granth as early as *Srī Gur-sobhā*.[22] One may see here perhaps the first step in what will be the transformation of Nand Lal's poetry, from Sikh poetry to sacred utterance. Indeed, it is but a small step from making sacred the darbar to making sacred the poetic compositions of that darbar.

EIGHTEENTH AND NINETEENTH CENTURY SIKH SOURCES

To such inquiring manuscripts one must add the regular appearance of other eighteenth- and nineteenth-century texts containing Nand Lal's Persian works, particularly the *Divān-i Goyā* and *Zindagī-nāmah* the vast majority of which are in Gurmukhi script,[23] although one does find the rare *nastalīq* version, at least in India.[24] These Gurmukhi–Persian manuscripts merit consideration beyond their beautiful poetic content as these possess features which make it clear that Sikhs of the eighteenth and nineteenth century were familiar with both Nand Lal and his works as well as the poetic darbar of which he was quite a significant member and in which these compositions were prepared.[25] Firstly, just below the Gurmukhi–Persian text of manuscript 115123 located in Punjabi University, Brajbhasha translations of individual Persian words appear in both Devanagari and Gurmukhi scripts.[26] In light of the fact that most Sikhs of the eighteenth century did not understand the now-classical Persian of the Mughal court, one could assume that the translations of specific terms indicate that the texts were indeed read, heard, and more likely studied by pious Sikhs or others.[27] It may well be that Sikhs in this later period turned to Nand Lal and his poetry as models in much the same way as some would turn to the Adi Granth, Dasam Granth, and vars of Bhai Gurdas, references to all of which occur intermittently throughout the eighteenth-century rahit-namas. Kahn Singh of Nabha would effectively use Nand Lal's Persian poetry to this end in both his Rahit compendiums *Gurmat Sudhākar* and the posthumously published *Gurmat Mārtand*.[28] The second feature of these texts which seems to also emphasize this point is their size. Many manuscripts of the *Divān-i Goyā* and *Zindagī-nāmah* are small, compact, and gutka-like, signifying breviaries.[29] Size in this case does matter for a number of interrelated reasons: it generally allows us to date the manuscripts to the mid to late eighteenth century as this was the period in which Khalsa Sikhs were generally mobile and often carried with them their sacred literature. As these texts were most likely shuttled from place to place easily (and so their size), we may assume that these were, once again, read by literate Sikhs.

As the number of such manuscripts implies that the baits and ghazals of Nand Lal were circulating throughout the Punjab in the late eighteenth and early nineteenth century, it seems likely that these may well have been a part of the repertoire of the many travelling professional singers who used the hymns of the Gurus and other Sufis and Bhagats in congregational singing or kirtan.[30] That the majority of manuscripts are written in Gurmukhi, the script of the Adi Granth, Dasam Granth, and the vārān of Bhai Gurdas, supports such a contention highlighting in effect the oral nature of transmission in the Punjabi culture of this period.[31] The recitation of such works in Persian, moreover, would most certainly have required a giānī (traditional Sikh intellectual) or kathākār (exegete) to elucidate both the meaning of individual words and couplets as well as their 'subtle' or *paramārath* meaning to gathered Sikhs (and so the existence of ms. 115123). As the kathakar's discussion of scripture and poetry involved supporting his interpretation with, among other things, 'anecdotes from the lives of the Gurūs [sic],'[32] it seems likely that in the case of both Bhai Gurdas and Bhai Nand Lal, an itihās of their lives would have been required for a well-rounded exegesis of their more demanding poems.[33]

Although in light of the manuscript evidence presented above it is clear that Nand Lal was generally understood to be a beloved disciple of the tenth Guru by the Sikhs of the eighteenth century, it is not until the mid to late eighteenth century as Sikhs occupied Lahore and began to secure more and more territory that the first narratives of Nand Lal's life were written down. This coincides with claims made earlier about the first narratives of the Guru's court which appear at this rather chaotic period in the history of the Sikhs. These initial Nand Lal narratives begin in the year 1769 CE with Kesar Singh Chhibbar's well known *Bansāvalī-nāmā Dasān Patshāhīān kā*.[34] Nand Lal appears in both Kesar Singh's tenth and twelfth sections, the latter of which deals with Mata Sundari's adopted son Ajit Singh (d. 1725) and the various Khatri Nanak-panthi sangats around Delhi, many of whose members recognized Ajit Singh as the legitimate heir to the guruship.[35] The first section is the initial appearance of the now-famous story of Nand Lal's extraordinary erudition. It is lengthy and differs in one very substantial way from the commonly accepted story which we will encounter in a moment. Here we find that Bahadar Shah and not his father Aurangzeb is troubled by an interpretation of a Quranic ayat that is less than satisfying. It begins with Guru Gobind Singh querying Nand Lal:

> The Guru then asked, 'Munshi ji, how did you get the name "Master Speaker" (*Mullā Goyā*)?'

To this Nand Lal responds that such came his way when he interpreted a passage from the Qu'ran to the satisfaction of the emperor Bahadar Shah:

> I carefully expained it all to the emperor [to which] he then said, 'You are indeed a master speaker.' The emperor himself commanded: 'You are the preserver (hāfez) of truth, a Master Speaker.' Right there such a name fell to me and all have fixed upon me the title Munshi Mulla Goya.'[36]

The second reference, however, is brief, comprising a single quatrain or chaupaī, and refers to Bhai Nand Lal only in passing, but it is very significant nevertheless:

> And then [Kirpal Singh] the revered maternal uncle [of Guru Gobind Singh] implored the audience to hear the entire truth [about Ajit Singh and the divine curse which caused sons to rebel against their fathers. He narrated his tale] just as Nand Lal sang [ghazals] in the [royal] darbar. When Nand Lal, likewise, spoke to Bahadar Shah the emperor commanded that Bhai Nand Lal be called by the name 'Master Speaker'.[37]

Since the non-Khalsa Khatri Sikhs of Delhi and its regions accepted Ajit Singh (and later his son Hathi Singh) as guru, our Chhibbar author may be here reminding them of past Khatri Sikh loyalty to the line of legitimate Gurus by alluding to Bhai Nand Lal, who though in Mughal service for a time remained both a staunch Sikh and friend to Bahadar Shah until our poet's death sometime around the first decade of the eighteenth century. This was unlike Ajit Singh who broke all ties with Mata Sundari sometime around 1715 CE after having accepted robe(s) of honour from the emperor Bahadar Shah and his more hostile successor, Farrukh Siyyar (d. 1719 CE), who according to Sikh tradition put all Sikhs down mercilessly.[38]

But such conclusions notwithstanding, there are two particular points to note here. Firstly, this is the earliest reference in Sikh literature in which we find Nand Lal's name associated with the sobriquet 'Goya', a penname which Kesar Singh makes clear the emperor

Bahadar Shah himself had affixed. Such a gift no doubt added an enormous prestige to the figure and image of Nand Lal and thus merited reiteration in the much longer narrative of Sarup Das Bhalla seven years later.[39] Whether or not this is true, the association allows us to connect to Nand Lal at a relatively early date, the *Divān-i Goyā* and the *Zindagī-nāmah* in which this 'Goya' sobriquet appears frequently within the signature line. Secondly as early as 1769 there were Sikhs who were aware of Nand Lal's intimate connection to the Mughal darbar and of his service to the court of the Mughal prince and emperor.

This connection is a particularly significant one and marks Nand Lal as unique among the other poets of the Guru's darbar. Now we do hear of a small handful of seemingly similar Sikhs in the eleventh vār of Bhai Gurdas,[40] but even taking into consideration the brief narratives of their lives which we discover in the later *Sikhān dī Bhagat-mālā*, claiming that some of these Sikhs were initially employed by the Mughal army, none of these devotees have lives as relatively detailed in nineteenth-century sources as Nand Lal's. Also, none of these characters were as intimate with Mughal nobility as Sikh tradition claims of our poet.[41] Certainly a very small number of Anandpur poets were likewise earlier employed, for example, Sukhdev who was apparently in the service of Aurangzeb's vazir Nawab Fazil Ali Khan and Kavi Alam who, according to Piara Singh Padam left Prince Mu'azzam's service after the latter was jailed in 1687,[42] but their stories too are extremely brief. Very little may therefore be said about them, a point to which the silences in Sikh tradition bear ample testimony. The accounts of Nand Lal's life as the *munshī* and then *mīr munshī* or 'scribe' and 'principal scribe' of the future emperor Bahadar Shah, Prince Muhammad Mu'azzam (who was also known as Shah Alam, a title he was bequeathed by the emperor Aurangzeb in October 1676)[43] make him stand out from amongst all the poets of traditional Sikh history whose poetry does not appear in the Adi Granth.

What makes him even more so, despite the claim that other poets also left the Mughal court for the Anandpur darbar is the fact that Nand Lal's popular narrative extends back into his childhood. As far as I can recall the only other famous Sikh the account of whose youth is available, is Baba Buddha.[44] This is a point which is truly worthy of examination. Although the allusion in question may, like the story of the child Baba Buddha, be an early verification of Nand Lal's brilliance, wisdom, and piety I believe it has a structural importance which extends beyond the figure of Nand Lal himself.

If one were to demonstrate an intimate connection between Nand Lal and the Sikh Gurus, one in which Nand Lal is portrayed as a pious Sikh from a very early period in his life, here is how one would do it, from Sarup Das Bhalla's text of 1776 CE, the *Mahimā Prakāsh Kavitā*. Nand Lal first appears at the conclusion of the fourth sakhi of the tenth chapter. Here our Perso-Sikh poet is initially described in a very conventional way:

Through contact with the Philosopher's Stone iron turns into gold. A devotee is both agreeable and happy when he meets with the True Guru who looks upon him mercifully. At that moment the resplendent light of the divine shines in the heart. [Such contact ensures that one is] free from doubt, his heart and mind achieve *samādhi*, a condition of deep meditation, and from the great bewitching sleep he is awakened. Bhai Nand Lal was one such beloved.[45] [As Guru Nanak says of such devotees,] 'It is through the grace of the Lord, the one who bestows grace, O Nanak, that one becomes blessed.'[46]

As we may infer, that since Nand Lal was blessed by the True Guru we are to expect great things from him. This pre-eminence we recognize as we are treated to the birth and childhood of this most pious devotee:

Nand Lal was born into a Khatri family. He was born into a pious family and through his father's virtue he had obtained birth. [And so as his father was] a practitioner of the Vaishnavite tradition [so was he]. One day a Vaishnav guru came [to his residence]. Nand Lal became troubled at heart. Nand Lal was twelve years old [at that time], the year during which Nand Lal [became] beautiful, wise, and virtuous. His father said this [to him]: 'Our guru has just arrived (*āe he tāt*). Take his sacred necklace, son, and repeat the mantra of the [Vaishno] guru which is our mantra. Nand Lal ji spoke words of understanding which did not persuade nor please his father. 'The bani [of the Gurus', he said,] 'is the sacred thread which I utter from my mouth. I will speak [*rākhī*, "employ"] this and utter nothing else.' The Vaishnav guru summoned Nand Lal near to him [and said,] 'O son, take this sacred thread and venerate the idol.' Nand Lal pressed both of his palms together and said, 'The word which is amrit, O bhagat, is the delight of bliss, [the desire of all hearts]. The bani is called the [true] sacred thread. This should be spoken. This is the necklace you should put around [my] neck.' Hearing of this [particular] necklace the Vaishno guru became delighted (*magnānā*) and recognized [Nand Lal] as a self-accomplished child. [He thought that] this is the type of [necklace] which should be given to him since a necklace of wood does not carry one across the ocean of existence.[47] Twice [more] the Vaishnav guru came instantly to see Nand Lal, questioning him about clinging to the feet of the Guru. This is [ultimately] the necklace which Nand Lal was given.[48]

This early narrative is especially important for a structural reason: it is purposefully modelled along the same lines as a popular eighteenth-century janam-sakhi account of Guru Nanak, in which the first Master is about to be fitted with the sacred thread.[49] Although the report of Guru Nanak's investiture takes place after the Guru's ninth birthday rather than twelfth, both accounts provide their respective protagonists the opportunity to censure external rituals and verify the inward acceptance of the sacred utterances which communicate the divine name; ultimately both of these students become in effect the teacher.

Here therefore, Nand Lal conveys the same message that we have heard the first Master enunciate on numerous occasions in both the Adi Granth and his hagiographic narratives. A more subtle connection is implied, however, through which Sarup Das Bhalla and later Santokh Singh (whose own account of Nand Lal is profoundly indebted to Bhalla's) relate Nand Lal even more intimately to Guru Nanak, fortifying our poet's bond to the Sikh tradition on the one hand and indeed making him into the image of the first Master on the other. It is true that both Nand Lal and the first Guru are Khatris which perhaps explains the Khatri Sarup Das Bhalla's keen interest in our esteemed poet.[50] But Nand Lal like Guru Nanak, achieves his insight into the transcendent Lord and interior religion intuitively without the assistance of a guru or a yogi, a shaikh or a pir.

This I believe marks Nand Lal as a Sikh of exceptional character, a trait which may explain why the early twentieth-century Sikh poet and theologian Puran Singh eulogizes Nand Lal so eloquently in his poem, *addhī mītī akkh bhāī nand lāl jī dī*, 'The half-closed eyes of Bhai Nand Lal ji', emphasizing the more mystical inclinations of Bhai Nand Lal.[51] For Sarup Das Bhalla it seems only natural therefore that Nand Lal's innate ability to discern the truth would attract

Muslim disciples to him,[52] and would ultimately compel him to seek out Guru Gobind Singh at Anandpur. This he does very soon after having secured employment with Prince Mu'azzam;[53] he selflessly served the Guru and the Panth as a *sevādār*, especially within the langar under his charge, in a capacity which far exceeds that of the tenth Guru's other Sikhs.[54]

Since the *Prashan-uttar* attributed to Nand Lal also includes a discussion of selfless service, it is little surprise that our poet would perfectly embody this particular lesson conveyed to him by the tenth Guru.[55] Although Max Arthur Macauliffe fails to note the similarity between the two investiture narratives in his *Sikh Religion*, most of Santokh Singh's contemporaries would no doubt have done so.[56] Keeping this in view, it comes as no surprise to hear the narrator of ms. 1060(s) at Guru Nanak Dev University, the *Dhiāu Guhaj Ustat Dasam Shabad* (Secret Meditations which Praise the Word of the Tenth Master), which records a conversation between Guru Gobind Singh and Nand Lal in part about the Bhagavad-Gita, claim the following on the final folio of his text:

The True Guru advises one with this advice: praise Gobind! Remember Nand Lal ji, o my heart, and you will easily cross over the ocean of existence.[57]

Now with this in mind we turn to Nand Lal's intimate association with the Mughal court. How this is related to our discussion of Nand Lal's childhood above will become clear. Although there can be no doubt that Sikhs had had their differences with the Mughals during the seventeenth century, Mughal rule was nevertheless believed to be authenticated by Guru Nanak who, according to tradition, bestowed sovereignty upon Babur, a point to which we earlier made reference.[58] There is moreover tentative evidence to suggest that Guru Gobind Singh himself recognized and accepted the suzerainty of the Timurid line of which Aurangzeb was most certainly a part without embracing the person of the emperor himself. Perhaps this helps explains why the image of Aurangzeb is so much softer in Sarup Das Bhalla than in Santokh Singh.[59] For Ratan Singh Bhangu as I have shown in another context, the Mughals rejected Baba Nanak's gift by executing both Guru Arjan and Guru Tegh Bahadar. For Bhangu this refusal ultimately led to the Mughal downfall of the mid-eighteenth century.[60] Nand Lal who as we have implied is a symbolic representation of Guru

Nanak at the Mughal court is made to buttress this point. In order to understand the process at work here let me provide some background.

Sarup Das Bhalla's Nand Lal embodies those other qualities of the Mughals to which the Sikhs have been privy since Akbar's meeting with Guru Arjan in 1598: the munificent, erudite, and tolerant characteristics represented by the emperor Akbar and elucidated in the bani of Guru Nanak and his successors. Also, since the time of the first Persianite courts Persian poets had been trained with the cultivation of particular features in mind, qualities which were first summed up by the famous twelfth-/sixth-century Persian court poet and prosodist Nizami-i Aruzi-i Samarqandi:

> ...[the court poet] must be of a tender temperament, profound in thought, sound in genius, clear of vision, quick of insight. He must be well versed in many divers [sic] sciences, and quick to extract what is best from his environment; for as poetry is of advantage in every science, so is every science of advantage in poetry. And the poet must be of pleasing conversation in social gatherings, and of cheerful countenance in social gatherings, of cheerful countenance on festive occasions...[61]

It is likely that Sarup Das Bhalla describes Nand Lal with these in mind. We are told for example that

> Nand Lal performed two tasks simultaneously: he studied Persian and acquired knowledge thereby sharpening his mind. [Nand Lal] became a proficient scholar of Persian reading and memorising a large number of [Persian] books. He became privy through constant study and practice to the knowledge and etiquette required of the [royal] darbar. [Through such dedication] he became a renowned servant [of the court securing a post in the retinue] of the prince whom the world [later] called Bahadar Shah. He was appointed the Shah's *mir munshi* and his reputation increased day by day.[62]

What we see at this point therefore is a very rare Sikh who manifests that same insight of Guru Nanak, is an accomplished scholar of the various Islamic disciplines as well as an ideal Mughal scribe. Indeed, Nand Lal is made to combine here in one person, two of the most important offices which surround the king according to the *Chahār Muqālah*, or the Four Discourses, a very rare distinction indeed. For Sarup Das Bhalla therefore Nand Lal not only exceeds the relatively ordinary Sikh of the Guru but he is likewise a savant set apart from all other Islamicate scholars of note.[63]

But these expertise are not enough for the author of the *Mahimā Prakāsh*. Sarup Das goes a step further to ensure that his readers and listeners know beyond doubt that Nand Lal is indeed the full moon of the Mughal court. Here we have one of the earliest references to the famous story in which Nand Lal is the only scholar in the entire assembly of Aurangzeb's very learned maulanas who can interpret an āyat (literally, 'a [miraculous] sign', a single verse of the Qur'an) to the satisfaction of the emperor.[64] This story provides an interesting twist to a familiar theme we discover in the janam-sakhis, a theme which Hew McLeod titles Guru Nanak's 'Triumph over Islam' and whose standard pattern shows Guru Nanak defeating both in debate and through a display of miracles various Muslim religious personnel.[65] Nand Lal too triumphs over these personnel: not through miracles or an elucidation of Sikh doctrine but rather (or so we are led to infer) through Islamic understandings themselves refracted through the personality, erudition, and wisdom of Nand Lal.

What makes this story so captivating is that Persian poets and erudite courtiers in the emperor's entourage did at times present their patron with commentaries on verses found in the Qur'an.[66] It is true as well that in a letter written in 1693, Aurangzeb does demonstrate a degree of impatience over the inability of his religious personnel and advisors to decipher both a hadith and the 101st āyat of the *Surat Yūsuf* (The 'Sura of Joseph,' Qur'an 12) to his liking, a failure which causes him to ask that his request for an adequate intepretation of these be sent to Asad Khan, the emperor's very learned vizier.[67] It is sad to say, however, that because we are never told the verse upon which Nand Lal exercises his extraordinary exegetical skill nor given his specific interpretation of the unknown ayat, it is likely that this story is pure fiction, a creation of Sarup Das Bhalla's imagination, whose aim is many sided. Not only is it a triumph for Nand Lal (and so Guru Nanak and Sikhism), but it is also a victory for the Sikh court of the tenth Master, underscoring the legitimacy of Guru Gobind Singh and his court as the true heirs of the empire of Babur, an empire which, let us repeat, was bestowed upon these descendents of Timur by Guru Nanak.

How is this so? What I have not mentioned is that Nand Lal is told of Aurangzeb's quest for the ayat's meaning by Prince Mu'azzam who is initially terrified of his father's wrath if he does not divine a satisfactory meaning (5:20–3). When Nand Lal recognizes the prince's anxiety he is told of its cause and almost immediately provides the prince relief by supplying the best possible interpretation. At that instant [Nand Lal] fulfilled ('spoke') the prince's desire (*maqāsid*) of [discovering the] meaning [of the ayat]. [As soon as] [Nand Lal] explained (*sunā*) [the meaning] to the him [the prince's] heart [was filled] with joy. Right at that moment [the prince] bestowed upon Nand Lal a distinguished robe of honour. [The prince] was calmed and all of his weariness departed.[68]

The prince is thus overjoyed.[69] He goes to his father and recites Nand Lal's commentary. Hearing it Aurangzeb is naturally amazed (5:27).[70] The emperor then questions Prince Mu'azzam, who informs Aurangzeb of his very intelligent mir munshi (5:28). The emperor proceeds to summon Nand Lal before him. It is only as Nand Lal stands in front of the emperor that Aurangzeb discovers that he is not a Muslim. Aurangzeb then thinks to himself:

I see with my own eyes that he is a Hindu and he is well [learned]. I am not encouraged by this; know that the strength [of Islam] will depart and be forsaken.[71]

The passage from Santokh Singh follows suit but with a dark addition which may have been implied in the earlier version:

So, [Nand Lal] is a Hindu and he is learned. This will not do [lit., 'this is an injustice']; this does not befit me. Bring him inside the faith. By any means necessary (*jayom kayom*) cause him to understand thoroughly.... Bring [Nand Lal] into the faith by any means at our disposal.[72]

Rather than comply, Prince Mu'azzam informs Nand Lal of his father's desire and permits him to leave. Nand Lal does so and flees to the court of Guru Gobind Singh along with his friend and disciple.

By forcing Nand Lal, a pious non-Muslim and learned scholar of all things Islamic to flee the court for fear of his life, our authors show that the authority of Babur really no longer lies at the court of Aurangzeb, a man who Santokh Singh claims

...treated hundreds of thousands of Hindus cruelly...[a man who was] a sinner...[who] placed the noose of the Sharia around the necks [of all people].[73]

When Nand Lal leaves the court it is not only Nand Lal in the image of the first Master leaving the court but the departure of the legitimacy bestowed upon that court by Guru Nanak. It comes full circle when Nand Lal arrives at the court of the tenth Master who is the ninth embodiment of the first Guru. This narrative of Nand Lal, in other words, is a symbolic dramatization of both, the delegitimization of the Mughal court of Aurangzeb and the authentication of the court of Guru Gobind Singh based on that very feature which legitimized the Mughal court in the first place, Guru Nanak. While Babur bows in humility before Guru Nanak in the Puratan Janam-sakhi account of their meeting, the self-righteous Aurangzeb fills both Hindus and his courtiers with dread at his intolerance as implied in the *Mahimā Prakāsh* and made explicit in the later *Sūraj Prakāsh*.[74] He would seem to be a twisted version of Babur and thus unfit to don the mantle of Mughal rule. It would not be until Bahadar Shah that the Mughal empire would be somewhat redeemed, in particular as tradition maintains (and historical sources support this contention) that Guru Gobind Singh helped (and therefore blessed) the then prince secure his claim to the Mughal throne against his brothers. Let us here note Gian Singh's early twentieth-century interpretation of these last events, beginning with the period just before the then prince's entry into the suba of the Punjab in 1696:

Along with the prince [travelled] his Mir Munshi, Bhai Nand Lal and Divan Hakam Rai of Agra. The latter was a Sikh minister of the Guru. The prince heard from [the Diwan] the story of the [ten] Gurus' grandeur and the battles of the sixth Guru, in which he defeated the army of Shah Jahan four times. He had heard the entire story and after having done so the prince put an end to the [royal] army's invasion [into the Guru's territory]. Instead [of incursion], the prince gave to Nand Lal presents [to put before the Sikh Master] and sent him to Guru Gobind Singh in Anandpur. Through Nand Lal the prince requested the Guru for his blessings so that he might become the king [of India one day] and should have the opportunity to serve him. In response to this plea the Guru conveyed to Nand Lal, 'Muazzam Shah should not worry at all. We will make him the emperor.' Hearing this Nand Lal was overjoyed. He obtained a siropa from the Guru and bid farewell to him. He [then] came [back] to the prince. When the prince was told of the Guru's blessing he also read the *al-hamdu*, the first sura of the Qur'an [which begins *al-hamdu il-'llāh* 'praise be to God!'] and celebrated joyously.[75]

This redemption would be short lived however, as the general order to persecute all Sikhs would be reissued with much vigour by Farrukh

Siyar who would kill a large number of Khalsa Sikhs in his attempt to eradicate the threat of Banda.

It would not have been lost on a late eighteenth- or early nineteenth-century Sikh audience that the departure of such a learned and illustrious figure as mir munshi Nand Lal from the court of the prince and the emperor to that of the Guru would have also increased the grandeur of the tenth Master's own court.[76] Indeed, it is within the context of such increasing grandeur that one of the very first acts undertaken by Nand Lal after having arrived in the tenth Guru's presence is to present Guru Gobind Singh with a composition which, we are told, was written in his honour, the *Bandagī-nāmah*, the Book of Servitude, the title of which the Guru famously alters:

[Nand Lal] prepared the *Bandagī-nāmā* and presented it as a gift to the True Guru. The True Guru effaced the title *Bandagī-nāmā* [Book of Servitude] and [in its place] named the text *Zindagī-nāmā*. The text was recited in the *Bahir Tavil* style in Persian and [afterwards] placed in front of the Guru.[77] Hearing it the True Guru was filled with mercy. [He noted that] it consistently pronounced (*ucharat*) the mystical knowledge of the divine. It makes dharma clear and always brings peace [upon its reader]. [Reading it] the mind will achieve glory and [be free] from adversity (*biparīt*). The splendour of the mystical awareness of the Fearless Lord will [then] become manifest within the heart. Indeed, without the true lord nothing can be known.[78]

This follows what Sarup Das Bhalla and his audience would have most certainly understood as a common occurrence in Indo-Timurid courts.

Since the time of Timur himself poets seeking audience or admission to august courts often presented their future patron with encomiums in their honour. A poem or good turn of phrase did not only increase a poet's prestige (and in many instances his income) but it could also usher him into the royal circle of poets and in turn bestow upon his patron an even more renowned reputation amongst his peers. The words penned by E.J.W. Gibb over a century ago may be cited here:

For a man of literary ability there is...no better introduction to the notice of the great [ruler] than a skillfully composed qasida or ghazel [*sic*]; and so we find that from this time [1450 CE] forward nearly all the greater poets are at least nominally either court functionaries or government officials of one class or another. When a clever young poet was brought under the notice of a vezir or other grandee, it was almost a point of honour with the great man to find him some berth where he would be provided with a competence and yet have the leisure to cultivate his talent.[79]

That the tenth Guru changes the name of the text, moreover, is also in accord with Indo-Timurid courtly etiquette: although not common, patrons could rename texts presented to them by courtiers and court poets as well as suggest modifications to the text of their poetry. The emperor Akbar, for example, exercised this prerogative in regard to the *Khulāsatulmulk* (The Essence of the Kingdom) presented to him by Qulij Khan. Akbar renamed the text *Haqīqatulmulk* (The Truth of the Kingdom).[80] As a spiritual king Guru Gobind Singh could act likewise.

It is perhaps in part as a result of this tradition that Nand Lal's poetry was ultimately elevated to bani. It is most likely with such precedents in mind that Santokh Singh also claims that the tenth Guru established the title of Nand Lal's famous collection of ghazals, the *Divān-i Goyā*. That Sarup Das Bhalla fails to note this in the last quarter of the eighteenth century implies that the tradition was most likely established later:

Having heard [Nand Lal recite his] delightful ['Holi' ghazal] Guru [Gobind Singh] was pleased. To [the collection in which] it [appeared] he fixed the title (*nām dhāri*) *Divān[-i] Goyā*.[81]

It is in the context of the relationship between Guru Gobind Singh and Prince Mu'azzam in which we once again see Nand Lal, though in this case unlike the *Mahimā Prakāsh* account of his life, the reference is all too brief. This occurs two decades later in 1797 CE within the gur-bilas text attributed to Sukha Singh, the *Gur-bilās Pātshāhī 10*, a hagiography narrating the events which eighteenth-century Sikhs associated with the tenth Guru. The specific portion we have in mind regards the journey of Prince Mu'azzam to the Punjab in 1696 (the prince's entry into the suba is briefly noted in the thirteenth chapter of the *Bachitar Nātak*)[82] to deal with the Raja Bhim Chand of Kahlur and the other troublesome hill rajas who had occasionally withheld their tribute to the emperor and had been frustrated by the Guru's apparent success (and perceived defiance) at Paunta, Makhowal, and later Anandpur Sahib. We are told that it was through the intercession

In the Tenth Master's Court 219

of Nand Lal that the prince ultimately excused Guru Gobind Singh and concentrated his punitive efforts solely on the hill rajas:

A Khatri Sikh [who was] a resident of Delhi [named] Nand Lal was the first among the [prince's] wise counselors. He advised the emperor's son in a number of ways. Through his conversation he successfully accomplished the task [of pleading on the Guru's behalf].
[Nand Lal's] good advice appealed to [Prince Mu'azzam's] heart. [As a result the prince] loved him dearly. As his heart was stolen by this devotee of the [true] Lord [the prince] took the word of the Sikh [Nand Lal] as true.[83]

The evidence here is problematic as is the entire text itself steeped as it is in a strong Udasi Sikh mixture.[84] Its lack of historical veracity notwithstanding (nowhere else do we hear of Nand Lal as a resident of Delhi for example),[85] the text does suggest one of the two possibilities. Nand Lal may either have not joined the court of the tenth Guru (which seems very unlikely indeed in light of the evidence we have thus far marshalled), or Nand Lal shifted his residence between the two courts. Such a commute is claimed by some scholars of the Sikh tradition although it does not seem to be generally accepted.[86] This passage also corroborates claims that by the mid to late eighteenth century, some Sikhs were convinced of Nand Lal's (continued) involvement in the affairs of the prince who would become the emperor Bahadar Shah, adding support perhaps to the contentious evidence one discovers in the Persian *Amar-nāmah* of Dhadhi Nath Mal.[87]

As we have noted in the *Mahimā Prakāsh* account, Nand Lal was known for his extraordinary erudition which included an ability to unravel complex riddles (such as the unknown Quranic ayat). This was a talent which was particularly prized among later Timurid and Indo-Timurid poets.[88] In a passage in the early nineteenth-century gur-bilas text attributed to Kavi Koer Singh which is also, like Sukha Singh's, entitled *Gur-bilās Pātshāhī 10*, Nand Lal is once again at his interpretive best.[89] In this passage also Nand Lal's faith in Guru Nanak and thus in the Sikh tradition is once again firmly established. The passage in question (2:13–20) places Nand Lal within the Mughal court before 1682 CE, indeed even prior the birth of Guru Gobind Singh, the only text to ever do so. It begins with a puzzling letter which the emperor Aurangzeb receives from the king (bhūp) of

Mazandaran in Persia in which there are regular allusions to the convoluted 'predictions' found in the *Bhavishya Purana*, an allegedly ancient Hindu text which foretells the Prophethood of Muhammad, the birth of Guru Nanak, and the coming of the British among other such prognostications.[90] The portion directly below picks up after the emperor has heard the letter's contents for the first time:

> When the emperor [Aurangzeb] tried to make sense of this letter none of his advisors could read it properly for him. From amongst his wise counselors there was one Nand Lal. [Nand Lal] clearly explained the letter's meaning, revealing his keen insight. [While] listening [to others, however,] the scribe began to tremble. [He was told, 'someone] will now slander you to the emperor and you will suffer terribly. [Indeed,] the emperor will now convert you to Islam. This is not a difficult task for him. He will even give you his daughter to bring you into the fold. He delights in seeing [such intelligent people] becoming Muslim. [If you choose] otherwise, he will just kill you.' Hearing this Nand Lal was weighed down with grief. At that time he thought of Guru Nanak Dev. Immediately the Guru came to his rescue in selfless service. [Nand Lal feared that] if he casts away the chain [of faith] he will betray the Guru, although he might get Zebunnisa, Aurangzeb's daughter [and thus be elevated in rank and prestige].[91] But he immediately left that place and ran away. In this way he remained faithful to the Guru who protected him in difficulty.[92]

Were this a Persian qasīdah one would clearly note the similarity to the rahīl mentioned earlier, the poet's arduous journey to the patron.[93] Unfortunately, in Nand Lal's Persian poetry such a journey narrative does not appear or if it does, it has been collapsed to an almost illegible point.[94] Within the rahīl-like narrative directly above, however, we recognize some interesting points. Firstly, the image of Aurangzeb is perhaps at its darkest here where he is even willing to use his own daughter to secure his orthodox ends. This is well in keeping with the early nineteenth-century attitude towards Aurangzeb as we see in the later *Sūraj Prakāsh*. Secondly, being a true Sikh of the Guru is far superior to being a member of the royal court or even in this case, the royal family.

Let us moreover note that this gur-bilas text was not at all well known, if at all, to scholars of the Sikh tradition in the early twentieth century. Indeed, only with its modern publication in 1968 did it become so.[95] The story of Nand Lal's learning mentioned above, however, was known it seems and was passed down through oral tradition. For this reason it was recorded by Max Arthur Macauliffe in his 1909 *The Sikh Religion* as a 'tradition preserved among [Nand Lal's] descendants.'[96] This is significant for the differences in the two versions of the story allow us to witness on the one hand Nand Lal's increasing importance in the later nineteenth century and on the other, the reliance upon stories provided by Nand Lal's family. In the family's and Macauliffe's rendition, Nand Lal writes not to the 'king' of Mazandaran (more likely the governor), but rather to the more important and powerful Safavid 'King of Persia' himself.[97]

The next text in which we find reference to Nand Lal is the *Sau Sākhīān* of 1834 attributed to Guru Gobind Singh himself. Although the relevant passage fails to mention Nand Lal's erudition, it implies it along with underscoring his intimacy with the tenth Guru:

[One day in Kesgarh the tenth Guru] ordered that the sangat direct the questions [which would normally be asked of the Guru] to [Bhai] Nand Lal. When Nand Lal heard this order he gathered together [all of] the writers [in the Guru's entourage from the] centre[98] [at which they were stationed]. He summoned [all of] the royal writers and poets. [Nand Lal often performed this task of summoning poets] into the presence of the True Guru for sessions of poetry [because their recitals] pleased the tenth Master.[99]

A few anecdotes further the *Sau Sākhīān* will show Nand Lal within a majlis-like setting. Here his insight into Sikh soteriology is demonstrated and, as he is the first of the poets to answer a question put to the gathered kavi darbar, one may infer that his place is the foremost one, a *malikushshu'arā* sans title:

One day Guru Gobind Singh was sitting in a meditative state of mind while a pandit was reading out the portion of the Mahabharata dealing with the Pandavas. After this account was recited someone spoke out: 'No one has ever come back after having died. And so what does one know of what occurs in the hereafter, whether anything at all occurs or not.' Nand Lal spoke in reply, 'Our actions accrue karma [even if such acts are] pleasing, but to those great Sikhs who turn towards the Guru the end result will be very good indeed.' Sainapati, the poet, then spoke, 'Taking the Guru's darshan allows one to cross over the Ocean of Existence. Whether he performs good or bad deeds the True Guru always sets these in order.'[100]

The text may exclude reference to Nand Lal's Persian skill as it was generally well known enough to be taken for granted, though in regard to a later passage we find in the *Sau Sākhīān*, in which Persian-knowing Sikhs are disparaged, it seems that the author may have purposefully excluded this fact to ensure that no negative light is cast upon this most devoted disciple.[101] An interesting feature of the first passage above is the tacit equation between the Guru and Nand Lal, a feature we earlier noted between Nand Lal and Guru Nanak.[102] In this case, moreover, one is reminded of the *nadīm* or the monarch's boon-companion, a special type of courtier/poet who was particularly versatile in the courtly arts in order to prove at times a pleasing companion and confidant to the monarch/patron and at others, a moral support and guide.[103] In the full sixty-second sakhi only part of which appears above, Nand Lal calls together poets and writers in a majlis in order to comfort the Guru whose ire had been raised for close to a year by reports of brahman slander and displeasure at the Guru's creation of the Khalsa.[104] This intimate picture of the relationship between the tenth Guru and his esteemed poet is also brought out in the famous narrative in which the Guru and Nand Lal celebrate Holi.[105]

We have already noted in traditions associated with the *Sikhān dī Bhagatmālā* that one of Nand Lal's roles in the Guru's darbar was that of messenger and emissary shuttling instructions and requests from the royal camps of Bahadar Shah to the camp of the tenth Guru and, after 1699, from the Guru's court to various disgruntled brahmans. Nand Lal adopts this position again in Ratan Singh Bhangu's famous *Gur-panth Prakāsh* of 1841 CE. Bhangu's narrative is relatively brief.[106] We first see Nand Lal summoned not by Bahadar Shah but rather by the Mughal emperor Farrukh Siyar who instructs Nand Lal to go and petition Mata Sundari to put an end to Banda's incursions into the Punjab.[107] The Mata ji then deputes Nand Lal to do this very thing:

After [having heard the request to persuade Banda to end his campaigns] Mata ji spoke to Nand Lal, '[Nand Lal] send a letter in our name [to Banda] conveying [my] order.' She continued, 'Now please write it [for me] and affix the seal of the [House of] Guru [Gobind Singh] onto the letter.' Bhai Nand Lal did exactly this, [writing down] that which the [wife of the true] king requested. Bhai Nand Lal hurriedly dispatched the Guru's command [to Banda].[108]

In the Tenth Master's Court 223

Here Nand Lal is emissary to both the Mughal emperor and the House of the Guru as represented by Mata Sundari. In the person of our poet, Bhangu allows the interests of both parties to merge together. Nand Lal is thus a figure who appears at home in both courts and while so positioned bestows legitimacy on the two, at least from Bhangu's perspective who most likely adds this hitherto unknown narrative to the Nand Lal story in order to display his own dislike of Banda, who never appears in a flattering light in Bhangu's text.[109] Now we once again do not hear of Nand Lal's Persian ability, but it is nevertheless implied by virtue of his situation in the court of the Mughal emperor. We infer that his position is a privileged one, since Farrukh Siyar immediately summoned only Nand Lal after reminding his courtiers that it is to the family of the Guru that the descendents of Babur, himself included, are indebted. Such is also the case in the second appearance of Nand Lal when the emperor's courtiers instantly implore Farrukh Siyar to summon our poet to once again deal directly with Mata ji and Banda.[110]

We have come to the end of our early sources. Of course Santokh Singh's account rounds off our narrative but since his almost exactly follows the trajectory of Sarup Das Bhalla's we have alluded to it in the context of the former. The principal difference between these two works which form the beginning and the end of the Nand Lal narrative respectively, apart from the poetic metres they employ in the telling, is their depictions of the nature of the Mughal emperor, Aurangzeb. The *Mahimā Prakāsh* version, in the context of the Nand Lal narrative, is not at all as dark as the version of Aurangzeb that we find in Santokh Singh's work.

FAMILY MEMORY

A glance at contemporary traditions regarding Nand Lal, as found in such texts as the introductions to both Ganda Singh's *Bhāī Nand Lāl Granthāvalī* and his *Kulliyāt-i Bhāī Nand Lal Goyā*, as well as the Nand Lal entry in the *Encyclopaedia of Sikhism* make it clear that the story does not end here.[111] In these eighteenth- and nineteenth-century Punjabi sources for example we hear nothing about Nand Lal's early life in Agra, Ghazna, or Multan before he made the acquaintance of Prince Mu'azzam apart from his birth and investiture.[112] It is only as communication networks increased after the annexation of the Punjab in 1849 and the journey between Punjabi towns such as Lahore, Amritsar, and Multan became far less arduous coupled with the rise of print and print-literate Punjabi Sikhs that we find the alleged descendants of Nand Lal, living in Multan, supplying this apparently lost segment of Nand Lal's narrative.[113] One can understand that for Nand Lal's family the stories about their famous ancestor which circulated orally amongst themselves and all those willing to hear these for well over a century would have been grand ones. Indeed, in this regard we are not disappointed. Let us therefore briefly add to our late eighteenth and early nineteenth-century narrative with the memories of Nand Lal's family which begin just as the Singh Sabha movement is beginning to make its indelible mark on the collective Sikh Panth.[114]

These begin with Nand Lal's birth in 1633 CE to Chhajju Mall (Chhajju Ram in some sources), a Hindu Khatri whose name does not appear in early accounts, who though a pious Vaishnav, was well learned in Persian and stationed in Ghazna in the employ of the Mughal court. Sikh tradition enhances this importance in its claim that Chhajju Mall's principal employer was none other than the Crown Prince Dara Shikoh himself, whose mīr munshī Chhajju Mall had eventually become, although contemporary Mughal records are utterly silent in this regard.[115] Sikh tradition is often confused about the place of Nand Lal's birth[116] but it is nevertheless sure that it was here in Ghazna that Goya was raised and educated by his father (when not officially engaged) according to the exacting Islamic standards of his day, a claim which certainly follows generally prescribed standards for munshis and their sons in seventeenth-century Mughal India.[117]

With the death of Chhajju Mall in 1652, Nand Lal led his servants south into India, eventually settling in Multan. Here he invested a part of his father's wealth in a house and land (a precinct of sorts later called Aghapur since Nand Lal was known as *āghā*, the Persian term for a great lord or nobleman while living in Multan), was married to a woman from a Sikh family (the poetry of whose Gurus he began to revere), and soon occupied the post of munshi under one Nawab Wassaf Khan in the Court of Multan. Although Sikh sources claim this Wassaf Khan to be a nawab, an inability to discover one so titled implies that he was most likely (if he existed at all)[118] not the nawab but rather a lesser noble. Through diligence and hard work, tradition maintains, Nand Lal was elevated to the position of mir munshi. Tradition claims that Nand Lal so excelled at his scribal art that he was able to prepare an *inshā*, a collection or compilation of stylized form-letters and correspondence which was, according to Jan Rypka, 'grist to the Indian mill...for it offered opportunity for extravagance of expression in the most brilliant form, both in word and thought.'[119]

This text of Persian letters is partially reproduced in Ganda Singh's Persian *Kulliyāt-i Bhāī Nand Lal Goyā* and abridged and translated into Punjabi in his *Bhāī Nand Lāl Granthāvalī*. This text is, however, very problematic and not only because of its nature as insha.[120] Some years ago I made claims regarding the signature line of this text without having seen the original manuscript from which Ganda Singh took the versions he placed in his respective books.[121] This was unfortunate for I made claims which I now would like to qualify, as upon examination of the said manuscript, ms. 332164/GS at Punjabi University, Patiala titled *Tasnīfat-i Goyā*, I have found that the signature lines in each of the texts mentioned were pencilled in by another hand after the writing of the original text.[122]

In notes in Urdu and Persian written into the margins of particular folios (by an unknown author though it was likely Ganda Singh since he owned this particular manuscript) and in a hand-written Urdu page inserted into the manuscript between the third and fourth folios of the *Ganj-nāmah* (which Ganda Singh certainly wrote), Ganda Singh claims that texts such as the *Dastūrulinshā* appear only partially within this particular manuscript because the original text was lost and had to be recopied. In these and the marginal notes, it is also mentioned that the scribe had unfortunately left out certain portions of the original text from which he copied especially, we may infer, the very significant signature lines. The elegant hand, crisp margins, the use of both red and black ink, the regular borders, and the sheer lack of scribal errors in this *Tasnīfat-i Goyā* manuscript suggest that the copyist worked *ad seriatum* from an original manuscript or manuscripts which implies that there is no reason to doubt Ganda Singh or the unidentified reader(s) who indulged in marginalia. One must nevertheless suspend judgement on the text in the light of these circumstances. There is also the text's own internal evidence which likewise suggests that scholars proceed cautiously.

It is true that there are passages which very much suggest the genuine nature of the *Dastūrulinshā*. Regarding the travel of one Chhotah Mall, for example, we find a typical insha passage noting the daily occurrences which would have come to the attention of a court scribe, a position which, as we have noted, Nand Lal is alleged to have held:

The Asylum of Love, Malik Chhotah Mall, was travelling from Iran to Multan together with Pir Kakun. Along the road highway robbers pillaged their caravan and looted approximately four lakhs of rupees (400,000) in cash and goods. The [aggrieved party] continued on and the aforementioned [Chhotah Mall] under the constraints of time once again departed[123] with one word and two ears (that is, he listened attentively to somebody's advice and spoke little himself) and wrote to Moti Ram noting that from now on he should guarantee the security of travellers on the way to Multan.[124]

There is it seems, an authenticity to this passage as the author of this piece was most likely well aware of how seriously the Mughals took such disruptions along their trade routes, especially along highways as supremely important as those going through Multan, an economic and cultural hub connecting the Mughal empire with the Safavid and beyond.[125] Ideally for such acts of highway robbery Mughal officials who failed to secure the perpetrators were mandated to pay compensation to the affected parties or their mansabdari ranks were dramatically reduced. This well known characteristic of Mughal economic policy is attested to by many contemporary observers, both European and Indian. Extant edicts from the period of Shah Jahan, for example, demonstrate just how keenly Aurangzeb's father endeavoured to punish the offending party and restore losses to those lodging complaints.[126] The same could be said for his son. In the famous seventeenth-century *Chahār Chaman* of Chandar Bhan Brahman, for example, we are told:

Owing to the justice and management of this great Government, such peace is maintained on the routes and halting places that merchants and traders and travellers journey forth to distant parts in tranquility of heart and joy. If at any place anything is lost, the officers who have jurisdiction there are obliged to pay compensation as well as a fine for their negligence.[127]

Indeed, even Aurangzeb's third and favourite son Muhammad Azam Shah (1653–1707 CE) was not free from censure in this regard.

Having shown indifference towards a highway raid conducted by the Maratha commander Janaji Dalia while the prince was governor of Ahmadabad, Aurangzeb scathingly wrote of his son:

Decrease five thousand from the substantive rank of the prince, and take from his agents money correspond-ing to the [loss] reported by the merchants. If it had been an officer other than a prince, this order would have been issued after an inquiry. For a prince the punish-ment is the absence of investigation.[128]

Yet these items notwithstanding, one must note as well the way that the author of the *Dastūrulinshā* attributed to Goya refers to a certain Gurbakhsh Singh:

...that respected brother (*bhā'ī sāhib*) and great lord whose face is as if it is turned towards the Guru (*gur-mukh sifat*), Bhai Gurbakhsh Singh jiv...[129]

It seems unlikely to me that a munshi of a sub-imperial Mughal darbar would, during the period of Shah Jahan refer to a Sikh in such flattering terms in a collection of stylized letters meant to be passed on as literary standards to follow in letter writing.[130] This form of address, 'Bhai Sahib...Bhai...', thus warrants concern as it appears most likely to have become a popular form of address amongst Sikhs not in the mid-seventeenth century but rather in the nineteenth century, during the period of Maharaja Ranjit Singh and the British afterwards. It is quite likely that this manuscript, and the original from which it had been copied, dates to sometime in the latter part of this period.

Whether the *Dastūrulinshā* document is genuine or not, tradition continues that Nand Lal's elevation to mir munshi in Multan would not be the last of his promotions. Recognized for both his literary talent and military acumen he was promoted to the deputy governorship (*nāib sūbādār*) of Multan[131] after which the future Bhai ji followed in his father's footsteps by somehow securing a station in Delhi on the staff of the future Mughal emperor Bahadur Shah, Prince Mu'azzam, the eldest but one son of Aurangzeb.[132] This too is well in keeping with the late seventeenth-century trend as we earlier noticed in the careers of other Persian poets who travelled to India from elsewhere and began writing within sub-imperial darbars in the hope to ultimately achieve prominent positions within the Mughal darbar itself.

Nand Lal's military skill seems very much like a later Sikh attempt to somehow read Nand Lal's life through a more martial Khalsa lens (a reinterpretation which often finds Nand Lal's name suffixed with the surname Singh). This certainly seems the most likely case to me. But we should nevertheless note that such activity on the part of munshis and poets, though undoubtedly rare, did in fact occur. One of these very exceptional cases was the career of the famous Abdurrahim Khan-i Khanan (1556–1627) whose takhallus was Rahim. Not only was Rahim a decent poet of both Persian and Brajbhasha but he was also a great patron of painting, calligraphy, poetry, and Sanskrit literature as well as one of Akbar's most skilled generals (and so his title the 'Lord of Lords') and the son of Bayram Khan (d. 1560 CE), Akbar's regent until he fell into disfavour and was sent on a pilgrimage to Mecca during which he was assassinated.[133] With the Khan-i Khanan as his example Muhammad Abdul Ghani makes the following claim,

...the titles atāliq [governor], munshī and malikushshu'ārā' [poet laureate], at the court of the Mughal sovereigns were decorations held not merely by virtue of literary ability, but their holders were practical officers commanding armies and leading them successfully in battles against veteran foes.[134]

The Nand Lal story at this point picks up by noting the material we have covered in the earliest Punjabi accounts described above, beginning with Nand Lal's arrival at the court of Guru Gobind Singh in 1682. Although the majority of these accounts agree upon the date of Nand Lal's birth, virtually every one disagrees about the dates of his death. The gamut runs from 1705 as noted in Kahn Singh Nabha to 1715, the latter dates allowing Nand Lal to indeed be present in Nander as Guru Gobind Singh meets with Bahadar Shah and to finally move back to Multan to establish a maktab to train students in Persian.[135] It was apparently here that Nand Lal's descendants remained in teaching or administrative capacities until the early twentieth century according to their own account and that of Ganda Singh.

The Seventeenth-Century Indo-Persian Khatri

Our reliance thus far on Sikh and family tradition should imply how devilishly complex it is to reconstruct the life of Nand Lal from contemporary sources. The reason for this is that there is simply no evidence outside the Sikh tradition which mentions Nand Lal. As we have noted, even Sikh traditions regarding our poet are not narrated until the mid to late eighteenth century. To do this therefore we must begin by working backwards, taking as our point of departure the works attributed to Nand Lal, in particular, the Persian works.

I single these Persian works out for good reason. I have shown elsewhere that it is highly unlikely that the Brajbhasha works attributed to Nand Lal are the product of the same Bhai Nand Lal Goya under discussion.[136] If there were indeed two Nand Lals (or more) they have been purposely conflated in Sikh history since, one may assume, the appearance of Bhai Nand Lal as an important figure in the early eighteenth century.[137] We have therefore no reason to dispute Hew McLeod's oft-repeated claim that the authors of the many rahit-namas attributed to Nand Lal probably used his name to grant authority to their texts and the ideas contained therein, in the same way as the Gur-pādhantī above. These certainly tell us a great deal about the Sikh perception of this esteemed poet but little about the man himself.[138]

Nevertheless, we do have grounds to briefly add to McLeod's claim. Indeed, the reasons for appending Nand Lal's name to Khalsa rahit-namas are perhaps far more complicated than contemporary published works on the rahit claim. First, it seems likely that the anti-Islamic/Islamicate injunctions in works like the *Tankhāh-nāmā* were attributed to Nand Lal, an intimate of Muslims who himself wrote Persian ghazals, to add a particular force to this enmity. This is a possibility, but it suggests that Nand Lal's alleged involvement with the Mughals was generally understood by the Khalsa Sikhs of the early eighteenth century as it was by Khalsa Sikhs of the later eighteenth century, a point sustained by Kesar Singh Chhibbar's reference to Nand Lal in his *Bansāvalī-nāmā*. Second, it is worth remembering that Nand Lal belonged to a birādarī to whom the newly established Khalsa was initially hostile, at least according to Sainapati's *Srī Gur-Sobhā* which, as Jeevan Deol reminds us, devotes two entire sections (*dhiāu/adhyāy*) to the conflicts between the nascent Khalsa and other non-Khalsa Sikhs, particularly the Khatri Sikhs of Delhi, who were most likely employed by the Mughals and thus drawing a 'salary' (*tankhāh*) a term of later repugnance in the rahit-nama literature.[139] In light of the fact that the earliest written Nand Lal rahit-nama, a version of the *Tankhāh-nāmā* whose original title is *Nasīhat-nāmā*,[140] was finalized in 1719 CE and was prepared from an earlier copy,[141] one could speculate that the reason for the Nand Lal attribution was to somehow demonstrate to Nanak-panthi Khatri Sikhs who avoided admission to the Khalsa that there were most certainly well-known Khatri Sikhs who could easily join the order without incurring any ritual impurity, especially that accrued from failing to shave the head of those recently bereaved (*bhaddar/ bhaddan*) as such activities were in themselves false and impotent ('error, and not duty at all' according to Sainapati).[142] On the other hand, it demonstrated Sainapati's belief that the Khalsa had indeed become the principal Sikh identity, a claim made all the stronger by designating a devoted Khatri Sikh (a group predominantly Nanak-panthi in the early eighteenth century) like Nand Lal as author of Khalsa rahit-namas such as the *Nasīhat-nāmā*.[143] It is, as well, possible though implausible that such attribution would convey to Khalsa Sikhs the importance of Khatris to the Panth. It is worth noting that both these views aim to end the hostility between the two groups and various other non-Khalsa members of the diverse eighteenth-century Panth. This termination may well prove to ultimately be the objective of the rahit-nama literature.[144]

Assuming that it was in fact the Persian-writing Nand Lal who was a figure in the court of Guru Gobind Singh is both a sensible and well-contextualized conclusion. It is very likely that Nand Lal's initial fame would in all probability have rested upon his very good Persian works rather than the pedestrian Punjabi ones attributed to him. This is implied in the Punjabi rahit-namas credited to Nand Lal as in none of these, including the portion of the Desa Singh rahit-nama in which he is the principal interlocutor, does one discover a condemnation of the Persian language, a criticism often found in eighteenth- and nineteenth-century rahit-namas.[145] With this in mind, moreover, it seems highly plausible that it was Nand Lal's skill as a poet which would have initially attracted the attention of the Guru.[146] This may have engendered the Guru's love for Nand Lal, a rare affection which has characterized later Sikh history and which is strongly implied in many eighteenth and nineteenth-century Sikh manuscripts. A bait which is considered to express Nand Lal's profound reverence for the tenth Guru, for example, appears in the tenth chapter of the *Ganj-nāmah* (Treasure Book) attributed to our Indo-Persian poet:

Lal, the slave-dog of Guru Gobind Singh, has been branded with the nām of the tenth Master.[147]

It is perhaps based on such couplets that Nand Lal's descendants claim the following:

Bhai Nand Lal ji so enjoyed [taking] the [tenth] Guru's darshan that he was not satiated even though he did so everyday. Guru Gobind Singh likewise remained very pleased with [Nand Lal] and was exceedingly happy to hear the poet's words of wisdom.[148]

Such conclusions are easily borne out by making reference to the standards that court poets of the various Persian courts of the Indo-Islamic period were expected to exhibit. We noted these earlier in our discussion as standards with which Sikh writers of the late eighteenth-century would have most likely been familiar. I do not of course mean to caricature Nand Lal by reducing him to the series of qualities or characteristics noted by Aruzi in the way that Gibb and Browne often do to both the Ottoman and Iranian poets of their famous histories, but if Nand Lal was cognizant of such ideals (a very likely conclusion since the *Chahār Maqālah* was very well known to both Central Asian and Indian Timurids and thus generally defined the standard criteria by which the Mughal emperors and various others judged its poets),[149] he may have cultivated these in his professional life which would have easily endeared him to his patron, Guru Gobind Singh. Both Sarup Das Bhalla and Santokh Singh may therefore be close to the mark when they claim as much of Nand Lal in their respective texts.

As both the *Dīvān* and the *Zindagī-nāmah*, among other Persian Nand-Lal texts, are sources of a relatively good quality one can be assured that they indicate considerable training in both Arabic and Persian, and a keen knowledge of the great Persian works which infused Indo-Islamic culture.[150] The possibility that the poet of these works was employed by the Mughal empire (or perhaps some other Indian administration modelling itself along the same lines as the hegemonic Mughal)[151] is strong, as Persian in particular was the language of high culture and thus in the late seventeenth century the formal language of the eastern Islamicate of which India was a formidable part. Though Sikh tradition makes it clear that Nand Lal was indeed a clerk of emperor Aurangzeb's son, Prince Mu'azzam, and that after the evacuation of Anandpur in late 1704–early 1705 he had managed to once again procure employment in the Mughal court, Mughal sources appear to say nothing in this regard. There is a mention of a courtier named Nand Lal who was a hazārī amīr or nobleman with a 1000 rank in the *Farhatulnazirin*, a Mughal document in which some of Aurangzeb's nobles are listed, although the very brief nature of the entry makes it impossible to tell if this is the Nand Lal Goya under discussion.[152] Such evidence at our disposal therefore should compel us to not deny Sikh tradition's claim, but rather to amend it. Since it is implausible to believe that every clerk in the empire's employ would have been noticed and mentioned by its Persian chroniclers, it may be possible that Nand Lal served the Mughal administration as a minor scribe in the court of a lesser noble or in an as-yet-to-be-determined capacity. Though one must indeed be cautious here for it is also very likely that such a royal pedigree was an apocryphal one, appropriated in order to enhance the reputation of this poet, his later family, and that of the court of the tenth Sikh Master to which he was pledged at one point in his life.

That such literary skills as we find in these Persian texts could only come about through long, perhaps a lifetime of study is a point worth repeating particularly when we combine this with internal evidence which suggests that the author was a non-Muslim poet. This leads one to assume that the author of these sources would probably have belonged to those Hindu or (though less likely) Sikh castes which valued literacy and whose traditional occupations tended towards bureaucratic employment, such as the Kayastha or the Khatri (in some cases the Brahman).[153] Such extensive training would have benefitted no other non-Muslim group though to be fair, a knowledge of Persian officialize and polite usage was certainly beneficial to all local rulers, managers, and village headmen as many official documents (arz-da*sht*, sanad, and many others) were composed in Persian. Such knowledge was also quite advantageous to Hindu traders throughout northern India and the eastern Islamicate. Sikh tradition easily supports this inference since it holds that Nand Lal was a Khatri, a group generally associated with trade. This is a point, moreover, which may be reinforced with a bait from the first ghazal of Nand Lal's Persian *Dīvān*. Here we are told that

I will sacrifice my life, heart, and body to the dust of the feet of the *muqaddam*, [who is] anyone who shows me the way to You.[154]

The reference to the muqaddam, the village headman in the Punjab and other parts of northern India is an unusual one as it is rarely, if ever, encountered in Persian ghazal poetry in India or elsewhere.[155] The muqaddam in the period under discussion would most likely have been a Khatri though there are examples of other groups also acquiring this position.[156]

Now that we have inferred from our evidence that the author was most likely a Khatri, that he was perhaps employed by the Mughal administration at one point in his life (in Multan according to a Sikh tradition, though this claim cannot be substantiated by written evidence),[157] and certainly by the Sikh court at another the obvious question one must ask is: were these texts the product of a Sikh? Here we are on surprisingly unstable ground and not simply because the line separating Sikhs and Hindus in the period under discussion was a rather fuzzy one (at least retrospectively).

It would be folly to claim that Nand Lal's *Dīvān*, easily his best work, was principally inspired by the bani of Guru Nanak, the central motivation behind the vars and kabitts of Bhai Gurdas and the hymns of the Sikh Gurus we discover in the Guru Granth Sahib.[158] It is impossible to show in Nand Lal's poetry the kind of hymn to hymn correspondence that we recognize between the hymns of Guru Nanak and his successors to the guruship[159] because Nand Lal's work is not written in what Christopher Shackle terms 'the Sacred Language of the Sikhs'.[160] The ghazals in the *Dīvān-i Goyā*, as I have shown elsewhere, may certainly be interpreted as Sikh but only insofar as there exists in many cases a general affinity between both the Sufi and Sikh traditions of the seventeenth and eighteenth centuries.[161] However, when we examine the other works attributed to Nand Lal, discussed earlier, we can establish a case for there being more than simple affinity.

Sikh tradition certainly claims that Nand Lal was not an ordinary Sikh disciple, but one of the most revered devotees whose literary acumen was exceeded only by his humility and his capacity for selfless service or sevā. The earliest Sikh narratives of Nand Lal's life make this utterly clear. Such a picture of Nand Lal, moreover, receives strong support from certain Persian couplets attributed to him which do seem to indicate that the author is a Sikh. The entire Persian *Joti Bigās* ([Divine] Light's Progress) for example is an encomium praising the ten Sikh Gurus underscoring both their magnificence and their superiority to the many personages and heroes of Indian, Iranian, and other mythologies.[162] Passages discovered within the *Arzulalfāz* (The Exposition of Terms) may be here also cited in support. According to the *Arzulalfāz*:

> Guru Nanak is the perfect spiritual guide whose excellence and wisdom encompass both this world and the next.
> How excellent is the [word] Satiguru! [How] wondrous is the wonder of the [word] Satiguru! (*satigūrū vāh vāh*). It is from this one word that this beautiful world (*jilwah gāh*) comes forth.[163]

So also suggests the *Sultanat Dahamm* or the 'Kingdom [of the] Tenth [Lord]', the tenth and concluding chapter of the *Ganj-nāmah* qasidah. Here we have a collection of 17 couplets in the first portion of the text and 56 couplets in the second.[164] As the *radīf* or 'word(s) repeated after an end-rhyme (*qāfiyah*)' of the final portion of the *Sultanat Dahamm* include 'Gobind Singh' let me provide the first three couplets and the last one by way of example:

> Guru Gobind Singh protects [the world] and is [himself] protected by the Lord. Chosen by the Lord himself is Guru Gobind Singh [who] is the treasury of [the Lord's] Truth and the sum of divine light effulgent. The knower of God's truth is Guru Gobind Singh, king over the greatest of kings... Let it be that this one's life is a sacrifice to Guru Gobind Singh at whose feet he places his head.[165]

Most likely written after the creation of the Khalsa in 1699 CE (according to tradition) these lines certainly suggest a fondness for the Guru and, perhaps, an attempt to undermine the grandeur of the Mughal emperor, Aurangzeb 'Alamgir.[166] Add these to other couplets found in Goya's works, especially in the *Ganj-nāmah*, the baits earlier cited from the *Arzulalfāz*, others from the *Zindagī-nāmah*, and the Persian *Joti Bigās* and *Dīvān-i Goyā*, and one could easily claim as many tacitly do that Sikh authorship is simply beyond doubt.[167]

But doubt nevertheless exists. Does such praise necessarily mean that the author was in fact a Sikh? What it certainly does suggest (and what to my mind is beyond doubt) is that the author was a poet in the court of the tenth Guru; the list of terms associated with the Guru above would not seem out of place in many a panegyric written for the patron by any number of Persian poets in Mughal India and elsewhere in the Islamicate. One need only observe the work of perhaps the most noted Persian writer in the history of Mughal India, Akbar's vizier or informal secretary, Abu'l Fazl 'Allami, author of the celebrated *Akbar-nāmah* and its *Āin-i Akbārī*. Based on Chingisid/Timurid precedent 'Allami, develops a remarkable chronology for his dearly loved emperor, tracing the miraculous light which entered the legendary Mongol queen Alankua (made of that same light—the Qu'ranic *nūr*—which maintains the universe), through the emperor's bloodline to finally become embodied within him.[168] To this we may add the Mughal court poet 'Urfi's qasidah in praise of the then Shahzada Salim (the future emperor Jahangir) and Abu-Talib Kalim's encomium in praise of Shah Jahan.[169] Both of these descriptions are easily as magnificent as the *Ganj-nāmah*'s praise of Guru Gobind Singh. Indeed the last line of the *Sultanat Dahamm* brings to mind the practice of *kurnīsh* made popular during the reign of the Emperor Jalaluddin Akbar (d. October 1605 CE) and continued in the courts of Jahangir and Shah Jahan.[170]

With this in mind we may allude to precedents set in earlier Persian courts, along which the Mughal court of Akbar, in particular, was in part purposefully modelled. Although the following quotation applies specifically to the Samanid court of Persia and its premiere poet Rudaki (*c.* tenth century) it would nevertheless hold a certain amount of truth for court poets of Mughal India regardless of the darbar in which they wrote:

The presence of a poet at court was an ancient [Persian] tradition of royalty, an essential part of the pomp and circumstance attaching to it. At the Persian courts he not only occupied himself in celebrating his master's triumphs but also performed a very practical function which corresponds in some measure with that of the press attaché or 'public relations officer' of today. The ode, intended to flatter the prince by an elaboration of his noble virtues and magnificent exploits in the field, might serve a secondary purpose by being distributed among rivals as a challenge, among potential usurpers as a warning, and among the general population subject to the prince as a manifesto of his greatness.[171]

Now this does not discount the belief that Nand Lal was a Sikh. Sikh tradition makes this claim vociferously, a claim which has been strongly reiterated since the early eighteenth century, and we have no need to challenge it in light of our earlier arguments, we seek merely to problematize the traditionally accepted narratives, not to reject them definitively, but rather to 'disturb the tranquility with which they are accepted.'[172] This will ultimately suggest an intriguing answer to the problem which has plagued many a scholar of Sikhism this last century (well, at least those scholars interested in Bhai Nand Lal like me): why did Nand Lal not become a member of the Khalsa, especially since so many Khalsa rahit-namas lay claim to him as their putative author? There are some Sikhs and scholars of the Sikh tradition who contend that despite the lack of evidence Nand Lal did indeed join the Khalsa, sometimes alluding to a Persian bait spuriously attributed to Nand Lal which mentions the five Ks.[173] Their opinion is, however, shared by very few scholars of Sikh history and may be dismissed forthwith.[174]

From a traditional point of view, Nand Lal's failure to join may be inferred from statements found in the early eighteenth-century gurbilas text of the poet Sainapati, *Srī Gur-sobhā* to which we have earlier referred: that is, Khatri Sikhs (like Nand Lal apparently) were not overtly happy at the creation of the Khalsa as its regulations (particularly cutting one's hair at the time of bereavement [bhaddar]), violated their traditional practices.[175] There is, moreover, a far more recent explanation which is echoed by Piara Singh Padam in his study of the poets of the tenth Master's literary court. Piara Singh implies that it was not Nand Lal who refused to join the Khalsa, but rather that Guru Gobind Singh asked Nand Lal specifically not to don the sword as the Guru understood the dire need for the heroic/pious variety of literature for which his court would become known in order to transform the people of India into courageous warriors who could finally stand up to the atrocities committed by the Mughals.[176] Nand Lal would be better put, in other words, as a littérateur/poet inspiring all Indians generally and the Sikhs specifically to stand up to tyranny than as a warrior. I reproduce a part of this exchange below:

Complying with the Guru's order [that all Sikhs should present themselves at Anandpur bearing arms] Bhai Nand Lal and Bhai Kanhia[177] donned swords. When all of the Sikhs were present within the darbar the Guru gazed upon every one of them with great affection. While first addressing Bhai Nand Lal he said, 'What need is there for you to put on the sword? Take up the pen [the nib of] which I have sharpened for you.' In this very same affectionate manner [Guru Gobind Singh] commanded Bhai Kanhia, 'You shall take up the sword of selfless service, *sevā*, while we will brandish the sword [of steel].'[178]

In light of my observations above, however, one could speculate that Nand Lal did not seek admission to this august assembly because he was not a Sikh to begin with, and perhaps had no intention of becoming one. Let us never forget that much of the poetry attributed to Nand Lal suggests that our writer was first and foremost a poet in the employ of the Guru's court. As we have regularly noted, Sikh tradition strongly implies that the Guru had kept a poetic entourage not just to translate Sanskrit and Persian poetry for the benefit of inspiring a Punjabi-speaking audience to perform great deeds but because it doubtlessly added grandeur to his court, a splendour which contemporary Sikh and Persian sources substantiate.[179] Here we may allude to certain cultural ideals and values which pertained to the Uzbek-Timurid courts of sixteenth-century Central Asia. Although the following observation is Central Asian to be sure, it is nevertheless relevant to the point at hand, especially since the Mughal emperors were also, like the Uzbeks, particularly cognizant of their descent from both Amir Timur and Chinggis Khan (despite the fact that the Mughal emperors collectively despised the Uzbeks), and that it was the Mughals who provided the dynastic model with which the Sikh Gurus were most familiar:

Poetry was a cultural staple that no self-respecting court could afford to do without and it was the determining factor in the assessment of its ultimate worth.[180]

And so in this light one may also assume that like the Mughal emperor himself the Guru kept many poets not so much for their religious allegiance but simply because of their skill. The traditional narratives which speak of imperial Hindu poets making their way to Anandpur support such claims as to the fact that the Mughal emperors allowed non-Muslim poets to write in their courts without personally expressing loyalty to Islam, the emperor's religious tradition.[181] As in the case of the *Ganj-nāmah* therefore Nand Lal's reasons for writing may have simply been professional ones:

> The poet himself benefitted [from writing elegant poetry for a patron] in more than one way.... Copies might be sent to neighbouring courts... to [perhaps] provide him with alternative markets for his wares should the first patron fail to provide rewards that came up to expectation.... It was not unknown for a poet to hawk his compositions about from one court to another, changing a name here and a line there as circumstances made expedient...[182]

Let me state categorically that this is simply speculation, but in light of the commonly held belief that Nand Lal returned to the employ of the then Mughal emperor Bahadar Shah sometime in the first decade of the eighteenth century or perhaps earlier[183] and continued to serve the Mughals under the latter's successors, Jahandar Shah and Farrukh Siyar, it is a merited conjecture.[184]

The Transformation of Nand Lal's Poetry

We have thus far focussed a great deal on showing Nand Lal in his multiple capacities: a figure of reverence whose poetry was recited and read by eighteenth- and nineteenth-century Sikhs; an ideal devotee and emissary of the tenth Guru whose career with the tenth Master allowed eighteenth-century writers to underscore the superiority of the darbar of Guru Gobind Singh over that of the imperial Mughals; Nand Lal as the courtier of the Multan darbar as recalled by his ancestors; and finally the historical Nand Lal based on the circumstantial evidence supplied in his poetry.

We have yet though to answer why Nand Lal's poetry was eventually transformed in the sacred writ, bānī. Let us now endeavour to do just this. Of course one simply cannot know whether Nand Lal's intention in writing any of his known poetry was to produce scripture nor can we know if Guru Gobind Singh did indeed nominate his work to this status, despite the claims of later Sikh tradition.[185] This said, we may here begin our discussion with the *Sikh Rahit Maryādā*, the normative Khalsa Sikh code of conduct. As is well known the *Sikh Rahit Maryādā* completed in 1950 CE is the Singh Sabha's testament to modernity, providing Khalsa Sikhs throughout the world

In the Tenth Master's Court 239

with a guide, supplementary to the Adi Granth, as to what proper Sikhs must do and must believe. Under the section headed kīrtan, the congregational singing of hymns, a pious Sikh is told that

> Within the community of the faithful only the utterances of the Gurus (gurbānī) or the commentaries upon those utterances, [that is] the bānī of [both] Bhai Gurdas ji and Bhai Nand Lal ji, can be sung as kirtan.[186]

As W.H. McLeod has noted those Khalsa Sikhs who drafted the *Sikh Rahit Maryādā* were very cautious in their use of language and it is perhaps for this reason that a great deal of ambiguity exists within this statement, probably by design.[187] First, Nand Lal's poetry here (as well as Bhai Gurdas') occupies two significant spaces, not one as is often assumed.[188] It is both, a commentary on the sacred utterances of the Adi Granth (*is dī viākhiā-sarūp* lit., 'having the form of its exposition'), and sacred utterance itself (bānī).[189] It is, however, unclear whether it is bani because of its nature as commentary, if it is bani independently in and of itself, or if it is both simultaneously though it seems the latter.[190] Second, as I have mentioned elsewhere, which of the texts attributed to Nand Lal is privileged with this status is left unsaid.[191] Since portions of the *Ganj-nāmah*, especially the *Sultanat Dahamm* cited earlier were and still are recited as part of amrit kīrtan on special *gurpurabs* (for example, the gurpurab commemorating the birth of Guru Gobind Singh on Poh *sudī* 7, S. 1723/ 22 December 1666 CE) one can assume that this part of the *Ganjnāmah* would be accorded such a status.[192] Moreover, since the earliest eighteenth-century Nand Lal sources refer only to the *Dīvān* and *Zindagī-nāmah* as his creations, and these two texts frequently appear as eighteenth- and nineteenth-century manuscripts one may also allocate this standing to them. These two collections are easily the best works attributed to Nand Lal.

Let us attempt to make some sense, however, of the decision to include Nand Lal's poetry at all. A question I have often asked myself is why in the final analysis was Nand Lal's Persian poetry, out of all the poetry produced by the poets in the tenth Guru's darbar, included in this august assembly? This is a compelling question as the vast majority of poets that tradition places in the Guru's court wrote in Brajbhasha, the lingua franca of seventeenth-century Punjab and thus the language best understood by later-day Punjabi Sikhs. Though quite different from today's modern standard Punjabi it is far more readily intelligible to Punjabi speakers than classical Persian. In an earlier article I mentioned that such inclusion was an attempt to underscore the various agenda of the Singh Sabha and the elite, print-literate Khalsa Sikhs who generally headed this organization. Perhaps members of the Singh Sabha educated in high-culture classical Persian included such poetry in an attempt to 'raise' Sikhism to the status of a 'world religion' rather than allowing it to remain simply a parochial tradition situated in a particular region of the world, the Punjab. Put simply, by appropriating texts written in a classical 'Oriental' language like Persian with which European Orientalist scholars had been familiar since at least the mid-seventeenth century[193] and perhaps earlier, Khalsa Sikhs of the Singh Sabha attempted to demonstrate to both non-Sikhs and non-Sikh scholars that Sikhism must be recognized as more than simply a religion of 'rugged' Punjabi peasants as many of the manuals for Sikh recruitment to the British Indian army and the various gazetteers seemed to imply.[194] Ultimately this would have had a beneficial legislative affect on the British Government's treatment of the Sikhs generally, who were at that time a minority community both within the Punjab and India, 'overwhelmed by both Hindu and Muslim numbers' a belief often decried in Singh Sabha newspapers of the early twentieth century.[195] This was an attempt therefore to ensure that Sikhism would become a tradition on a footing equal to that of other 'world religions' such as Islam and Christianity. There may also be another type of elitism at work here, as Marshall McCluhan's famous dictum so aptly states: 'The Medium is the Message.' Persian as a medium to communicate Sikh thought was one shared by only a very small number of classically educated Punjabi Khalsa Sikhs of the early twentieth century, an elite in Oberoi's understandings, in part by virtue of their intimate familiarity with the new print capitalism culture of the late nineteenth century.

One can, moreover, see a symmetry in the kirtan section noted above from the *Sikh Rahit Maryādā*. I will adapt McLeod's hierarchical ladder of bani here with a minor modification. At the top appears gur-bani, the bani of the Gurus (including that attributed to Guru Gobind Singh) while below it on the second rung appears on the one hand, the vars of Bhai Gurdas, odes which draw primarily upon Hindu myths, tropes, and symbols and on the other, the more Islamically flavoured Sikh material of Bhai Nand Lal, poetry well centred within a symbolic universe drawn mainly from Islamicate materials. Such a picture opens up the Sikh tradition to multiple interpretations (the universal message of the Sikh tradition, the atmosphere out of which the Sikhism of Guru Nanak evolved, the affinities between the respective traditions tacitly noted, etc.) which need not detain us here, though we must keep in mind that all such meanings will ultimately give vent to the single most important agendum of the Singh Sabha: to demonstrate that Sikhism was, to paraphrase a well-worn expression, neither Hindu nor Muslim.

To these we may easily add other possibilities but in light of recent researches I would like to propose a different understanding to what I rather crudely call the 'banification' of Nand Lal's poetry, and to do this I would like to turn our attention to a factor which is so prevalent in eighteenth- and nineteenth-century Sikh manuscripts of Nand Lal's poetry as to have been taken for granted by us all: the script in which this Persian poetry is preserved. It seems likely to me that the large number of eighteenth and nineteenth-century Nand Lal Persian manuscripts in Gurmukhi script as opposed to those in Perso-Arabic script not only aided in the identification of this material as Sikh literature (obviously the first step in granting the poetry its contemporary sacrosanct status) but also encouraged its transformation.

Although there were other poets in the Guru's darbar, eighteenth-century accounts of their poetry and stories are nowhere near as abundant as those of Nand Lal. It therefore seems likely based, on all the evidence we have thus far examined, that Nand Lal's connection to the court of the tenth Guru and to the tenth Guru himself would have initially inspired the Panth's dedication to the former's works. But the fact that this material was in Persian, the language of those opposed to the Khalsa of the tenth Master most likely made such reverence problematic for eighteenth-century Khalsa Sikhs. Like Islam and Muslims themselves Persian had in the eighteenth and early nineteenth century a dubious reputation amongst Sikh writers. There are two principal, interrelated reasons for this. On the one hand Persian was implicitly condemned as the language of the Islamicate in general and the Mughals in particular. Such censure we discover in the rahit-namas, particularly the controversial Khalsa rahit-nama of Bhai Daya Singh. Although Daya Singh was allegedly one of the original *panj piāre*, it is clear his rahit-nama is a late eighteenth-century text.[196] Assuming that Daya Singh wrote with regard to the general understandings of his audience, one can assume that the majority of statements in his rahit-nama captured the prevalent attitude of many Khalsa Sikhs. Daya Singh provides, in other words, a descriptive rather than prescriptive text. On three separate occasions Daya Singh tells us of his disdain for the Persian language, a dislike we also find in numerous contemporary Sikh texts.[197] In one such instance we are told the following:

Read the bānī in Gurmukhi. Study neither Arabic nor Persian.[198]

One does not know what Daya Singh actually means here by the word bani, though one can assume he refers to the Guru Granth Sahib at the very least. Even the word Gurmukhi is open to interpretation though here too it seems likely that the author conflates Gurmukhi, the script, with the language of both the Guru Granth Sahib and the Dasam Granth, an error which is still quite common today.[199]

A similar type of conflation appears in the rahit-nama attributed to Chaupa Singh Chhibbar though in this case it regards languages generally written in the Perso-Arabic script.

The [Khalsa Sikh who] places [anything written] in the script of the Turks (Perso-Arabic) on his sanctified hair is deserving of punishment (*tankhāhīā*).[200]

Here too though the denunciation of Persian is intended: although Hew McLeod translates the terms *turk akhar* 'Turk characters' as 'Arabic' based most likely on the reverence Muslims generally accord to the language and the script of the Qur'an, it is possible that Arabic is not what Chaupa Singh here has in mind.[201] In the light of the injunctions condemning Sikhs who know and study Persian, it seems more likely that the intended language is the one formally used by the Mughal establishment. Indeed, explicit condemnations of Arabic in the rahit-nama or gur-bilas literature are far more rare than those of Persian, appearing for example in the Daya Singh rahit-nama and in the sixty-fifth sakhi of the controversial *Sau Sakhīān*.[202]

While all these allusions to the language in eighteenth-century Sikh literature condemn it for its implicit association with Muslims and the Islamicate, Kesar Singh Chhibbar, on the other hand, does so for another reason. It is not because Persian is an 'Islamic' language per se but because Persian is not the sacred language of the Sikhs. Kesar Singh demonstrates his anxiety of Persian-knowing Sikhs (and by extension Persian itself) in his tenth chapter (10:365– 9) by alluding to and in parts paraphrasing the Bhagavad-Gita's famous teaching that it is better to perform one's own caste duty (*svadharma*) poorly than to perform another's well (Bhagavad-Gita 3:35).[203] The respective passage begins with a description of the *maleccha-bhākhā* or 'language(s) of the Muslims' to which Guru Nanak alludes in his *Dhanāsarī* 3.[204] Having specifically named these languages ('Arabic, Turki, and Persian') Kesar Singh then acknowledges the existence of Sikhs and Hindus whose livelihood inevitably involves a knowledge of these (this is well in keeping with Kesar Singh's generally derisive comments regarding Khatri Sikhs who as we noted would have known at least some Persian in their professional capacities as traders and scribes). He concludes by issuing the following warning:

And having studied Persian [and the other] language[s] of the Muslims (maleccha-bhākhā) [a Sikh or Hindu] will [inevitably] praise the Qur'an and the other Semitic scriptures (kateb) [forgetting the reverence due to the Guru Granth Sahib]. When one protects the central tenets of another's [dharam in such a way] one is separated from one's own dharam. One leaves [this world] only within [the sphere of] one's own dharam. At the end [of life] one will [therefore] be sorry [for having performed] the dharam of another.[205]

It should be noted that such attitudes towards Persian and the script in which it was written run contrary to those we discover in the *Akāl Ustati* attributed to Guru Gobind Singh himself, and which we find in the Dasam Granth. In one passage elaborating upon the magnificence of the many attributes of Akal Purakh, the tenth Guru expresses the divine's ubiquity in this way:

At times You are Arabic, Turki, and Persian; at others Pahlavi, Pushto, and Sanskrit. [Indeed,] You [exist] in [all] human language at [all] times [as well as within all] divine utterance at [all] times. At times you are the knowledge [behind the establishment of] rule at others you are the rule itself.[206]

We may once again take a cue from the Daya Singh Rahit-nama. Although this rahit-nama recognizes the importance of this composition of the tenth Guru for the Akali, that is the Sikh who 'has memorised the *Srī Akāl Ustati*', yet Daya Singh advocates censure for Sikhs who know Persian.[207] Such statements in the *Akāl Ustati* notwithstanding, it is clear that Khalsa Sikhs of the eighteenth century would have encountered Persian principally as the language of the Mughal or Afghan state whose persecution of Khalsa Sikhs was commonly noted in both eighteenth-century Sikh literature and certain Persian chronicles, and so the prevailing attitude towards these. Now it is unlikely that literate Sikhs would have discriminated between written and spoken Persian and so the simple act of transliterating the poetry would not have altered Nand Lal's texts linguistically at all or made them any better understood. Persian is Persian in whatever script it appears, a fact to which Khalsa Sikhs of this period would probably have been privy.

But the transliteration I believe had an effect nevertheless. At the least the transliteration of the Persian poetry of Nand Lal into Gurmukhi would have most likely served two purposes. The first and most obvious was to simply allow Sikh exegetes and traditional intellectuals whose expertise extended to Gurmukhi alone to sound out the poems to their gathered sangats. The second, less obvious purpose was probably to ensure that Sikhs did not immediately disregard Nand Lal's poetry.[208] But when one takes into consideration the reputation of the Gurmukhi script, an intriguing possibility suggests itself: the transliteration in concert with the meaning of the words, the author's relation to the tenth Guru, the regular appearance of Nand Lal in the eighteenth and nineteenth-century manuscript record, and of course the reputation of Persian as the language of high culture and empire had a significant effect on the growing Sikh reverence for Nand Lal's Persian poetry.[209]

The adoption of the Gurmukhi script for the sacred writings of the Sikhs was, according to Pashaura Singh, an explicit rejection of other scripts, a rejection which bolstered a sense of separate Sikh identity. In his words: 'The use of the Gurmukhi script certainly added an element of demarcation and self-identity to the early Sikh tradition.'[210] I believe one can extend and modify this equation in order to understand the increasing popularity of Nand Lal's poetry in the eighteenth century and perhaps its eventual incorporation into the sacred Sikh canon.

This trajectory seems to me analogous to the one witnessed with the increasing Islamicization of Iran, Central Asia, and northern India, a process in which the Perso-Arabic script was eventually adopted for the many languages of these regions (Persian and Urdu in particular). According to Richard Eaton,

The transliteration of any language into Arabic script not only facilitates the assimilation of Arabic vocabulary but fosters a psychological bond between non-Arab and Arab Muslims.[211]

Though akin, the process I have in mind differs somewhat from the one narrated directly above. In our case, the transliteration of the Persian-language literature of Bhai Nand Lal into the Gurmukhi script may have unconsciously fostered a link to the greater corpus of sacred Sikh literature, in particular the Guru Granth Sahib and the Dasam Granth, among others, especially since it was believed that the script was created by the second Sikh Guru, Guru Angad, a tradition which is noted in some of the earliest Sikh writings predating the compilation of the Adi Granth in 1604 CE and which, as was implied in the Daya Singh rahit-nama, conveyed a particularly sacred status to Gurmukhi.[212] Indeed, many rahit texts either imply the importance of learning Gurmukhi or state it outright as do the rahit-namas of Chaupa Singh Chhibbar and Desa Singh as well as both the apocryphal *Gurū kīān Sākhīān* attributed to Sewa Singh Kaushish and the mid-nineteenth century *Sau Sakhīān*.[213] This link in turn encouraged a Sikh bond to this Persian-language material, an attachment which became all the stronger in the light of the increasing attention which the 'historical' Nand Lal began to receive in Sikh literature of the mid to late eighteenth century. Put succinctly, even though reverence for the poetry of Nand Lal probably originated with the Sikh belief that its author was a devoted disciple of the tenth Guru (as evinced by his regular appearances in the rahit-nama literature), the poetry itself was transformed, albeit unknowingly, from mere 'courtly poetry' to Sikh religious poetry, to bani, when it was transliterated into the Gurmukhi script, the sacred script of Sikhism. And this may perhaps be why Sikhs have generally tended to favour Guru Gobind Singh's statements in the *Akāl Ustāti* as against those of Bhai Daya Singh in the case of Nand Lal and also may explain why Santokh Singh refers to Nand Lal's poetry as bani in the mid- nineteenth century.

What seems to argue this case effectively to my mind is the fact that there exist no eighteenth or early to mid nineteenth-century Brajbhasha/Punjabi translations or reinterpretations of Nand Lal's Persian poetry.[214] Assuming as I do that few Sikhs of this period understood the Persian of Nand Lal's works, this absence demonstrates an eighteenth- and nineteenth-century Sikh attitude towards these texts which seems to differ substantially from that evinced today to works generally described as Hindu, literature such as the Mahabharata, the Ramayana, the Puranas and various others, contemporary Brajbhasha-Gurmukhi translations of which are abundant within the Punjab.[215] It is tempting to assume therefore that by this time, the mid to late eighteenth century, Sikhs regarded the works attributed to Nand Lal as somewhat inviolable, thus allowing these to continue in their original language (albeit in Gurmukhi script) and be read out in Persian. In the *Mahimā Prakāsh*, we have a description of Nand Lal and his langar which can be easily extended to the poetry of Nand Lal itself, implying that already by the mid to late eighteenth century some Sikhs allocated to this Persian poetry a reverential space alongside that of more traditionally accepted bani. In a clear reference to the *Dhanāsarī ashtapadīān* hymn of Guru Nanak,[216] Sarup Das Bhalla has Guru Gobind Singh proclaim the following after having tested Nand Lal's commitment to sevā, selfless service by visiting his langar incognito:

[The tenth Guru] explained this to all of the Sikhs [present]: '[Nand Lal] spoke the language of love and affection [when I came upon his langar in disguise]. Nand Lal is our giver whose devotion is pleasing and who sets out the net whose form is love and there ensnares the bird/soul. Love is the food which these birds peck up thus becoming dyed with the colour of the Lord's love. Running such a langar a Sikh acquires riches. [In this regard] Nand Lal's langar is most successful.[217]

Indeed, the success lies more likely with the Persian poetry of our poet as becoming dyed in the colour of the Lord's love, a feat which awaits the truly pious Sikh and is the ultimate goal of bani. Therefore, the equation between Nand Lal's poetry and sacred utterance is implicit.

We may in this light, speculate as to later developments in regard to Nand Lal. Certainly reverence for Nand Lal's poetry (among other factors) has led to its inclusion into the sacred canon of the Sikhs by the mid-twentieth century Sikh intelligentsia weaned on the values and ideals of the Singh Sabha and Chief Khalsa Diwan. Indeed, in Vir Singh's footnotes to his early twentieth-century edition of Santokh Singh's *Suraj Prakāsh* such is claimed of this poetry:

> Amongst the Sikhs [Bhai Nand Lal] is ranked alongside Bhai Gurdas. His bani is accepted in Sikhism as authentic [scripture, and thus commanding authority].[218]

This makes clear that already by the early 1900s Tat Khalsa ideologues had incorporated the poetry of Nand Lal into the canon if not de facto (as within the *Sikh Rahit Maryādā*) then certainly de jure. Vir Singh's work and that of Kahn Singh Nabha, therefore, insofar as Nand Lal's Persian poetry is concerned, seems to be the fulfilment of an idea which begins perhaps unconsciously with Sikh writers, exegetes, and gianis of the eighteenth and early nineteenth centuries rather than something altogether novel.[219] This is a departure from my earlier understandings of Nand Lal's inclusion into the sacred canon but indeed a welcome one which once again underscores a point made by Hew McLeod many years ago that the tradition formulated by the Singh Sabha was both old and new.[220]

Notes

1. An earlier version of this chapter appeared as 'The Two Lives of Bhai Nand Lal Goya', in Tony Ballantyne (ed.), *Textures of the Sikh Past* (New Delhi: Oxford University Press, 2007).
2. *Gur-pādhantī*, ms. 115682 Sikh Reference Library, Punjabi University, Patiala, folios 1a–b. It is interesting to note that the quotation above actually begins with the words *prashan karī [nand lal jī sabh sikhan mai chand]*. Although the context suggests that the principal meaning of prashan karī is 'he asked a question' there may here be a double entendre as prashankarī taken as one rather than two words (in virtually all early Punjabi/Brajbhasha manuscripts breaks between words are nonexistent) means 'greater than Lord Shiv himself' (intriguing since traditionally the moon is lodged in Shiva's headdress). In the light of the epigraph above this is not an invalid reading. This passage, however, may also indicate Vaishnava leanings as 'Nand Lal' is also an epithet of Krishna, 'the beloved of Nanda' (Nandalal), an epithet often used in the poetry of Sur Das and Mira Bai (perhaps the *lāl* here puns on the moon's intimate connection with love in Indic poetry).

There are many allusions to the auspicious nature of the glowing full moon in the *Zindagī-nāmah* attributed to Bhai Nand Lal. One such appears in the twelfth couplet, playing upon the notion of the sun and moon's revolutions: Anyone who has discovered how to take a turn around the lane of the Lord's devotees (*kū-ye shān*) shines like the sun [in the morning] and the moon [at night] in both this world and the next. *Zindagī-nāmah* 12. Ganda Singh (ed.), *Kulliyāt-i Bhāī Nand Lal Goyā* (Malaka, Malaya: Sikh Sangat, 1963), p. 77.

3. Pashaura Singh claims that it was the fifth Sikh Master who excused Mira Bai's hymn in rag Maru. Pashaura Singh, *The Guru Granth Sahib*, pp. 193–5. For an interesting discussion as to how Mira Bai got into the Adi Granth in the first place see John Stratton Hawley's 'Mirabai at the Court of Guru Gobind Singh.'

4. For the *Prem Abodh* see '*Prem Ambodh Pothī*', in *EoS* III, p. 364. Also see, John Stratton Hawley's, 'Mirabai at the Court of Guru Gobind Singh.' Hawley claims that the title of the work is more likely *Premān Bodh*, 'An Understanding of Love'.

5. The *Gur-pādhantī* manuscript from which the epigraph is taken for example records a conversation in Anandpur Sahib between Nand Lal, Mani Singh, and Guru Gobind Singh in which Nand Lal questions the Guru about the nature of the Nirmala Sikh panth. As the Nirmala Sikhs interpreted Sikh theology through a Vedantic lens it is only fitting that the title of this work is *Gur-pādhantī*, 'the end of the Guru's instruction' alluding it seems to the Vedantic Darshanas.

6. The first reference I have discovered to Bhai Gurdas' vars as bani is *MPV* 77, p. 121. Bhai Gurdas also wrote a large number of kabitts in Brajbhasha. Although the word bani is commonplace in devotional Hindi and Brajbhasha literature (appearing also as *vānī*) of the fifteenth to the eighteenth centuries, literature referring to just about any writing dealing with a sacred subject, especially that attributed to the sant Sur Das, rarely in a Sikh context does it indicate anything apart from the hymns of the Adi Granth and the Dasam Granth. The exceptions are the poetry of Bhai Gurdas and that of the tenth Guru's court poets though of these only Nand Lal's survives as sacred writ. For the term vānī in Hindi and Brajbhasha see R.S. McGregor, *Hindi Literature*, p. 58.

7. Such stray references include the online edition of *SP* 3:41:47, p. 459.

8. The earliest manuscript in which Nand Lal figures is a version of the *Tankhāh-nāmā* ms. 770, Guru Nanak Dev University, Amritsar which bears a date of *sammat* 1775 (1719 CE) and the title *Nasīhat-nāmā* (letter of advice). One should note that although there are indeed many Nand-Lal manuscripts, I have not yet seen an illuminated one. This absence may suggest that the scribes of the eighteenth and nineteenth century who prepared such works allocated the works of Nand Lal to a status below that of the Adi Granth, of which there are many such beautifully decorated manuscripts.

For manuscripts of the Adi Granth consult Pashaura Singh's *The Guru Granth Sahib*, pp. 28–82.
9. Although there are critical editions of the three rahit-namas attributed to Nand Lal it is worth pointing out that there are different versions of each one, in particular the *Prashan-uttar* which enjoys a number of various manuscript recensions. See W.H. McLeod, *The Sikhs of the Khalsa*.
10. Ms. 1060(s), Guru Nanak Dev University, Amritsar, folios 46b–52a.
11. Among others are *Shardhā Puran*, ms. 1097, Guru Nanak Dev University, Amritsar, folios 20a–36a; *Shardhā Purak*, ms. 973, Reference Library, Punjabi Sahitya Academy, Ludhiana, folios 1b–24b. Clearly these manuscripts may be tentatively dated to the late nineteenth or early twentieth centuries as the akhand path became a matter of importance under the Singh Sabhas and Chief Khalsa Diwan at that time.
12. *Prashan-uttar*, ms. 684, Punjab State Archives, Patiala, fols 215b–17a. The passage here discussing the Kaliyug is reminiscent of a similar discussion which occurs in the *Prem Sumārag* although the latter is sans Nand Lal. See W.H. McLeod (ed. and trans.), *The Prem Sumārag*, pp. 11–13. As well the *Sākhī Gurū jī dī Bhāī Nand Lāl jī dī Pātishāhī Dasvīn* (ms. 91, Guru Nanak Dev University, folios 172b–8a), folios 173a–b (a unique recension of the *Prashan-uttar*) which likewise mentions the Kaliyug and the Guru's descriptions of the proper pattern of conduct.
13. *Dīvān-i Goyā* 8, 40, and 42 amongst others. See *Kulliyāt*, pp. 52, 65, and 66. The signature line of the *Kulliyāt's* ghazal 42 makes such a theme implicit in its following command:
    Desist from avarice Goya so that you can see in a special way [the abundance of] God within your own house.
14. *Sākhī Bhāī Nand Lāl jī*, ms. 91 Guru Nanak Dev University, folios 163a–b. This manuscript appears to combine elements from a number of sources including the *Sākhī Rahit kī* of Nand Lal and the *Sikhān dī Bhagatmālā*.
15. Mss. 115373 and 115620, Punjabi University, Patiala are versions of the *Sikhān dī Bhagatmālā*. The quotation is, however, from the critical edition: Tarlochan Singh Bedi (ed.), *Sikhān dī Bhagatmālā* 161 (Patiala: Punjabi University Press, 1994), pp. 152–3. In sakhi 155 (esp. pp. 146–7) Guru Gobind Singh sends along with our poet the *Khālsā Mahīmā* (Svaiya 1–4, Dasam Granth, p. 716) which was written for the occasion and which Bhai Nand Lal recites to the brahmans who are worried that the creation of the Khalsa will exclude them from the offerings they were previously given. See also Gian Singh, *Tavārīkh Gurū Khālsā* I, p. 877.
16. Tarlochan Singh Bedi (ed.), *Sikhān dī Bhagatmālā*, pp. 156–7. The text is also known as the *Bhagat Ratnāvālī*. The *Sākhī Bhāī Nand Lāl jī* also contains a conversation between Nand Lal and brahmans. In this instance the brahmans were angry at the fact that the Sikhs, not they, made the goddess manifest herself during the *hom* ceremony. Ms. 91 Guru Nanak Dev University, fols. 163b ff.

250 The Darbar of the Sikh Gurus

17. Guru Nanak, *Vār Mājh, shlok* 1 of *paurī* 7, Adi Granth, p. 140. Also see Guru Nanak's *Basant Hindol* 9, Adi Granth, p. 1171. Of course Guru Nanak is not the only author to make use of such a technique within the Adi Granth nor is such a practice absent from other Sikh literature. The *Shabad Hazāre* attributed to Guru Gobind Singh for example likewise exhibits this style: O my mind, practice yoga in this way: make truth your trumpet, sincerity your necklace, and contemplation the ashes you apply to your body. *Rāmkalī pātishāhī* 10 [*Shabad Hazāre*] 2(1), Dasam Granth, p. 709.
18. Although there is no mention of a date on this manuscript I base my conclusions on the period of its preparation on the character of the Gurmukhi script. In many instances in the place of the short vertical stroke which represents a lengthening of the vowel 'a' common to printed Gurmukhi there is the older small circle or dot which one often finds in early eighteenth-century manuscripts. In this manuscript's case this dot usually appears in the margins when the scribe had inadvertently left out the short vertical stroke. See *Prashan-uttar*, ms. 684, Punjab State Archives, Patiala, folios 216a, b; 219b; 221b; 222b; 225a; 227b; 228a; 229a.
19. See Piara Singh P.S. Padam, *Rahit-nāme* (5th ed., Amritsar: Bhai Chatar Singh Bhai Jivan Singh, 1991), p. 54 and Ganda Singh (ed.), *Bhāī Nand Lāl Granthāvalī* (Patiala: Punjabi University Press, 1989), pp. 220–1. [hereafter *BNLG*]. A translation appears in Hew McLeod, *Sikhs of the Khalsa*, pp. 265–6. In this version we are told of three forms the Guru will assume: the visible (*saguna*), the invisible (*nirguna*), and the *gurshabad*.
20. *Prashan-uttar*, ms. 684, Punjab State Archives, Patiala, fols 221a–b.
21. This last reference though would be superfluous. See the discussion in 'Darbār', in *EoS* I, pp. 506–7.
22. Ganda Singh (ed.), *Srī Gur-Sobhā* 18:42, p. 170.
23. Among many are mss. 752 and 764 Central Public Library, Patiala; ms. 90272, Punjabi University, Patiala; ms. 104, Bhasha Vibhag Punjab, Patiala; mss. 464, 1059(b), 177(a, c), 790, 609(s), 439(b), Guru Nanak Dev University, Amritsar.
24. GS/MSS 332121, Punjabi University, Patiala and the incomplete ms. 2311 Sikh Reference Library, Khalsa College, Amritsar. The former is dated to 1906 sammat (1849 CE). I was unable to check for Nand Lal manuscripts in Pakistan in 2002 because of the political standoff between India and Pakistan at that time.
25. The general content of Nand Lal's poetry has been examined elsewhere. See my 'Persian Sikh Scripture: the Ghazals of Bhai Nand Lal Goya', in *International Journal of Punjab Studies* I:1 (1994), pp. 49–70.
26. Ms. 115123, Punjabi University, Patiala. Other features of this manuscript which merit consideration are that it may have been consulted by numerous scribes as there are many different hands at work in the translations, some on the same folio (on a number of individual folios for example both Devanagari and Gurmukhi appear). The production of this text in Gurmukhi

along with its sporadic translations suggests that there were indeed Sikhs who were not only aware of Nand Lal's *Dīvān* but used it to recite his hymns, perhaps according to it a revered place among the compositions of the Gurus thus foreshadowing its eventual incorporation into the Sikh Canon. Some may, moreover, have used the occasional bait as an augury in the same way that cultured Muslims used the ghazals of Hafez and Rumi. For the emperor Jahangir's use of such see Wheeler M. Thackston (trans.), *Jahangirnama*, pp. 132, 222.

27. For a similar phenomenon regarding the Puranas, in which commentators translate the texts into the vernacular and comment upon them, see Giorgio Bonazzoli, 'Composition, Transmission, and Recitation of the *Purānas*,' in *Purāna* 25 (July 1983), pp. 254–80.
28. Kahn Singh, *Gurmat Sudhākar* (5th ed., Patiala: Bhasha Vibhag Punjab, 1988), pp. 237–76 and his *Gurumat Māratand* (3rd ed., Amritsar: SGPC, 1993), p. 796.
29. By way of illustration consult ms. 764, Central Public Library, Patiala. Many Sikh scholars hold that the small size of such manuscripts were essential at a time when Sikhs (particularly Khalsa Sikhs) were hounded by the authorities.
30. For this emphasis on oral transmission of ghazals and hymns within the broader Islamicate see Canfield, *Turko-Persia*, p. 30. Winand M. Callewaert, 'Singers Repertoires in Western India', in R.S. McGregor (ed.), *Devotional Literature in South Asia: Current Research 1985–1988* (Cambridge: Cambridge University Press, 1992), pp. 29–35 deals with this type of communication within India itself. As Nand Lal's bani is, according to the *Sikh Rahit Maryada*, today accepted for recitation within gurdwaras along with the hymns of the Gurus and those of Bhai Gurdas, it is clear that it is still orally transmitted.
31. Although such seems obvious one may consult for background Pashaura Singh, *The Guru Granth Sahib*, pp. 270–1 and Callewaert, 'Singers Repertoires'. An insightful definition and discussion of katha in a Vaishnava context, especially its performative dimension which is excluded from discussions of Sikh katha, appears in Philip Lutgendorf's *The Life of a Text: Performing the* Rāmcharitmānas *of Tulsidas* (Berkeley: University of California Press, 1991), pp. 115–19.
32. *EoS* II, p. 460. Also Callewaert, 'Singers' Repertoires,' p. 29.
33. Bhai Gurdas also authored 675 kabitts in Brajbhasha. These all appear along with commentary, text, concordance, and an explanation of difficult words in Onkar Singh, *Kabitt Savaiye Bhāī Gurdās: Pāth, Tuk-tatkarā, Anukramnikā ate Kosh* (Patiala: Punjabi University Publication Bureau, 1993).
34. The portion of the twelfth chapter of the *Bansāvalīnāmā* which refers to Nand Lal is missing in Rattan Singh Jaggi's edition of the text: R.S. Jaggi (ed.), *Kesar Singh Chhibbar dā Bansāvalīnāmā Dasān Pātshāhīān kā* in S.S. Kohli (ed.), *Parkh: Research Bulletin of Panjabi Language and*

252 The Darbar of the Sikh Gurus

Literature (Chandigarh: Panjab University, 1972). The expanded *Bansāvalī-nāmā* appears in Piara Singh Padam edition of the *BSVN*.
35. Jeevan S. Deol, 'Eighteenth Century Khalsa Identity', pp. 27–30. Also, 'Ajīt Singh Pālit', in *EoS* I, pp. 31–2.
36. *BSVN* 10:500, 504, p. 171.
37. *BSVN* 12:11, p. 204. For Kirpal Singh the brother of Mata Gujari who first distinguished himself in the Battle of Bhangani see 'Kirpāl Chand' in *EoS* II, p. 512.
38. Muzaffar Alam, *The Crisis of Empire in Mughal North India: Awadh and Punjab 1707–1748* (Delhi: Oxford University Press, 1986), p. 175. Of course Guru Gobind Singh also accepted a robe of honour from Bahadar Shah.
39. *MP* II, 5:30, p. 772:
    [Nand Lal] was then given the title Mullah Goya.
    Although we are not told who bestowed this title upon Nand Lal it is given to our poet just after he successfully interprets a passage from the Qur'an for the emperor Aurangzeb. See below. Interestingly, this story is absent from Santokh Singh's account which implies that he purposefully omitted it.
40. There are well over one hundred devotees of the Gurus mentioned in this var but only a small number of these were employed by the Mughal administration or army. *BG* 11, pp. 174–96.
41. A critical edition of this text is Tarlochan Singh Bedi (ed.), *Sikhān dī Bagatmālā*, pp. 61–143. Also Vir Singh (ed.), *Bhai Gurdās jī dī Yarvhīn Vār dā Tīkā Arthāt Sikhān dī Bhagat Māllā Rachit Sacchkhand Vasī Srī Bhāī Sāhib Shahīd Bhāī Mani Singh jī Gayānī*, pp. 28–165. Most of the Sikhs mentioned in var 11 also have very brief entries in Kahn Singh's *Gur-shabad Ratanākar Mahān Kosh*.
42. *Darbārī Ratan*, pp. 161, 171. Bharatbhushan Chaudhari, *Ālam aur unkā Kāvya*, pp. 10 ff.
43. Background on Prince Muhammad Mu'azzam appears in Jadunath Sarkar, *History of Aurangzeb Based on Original Sources* III, IV (second edition, Calcutta: M.C. Sarkar & Sons, 1928, 1930), esp. III: pp. 44–7.
44. *EoS* I, pp. 399–400.
45. There is a poetic conceit here as lāl 'beloved' in this context, is also the penname associated with Nand Lal.
46. *MP* II 10:4, p. 767. For the Philosopher's Stone see amongst many others Guru Ram Das' *Kānrā ashtpadīān* 1(6), Adi Granth, p. 1311. The hymn noted at the end of this quote is Guru Nanak, *Japji* 38, Adi Granth, p. 8. The *MP* narrative is clearly the basis for Santokh Singh's section dealing with Nand Lal. See *SP* XII 3:24–7, pp. 5075–92. This very same passage from Japji is, for example, reproduced at *SP* XII 3:24:33, p. 5078 although in this version Nand Lal recites the line:
    At that time Nand Lal pressed both palms together and prayed (*bolyo*): 'O Nanak, [it is only] through the grace of the merciful Lord that one

becomes blessed.' [As a result] he obtained mercy such as [that which was] the True Guru's [to give] and much love [began to] reside in his heart.
47. This passage is reminiscent of *Bachitar Nātak* 1:100, Dasam Granth, p. 46: One cannot realise the Lord by wearing wooden necklaces around one's neck nor does such knowledge come from keeping one's hair matted upon one's head.
48. *MP* II 11:2–9, pp. 768–9.
49. This sakhi appears in the mid-eighteenth century *MPV* 4, pp. 34–5 as well as within the Miharban janam-sakhi. See W.H. McLeod, *Guru Nanak and the Sikh Religion* (Oxford: Clarendon Press, 1968), p. 52 and his *Early Sikh Tradition: A Study of the Janam-sākhīs* (Oxford: Clarendon Press, 1980), p. 283. An English version appears in M.A. Macauliffe, *The Sikh Religion* I, p. 16.
50. For Sarup Das Bhalla's interest in his family and by extension Khatri devotees of the ten Sikh Gurus see Surjit Hans, *A Reconstruction of Sikh History from Sikh Literature* (Jalandhar: ABS, 1988), pp. 285–7.
51. Mahinder Singh Randhawa (ed.), *Pūran Singh Jīvanī te Kavitā* (New Delhi: Sahit Akadami, 1965), pp. 363–6.
52. *MP* II 6:10, p. 775. Also see *SP* XII, 3:26:36, p. 5082 where the *dīvān khās kā daroghā* (The Superintendant of the *Diwan-i khass* [5:16]) of *MP* is named Ghiyasuddin, simply a superintendent of the Mughals and a Muslim friend of Nand Lal who accompanies Nand Lal to Anandpur. He here claims:

[Nand Lal,] I acknowledge you as my *murshid*. [Thanks to your teachings] I cleanse my mind of evil day and night (*dinprati*); [Thanks to your teachings] I meditate on the [glories of] the Lord day and night (*nit*, always). I consider you to be the one who will help [me] at the end [of my life].

Later in the *MP* narrative Mir Sahib presents the tenth Guru with an offering of 1500 mohars after which Guru Gobind Singh asks him whom he calls guru:

The Guru then spoke to him: 'Tell me whose disciple you are.' He joined his palms together and then uttered these words: 'I am a disciple (sikh) of the teacher (gurū) Nand Lal.

MP II 6:19, p. 19, p. 777. Also see *SP* XII, 3:26:11–12, p. 5083.
53. Whom both Sarup Das Bhalla and Santokh Singh mistakenly refer to by his later title Bahadar Shah. See *MP* II, 5:13, p. 770 and *SP* XII, 3:24:14, p. 5077.
54. The famous story notes that one evening Guru Gobind Singh had toured the various langars throughout Anandpur incognito and had found only Nand Lal's to be in perfect order, and to give food to all regardless of their caste or the time they arrived at the kitchen. *MP* II, 9:1–16, pp. 787–9. The Guru afterwards recites his tale and:

254 The Darbar of the Sikh Gurus

> The Guru demonstrated to all of the Sikhs [present the nature of Nand Lal's service.] He said, '[Nand Lal] spoke the language of love and devotion. Nand Lal is our benefactor whose commitment is pleasing and who sets out the net whose form is love and there ensnares the bird. Love is the food which these birds peck up thus becoming dyed with the colour of the Lord's love. Running such a langar the Sikhs acquire riches. [In this regard] Nand Lal's langar is most successful.'

See also *SP* XII, 3:26:42, p. 5086. There may be some merit to this tradition as within the rahit-nama credited to Desa Singh there are lengthy descriptions attributed to Bhai Nand Lal, of the langar and the method of conducting one. The tradition of Nand Lal's pristine langar, however, may have arisen from just such claims. See lines 90–120 in the Desa Singh Rahit nama which appear in Piara Singh Padam, *Rahit-nāme*, pp. 153–5.

55. *Prashan-uttar* 19 as found in P.S. Padam, *Rahit-nāme*, p. 55:

> Listen, Bhai Nand Lal, [as you are a true] Sikh, to the divine message which I convey to you. Acknowledge the visible form of the Guru within the one whose face is turned towards the Guru. The first step in selflessly serving me is to serve them attentively.

Our earlier mentioned manuscript copy's portion dealing with sevā is far more brief, compromising but one line. Punjab State Archives, Patiala ms. 684, f. 222a:

> And Bhai Nand Lal ji, you [also] asked about serving selflessly. Listen, this is selfless service: what the Wonderful Lord finds acceptable is the service of that person who selflessly serves the Sikhs and the sants.

56. Macauliffe's references to Nand Lal are clearly based on Santokh Singh. See *The Sikh Religion* V, pp. 79, 102–4, and 230.
57. The manuscript begins on folio 46a with the phrase *dhiāu guhaj ustat dasam shabad* which we may assume is the title of the work. Ms. 1060(s) Guru Nanak Dev University, folio 52a. Incidentally, both Gobind and Nand Lal are epithets of Krishna.
58. See again Jit Singh Sital (ed.), *Srī Gur-panth Prakāsh*, p. 186 and Macauliffe *The Sikh Religion* IV, p. 379. Richard Eaton discusses the 'connection between political fortune and spiritual blessing' in regard to the Chishti Sufi order and the sultans of Bengal in his *The Rise of Islam and the Bengal Frontier: 1204–1760* (Delhi: Oxford University Press, 1994), p. 84.
59. As mentioned earlier this 'acceptance' is based upon statements found in both the *Bachitar Nātak* and the *Zafar-nāmah* both attributed to Guru Gobind Singh. See *Bachitar Natak* 13:9 and *Zafar-nāmah* 89–94, Dasam Granth, pp. 71, 1393.
60. Louis E. Fenech, *Martyrdom in the Sikh Tradition: Playing the 'Game of Love'* (New Delhi: Oxford University Press, 2000), p. 150.
61. These statements appear in Nizami-i 'Aruzi's *Chahār Maqāla* or 'Four Discourses'. Edward G. Browne (ed. and trans.), *The Chahār Maqāla ("Four Discourses") of Nidhāmī-i-'Arūdī-i-Samarqandī* (London: Luzac & Co.,

1900), p. 49. As a text regularly quoted throughout the Islamicate it is quite likely that the contents of the *Chahār Muqālah* were well known within Timurid Central Asian and Indo-Timurid Mughal India.

62. *MP* II, 5:11–13, pp. 769–70. Also *SP* XII, 3:24:15–16, pp. 5076–7:
    [As time went on] Nand Lal went to the *maktab* [for his education] on a daily basis. Here he was made to study Persian and all forms of Islamic knowledge (*ilm*; Persian: *alm*). His brilliance (*tīcchan* 'sharpness') and wisdom improved through steady practice (*punahi abhbhayāse*). The great light of knowledge began to shine within him through his relentless learning. [Nand Lal] read large collections of books and as a result became knowledgeable/very accomplished in the subject of Islamic literature and learning. Within society [Nand Lal] was quick witted and spoke on important subjects intelligently. [In this way] his excessive knowledge in all things became most apparent.

    For a mid-seventeenth century understanding of what went into preparing a student for the career of munshi see the delightful letter sent by the famous court poet and writer Chandar Bhan Brahman to his son, Khwaja Tej Bhan. A translation into English of the relevant portion is found in Muzaffar Alam and Sanjay Subrahmanyam, 'The Making of a Munshi', in *Comparative Studies in South Asia, Africa and the Middle East* 24:2 (2004), pp. 61–72, esp. pp. 62–3.

63. Edward G. Browne (ed. and trans.), *The Chahār Maqāla*, p. 22: '…the wise king cannot do without these four persons—the Scribe, the Poet, the Astrologer, and the Physician.'

64. *MP* II, 5–6, pp. 768–78. The account does indeed appear in the *BSVN* but is not as detailed as the one found in *MP*. See *BSVN* 10:499–504, p. 171. Also see the account in *SP* XII, 25, pp. 5079–82. A narrative which is reminiscent of this story, perhaps forming an epilogue or an interlude appears in the *Sākhī Gurū jī dī Bhāī Nand Lāl jī dī Pātshāhī Dasvīn*, ms. 91 Guru Nanak Dev University, folios 174a–b. This manuscript includes the entire version of the *Prashan-uttar* attributed to Nand Lal although with a substantial narrative portion (stanzas 1–7 and 9–54, fols. 172b–3b; 173b–6a) preceding today's standard text (Piara Singh Padam, *Rahit-nāme*, pp. 54–5). It is difficult to say whether this narrative was written before the *Mahimā Prakāsh* story or not. A later version of this tale is Gian Singh, *TGK* I, pp. 865–6.

65. *EST*, p. 142.

66. According to Badauni Abu'l Fazl presented the emperor Akbar with a commentary on the *āyatulkursī* (the 'Sign of the Throne', Qur'an 2:255) of the *Surat al-Baqarah* (the longest Sura of the Qur'an) which the emperor afterwards praised. See Muhammad Abdul Ghani, *A History of Persian Language and Literature at the Mughal Court: part III—Akbar the Great*, p. 236.

67. Aurangzeb wrote a number of letters to Asad Khan who at the emperor's death possessed a mansab of 7000/7000. For Asad Khan himself see

M. Athar Ali, *The Mughal Nobility Under Aurangzeb*, pp. 105–9, 178, 217. The event noted in the specific letter mentioned above is certainly symmetrical to the Nand Lal story cited and appears in Bilimoria (trans.), *Ruka'at-i-Alamgiri*, letter 125, pp. 124–5. Aurangzeb identifies neither the sura nor the hadith in question although the hadith is in the same spirit as Qur'an 12:101: 'Take my soul at death, and as a true believer, a Muslim, unite me with the righteous.'

68. *MP* II 5:25, p. 771.
69. See *SP* XII 3:25:18, p. 5080:
    On hearing [the meaning the prince] became blissful. He exalted [Nand Lal] morning, noon, and night [and proclaimed that Nand Lal's] profound wisdom could understand all things. In great joy he gave Nand Lal a splendid robe of honour.
70. Santokh Singh enhances Aurangzeb's appreciation of Nand Lal's explanation:
    When Aurangzeb heard [Nand Lal's] interpretation from his son he was amazed through and through. [He exclaimed,] 'There is nothing more intelligent than this!'
    SP XII 3:25:20, p. 5080.
71. *MP* II 5:29, p. 772. As well ms. 91, Guru Nanak Dev University, line 24, folio 174b has Aurangzeb declare:
    A Hindu [who is] very intelligent must accept our pirs and our paikambars. He should take a name which reflects our faith. The Sharia commands that they become Muslim.
72. *SP* XII 3:25:26–8, p. 5081. In the printed edition of *Mahimā Prakāsh* (both the Gurmukhi and Devanagari editions) the following passage is explained in the footnotes as being absent from the archival manuscripts of the *MP*:
    The emperor desired that he be brought into the fold of Islam. However, seeing the passion of his devotion no one could convert him; they gave him [instead] the title 'Mulla Goya.'
    In this instance it is not possible to say who bestows such a title upon Nand Lal. *MP* II, p. 772. The Devanagari edition is Bhagat Singh Vedi (ed.), *Mahimā Prakāsh krit Sarūp Dās Bhallā (Bhāg Dūsrā)* (Chandigarh: Bhasha Vibhag Punjab, 1989), p. 407. My claim that the dark addition is implied in the *MP* (rather than altogether not) is based on the following passage (*MP* II 5:30, p. 772) regarding the emperor's attitude:
    At that time Nand Lal was given the title Mulla Goya and [Aurangzeb's] desire to have [the munshi] punished (*hovai azāb*) increased dramatically.
73. *SP* XII 3:25:24, 37, pp. 5081, 5082. Santokh Singh also strongly implies that Nand Lal had been aware of Aurangzeb's reputation for cruelty well before his disciple's comment. Before knowing the reason for the prince's unease he asks: 'What has your father asked you to say?' *SP* XII 3:25:13, p. 5080. Interestingly Santokh Singh's image of Aurangzeb is far darker than the Aurangzeb we discover in Sarup Das Bhalla's text.

In the Tenth Master's Court 257

74. The story of Babur and Guru Nanak's meeting may be found in Macauliffe, *The Sikh Religion* I, pp. 113–15. Though this meeting is most likely apocryphal Babur's penchant for holymen and mystics is well known.
75. *TGK* I, p. 863.
76. In fact Sikhs of Santokh Singh's era may have witnessed such movement of poets first-hand. It is well known that the nineteenth-century Awadhi nawabs wooed great Urdu poets from Delhi, believed to be at the time the centre of Indo-Muslim cultural life, to Lucknow in order to enhance the status of the Awadhi court itself and augment their own stature as legitimate rulers within the hegemonic (though then impotent) Mughal empire. See for example Carla Petievich, *Assembly of Rivals: Delhi, Lucknow, and the Urdu Ghazal* (New Delhi: Manohar, 1992), pp. 27–8.
77. Literally, *bahir tavil* means 'the long tune'. According to Kahn Singh, the bahir tavil style was the name given especially to eminent and lengthy songs in either Persian or Pushto sung in Tilang rag, the rag of the Adi Granth generally associated with Islamically flavoured hymns. *MK*, p. 828.
78. *MP* II 6:6–8, p. 775. The account of the *Zindagī-nāmah* in the *Mahimā Prakāsh* is most likely an expansion of *Zindagī-nāmah* 498 in which the text of the *Zindagī-nāmah* is likened to the cup of Jamshed whose waters are generally assumed to bring everlasting life.

[This collection] is like the Cup [of Jamshed] filled with the water of [everlasting] life. It is for this reason that it has been named *Zindagīnāmah*, the Book of Life.

This bait suggests a number of possibilities: that the story in *Mahimā Prakāsh* is a fabrication to enhance the image of the tenth Guru or that Nand Lal gave to Guru Gobind Singh an incomplete version of the text. *Zindagī-nāmah* 498 in Ganda Singh (ed.), *Kulliyāt*, p. 108. Nand Lal's family traditions claim that Guru Gobind Singh himself added this last bait to the text. Bhai Megh Raj ji 'Gharib', *Prem Phulvarī arthat Srī Gurū Gobind Singh jī de annanay Sikh Bhāī Nand Lāl jī krit 'Dīvān Goyā'* (Amritsar: Bhapedi Hatti, 1912), pp. 21–2.
79. E.J.W. Gibb, *A History of Ottoman Poetry* II (London: Luzac and Company, 1900), pp. 19–20; and volume I, p. 262. We are here told that the poet Ahmedi was requested by the emperor Timur to join his private circle after he had presented him with a particularly enjoyable Persian qasidah.
80. Muhammad Abdul Ghani, *A History of Persian Language and Literature at the Mughal Court: with a brief survey of the growth of Urdu [Babur to Akbar]* volume 3, *Akbar* (Allahabad: The Indian Press, Ltd., 1930), pp. 24–5, 26.
81. *SP* XII 3:27:16, p. 5091.
82. *Bachitar Nātak* 13, Dasam Granth, pp. 71–3. Also Jadunath Sarkar, *History of Aurangzeb* V, p. 11.
83. Sukha Singh, *Gur-bilās Pātishāhī 10* 16:171–2 [ed. Gursharan Kaur Jaggi] (Patiala: Bhasha Vibhag Punjab, 1989), p. 248. Indubhushan Bannerjee claims that such intercession was provided not by Nand Lal but by Nand

258 The Darbar of the Sikh Gurus

Chand. See his *Evolution of the Khalsa* II (3rd edn., Calcutta: AMC, 1972), p. 91.
84. Surjit Hans, *A Reconstruction of Sikh History from Sikh Literature*, pp. 250–3.
85. Kesar Singh Chhibbar's *BSVN* does imply such residence, however.
86. Uttam Singh Bhatia, *Gurū Bhagat Bhāī Nand Lāl Goyā* (Patiala: Pavitar Pramanik Prakashan, 1987), pp. 15, 17 suggests that Nand Lal went to Agra to be with Prince Mu'azzam after 1695, implying that after this year he shared his time between the two courts. This is a plausible conclusion as the prince was that year released from the confinement in which his father placed him in February 1687 and did indeed make his way to Agra immediately upon such release. Background on the alleged treason and imprisonment of Prince Mu'azzam during his siege of Golconda appears in Jadunath Sarkar, *History of Aurangzeb* IV, pp. 430–3. Also Jadunath Sarkar, *History of Aurangzeb* V (Calcutta: M.C. Sarkar & Sons, 1924), p. 302.
87. Ganda Singh (ed. and trans), *Amar-nāmā: Fārsī mūl, Panjābī Utārā te Arath* (Patiala: Sikh History Society, 1975), line 43, pp. 23–4 for the Gurmukhi text and page 45 for nastaliq text.
    Amongst the privy counselors of the Sultan was Nand Lal. He became the travel companion of the perfect emperor [Bahadar Shah].
88. Maria Eva Subtelny, 'A Taste for the Intricate: The Persian Poetry of the Late Timurid Period', in *Zeitschrift der Deutschen Morgenländischen Gesellschaft* 136:1 (Stuttgart: DMG, 1986), pp. 56–79.
89. According to Surjit Hans this text although claiming a traditional date circa mid eighteenth century is actually a product of Ranjit Singh's period (1799–1839 CE). See Surjit Hans, *A Reconstruction of Sikh History*, pp. 266–9.
90. *MK*, p. 909. In the note marked with an asterisk attached to the respective entry Kahn Singh includes the Sanskrit portion of the Purana which seems to tell of Guru Nanak's birth and a modern Punjabi translation of it.
91. Zebunnisa (1637–1702 CE) was Aurangzeb's eldest daughter and a favourite of Dara Shikoh. An accomplished Persian poet writing under the takhallus *Makhfī* 'hidden' a penname common to the majority of women ghazal poets of Mughal India [Ellsion Banks Findly, *Nur Jahan Empress of Mughal India* (New York: Oxford University Press, 1993), p. 113], Zebunnisa herself held her own darbars to which poets and scholars would flock. For an introduction to Zebunnisa and samples of her poetry see Magan Lal and Jessie Duncan Westbrook (trans.), *The Diwan of Zeb-un-Nissa: the First Fifty Ghazals* (New York: Dutton, 1913).
92. Shamsher Singh 'Ashok' (ed.), *Gurbilās Pātshāhī 10 krit Kuir Singh* 2:16–20 (Patiala: Punjabi University Press, 1968), p. 27.
93. Meisami, *Medieval Persian Court Poetry*, p. 52.
94. The work attributed to Nand Lal which best qualifies as a panegyric (with some qualifications) is the *Ganj-nāmah* and within this text no such passage

In the Tenth Master's Court 259

is readily apparent. Perhaps the bait with which the *Dīvān-i Goyā* begins may be construed as such:
The desire of servitude has brought me into existence. If not for the [taste] of such coming I would have no pleasure.
Dīvān-i Goyā 1:1, *Kullīyāt*, p. 49.

95. *EoS* II, pp. 135–6. This may be confirmed by referring to Kahn Singh's *Mahān Kosh*. In his entry, *guruvilās* there is no mention of Koer Singh's text while both Sukha Singh's and Kavi Sohan's appear. Kahn Singh, *MK*, p. 421.
96. M.A. Macauliffe, *The Sikh Religion* V, p. 103.
97. Ibid.
98. The actual word used here is *akhārā* a 'wrestling pit' literally but also the name used to designate Nirmala as well as Udasi Sikh centres.
99. See sakhi 62 in Gurbachan Singh Naiar (ed.), *Guru Ratan Māl: Sau Sākhī*, p. 71.
100. Naiar (ed.), *Guru Ratan Māl* 66:1–4, p. 80. The sakhi in which we find this majlis setting continues to vet the responses of a number of the tenth Guru's poets (66:5–18) ending with the Guru's own comments upon knowledge of the afterlife (66:19–30). The sakhi concludes (66:31) with the following statement representative of at least one interpretation of the rationale behind the Guru's darbar:
    Discussions regarding knowledge of the divine are always discussed with the mercy of the Guru [in the Guru's Darbar]. The Sikh who hears and attends to these diligently will be saved from the fears of the world.
101. Sakhi 65 of the *Sau Sākhī* places the following words in the mouth of Guru Gobind Singh:
    I will have nothing to do with the Sikh who commits adultery, gambles, or learns Persian. I will take nothing from this person. Never drink water [from the hands of this Sikh]. Never accept anything from the house of the person who reads Persian. Trust him at no time. Do not touch his food [as it is polluted] since he has strayed from the path of dharam.
    Gurbachan Singh Naiar (ed.), *Gur Ratan Māll: Sau Sākhī*, p. 79. What is probably closer to the truth is that such inconsistency underscores the composite nature of the *Sau Sākhīān*.
102. Piara Singh Padam references this passage to underscore the democratic character of Guru Gobind Singh's court. And so according to Padam, 'Even when the Guru was himself gracefully seated within the assembly there were several instances when learned scholars and even honourable friends such as Bhai Nand Lal ji or Bhai Daya Singh managed the darbar. Signs of such management are available in many sources.' Padam, *Darbārī Ratan*, p. 44.
103. For the early history of the nadim and of *munādamah* (boon-companionship) and the rigorous discipline involved in the latter see Anwar G. Chejne, 'The Boon-Companion in Early 'Abbāsid Times,' in *Journal of the American Oriental Society* 85 (1965), pp. 327–35; as well, Julie Scott Meisami,

Medieval Persian Court Poetry, pp. 6–7; Hubert Drake (trans.), *The Book of Government or Rules for Kings: the Siyāsat-nāma of Siyar al-Mulūk of Nizām al-Mulk* (New Haven: Yale University Press, 1960), pp. 92–4; and Reuben Levy (trans. and ed.), *A Mirror for Princes: The Qābūs Nāma by Kai Kā'ūs ibn Iskandar Prince of Gurgān* (London: Cresset Press, 1951), pp. 196–200. The courtier confidant also exists in early Hindi court poetry. See R.S. McGregor, *Hindi Literature*, p. 17.

104. Naiar (ed.), *Guru Ratan Māl: Sau Sākhī*, pp. 71–2. The initial portion of this sakhi is reminiscent of sakhi 155 of the *Sikhān dī Bhagatmālā*. Tarlochan Singh Bedi, *Sikhān dī Bhagatmālā*, pp. 146–7.

105. *MP* II 10:1–11, pp. 790–1. At line 10 we find that

At that time [the celebration of] Holi was praised. Nand Lal sang a ghazal in Persian which when heard by the merciful Guru brought delight. Fortunate indeed is the sangat, great is its glory.

106. Jit Singh Sital (ed.), *Srī Gur-panth Prakāsh*, pp. 57–8, 185–92.

107. According to Bhangu, Farrukh Siyar is unwilling to follow the advice of his Turks who wish him to ultimately jail Mata ji in order to force Banda to cease and desist. He replies to their request as follows:

This course of action which you advise is not at all a good one. I owe my crown to that very family; [it was the line of Sikh Gurus who] blessed us [and my family] with the royal title.

Sital (ed.), *Srī Gur-panth Prakāsh*, 57:7, p. 186.

108. Jit Singh Sital (ed.), *Srī Gur-panth Prakāsh* 57:14–16, p. 187. Gian Singh's version of this story excludes Mata ji and deals directly with Guru Gobind Singh, Nand Lal, and Bahadar Shah rather than the latter's successor. Gian Singh, *TGK* I, pp. 1133–4.

109. Ratan Singh Bhangu was descended from the family of Bhai Mehtab Singh who according to tradition avenged the Sikh Panth by killing the despoiler of Harimandir Sahib, Massa Ranghar. As a member of the true or Tat Khalsa Mehtab Singh would have taken issue with Banda's more questionable activities and that of the Sikhs who surrounded Banda known as the Bandai Khalsa.

110. Jit Singh Sital (ed.), *Srī Gur-panth Prakāsh* 58:5, p. 188.

111. A contemporary retelling of Nand Lal's brief biography and reputation is found in *EoS* III, pp. 195–6. A more critical appreciation of Nand Lal's 'biography' is my 'Bhāī Nand Lāl "Goyā" and the Sikh Tradition', in Pashaura Singh *et al.* (ed.), *Sikhism and History* (New Delhi: Oxford University Press, 2004), pp. 111–34.

112. Ganda Singh speculates that Nand Lal was probably born somewhere near Agra if not in the city itself. *BNLG*, p. 2.

113. I base this brief narrative of Nand Lal's early life on the text prepared by his ancestors Megh Raj and the latter's son, Ram Dyal. Bhai Megh Raj ji 'Gharib', *Prem Phulvarī* and Ram Dyal, *The Life of Bhai Nand Lal Goya* (Amritsar: The Sikh Tract Society, 1923). Ram Dyal is noted in Ganda

In the Tenth Master's Court 261

Singh's family tree of Nand Lal which appears at *BNLG*, pp. 22–3. For a brief history of Nand Lal's family see *BNLG*, pp. 17–21. A glance through any early twentieth-century Singh Sabha tract or text dealing with Nand Lal will invariably rely on these, particularly the former, in the construction of their narrative. See for example both See Vir Singh (ed.), *Ganjnāmah* (rpt; New Delhi: Bhai Vir Singh Sahitya Sadan, 1966) and Karam Singh Zakhmi, *Srī Gurū Gobind Singh jī de Annanay Sikh Bhāī Nand Lāl jī krit Tausīfo Sanā* (Amritsar: Bhape di Hati, 1930). The title of this last work is misleading as it is not the *Tausīf o Sanā'* which is supplied but rather a translation (with accompanying Persian-Gurmukhi text) of the *Ganj-nāmah*.

114. For the Singh Sabha the best account remains Harjot Oberoi's *The Construction of Religious Boundaries: Culture, Identity and Diversity in the Sikh Tradition* (Delhi: Oxford University Press, 1994).

115. Although emperors and princes could alter their selection of mir munshis on a whim, according to contemporary accounts, most notably the *Mirāt-i Jahān-nāmah*, the famed Chandar Bhan Brahman was at one point in time appointed the mir munshi of Dara Shikoh. See Mohiuddin, *The Chancellery and Persian Epistolography*, p. 228 and Hasrat, *Dārā Shikoh*, p. 244. Perhaps telling are two statements about Chhajju Mall which were made some forty years apart. While Kahn Singh Nabha refers to Chhajju Mall as *jo fārsī dī vidhvān sī* '[A man] who was a scholar of Persian' [*MK*, p. 723] Ganda Singh describes him as *fārsī ate arabī change vidavān mālūm hunde han* 'A very famous scholar of Persian and Arabic.' *BNLG*, p. 2.

116. Ganda Singh speculates that Nand Lal was probably born somewhere near Agra if not in the city itself. *BNLG*, p. 2.

117. These standards are outlined in Mohiuddin, *The Chancellery and Persian Epistolography*, pp. 40–4. Such an education emphasized history, Islamic jurisprudence (fiqh), theology, linguistic science, epistolography (inshā), and Quranic exegesis (*tafsīr*) as well as traditional *yunānī* (Graeco-Arab) medicine. To this was added the study of prosody, panegyrics (qasīdas), and Persian mystical poetry, particularly the ghazals and masnavis of Hafez, Jalaluddin Rumi, Attar, Sa'di, Amir Khusrau and other famous poets. If the Persian works attributed to Nand Lal are actually the product of the Nand Lal of Sikh tradition then it is clear that he was indeed well learned in all of these areas. A comprehensive examination of Muslim education prior to the modern period appears in Aziz Ahmad, *An Intellectual History of Islam in India* (Edinburgh: Edinburgh University Press, 1969), pp. 53–7; 78; and his *Studies in Islamic Culture in the Indian Environment* (Oxford: Clarendon Press, 1964), pp. 234–5. For the poetic contributions to an education see Annemarie Schimmel, 'Persian Poetry in the Indo-Pakistani Subcontinent', in Ehsan Yarshater, *Persian Literature* (New York: Columbia University Press, 1988), pp. 405–21. It is worth mentioning that for those men and women who desired to become Persian poets the ideal

to which they aspired was to memorize as many couplets as they could. In fact, some poets are said to have memorized anywhere from 25,000 to 50,000 baits. Maria Eva Subtelny, 'A Taste for the Intricate: The Persian Poetry of the Late Timurid Period', esp. pp. 60–4.
118. Sikh tradition only provides his title, 'Lord Virtue'. I have been unable to discover any reference to a Wassaf Khan in Multan during the seventeenth century. Perhaps the most telling is the lack of reference in M. Athar Ali, *The Apparatus of Empire: Awards of Ranks, Offices, and Titles to the Mughal Nobility, 1573–1658* (New Delhi, 1985). For a list of Nawabs in seventeenth-century Multan see Humaira Faiz Dasti, *Multan: A Province of the Mughal Empire (1525–1751)* (Karachi: Royal Book Company, 1998), pp. 148–56. According to the *EoS* III, p. 195 Wassaf Khan was the Subadar of Multan.
119. Rypka, *Iranian Literature*, p. 315. The best analysis of insha materials in India remains Momin Mohiuddin, *The Chancellery and Persian Epistolography*.
120. One must, moreover, read such texts guardedly for as recent studies on insha literature in India have made clear scribes and clerks sometimes fabricated letters to dignitaries and members of the Mughal royal family and others to serve as stylistic examples. In fact, Zahuruddin Ahmad has determined that such was done by the great Abu'l Fazl himself. Zahuruddin Ahmad, *Abu'l Fazl—Ahwāl o Āsār* (Lahore: Punjab University Press, 1975), pp. 185–97 as noted in Ishtiyaq Ahmad Zilli, 'Development of *Inshā* Literature to the End of Akbar's Reign', in Muzaffar Alam et al (ed.), *The Making of Indo-Persian Culture: Indian and French Studies* (New Delhi: Manohar, 2000), pp. 309–49. This wonderful article also constructs a history of insha literature from its earliest period to the sixteenth century both within and outside of India. Ahmad Zilli notes that even the fabricated letters are significant in the proper context as it allows historians to understand the principles and norms of political and social behaviour of the compiler's period.
121. The line appears directly below and may be found in Ganda Singh's *Kulliyāt*, p. 205:
My book the *Dastūrulinshā* is here completed. It was completed by Munshi Nand Lal Goya Multani.
Fenech, 'Bhai Nand Lal "Goya" and the Sikh Tradition', p. 120.
122. Also the signature line in the final *Khatimah* of the *Tausīf o Sanā'* (f. 25b) was clearly added later in an unsteady hand and in pencil. On this same folio there are marginal notes providing alternatives to the final bait. I have in my possession a photo of this folio. Manuscript 332164/GS at Punjabi University, Patiala contains the *Tausīf o Sanā'* (folios 2a–25b); *Ganj-nāmah* (folios 27a–38b); *Tarjumah Joti Bigās* (folios 40a–8a); *Dastūrulinshā* (folios 48b–63a); and the *'Arzulalfāz* (folios 63b–124b). After three months of scouring the archives and libraries of the Punjab during the summer of 2002 this was the only manuscript copy I discovered which includes these

particular works of Nand Lal. In other words, while manuscript copies of the *Dīvān* and *Zindagī-nāmah* are plentiful this may be the only available manuscript of these lesser known texts. Unfortunately Vir Singh does not mention the manuscript on which he relied for his version of the *Ganj-nāmah*. See Vir Singh (ed.), *Ganj-nāmah* (New Delhi: Bhai Vir Singh Sahitya Sadan, 1966).

123. It is exactly this term *kaharah* which appears in the *Kulliyāt*, p. 190. As it stands here this word makes no sense unless it is the name of some place I have yet to discover. I have therefore taken it to be a combination of the terms *gāh* (in Persian manuscripts the 'g' character rarely appears with the second top bar so every *kāf* or 'k' character may be a potential 'g') and *rāh* though there are certainly other possible readings.

124. *Kulliyāt*, p. 190.

125. Chetan Singh, *Region and Empire: Panjab in the Seventeenth Century* (New Delhi: Oxford University Press, 1991), pp. 206ff.

126. Linda Darling, 'Middle Eastern Advice for Indian Muslim Rulers,' p. 11.

127. The translation appears in Irfan Habib, *The Agrarian System of Mughal India 1556–1707* (second revised edition, New Delhi: Oxford University Press, 2002), p. 75, n. 41.

128. See Jadunath Sarkar (trans.), *Anecdotes of Aurangzib* (English Translation of *Ahkam-i-Alamgiri*), p. 68.

129. *Kulliyāt*, pp. 194–5. Ganda Singh's Punjabi translation of this address follows:

> The great and respected brother, the person who is a Gurmukh, Bhai Gurbakhsh Singh ji…

BNLG, p. 235.

130. What governed the choice of letters to prepare or include within an inshā was based far more on style, expression, and even penmanship than on the particular events narrated within. These letters, in other words, are not without importance in terms of biographical or historical data, but 'their factual contents stand in inverse ratio to their verbosity.' Rypka, *Iranian Literature*, p. 316. This verbosity was telling in itself however. Note the words of Momin Mohiuddin: 'There is hardly any other branch of Persian literature which mirrors the social set up and reflects the character of the society of that period so clearly as the epistolography…. Distinction of class was maintained and recognized [within the eloquence of the inshā] as determining their relations with one another.' Mohiuddin, The Chancellery and Persian Epistolography, p. 19.

131. Apparently Nand Lal was at the head of a powerful army which had defeated a 'wealthy and famous' dacoit operating in the areas around Multan. *BNLG*, p. 5. It seems unlikely that Nand Lal did succeeded to the deputy governorship as a list of men who held the title *nā'ib* is provided in Humaira Faiz Dasti, *Multan*, pp. 148–77.

132. According to Megh Raj Nand Lal travelled to Agra where Prince Mu'azzam resided as the governor and recited an encomium in praise of Aurangzeb. Pleased by Nand Lal's literary abilities the prince awarded him the post of mir munshi. Megh Raj, *Prem Phulvarī*, pp. 13–14. Also Ram Dyal, *Life*, pp. 10–11.

133. Rahim's biography and Brajbhasha poetry appears in Samar Bahadar Simha, *Abdurrahīm Khānkhānā* (Chirganv: Sahitya Sadan, 1961).

134. Muhammad Abdul Ghani, *A History of Persian Language and Literature at the Mughal Court: with a brief survey of the growth of Urdu* [Babur to Akbar] *volume 3, Akbar* (Allahabad: the Indian Press, Ltd., 1930), p. 226, n. 1. Compare this with Ganda Singh's statements *BNLG*, pp. 4–5.

135. *MK*, p. 723 Ganda Singh claims it was 1712 (*BNLG*, p. 13).

136. Fenech, 'Bhāī Nand Lāl "Goyā" and the Sikh Tradition', pp. 111–34.

137. According to Sikh tradition there were other Nand Lals associated with the history of the Sikhs and indeed within the court of the tenth Guru. Piara Singh Padam, *Darbārī Ratan*, p. 217. For the reasons behind the elimination of this Nand Lal and various other namesakes in Sikh tradition see my 'Bhāī Nand Lāl "Goyā" and the Sikh Tradition', pp. 117–18.

138. For example W.H. McLeod, *Sikhs of the Khalsa*, p. 16.

139. Ganda Singh (ed.), *Srī Gur-Sobhā*, chapters 5 and 6, pp. 78–96. Jeevan S. Deol, 'Eighteenth Century Khalsa Identity, pp. 25–46. Let us recall that in some eighteenth- and nineteenth-century sources Nand Lal resided in Delhi, the home of many Khatri Sikhs.

140. Renaming the text *Tankhāh-nāmā* probably had something to do with the early to mid eighteenth-century enmity between the Sikhs and the Mughals as well. As is well known, the nasihat-nama genre was a common variety of Islamicate literature found within the territory covering Ottoman Rum to Mughal India, which contained letters advising monarchs in all sorts of matters, particularly economic. And so according to Stephen Dale: '[The Emperor] Akbar might have been sitting with one such nasihat nama in hand when he formulated Mughal commercial policies...' Stephen F. Dale, *Indian Merchants and Eurasian Trade, 1600–1750* (Cambridge: Cambridge University Press, 1994; paperback edition, 2002), pp. 31–2. Such a title may have therefore been understood by Sikh scribes and writers after 1719 as relating to the type of advice given specifically to Mughals and as such required recasting in the light of the anti-Mughal and anti-Islamic bias found in some of the Sikh literature of this later period. Indeed, the seventeenth and eighteenth-century Sikh association between the title nasihat-nama and Islam is also evinced in manuscript IOL MS Panj B41 at the India Office Library, the latter portion of which is titled *Nasihat-nāmā* and in which we discover the *Tilang kī vār* of Guru Nanak. As Christopher Shackle reminds us 'this *rāg* [*rag tilang*] was clearly felt to have a special appropriateness for poems associated with Islam.' C. Shackle, 'Approaches to the Persian Loans in the Ādi Granth', p. 81, n. 34. Interestingly, it is very

likely that as a Khatri, the Hindu/Sikh trading community par excellence in later Indo-Islamic northern India and the rest of the eastern Islamicate, Nand Lal would have been familiar with the contents of nasihat-namas. See Scott C. Levi, *The Indian Diaspora in Central Asia and its Trade, 1550–1900* (Leiden: Brill, 2002), pp. 38, 110–11.
141. Based on the examinations of Hew McLeod: W.H. McLeod, *Sikhs of the Khalsa*, p. 69.
142. *Srī Gur-Sobhā* 5:23, p. 80: *bhaddar bharam dharam kacchu nāhī*. This statement is noted by both Deol ('Eighteenth Century Khalsa Identity', p. 26) and McLeod (*Sikhs of the Khalsa*, p. 270). What seems disregarded, however, is that Sainapati later implies that such advice to the Khatri Sikhs of Delhi regarding bhaddar may well have convinced them to give up the practice as in the sixteenth chapter of *Gur-Sobhā*, we find the Delhi sangat's rejoicing at the prospect of Guru Gobind Singh's arrival near Delhi while on his way to meet with the newly crowned Bahadar Shah. *Gur-Sobhā* 16:1, p. 153. Indeed, having earlier equated bhaddar with bharam Sainapati claims that the Delhi meeting between the sangat and the Guru was very efficacious in obviating error:

> The shabad was uttered and the [sangat] saw the one [true Lord]. [As a result its members] were liberated from both fear and the cycle of existence, and delusion was destroyed (*bharaman bidār*).

Gur-Sobhā 16:3–4, p. 153; also 18:24, 28, p. 168.
143. In Nand Lal's *Sākhī Rahit kī* for example the proscription regarding bhaddar/bhaddan is once again emphasized. *CSRn*, pp. 133, 202.
144. For the enmity between the emerging Khalsa and the Khatri biradari see Deol, 'Eighteenth Century Khalsa Identity, pp. 25–46.
145. McLeod, *Sikhs of the Khalsa*, pp. 131, 147.
146. Hari Ram Gupta's *History of the Sikhs* I (Delhi: Munshiram Manoharlal Publishers, 1984), p. 381 retells that story which notes that prior to presenting himself before the Guru Nand Lal presented his poetry. It was only after this that the Guru invited the poet before him.
147. *Sultanat Dahamm* 2:52 of the *Ganj-nāmah*, Ganda Singh (ed.), *Kulliyāt*, p. 125. (in other editions of the *Ganj-nāmah* this is bait 53). The *nām* (name) here probably refers to both the nām of Sikh theology, that aspect of the divine which permeates the universe and the very name of Guru Gobind Singh.
148. Bhai Megh Raj 'Garib', *Prem Phulvarī*, p. 23.
149. Maria Eva Subtelny, 'The Poetic Circle at the Court of the Timurid Sultan Husain Baiqara, and its Political Significance', (PhD thesis, Harvard University, 1979), pp. 30, 84–6, 90, 91. On page 71 there is a quote from Dawlatshah's famous *Tadkiratushshuarā* which criticizes contemporary poets (circa early sixteenth century). The criticisms tell us of the ideal qualities which were sought in poets.
150. The works attributed to Nand Lal Goya are the *Dīvān-i Goyā* (Persian), *Zindagī-nāmah* (Persian), *Ganj-nāmah* (Persian), *Joti Bigās* (Punjabi), *Joti*

Bigās (Persian with Punjabi. The title of this work is in Punjabi as it is, according to tradition, an attempt in Persian to expand upon the 43 couplets of the Punjabi *Joti Bigās*. Indeed, ms 332164 at Punjabi University, Patiala titles this Persian work *Tarjumah Joti Bigās* or '[An] Interpretation of the *Joti Bigās*), *Tanakhāh-nāmā* (Punjabi), the *Sākhī rahit kī* usually appended to the text of the Chaupa Singh rahit-nama (Punjabi), *Prashanuttar* (Punjabi), *Dastūrulinshā* (Persian), *Arzulalfāz* (Persian with some Punjabi and Arabic), and the *Tausīf o Sanā* (Persian). All of these are included in the *Kulliyāt-i Bhāī Nand Lal Goyā*. For the education required to write such works see Aziz Ahmad, *An Intellectual History of Islam in India* (Edinburgh: Edinburgh University Press, 1969), pp. 53–7; 78; and his *Studies in Islamic Culture in the Indian Environment* (Oxford: Clarendon Press, 1964), pp. 234–5.

151. Grewal and Bal plot a similar trajectory when they claim that 'some of the [hill] Chiefs (*sic*) [of the Punjab] of their own accord could try to assimilate their administration to that of the Mughals,' Grewal and Bal, *Guru Gobind Singh*, p. 12.

152. M. Athar Ali, *The Mughal Nobility Under Aurangzeb*, noble no. 563, p. 270. A discussion of Mughal nobles who formed a very small portion of the combined nobility and were 'recruited from those who had no claims to high birth but were pure administrators or accountants' is noted on page 14 of *The Mughal Nobility Under Aurangzeb*.

153. Case in point would be the famous Chandar Bhan 'Brahman', the court poet and mir munshi of Dara Shikoh, author of the *Chahār-Chaman* (The Four Orchards). See F.M. Asiri, 'Chandar Bhan Brahman and His Chahar Chaman', in the *Visva-Bharati Annals* 4 (1951), pp. 51–64 and Ahmad Gulchin-i Ma'ani, *Tārīkh-i Tazkirah-hā-ye Fārsī* I, pp. 631–5. Also in southern India, particularly the later Maratha homeland including the district of Bijapur many brahmans took to Persian and Islamic learning. Richard Eaton, *The Sufis of Bijapur 1300–1700* (Princeton: Princeton University Press, 1978), pp. 90–1. Indeed, as James Laine reminds us to this day many high caste Hindus in Maharashtra have the surname Parasnis indicating 'a former profession as a clerk literate in Persian'. See James W. Laine, *Shivaji: Hindu King of Islamic India* (New York: Oxford University Press, 2003), p. 10. For the role which Khatris and Kayasthas played in Mughal bureaucracy and administration see Aziz Ahmad, *Studies in Islamic Culture in the Indian Environment* (Oxford: Clarendon Press, 1964), pp. 105–7.

154. Ms. 332121 (1851 CE), Punjabi University, Patiala, folio 2a. This rare nastalikh ms. copy of the *Dīvān*, whose scribe was one Faqir Dharam Das of village Naulari (the name is noted on folio 33b while the date appears on folio 16b), is the only manuscript of Nand Lal's works I have seen which begins with the Arabic invocation *bismallah*, 'In the name of God…' Other versions of this ghazal substitute the word *mardum* or 'man' for muqaddam.

Although Ganda Singh supplies *mardum* in this spot he does note that other versions supply muqaddam. See *Kulliyāt*, p. 49.
155. I base this conclusion on information in the entries for *muqaddam* and *muqaddamī* in the recently released CD-ROM version of Ali Akbar Dehkhoda's famous *Lughat-nāmah*.
156. C.A. Bayly, *Rulers, Townsmen and Bazaars: North Indian Society in the Age of British Expansion 1770–1870* (Delhi: Oxford University Press, 1993), pp. 140–1, 240; J.S. Grewal and Indu Banga (eds), *Early Nineteenth Century Punjab: From Ganesh Das's Chār Bāgh-i-Panjāb* (Amritsar: Guru Nanak Dev University, 1975); Irfan Habib, *The Agrarian System of Mughal India 1556–1707* (second revised edition, Delhi: Oxford University Press, 2002), pp. 160–8.
157. *BNLG*, pp. 4–5. Ram Dyal, *The Life of Bhai Nand Lal Goya* (Amritsar: Sikh Tract Society, 1923), tract no. 47. This tract is almost a word for word translation of Ram Dyal's father's *Prem Phulwarī*.
158. That the first Guru's bani provided the motivation behind the works of the subsequent Gurus and Bhai Gurdas is a point made most persuasively by Pashaura Singh, *The Guru Granth Sahib*, pp. 151–76. It seems likely that any writing inspired by the faithful understanding of the first Guru's bani would be generally acceptable as 'Sikh'.
159. For example note once again the association between the hymns of Guru Nanak and Guru Amar Das mentioned in ibid, pp. 158–9 and those between Bhai Gurdas and the first Guru in ibid., pp. 245–6.
160. Christopher Shackle, *An Introduction to the Sacred Language of the Sikhs* (London: School of Oriental and African Studies, 1983).
161. This is outlined in both my 'Bhāī Nand Lāl "Goyā" and the Sikh Tradition' and 'Persian Sikh Scripture: the Ghazals of Bhai Nand Lal Goya', in *International Journal of Punjab Studies* I:1 (1994), pp. 49–70. Sufi/Sikh affinities are noted in W.H. McLeod, *Gurū Nānak and the Sikh Religion* (Oxford: Clarendon Press, 1968), p. 158 among other works. In the same vein Uttam Singh Bhatia, *Gurū Bhagat Bhāī Nand Lāl Goyā* (Patiala: Pavitar Pramanik Prakashan, 1987), pp. 36–50; 88–101 attempts to discuss both the bhakti and the Sufi elements which infuse Nand Lal's *Zindagī-nāmah*. Rather than actualities though Bhatia relies on affinities.
162. *Joti Bigās, Kulliyāt*, pp. 159–69.
163. *Arzulalfāz baits* 127 and 132, *Kulliyāt*, p. 213.
164. I shall therefore consider the first 17 couplets as part 1 and the final 56 couplets as part 2. This text is, as far as I know, the only Persian work attributed to Nand Lal which begins with a shabad from the Guru Granth Sahib (Although the opening couplet of the Punjabi *Joti Bigās* seems to allude to the shabad in question, *BNLG*, p. 217):
The Guru is Gobind, the Guru is Gopal, the Guru is the Perfect Narayana. The Guru is merciful and mighty indeed. The Guru, O Nanak, is the support of all those who have fallen by the wayside (*patit*).

Guru Arjan, *Jaitsarī dī Vār* 19, Adi Granth, p. 710. This hymn by the fifth Sikh Master, appropriating names and titles characteristically associated with the Hindu deities Krishna and Rama, is particularly apt as it includes the names of both the terminal and initial human Gurus (Gobind and Nanak, at the beginning and end respectively) thus in a sense collapsing the entire content of the *Ganj-nāmah* in the same way that the *Mūl Mantar* which begins the Adi Granth condenses the nature of Akal Purakh and by extension the content of the Sikh scripture (Pashaura Singh, *The Guru Granth Sahib*, p. 84). The hymn appears in Perso-Arabic script in the *Kulliyāt*, p. 109; in Gurmukhi, *BNLG*, p. 162.

165. *Sultanat Dahamm* 2:1–3, 56 of the *Ganj-nāmah*, *Kulliyāt*, pp. 122–3, 125. The *Ganj-nāmah* includes a brief introduction as well as ten further chapters each of which is broken up into two further parts (perhaps in an attempt to mimic the format of Sa'di's *Būstān*?). Each of the ten deals with one of the Sikh Gurus in the traditional sequence of their guruship. In the *Sultanat Dahamm* portion the first 17 baits glorify both God and Guru Gobind Singh and then proceed to allude to the Guru's metaphysical qualities based on the Persian letters of his name [G-O-B-N-D-S-N-G-H], tacitly noting the cosmic and worldly processes which occur as the pious devotee speaks the name of the Guru. And so, for example,

The Persian letter 'G' (here, *kāf-i fārsī*) [refers to] the name of the ultimate truth of the universe while the letter 'o' (*vāv*) is the beginning of the cause of the movements of both earth and time.

Sultanat Dahamm 1:6, *Kulliyāt*, pp. 121–2.

166. According to Robert Canfield, '[Persian] Poetry has often been a powerful idiom of popular protest', *Turko-Persia*, p. 4. The specific challenge to which I allude above may be discerned through *ihām* or ambiguity. Such we discover in the awkward phrase *shāh-i shāhanshāh* literally meaning 'the king of the king of kings'. Of course my reading above simply translates the honourific *shāhanshāh* as 'king of kings' a statement one could easily imagine a disciple attributing to his spiritual master in seventeenth-century northern India. In fact one discovers such descriptions of Guru Gobind Singh in other Sikh works one example of which is the fifth *adhiāi* of Koer Singh's early to mid nineteenth-century *Gurbilās Pātshāhī 10*, 5:25:

Guru Gobind [Singh] is the king of kings (*shāhanshāh*), the lord who is the greatest of the God's incarnations.

Shamsher Singh 'Ashok' (ed.), *Gurbilās Pātshāhī 10 krit Kuir Singh*, p. 68. But as this honourific *shāhanshāh* often appears as an epithet of the Mughal emperors the poet may here be attempting to proclaim Guru Gobind Singh the greater of the two by presenting the appellation as shāh-i shāhanshāh. The rest of the *Sultanat Dahamm* may be easily read with such dissension in mind. Indeed in light of Nand Lal's traditional history such a reading may not be far from the mark. The subtitle of this work, moreover, 'the Tenth [Lord's] Kingdom' of the 'Treasure Book' certainly seems to imply that our poet thought of the Guru as a great king, the tenth of ten 'true' treasures if you will, all of whom rivalled the Mughal emperors. For dissension in South Asian ghazal poetry (both Persian and Urdu despite the title) see Harbans Mukhia, 'The Celebration of Failure as Dissent in Urdu Ghazal', in *Modern Asian Studies* 33:4 (1999), pp. 861–81.

167. Often, Punjabi commentary on the Persian baits suggest that Nand Lal is referring to Guru Gobind Singh when ambiguous phrases such as *murshid-i kamāl* 'the perfect spiritual guide' appear. See the Punjabi translations and commentary in Haribhajan Singh, *Sāchī Prīti Ghazalān Bhāī Nand Lāl jī Satīk* (2nd. ed. Amritsar: Singh Brothers, 1975).

168. Henry Beveridge (trans.), *The Akbar Nama of Abu-L-Fazl* I, II, pp. 50–68. N. Elias and E. Denison Ross (trans.), *The Tarikh-i Rashidi of Mirza Muhammad Haidar Dughlat A History of The Moghuls of Central Asia* (Patna: Academia Asiatica, 1973), p. 5 describes the pre-Akbar version of the myth of Alankua. For background on Abu'l Fazl's situation see Peter Hardy, 'Abul Fazl's Portrait of the Perfect Padshah: A Political Philosophy for Mughal India—or a Personal Puff for a Pal?' in Christian Troll (ed.), *Islam in India, Studies and Commentaries*—vol. 2, *Religion and Religious Education* (New Delhi: Vikas Publishing House, 1985), pp. 114–37.

169. Muhammad Abdul Ghani, *A History of Persian Language and Literature at the Mughal Court: part III—Akbar the Great*, pp. 160–71. Also Wheeler M. Thackston, 'The Poetry of Abu-Talib Kalim Persian Poet-Laureate of Shahjahan Mughal Emperor of India.' (Harvard University, Dept. of Near Eastern Languages and Civilizations, 1974), p. 181.

170. *Kurnish (körünüsh)* was a practice of the Turco-Mongolians which literally means 'interview' and became a ritual during the time of Amir Timur while under the Mughals it became the formal ritual of obeisance before the emperor. For the kurnīsh under the Mughals see H. Blochmann (ed. and trans.), *AA* I, pp. 166–7; Streusand, *The Formation of the Mughal Empire*, p. 124; and Wheeler Thackston (trans. and ed.), *The Baburnama: Memoirs of Babur, Prince and Emperor* (New York: The Modern Library, 2002), pp. 432, 509. As well, there could be a hint of Guru Nanak's hymns here though let us note that symbolically offering the head was a common phrase signifying the need for humility.

171. Rueben Levy, *An Introduction to Persian Literature* (New York: Columbia University Press, 1969), p. 26.

172. Michel Foucault, *The Archaeology of Knowledge and the Discourse on Language* [trans. A.M. Sheridan Smith] (New York: Pantheon Books, 1972), p. 25.

173. The bait is noted in Anok Singh (ed.), *Maskīn jī de Laikchar: Bhāg Pahilā* (6th edition. Amritsar: Singh Brothers, 1992), p. 80 (where it appears in Gurmukhi script) although I have heard that the earliest appearance of this bait is within a manuscript copy of the Dasam Granth. Personal communication with Pashaura Singh.

The sign of the Sikh are these five ks (*kāfs*). A Sikh should never be excused from wearing these five things. Hew McLeod's *Sikhs of the Khalsa*, pp. 204–5 succinctly and rightfully dismisses the attribution.
174. One such scholar is Haribhajan Singh (trans.), *Sāchī Prīti: Ghazalān Bhāī Nand Lāl jī "Goyā" ate "Ganj-nāmā" chon "Salatanati Dahamm" Satīk* (Amritsar: Singh Brothers, 1989), p. 22. The author here refers to Nand Lal as 'Bhai Nand Lal Singh'. It seems unlikely in the extreme that the Mughal emperor would have allowed Nand Lal to serve if he were a Khalsa Sikh complete with beard and turban.
175. Ganda Singh (ed.), *Gur-Sobhā*, esp. pp. 88–90.
176. This line of reasoning appears in *Darbārī Ratan*, pp. 17–25. This argument is problematic since Nand Lal's most prominent poetry (the *Dīvān* and *Zindagī-nāmah*) tends to downplay the martial themes so prevalent in literature attributed to Guru Gobind Singh and his courtly poets. Padam's conclusion though may be supported since baits found in the Persian *Joti Bigās* attributed to Bhai Nand Lal compare the ten Gurus collectively to the warrior heroes of the Mahabharata and the Shah-namah among others (see especially bait 160, *Kulliyāt*, p. 169). Here as well appear numerous martial allusions. For example:
   When his arrow is quickly shot from its bow the livers of all [his] enemies are rent in two.
Joti Bigās 164, *Kulliyāt*, p. 169. (There is a pun here as the *shagā* of *shigāfad* [*sic: shikāfad* 'cleaving'] means 'quiver'.)
177. For Bhai Kanhia see 'Kanhaiyā', in *MK* p. 294.
178. *Darbārī Ratan*, p. 25. Now it is apparent why I use the term implied in the statement above. Padam is not actually saying that the Guru kept Nand Lal from joining the Khalsa but rather that he asked him not to wear a sword. Piara Singh seems to be saying that there are members of the Khalsa who did not need to carry weapons. Unfortunately our author does not cite the source of this exchange though it is quite reminiscent of a passage we discover in the rahit-nama of Chaupa Singh Chhibbar in which Guru Gobind Singh instructs Rai Singh, a Sikh scholar learned in Persian, to leave the battlefield. See *CSRn* 571, pp. 117–18 (Punjabi), p. 191 (English).
179. Nand Lal, the putative author of the *Sultanat Dahamm*, was too familiar with symbols of royalty:
   Guru Gobind Singh kisses the feet of the One who exists without a place (*lā-makān*) [and for this reason] the tenth Guru's kettledrum (*kos*) is sounded throughout both this world and the next.
Within Islamic thought the term lā-makān designates the divine, Allah, as existing without a place for existence, a point noted within the Hadith and apparently originating with the Prophet's son-in-law Ali. It can mean 'homeless' as well and so the first mesra may be read as 'the destitute kiss the feet of Guru Gobind Singh.' *Sultanat Dahamm* 2:17, *Kulliyāt*, p. 123. Also

see for symbols of courtly legitimacy under the Central Asian Timurids, particularly poetry as one such, Maria Eva Subtelny, 'Art and Politics in Early 16th Century Central Asia', in *Central Asiatic Journal* 27 (1983), pp. 121–48, esp. p. 130. Here she notes that

> In Central Asian Islamic history, every ruler, particularly the petty parvenu, sought to make his court a cultural showplace through patronage, especially of literary activity.

180. Subtelny, 'Art and Politics', p. 129. Let us be wary of exaggerating the Guru's adoption of such dynastic ideals, however. Certainly the task of copying and illuminating manuscripts of the Adi Granth was a highly respected one and may have been one of the principal functions of what we may assume was the Guru's equivalent to the Timurid kitāb-khānah or atelier. Indeed, many such manuscripts are extant, especially those prepared by one Bhai Harijas (Pashaura Singh, *The Guru Granth Sahib*, pp. 60, 72–3 for example), and those with Guru Gobind Singh's own autograph (nishān). Personal communication with Pashaura Singh. But it seems certain that artistic productions such as painting and architecture, and numismatics, all significant indicators of authority, prestige, and legitimacy amongst the Timurids were not, we may assume by their general absence, particularly prized by the Guru's court although we do find the rare painting of the tenth Guru during his lifetime as noted in Chapter 1. This may indicate that the Guru had no interest in challenging the claims of Aurangzeb or the Hill Rajas to rulership and was content with his possession of Anandpur alone. The importance of the Timurid atelier is outlined in Thomas W. Lentz and Glenn D. Lowry, *Timur and the Princely Vision: Persian Art and Culture in the Fifteenth Century* (Los Angeles: Los Angeles County Museum of Art, 1989), pp. 63 ff.

181. Lists of such Hindu poets in Mughal and earlier courts may be found in both Muhammad Firishta's *Gulshān-i Ibrāhimī* (*Tarikh-i Firishta*) and Abu'l Fazl's *Ā'in-i Akbārī*. See Aziz Ahmad, *Studies in Islamic Culture in the Indian Environment*, pp. 234–8 and Blochmann, *AA*, pp. 606–80, esp. 608, 611.

182. Levy, *An Introduction to Persian Literature*, p. 26. Here we may situate the story narrated by Koer Singh of Nand Lal's reply to the King of Mazandaran.

183. Uttam Singh Bhatia, *Gurū Bhagat Bhāī Nand Lāl Goyā*, pp. 15, 17 suggests that Nand Lal went to Agra to be with Prince Mu'azzam after 1695, implying that after this year he shared his time between the two courts. This is a plausible conclusion as the prince was that year released from the confinement in which his father placed him in February 1687 and did indeed make his way to Agra immediately upon such release. Background on the alleged treason and imprisonment of Prince Mu'azzam during his siege of Golconda appears in Jadunath Sarkar, *History of Aurangzeb* IV, 430–3. Also Jadunath Sarkar, *History of Aurangzeb* V (Calcutta: M.C. Sarkar & Sons, 1924), p. 302.

184. There are as far as I know no Sikh sources which claim Nand Lal had relations with Jahandar Shah which is somewhat surprising as Jahandar Shah was the governor of Multan (apparently Nand Lal's ancestral town) at one point in his career. Perhaps this is because Jahandar Shah was on the throne for less than a year.
185. Such traditions are flawlessly recounted in Trilochan Singh and Anurag Singh, *A Brief Account of the Life and Works of Guru Gobind Singh* (3rd revised edition; Amritsar: Bhai Chattar Singh Jiwan Singh, 2002), p. 7.
186. *Sikh Rahit Maryādā* (16th ed., Amritsar: SGPC, 1983), p. 13. Nand Lal and his poetry are also mentioned as material acceptable for exposition within a congregational setting. See the portion titled kathā, 'homily' in *Sikh Rahit Maryādā*, p. 16. Interestingly, in both of these cases Nand Lal appears without his penname Goya.
187. W.H. McLeod, *Who is a Sikh? The Problem of Sikh Identity* (Oxford: Clarendon Press, 1989), pp. 95–6.
188. W.H. McLeod (ed. and trans.), *Textual Sources for the Study of Sikhism* (Manchester: Manchester University Press, 1984), p. 2 very cautiously states that Bhai Nand Lal's writings occupy a third rung in the scriptural hierarchy as these are 'compositions traditionally approved for recitation in gurdwaras.'
189. For a detailed explanation of viākhiā in the tradition of *Rāmcharitmānas* recitation (Hindi/Brajbhasha: *vyākhyā*). See Lutgendorf's *The Life of a Text*, pp. 210–12. Having myself heard a number of giānīs and kathākars expound the text of the Sikh scripture it seems that this definition also accords well with such exposition within the Sikh tradition. The term viākhiā to describe Nand Lal's bani therefore may be something of a stretch. Indeed, this may be perhaps the reason for the SGPC's failure to mention just which works attributed to Nand Lal form *viākhiā-sarūp*.
190. There is a very palpable vacuum in recent studies dealing with the wider understanding of Sikh scripture and this perhaps is part of the reason why a definition of bani which includes all the respective literature understood as such by contemporary normative Khalsa Sikhs is still wanting. Would Nand Lal and Bhai Gurdas' poetry be understood, for example, as *dhur kī bānī* 'the bani from the beyond' in the same way as gurbani? Certainly Sikhs would agree that such a distinction exists but I have yet to discover a meticulous detailed statement to this effect and an assessment of the different types of bani. For current discussions see *EoS* I, p. 276–7. Also see Pashaura Singh, *The Guru Granth Sahib*, pp. 6–15 for some insightful observations.
191. For a supplementary discussion regarding which of Nand Lal's poetry the Singh Sabha considered bani see my 'Bhāī Nand Lāl "Goyā" and the Sikh Tradition', pp. 111–34. I do not include as bani the non-Persian writings attributed to Nand Lal.
192. Amrit Kirtan, finalized in the early twentieth century, is a liturgy which instructs professional ragis in regard to which shabads should be sung on

which special day. Nand Lal's *Sultanat Dahamm* beginning with the mesra *nāsr o mansūr gurū gobind singh* (*Sultanat Dahamm* 2:1 of the *Ganj-nāmah, Kulliyāt*, p. 122) finds a revered space within it. Every so often, moreover, one hears Persian hymns attributed to Bhai Nand Lal broadcast as kirtan from the Golden Temple though one should add that it is only on very rare occasions that one may discover audio performances of Nand Lal's works. After a decade or so of searching for example I have only recently acquired a CD recording of kirtan involving Nand Lal's Persian poetry thanks to the kindness of the late Baba Sucha Singh of Javvadi Taksal, Ludhiana.

193. The first translation of Sa'di's *Gulistān* appeared in Europe in 1634 in French and then in German in 1651 and again in 1654. Annemarie Schimmel, 'The Genius of Shiraz: Sa'di and Hāfez', in Ehsan Yarshater (ed.), *Persian Literature* (New York: Columbia University Press, 1988), p. 214.

194. For example, R.W. Falcon, *Handbook on Sikhs for the Use of Regimental Officers* (Allahabad: Pioneer Press, 1896) and E.D. MacLagan and H.A. Rose, *A Glossary of the Tribes and Castes of the Punjab and the North-West Frontier Province* I (1st ed., 1883; Patiala: Language Department, Punjab, 1990), pp. 676–730.

195. The best account of the agenda of the Singh Sabha and its history is still Harjot Oberoi, *The Construction of Religious Boundaries*. Such endeavours did succeed to a certain extent as a share of seats proportionately higher than the number of Sikhs warranted was eventually secured by Sikh leaders in the early twentieth century.

196. W.H. McLeod, *Sikhs of the Khalsa*, p. 72.

197. See for example Sakhi 8 [known as the *Mukti-nāmā*], stanza 32 and Sakhi 65, stanzas 10, 35 of the *Sau Sakhīān*. Gurbachan Singh Naiar (ed.), *Gur Ratan Māll: Sau Sākhī*, pp. 17, 76, 79. Once again, the quote on page 79 is worth singling out in its polemic against Persian-knowing Sikhs who are compared to adulterers.

198. All three occurrences including the one quoted appear in P.S. Padam, *Rahit-nāme*, p. 77. The emphasis on the use and study of Gurmukhi is also found in the non-Khalsa Sikh rahit-nama. *The Prem Sumārag*, section 8:9:1–4. See W.H. McLeod (trans.), *The Prem Sumārag* 8:9:1–4, pp. 89–90.

199. The conflation between Gurmukhi and Brajbhasha/Punjabi may also be found in other eighteenth-century Sikh texts. See for one Kesar Singh Chhibbar's *BSVN* 10:7, p. 125. One can also argue that the verb *parhe* is itself ambiguous as the term can mean 'read', 'study' or 'learn'. Considering the attitude towards Muslims, especially those who helped further the aims of the Mughals in India it appears that Daya Singh is here telling Sikhs not to study Persian as a way of telling them not to take up any administrative post. This is certainly the idea behind Hew McLeod's translation as it appears in his *Sikhs of the Khalsa*, p. 322 and the implication underlying the pejorative nature of the Punjabi word tankhāh (punishment) which is taken from the Persian word tan<u>kh</u>āh 'salary'. Although it seems

unlikely given the context one can also translate the second sentence as 'do not read [the bani] in Arabic or Persian.' (Perhaps implying the sacred status of Nand Lal's poetry?)
200. *CSRn*, pp. 104, 180, 236. The assumption is that any Sikh who treats the Perso-Arabic script with the same reverence one treats the Gurmukhi script is so branded.
201. Ibid., p. 180.
202. Sakhi 65:10. Gurbachan Singh Naiar (ed.), *Gur Ratan Māll: Sau Sākhī*, p. 76:
   Study neither the Arabic nor Persian characters.
   Referencing Guru Nanak's *Dhanāsarī* 3, Adi Granth, p. 663 Kesar Singh Chhibbar describes the language of the malecchas (Muslims) as 'Arabic, Turki, and Persian'. These may also be understood as a criticism of Arabic. See *BSVN* 10:366, p. 158.
203. Bhagavad-Gita 3:35:
   Better one's own duty to perform though devoid of merit than to perform another's duty well. It is better to die within the realm of one's own duty: perilous is the duty of others.
   R.C. Zaehner (ed. and trans.), *The Bhagavad-Gita with a Commentary Based on the Original Sources* (London: Oxford University Press, 1973), p. 175. It should elicit no surprise that Kesar Singh alludes to the Gita as his text is very much situated within a Sikh symbolic universe whose principal components are derived from the Puranas and the Epics. *BSVN* 10:367, pp. 158–9. For a reference to this same passage in the context of a Nand Lal narrative see Shamsher Singh Ashok (ed.), *Gurbilās Pātshāhī 10 krit Kuir Singh* 2:20–4, p. 27.
204. *BSVN* 10:365, p. 158 includes Guru Nanak, *Dhanāsarī* 3, Adi Granth, p. 663 as its final line:
   The Kshatriyas (Khatris) have abandoned their religion and adopted the language of the malecchas.
   The naming of these languages is Kesar Singh's own. A similar criticism levelled by the famous Marathi bhakti poet Tukaram, censuring the current Kaliyug, appears in his poetry which, Sumit Guha notes, was a powerful critique of the new Hindu urban elites who adopted new trends and styles ushered in by Muslims. This may also partially be the case here with Guru Nanak. See Sumit Guha,' Transitions and Translations', p. 25.
205. *BSVN* 10:368; also 10:365–7, pp. 158–9. The *Sau Sākhīān* also notes the fact that there are Sikhs who learn Persian for their livelihood, though it condemns these Sikhs in no uncertain terms. Gurbachan Singh Naiar (ed.), *Sau Sākhīān* 8:32, p. 17.
206. *Akāl Ustāti* 116, Dasam Granth, p. 22. In 1769 Kesar Singh Chhibbar claimed numerous times in the initial portion to his tenth chapter that Guru Gobind Singh himself was very well learned in Persian; that he in fact spent a year studying it under one Sikh munshi named Bhai Harijas Rai

(perhaps the Bhai Harijas who copied a number of Guru Granth manuscripts during the tenth Master's period?) the same Sikh who along with Chaupa Singh tutored the tenth Master in Gurmukhi. Since the list provided by Kesar Singh Chhibbar precisely corresponds to the sequence noted here in the *Akāl Ustati* it is likely that our Chhibbar brahman author was aware of this passage. This may perhaps be why Kesar Singh is able to easily include in his text two divergent attitudes towards the study of Persian. See *BSVN* 10: 6, 7, 9, 10; 365–8, pp. 125, 158–9. Also see Grewal and Bal, *Guru Gobind Singh*, p. 38.

207. P.S. Padam, *Rahit-nāme*, p. 78: *Srī akāl ustati kare chandī kanth sudhāri* (lit. '...[the Khalsa Sikh] who has memorised (*kanth sudhāri*) [both the] *Srī Akāl Ustāti* and *Chandī* [*kī vār* is an Akali].'

208. It is certain that Nand Lal originally penned his poetry in Perso-Arabic script. The extant Gurmukhi manuscripts which I have seen seem to be late eighteenth-century products. I base this on orthography in particular as in only some cases does the *kannā* appear as a dot rather than as a small vertical stroke.

209. It is urgent to realize that these aspects of the argument worked in collaboration with one another. The fact notwithstanding, there exist numerous eighteenth and nineteenth-century manuscripts containing Gurmukhi/Brajbhasha translations (rather than transliterations) of Sanskrit texts such as the Ramayana, Mahabharata and Bhagavad Gita, and the Puranas, demonstrating that these texts were also very much a part of the symbolic and ritual universe of the eighteenth-century Khalsa. (Many such manuscripts are held by the Sikh History Research Department at Khalsa College in Amritsar. Kirpal Singh (ed.), *A Catalogue of Punjabi and Urdu Manuscripts* (Amritsar: Sikh History Research Department, Khalsa College, 1963), pp. 50–67). For the traditional history of how this translation/transliteration came about see *Mahimā Prakāsh*'s discussion regarding the writing of the *Bachitar Nātak* (here meaning the whole of the mythological portions of the Dasam Granth) and the *Vidyā Sāgar* which appears as 10:11, pp. 794–6 especially the fifth chaupaī on p. 795:

The writers of Gurmukhi were summoned near [to all of whom] all of [the pandit's] sacred texts (*bidh*) were given and explained. [The Guru then ordered:] 'Translate these into the local language (*kar bhākhā*) and write it into Gurmukhi script. Then please give these to me so that I may tell their stories (*kathā sunāi*)'.

That Nand Lal's work has retained this status in today's Khalsa Panth (as too with non-Khalsa Sikhs) shows that his Persian poetry was commensurate with the understandings of the later Singh Sabha/Tat Khalsa.

210. Pashaura Singh, *The Guru Granth Sahib*, p. 17 refers the reader to G.B. Singh's pioneering work on the birth and evolution of the Gurmukhi script. Unfortunately G.B. Singh's work does not speak to the type of trajectory I have outlined above. For some background on the script and Guru Angad's

relation to it see his twenty-second chapter, 'How did the legend of Guru Angad's creation of the Gurmukhi script come about?' G.B. Singh, *Gurmukhī Lippī dā Janam te Vikās* (2nd ed., Chandigarh: Panjab University Press, 1972), pp. 109–10.
211. Richard M. Eaton, *The Rise of Islam and the Bengal Frontier: 1204–1760* (Delhi: Oxford University Press, 1994), p. 294.
212. Pashaura Singh, *The Guru Granth Sahib*, p. 17.
213. *CSRn*, p. 78:
A Sikh of the Guru should respect the letters of the Gurmukhi script.
W.H. McLeod, *Sikhs of the Khalsa*, p. 76. And Desa Singh's rahit-nama, line 36:
A Sikh should learn Gurmukhi characters from another Singh.
Piara Singh Padam, *Rahit-nāme*, p. 148. *Sau Sākhī* 65:9, p. 76:
Apart from the sacred utterances of the Guru a true Sikh will read no others. He will read these in Gurmukhi abandoning other writings (*thāt*).
214. I do not consider ms. 115123, Punjabi University, Patiala mentioned in Chapter 3 a translation, but an aide-mémoire. As mentioned individual terms are translated into Brajbhasha rather than entire baits or ghazals.
215. Again, see Kirpal Singh (ed.), *A Catalogue of Punjabi and Urdu Manuscripts*.
216. Guru Nanak, *Dhanāsarī ashtapadīān* 1:1, Adi Granth, p. 685:
The Guru is the pearl-filled ocean. The sants [are like birds which] peck at the amrit and do not go far. They peck the seed which contains the Lord's essence and are loved by Him. It is within this ambrosial ocean that the swans obtain the Master of their breath.
217. *MP* II 10:9, p. 789.
218. See the note marked with an asterisk on *SP* XII, p. 5075. In the precursor to the *Sikh Rahit Maryada*, the Chief Khalsa Diwan's *Gurmat Prakāsh Bhāg Sanskār* (Amritsar: Chief Khalsa Diwan, 1915), p. 12 there is no mention of what compositions may be recited as kirtan. There is a section on kirtan but this simply reaffirms that it is a vital component of the Sikh tradition:
(2) Kirtan is a fundamental part of Sikhism, fitting for every Sikh whether male or female. It is for this reason that sangats (whether of men or of women) of all countries and in all conditions and at all times can perform kirtan during Sikh rituals.
219. The same trend may perhaps hold true for the stories we discover in the Dasam Granth. There versions given invariably in Gurmukhi script may have allowed Sikhs to gradually assimilate this material as their own to foster a sense of legitimacy amongst the groups over whom the Guru held sway. This alas does not explain how other material in Gurmukhi script failed to be accorded reverence. A comparison with the other material produced at the Guru's court as noted in Padam's *Darbārī Ratan* demonstrates that none of the Brajbhasha poetry supplied is of the same calibre as Nand Lal's.
220. W.H. McLeod, *Who is a Sikh?*, pp. 62–81.

6
Conclusion

خاک درگاه تو صد تاج است بهر فرق من
عاصیم گر دل هوای تاج و افسر میکند!

The dust of your court is a hundred crowns for my head (*faraq-i man*). A rebel/sinner am I if my heart desires the trappings of worldly empire (*tāj o afsar* i.e. 'crown and diadem').

It is perhaps fitting that the previous and penultimate chapter of this book dealt with the history and poetry of Bhai Nand Lal Goya for in many ways the trajectory of his career after the evacuation of Anandpur is representative of those of his fellow poets. Indeed his career mirrors that of the Guru's darbar itself: its gradual dissolution. While Nand Lal's history is often taken up by his ancestors the history of other darbari kavis is only fleetingly found in the annals of traditional Sikh history. We should not disregard this but treat it as cautiously as all the narratives thus far engaged.

In the confusion of the Sikh flight from Anandpur in 1704–5 we can assume that most of the poets of the Guru's darbar scattered while others may have died in the battle and consequent siege. Forced to leave the fort, the tenth Guru and a small number of his disciples took a circuitous route from the sacred city with stops at Macchiwara and Dina amongst many others, which would eventually find them in Talwandi Sabo or Damdama Sahib, where the Guru would reside for about nine months until the end of 1706. While Sikh tradition (with some support from contemporary Persian letters) notes that some of this journey was occupied with battling Mughal forces (the

Battle of Chamkaur for instance, at which the poets Hari Das, to whom the *Prem Abodh* is attributed, and Dhian Singh were 'martyred' as well as the Battle of Mukatsar in which the famed *Chālī Mukte* 'the forty liberated' died fighting)[2] and travelling incognito (as *Uch kā pīr*, the Sufi Master of Uch), it also states that a good part of this sojourn was spent within the Lakkhi Jungle (just south of today's Firozpur), 'the forest of one hundred thousand trees.'

Although there is no forest found in this precise area today, the early eighteenth-century Lakkhi Jungle was a locale well known to the Mughal authorities as a region in which rebels operated. Indeed, it appears that insurgents did so with such impunity that just after the tenth Guru had left the area sometime in mid to late 1705, Aurangzeb's grandson, Prince Muhammad Ma'azuddin Bahadar (the future, short-lived emperor Jahandar Shah, d. 1713) had been made *faujdār* of the area by the emperor in 1706.[3] The Guru thus appears to have chosen this refuge with the obvious object of avoiding detection by the authorities, blending in as it were with numerous others disaffected by Mughal policies in the Punjab or others who simply wished to go unnoticed. He may also have chosen this specific location to rest his nascent Khalsa as this was an area particularly well known for horse breeding.[4] Sikh tradition claims that while interred here, the Guru spent much of his time preaching and further training his Khalsa in the martial arts among which riding, hunting, and swordsmanship were most certainly included.[5]

Tradition continues however that during more sedate moments Guru Gobind Singh also spent the time writing poetry and having such poetry prepared, presumably not by the poets of Anandpur.[6] According to a well-known tradition word of the Guru's forest residence spread quickly amongst scattered sangats whose members ran as quickly as possible to have the Guru's darshan and reside with him for a time.[7] While the Guru and his Khalsa Sikhs dwelled here for a brief period of time a number of poets had also heard of the Guru's presence and subsequently made their way to him, ultimately forming what we previously called, in Piara Singh Padam's words, the Lakkhi Jungle Darbar. That many of these poets had previously belonged to the order of ecstatic (divānā) Udasis may have allowed them to pass through various towns and villages to the Guru with little trouble, appearing as little more than common recluses.[8]

As a whole, the poetry here is of a far more mystical and devotional character than that of either the darbars of Paunta Sahib or Anandpur, which mainly (though not solely) manifest the heroic sentiment. Although this may be due to the belief that its authors were principally Udasis, it may perhaps reflect the more unstable and near hopeless context in which these later poets wrote, especially as their poetry was prepared some months after word of the execution of Guru Gobind Singh's two youngest sons.[9] The poet Lal Das Khiali, for example, implies just such an atmosphere,

[I have] become the dust of the feet of the True Guru for in so dying I am reborn.[10]

As too does his fellow Lakkhi Jungle poet, Bihari:

Daily both one's very body and soul are wounded by the Beloved's pain. Although constantly seeking a grand remedy the heart suffers everyday. [Such] pain is cast out from within the heart [however] as the secret resides within the eyes. Gobind Singh, Beloved, praise him who has brought the news [which liberates] hearts.[11]

Fitting here therefore are the comments of both Grewal and Bal who point out that the Guru's own 'poetic sensibility' (and by extension that of his poets) was at this time 'heightened by his personal grief as much as by his unwavering and deep faith.'[12] In spite of everything, the Guru and his Sikhs were forced to leave Anandpur after a two-year period of relative peace and stability, drawn out of the fort during a siege by both Pahari and Mughal forces, and had been parted from their loved ones, a separation which resulted in tragedy in the Guru's case, having now lost a number of his devoted disciples, his mother, and all four of his sons, the eldest two in the Battle of Chamkaur and the youngest to perfidy.[13] Tradition exacerbates this tension by repeatedly noting that Mughal forces relentlessly pursued the Guru and his Sikhs intent on capturing and killing them.

This darbar was however shortlived and most likely understaffed and seems to have brought an end to the literary output produced in honour of the tenth Guru as patron. Of course this excludes the few works attributed to the tenth Guru during this period (according to tradition the Persian *Zafar-nāmah* was written at Dina a few weeks before the Guru entered the Lakkhi Jungle) as well as the alleged compilation of the Dasam Granth by Bhai Mani Singh. Put simply, after the Guru's Lakkhi Jungle interlude his darbar, at least his literary darbar, becomes negligible notwithstanding tradition's claims that some of the Lakkhi Jungle poets followed the Guru south when he left Talwandi Sabo/Damdama to meet the emperor in late 1706/ early 1707.[14] The only literary activities to which we become privy are the continued issuing of hukam-namas once again indicating the presence of scribes, and the task of transcribing and copying the Adi Granth, the most famous story of which is the tenth Guru's recital of the text from memory at Damdama Sahib. It is likely that many of the poets of either Paunta or Anandpur may simply have felt it too precarious to once again meet up with the Guru. Indeed, the dangerously heightened circumstances may be inferred from the regular pleas in the tenth Guru's post 1700 CE hukam-namas for Sikhs to come armed into the presence of the Guru.[15] One such entreaty written in Guru Gobind Singh's own hand in 1704 may be claimed as representative:

The sangat is my Khalsa. Come into my presence and take along with you a number of well-trained young men: horseriders, footsoldiers, and riflemen.[16]

Certainly one may assume that Sikhs around Guru Gobind Singh at Damdama Sahib continued to comport themselves in the same courtly manner that they did at Anandpur prior to evacuation. It seems likely though, given the unstable circumstances, that those Sikhs surrounding the Guru would have belonged to the more martial Khalsa. Tradition tells us that a number of the Guru's poets had become members of the Khalsa but both traditional and near-contemporary Sikh accounts suggest that as the strength of the Guru's newly emergent Khalsa began to grow, the importance of the Guru's poetic darbar waned. The arrival of the Guru's 'arz dasht petition mentioned in Inayatullah Khan Ismi's *hasbulhukam* of the first decade of the eighteenth century[17] (which may have been the *Zafar-nāmah*) could have thus been a last ditch effort on the part of the Guru to engage Aurangzeb diplomatically, in a courtly style with which emperor was keenly familiar, a point which tradition supports in the fact that it has focussed attention principally upon a single bait of this text, one which repeats almost verbatim the eighth admonition of Shaikh Sa'di's *Gulistān* imploring the use of force as only the absolutely last resort.[18] Such diplomacy seems to have succeeded as the Guru was allowed free passage as he made his way southwards towards Aurangzeb and had the emperor not died, it is likely that a face to face meeting would have ensued.[19]

To tacitly explain the disappearance of the poetic darbar traditional accounts suggest a tension between the more martial and the more literate segments of the Guru's court.[20] Certainly the friction between the martial Khalsa and the more literate Khatri and Arora Sikhs—a group well represented amongst the Guru's poets and many of whom we may assume retained a Sikh Nanak-panthi identity perhaps at odds with the more martial Khalsa—was very evident during the period of Banda (d. 1716). As we have mentioned, this also garners a relatively great deal of attention from both contemporary Persian reports and early eighteenth-century Sikh writers such as Sainapati. The latter in particular pointing to the more urban-Sikh practice of tonsure, bhaddar/bhaddan, as a procedure no doubt vilified amongst Khalsa Sikhs enjoined to never cut their hair.

The rahit-nama of Chaupa Singh, although prepared almost forty years after *Gur Sobhā* also explains the vanishing literary darbar by pointing to such Khatri/Khalsa tension in an interesting exchange between the tenth Guru and a Khatri Sikh named Rai Singh which occurs in the section of the famous text to which Hew McLeod appends the heading Apocalyptical Prophecies.[21] The portion is rather lengthy but nevertheless deserves to be reproduced. At line 571, we are told of the tenth Guru's nameless *naqīb* who noticed after he had instructed the Sikhs attending the Baisakhi celebrations of 1702 (sammat 1759) at Anandpur to leave, that one Sikh remained behind. He brought this to the Guru's attention who then turned towards the Sikh, Rai Singh Khatri, and exclaimed:

'If you want to be a faithful Sikh [obey my command and] go to your home,' [the Guru] said to him.

'O True King,' [Rai Singh] answered 'I have remained here because I have abandoned my home. How can I be a faithful Sikh in my home when I have no home?'

'Only at home can you be a faithful Sikh, not here,' said [the Guru. 'This is no place for you at present.] You are a literate person, one who knows Persian, whereas here our business has to be war. Because of the designs of [evil] people I must bring about a time of tumult, for only thus can our ends

be attained. [In such circumstances you will be a hindrance.] When you witness the turmoil you will think up all sorts of suggestions concerning the way this should be done and that should not be done. You will then say that the Master has made a mistake.
[Instead of flinging yourself into battle] you will sit and listen to what others say. You will think, you will observe, and you will make calculations. But we shall be in the midst of tumult and when the Panth is plunged in tumult it has to fight! If all is calm [my] Sikhs will stay at home and there fall prey to excessive affection for family and possessions . But now, in the coming tumult, there will be no such distractions.' And so [the Guru] sent [Rai Singh Khatri] home.[22]

For the author of this text, it appears that in the light of Mughal and Pahari assaults on the Guru and his Sikhs the time for poetry had come to an end as early as 1702 and that the direction of the Panth would now be determined by the more martial segment of the Guru's companions, the Khalsa.

Unfortunately there is little more we can say with regard to the history of the darbar in the last two years of Guru Gobind Singh's life. Indeed, with the Guru's death, the darbar itself clearly comes to an end. It is likely that Banda possessed scribes as he too issued hukam-namas and after his capture of Rai Kot had in his entourage those who cast those coins that we noted in Chapter 1. Given his forced peripatetic activities and the discord he appears to have sown between Khalsa and non-Khalsa Sikhs, not to mention the havoc he caused the emperors Bahadar Shah and Farrukh Siyar, it is unlikely that he would have had the time to invest in such a coterie, Ganda Singh's implicit claims to the contrary notwithstanding.[23] Though what seems likely is that Banda did indeed desire to establish a symbolic connection to the Guru's court, as the inscriptions on his coins clearly suggest. There is as well a hint that the tenth Guru's wives, Mata Sundari and Mata Sahib Devi may have possessed a small darbar while in Delhi since they too issued hukamnamas.[24]

Certainly Sikh literature which praises the Guru and his prowess in battle continues to be written, the earliest example of which is Sainapati's *Srī Gur-sobhā* (which although prepared in 1711 ignores Banda and his depredations altogether). Such eulogistic works including other examples of the gur-bilas genre and the janam-sakhi and rahit-nama literature dominate the eighteenth century, but these it seems were not written within anything resembling a proper darbar. Patrons were certainly present, though as we see once again in the rahit-nama of Chaupa Singh Chhibbar, their aims in patronizing such literature were not always in consonance with what they most likely felt were the aims of the collective Sikh Panth.[25] Indeed, within the works of the brahman Chhibbar Sikhs we find the vilification of many contemporary mid-eighteenth century Khalsa Sikhs, the notoriously corrupt *māikī* or rapacious Sikhs, in what is likely Chhibbar attempts to seek a proper patron and regain what they probably felt was their earlier importance to the Khalsa Panth.[26] In describing these predatory Khalsa Sikhs Kesar Singh Chhibbar alludes to a shalok by Guru Amar Das to sanction his own understanding of them:

Those who are ensnared by delusion are completely blind and totally deaf. They cannot hear the shabad and as such engage in constant tumult.[27]

Such understandings imply that the literature of this period was not produced in a court as even under Nawab Kapur Singh, the misldars, and those closest to them, most likely the very rapacious Sikhs to whom Kesar Singh alludes, we find little literature prepared at their request apart from the rare encomium.[28]

Even before the advent of the misls however, courtly understandings of patronage had adapted to the new, less stable circumstances in which the Sikh Panth found itself.[29] A clue here is offered in one of the two notes attached to the manuscript copy of the B40 janamsakhi at the India Office Library, both of which suggest an alternative courtly arena for the production of such devotional works, though one certainly implied in earlier Sikh literature. The first claims:

The sangat is the court of the Supreme Guru. It speaks as His voice.[30]

It may well be that the collective imagination of this particular Sikh sangat viewed this congregation not only in the light of the Guru Panth doctrine but also as the inheritor of the grandeur of the Guru's court and as such saw itself embracing and expanding the legacy of the tenth Master in patronizing Sikh devotional literature.[31] As such it was one of its members, Bhai Sanghu (noted in the second of the two notes) who appears to have borne the cost of its preparation, not a modest one to be sure when we take into consideration the obvious skill of the professional artist whose paintings grace the manuscript copy in the India Office Library.[32] As the court of the Guru it seems likely that this particular sangat's more literate members (which may include the B40's author, Daia Ram Abrol)[33] would have been accorded a status akin to that of the Guru's courtly jewels, its litterateurs and poets. Whatever the mid to late eighteenth-century case may be, it is with the dawn of the darbar of Maharaja Ranjit Singh that we once again discover Sikh literature patronized by a Sikh ruler within a darbar expressing all of the traditional trappings of the Indo-Timurid court. But these of course are topics for future reckoning.[34]

Let us end by noting that although courtly literature may no longer be produced within the Sikh Panth the courtly legacy of the ten Gurus persists, and finds expression in so many diverse ways in Sikh tradition today. The sign to Sikhs the world over that a gurdwara is nearby for example is the famous Nishan Sahib, or saffron-coloured (sometimes dark blue) pennant strung upon the mast of a high saffron-cloth-covered flagpole usually found on a gurdwara's precincts. The nishan, a long-held symbol of Mughal imperium was adopted, according to one Sikh tradition, during the period of Guru Gobind Singh as a symbol of authority and empire in much the same way as it was by the Mughals: announcing visually to all those within the immediate viewing distance and beyond the emperor's proximity.[35]

Today's Sikh nishan, on which is emblazoned the Sikh Khanda, the double-edged sword superimposed over a quoit on either side of which is a kirpan, clearly invokes this regal image. Indeed, within the Punjab it is not uncommon to see Sikhs first pay reverence to the Nishan Sahib as the sign which leads them towards the darbar of the historical Gurus and of the Eternal Guru, the room in which the Guru Granth Sahib holds court so to speak (also called the Prakash Asthan). And while within that court, on special occasions, it is not exceptional to hear the gurdwara's nagārā or kettledrum being sounded or even the S-shaped horn. As mentioned earlier, among the Mughal emperors and their sub-imperial rajas and ranas, the kettledrum provided the audial component of empire establishing an audioscape informing everyone within hearing distance of the emperor's presence and of the empire's stability. Indeed, since the time of Humayun these drums were also sounded at least theoretically to announce the emperor's availability to administer justice.[36]

We have moreover made reference to the etiquette and procedures which Sikhs and others generally observe during worship at a gurdwara or elsewhere, procedures which may re-enact the customs and comportment believed to be observed within the historical darbars of the Sikh Gurus. Certainly the reverence shown to the Adi Granth corresponds in much detail with that earlier exhibited towards worldly sovereigns: it is 'cooled' by a whisk, placed underneath a canopy and, particularly at the Golden Temple, carried between the Akal Takht and the Prakash Asthan within the golden palanquin known as Palki Sahib in the late evening and the early morning.

Such royal symbolism is also implied in the title of the Sikh communal prayer, the *ardās*, recited at the end of Sikh worship, an important part of the Sikh liturgy which asks Sikhs to call to mind Akal Purakh, the ten Sikh Gurus, its martyrs, and symbols.[37] The designation is clearly derived from one of the official Indo-Timurid Mughal documents which Sikhs would have encountered in the seventeenth and eighteenth centuries, namely the 'arz da<u>sh</u>t or petition, the same type of request which Guru Gobind Singh wrote and sent to Aurangzeb. Although this Sikh Ardas/'arz da<u>sh</u>t does not play upon the format of the official petition, mimicking neither its structure nor its tone, the appropriation of the name nevertheless suggests the courtly procedure whereby a subject petitions his or her Lord.[38]

We see such a legacy also expressed in references to sartorial symbols known from the Mughal court such as the tenth Guru's epithet kalgidhār, 'the one who wears the aigrette's plume,' after the royal feather placed upon the sovereign's turban, a symbol of importance often given by the emperor to his favourites.[39] We would do well here to also include the omnipresent siropa which is often today granted to Sikhs or others of distinction by the SGPC or just about any other official Sikh body. This courtly legacy still lives on therefore and its regular re-enactment and inscription onto the general collective memory of the Sikh community confers upon the collective Panth what is believed to have been the grandeur of the court of Sikh Gurus.

But it also goes beyond such collective re-enactments and memories. Activities, rituals, and understandings which reflect this grandeur are also, one may argue prescriptions for the Sikh community's glorious future. Put another way, these are attempts albeit unconscious ones, to produce the divine court in the human world. These activities are indeed reminiscent of a scene we discover in what is at this time the earliest of the Khalsa rahit-namas. When Guru Gobind Singh is made to articulate a vision of the future, describing what is clearly his kingdom on earth (lit. *apnā rāju* 'my rule') to Bhai Nand Lal as we approach the denouement of the 1719 CE *Nasīhat-nāmā* attributed to our Perso-Sikh poet, it is obviously set within an Indo-Islamicate paradigm in which Khalsa Sikhs manifest the martial codes of the Mughal court while displaying a number of its courtly symbols, that is signs of dominion. It is best to complete this book with the same prophecy with which the *Nasīhat-nāmā* ends: 'Listen Nand Lal and hear this,' the tenth Master begins, 'I shall establish my [i.e. the Khalsa's] rule in which all human beings will be treated equally (lit., "the four varnas will become one"). [The Khalsa] shall ride fast horses which fly at the speed of hawks.'

[The] banners [of the Khalsa] (*neje*) shall wave and [they will ride] harnessed elephants. Their imperial ensemble (*naubat*) shall resound at every gateway. When a lakh and a quarter have fired their matchlocks the Khalsa shall then rise and will be victorious everywhere the sun sets and rises. The Khalsa shall rule and no traitor shall remain (*tikai*, 'dwell'). Those who are dishonoured will all be protected by taking refuge [with the Khalsa].[40]

NOTES

1. Nand Lal's Ghazal 31:2, *Kulliyāt*, p. 61. Although here the term *faraq* indicates the 'parting of the hair' and thus by extension the head, it also alludes—once again through ihām—to the lover's separation or 'parting' from the beloved. Indeed, the word evokes the intensity of feeling associated with one's separation from one's true love, a notion not dissimilar from the idea of *virāha* in Sanskrit and Brajbhasha poetry. A seventeenth-century listener would here have understood that the dust on which the beloved had trampled would be placed on the lover's head and would shine almost blindingly like a hundred polished crowns proclaiming to all within viewing distance the agony of parting which the lover was experiencing.
2. Padam, *Darbārī Ratan*, pp. 180, 226. Padam also claims that a number of bards (bhatts) were also martyred in October 1711 in the general arrest of all Khalsa Sikhs issued by Bahadar Shah. Amongst these are included Keso Singh Bhatt and Desa Singh Bhatt. *Darbārī Ratan*, pp. 213–15. For

the battles themselves see Gian Singh, *TGK* I, pp. 1009–20; 1046–50. A Mughal *hasbulhukum* in which a reference to the Battle of Chamkaur appears is found in the *Ahkām-i 'Alamgīrī* and reproduced in Ganda Singh (ed.), *Ma'ākhiz-i Tavārīkh-i Sikhān*, p. 74.
3. It is thus likely that Aurangzeb had heard of the presence of the Guru and his followers here as within a letter found in his *Ruqa'āt-i 'Ālamgīrī* penned to his grandson Prince Muhammad Ma'azuddin Bahadar (the son of Prince Mu'azzam) in 1706 he urges the prince to rid the Lakkhi Jungle district of rebels. Jamshid Bilimoria (trans.), *Ruka'at-i Alamgiri or Letters of Aurangzebe [with Historical and Explanatory Notes]* (London: Luzac & Co., 1908), letter no. 74, p. 75.
4. Jos Gommans, 'The Silent Frontier of South Asia, c. AD 1100–1800,' in *Journal of World History* 9.1 (Spring 1998), pp. 19–20.
5. Gian Singh, *TGK* I, pp. 1059–63.
6. Within traditional Indian epic literature (particularly the Mahabharata, Ramayana, and Ramcharitmanas), the forest ashram, which the Lakkhi Jungle phase of the Guru's life seems to resemble, was a time and an environment preferred for the recitation and performance of religious narratives. Lutgendorf, *The Life of a Text*, p. 124.
7. The popular verse claims:
    The Khalsa came to the Lakkhi Jungle to take the Guru's darshan in the same way that water buffaloes hearing the call of their herdsman [rush to him], leaving behind both food and water [in their haste]. To obtain their beloved (*shauq*) they rushed towards him without paying heed to those others likewise engaged (lit: 'no one joined with anyone'). Their pain of separation departed when they met their Guru-herdsman, and they gave thanks.
    This quatrain is taken from *Mājh Srī Mukhvāk Pātshāhī 10* in *Amrit Kīrtan Gutkā*, p. 555 as noted in Padam, *Darbārī Ratan*, p. 231 (Padam excludes the first verse however). Ultimately, such statements beg the question as to why the authorities were unable to discover the tenth Guru during this period while his disciples found him so easily.
8. A brief account of the Divana Udasis appears in H.A. Rose, *A Glossary of the Tribes and Castes of the Punjab and North-West Frontier Province* II (rpt, Patiala: Language Department, 1990), p. 243.
9. Padam refers us to Giani Gian Singh's account of Bihari in this regard noting that Bihari was so enraptured by the Guru that he only recited verses in the Majh metre dyed with the colour of the Guru's love. *Darbārī Ratan*, p. 232. One does discover it should be noted some martial metaphors in the poetry of Bihari. Once again, see Padam, *Darbārī Ratan*, p. 233:
    Eyelashes sharper than [the points of] arrows, tyrants [slaughter mercilessly and] recite the *takbīr*, the battlecry Allahu Akbar, 'God is Great!'
10. Padam, *Darbārī Ratan*, p. 237.
11. Ibid., p. 233.

288 The Darbar of the Sikh Gurus

12. Grewal and Bal, *Guru Gobind Singh*, p. 144.
13. The two-year period is described in Sainapati's *Srī Gur-Sobhā* 11:2–4, p. 116: Daily the Khalsa took the Guru's darshan and was pleased. Regularly such divine vision was obtained. The Sikhs of the Khalsa served the True Guru selflessly and love blossomed within their hearts. They came from towns [throughout the Punjab] and settled at that place [Anandpur]. They took the darshan of the Lord (*prabh purakh*) and no doubt whatsoever remained. The Khalsa overcame as many villages as resided nearby. Two years and a number of days were passed in this way.
    Most post-Khalsa-creation accounts tell us that the reasons for the enmity of the Hill Rajas after 1700 was because the Khalsa in the light of the growing numbers of Anandpur, began to raid nearby villages for supplies, provisions, and cash. Sainapati says as much in *Srī Gur-Sobhā* 11:5, p. 116. See also Indubhusan Bannerjee, *Evolution of the Khalsa* II, p. 130.
14. Of the Lakkhi Jungle poet Lal Das Khiali for example Padam says that he 'remained with the Guru until the end.' *Darbārī Ratan*, p. 237. Southwards too went the poets Ada and Jado Rai Udasi (*Darbārī Ratan*, pp. 240, 242).
15. Ganda Singh, *Hukam-nāme*, nos 54–65, pp. 168–91.
16. Hukamnama 60, Ganda Singh, *Hukam-nāme*, p. 181.
17. Ganda Singh (ed.), *Ma'ākhiz-i Tavārīkh-i Sikhān*, p. 74.
18. Note the comparison below between the the *Zafar-nāmah*'s bait 22 and the eighth admonition (*pand*) of the *Gulistān*:
    When all strategies brought to bear are exhausted it is then lawful to draw the sword [from its scabbard].
    When the hand is foiled at every turn it is then permitted to take the sword in hand.
    Zafar-nāmah 22, Dasam Granth, p. 1390 and M.H. Tasbihi (ed.), *The Persian-English Gulistan or Rose Garden of Sa'di* [trans. Edward Rehatsek] (Tehran: Shargh's Press, 1967), p. 575. Once again, we simply do not know if the *Zafar-nāmah* comprised the petition.
19. Ganda Singh (ed.), *Ma'ākhiz-i Tavārīkh-i Sikhān*, p. 75.
20. Tradition seems to imply that even the poets who took amrit and became Khalsa Sikhs brought their writing to an end upon their initiation. Allied to this is the tacit suggestion that as the ultimate goal of the Guru's vīr-rasa poets was achieved namely, to produce warriors of the Khalsa's calibre, the presence of such poets would now be redundant.
21. *CSRn*, p. 191.
22. *CSRn* 571–2, pp. 117–18; (English translation, p. 191). The translation above is only slightly adapted from McLeod's. Rai Singh is also noted in Padam's *Darbārī Ratan*, pp. 222–3 as the younger brother of Bhai Mani Singh.
23. Ganda Singh, *Life of Banda Singh Bahadur* (Patiala: Publication Bureau Punjabi University, 1990), p. 67.
24. *BSVN* 14:192, p. 238:
    In the darbar at Delhi of Mata Sundari and Mata Sahib Devi.

Conclusion 289

Although this could simply mean in the company of both mothers. For both of the Matajis' hukamnamas see Ganda Singh (ed.), *Hukamnāme*, pp. 196–231.

25. The patron of a mid-eighteenth century manuscript copy of the Chaupa Singh Rahitnama for example was the son of Dharam Chand who was allegedly the treasurer of the tenth Guru. It certainly seems with this in mind that the purpose of preparing this text was to glorify the Chhibbar household. See *CSRn* 643, pp. 130–1 (Gurmukhi text), 200 (English translation).
26. Hew McLeod discusses this interpretation very persuasively. *CSRn*, pp. 16–18; 46. The description of rapacious and other contemporary Sikhs appears at *BSVN* 10:142–3 and 14:116–23, pp. 137–8; 230–1. *BSVN* 14:189–92, pp. 237–8 gives the alleged history of the *Bansavālīnāmā*'s writing.
27. *BSVN* 10:143, p. 138 (repeated at 14:123, p. 231). The shalok itself is Guru Amar Das, *Gaurī kī vār* 24:2, Adi Granth, p. 313. Hew McLeod points out that a common theme of the contemporary Panth as far as the Chhibbars were concerned was *raula* or tumult. *CSRn*, p. 27.
28. Misldars did, however, give religious and charitable grants to gurdwaras and temples. Bhagat Singh, *A History of the Sikh Misals* (Patiala: Punjabi University Publication Bureau, 1993), pp. 365–6. For the very few coins attributed to certain misls see Hans Herrli, *The Coins of the Sikhs*, pp. 23–4. As well, it seems clear from the late eighteenth-century *Prem Sumārag* that misldars themselves most likely possessed rather modest courts as evinced by the reference to a small number of courtly accoutrements (8:19:1–7). W.H. McLeod, *Prem Sumārag*, pp. 100–1. That these were modest darbars reflects the political instability of eighteenth-century Punjab.
29. Other different courtly or pseudo-courtly arena of the eighteenth century in which literature was produced is noted in Rao, Shulman, Subrahmanyam, *Textures of Time*, p. 225.
30. W.H. McLeod (trans.), *The B40 Janam-Sakhi* (Amritsar: Guru Nanak Dev University, 1980), p. 19.
31. The Guru Panth doctrine claims that whenever five Sikhs (usually Khalsa Sikhs) gather together to determine what action to pursue their ultimate determination has the sanction of the eternal Guru. A history of the Guru Panth idea appears in J.S. Grewal, 'The Doctrines of Guru-Panth and Guru-Granth', in his *From Guru Nanak to Maharaja Ranjit Singh* (Amritsar: Guru Nanak Dev University Press, 1982), pp. 100–6.
32. W.H. McLeod (trans.), *B40*, p. 20. The name of the artist was Alam Chand Raj. The paintings themselves appears in Surjit Hans (ed.), *B-40 Janamsakhi Guru Baba Nanak Paintings* (Amritsar: Guru Nanak Dev University, 1987).
33. The second note claims that 'Bhai Sanghu had this volume written by Dasvandhi's son, servant of the sangat.' McLeod (trans.), *B40*, p. 20.
34. For a brief view of Ranjit Singh's darbar see my forthcoming 'Maharaja Ranjit Singh (1780–1839 CE): A Diamond in the Rough', in Kate Brittlebank (ed.), *Tall Tales of the Raj* (forthcoming). Also see Henry Fane, *Five Years*

in India; comprising a narrative of travels in the Presidency of Bengal, a visit to the court of Runjeet Singh, residence in the Himalayah mountains, an account of the late expedition to Cabul and Affghanistan, voyage down the Indus, and journey overland to England I (rpt, Patiala: Language Department, 1970), p. 71.

35. Tradition claims that Guru Gobind Singh gave both a nishan and a kettledrum to Banda to announce the coming Sikh kingdom both audially and visually. Of course today most gurdwaras throughout India possess both a nishan and a nagara. Another tradition maintains that the nishan originated with Guru Hargobind who erected it over the Akal Takht in 1606. *EoS* III, p. 240. There is too a reference to a 'white flag' erected by Guru Amar Das in Goindwal in the *Bhattan de savaīe*:
    Since time began patience has been the white banner of Guru Amar Das, a flag planted on the bridge to paradise.
    Savaīe mahale tīje ke 7, Adi Granth, p. 1393. I would like to thank Pashaura Singh for pointing me to this passage.

36. Linda Darling, 'Middle Eastern Advice for Indian Muslim Rulers', p. 8.

37. Today's official Ardas appears in the third segment of the section titled *shaksī rahinī* 'personal life' in *Sikh Rahit Maryādā*, pp. 9–10. Although early Sikh manuscripts contain the term it is not altogether sure what the Ardas entailed in the eighteenth century. A reference appears for example in the 1719 CE *Nasīhat-nāmā* attributed to Nand Lal, Guru Nanak Dev University's ms. 770, f. 34a:
    He who undertakes anything without [first] performing an ardas...finds no honour in the Lord's *dargah*.
    Versions of the Ardas predating the SGPC's differ considerably.

38. In fact, in the seventeenth and eighteenth centuries this form of correspondence was so commonplace that the famous Hindu saints, Eknath and Tukaram both prepared devotional works adopting the 'arz dasht format. Sumit Guha, 'Transitions and Translations', pp. 26–8. Guru Nanak certainly has the official petition in mind when he claims in his typical style:
    The supplication is true; the written petition likewise. Within his court (here, *mahalī* 'palace') the Lord hears these and congratulates those who so implore. Those very ones who are true are thus summoned before the throne and greatness is conferred upon them. Whatever the Lord does is whatever comes to pass.
    Guru Nanak, *Āsā rāg* 2(21), Adi Granth, p. 355. Also Guru Nanak, *Tilang rāg* 1(1), Adi Granth, p. 721 which is composed almost entirely of Persianite terms.

39. Aurangzeb gifts such a kalgi to his son, Prince Akbar, upon his wedding to Salima Banu Begam, the daughter of Sulaiman Shukoh. Jadunath Sarkar (trans.), *Maāsir-i-'Ālamgīrī*, p. 73. Also see Bernard Cohn, 'Cloth, Clothes, and Colonialism: India in the Nineteenth Century', in his *Colonialism and*

its Forms of Knowledge (Princeton: Princeton University Press, 1996), pp. 106–11.

40. *Nasīhat-nāmā*, Guru Nanak Dev University, ms. 770, folios. 36a–b. The term *apnā rāju* appears on folio 36a. Also Piara Singh Padam, *Rahit-nāme*, p. 59. There are recensions of the *Tankhāh-nāmā* which include the following line 'He is a Khalsa who bears a canopy over his head.' Hew McLeod, *Sikh of the Khalsa*, p. 284. Note however that McLeod mistakenly states that this line appears in ms. 770 (p. 419).

Bibliography

UNPUBLISHED MANUSCRIPTS

Das Gur Kathā 232–3, Khalsa College ms. 1797A, f. 32.
Gur-pādhantī, ms. 115682 Sikh Reference Library, Punjabi University, Patiala.
Tankhāh-nāmā ms. 770, Guru Nanak Dev University, Amritsar.
Shardhā Puran, ms. 1097, Guru Nanak Dev University, Amritsar.
Shardhā Purak, ms. 973, Reference Library, Punjabi Sahitya Academy, Ludhiana.
Prashan Uttar, ms. 684, Punjab State Archives, Patiala.
Sākhī Gurū jī dī Bhāī Nand Lāl jī dī Pātishāhī Dasvīn, ms. 91, Guru Nanak Dev University.
Mss. 115373 and 115620, Punjabi University, Patiala are versions of the *Sikhān dī Bhagatmālā*.
mss. 752 and 764 Central Public Library, Patiala.
ms. 90272, Punjabi University, Patiala.
ms. 104, Bhasha Vibhag Punjab, Patiala.
mss. 464, 1059(b), 177(a, c), 790, 609(s), 439(b), Guru Nanak Dev University, Amritsar.
GS/MSS 332121, Punjabi University, Patiala.
incomplete ms. 2311 Sikh Reference Library, Khalsa College, Amritsar (1849 CE).
Manuscript 332164/GS at Punjabi University, Patiala.

BOOKS AND ARTICLES

Ahmad, Aziz (1964), *Studies in Islamic Culture in the Indian Environment*, Oxford: Clarendon.
——— (1969), *An Intellectual History of Islam in India*, Edinburgh: Edinburgh University Press.

——— (1975), 'The British Museum Mirzānāma and the Seventeenth Century Mirzā in India', in *Iran: Journal of the British Institute of Persian Studies* 13, pp. 99–110.

——— (1976), 'Safavid Poets and India', *Iran* 14, pp. 17–32.

Ahmad, Zahuruddin (1975), *Abu'l Fazl—Ahwāl o Āsār*, Lahore: Punjab University Press.

Alam, Muzaffar (1986), *The Crisis of Empire in Mughal North India, Awadh and the Punjab 1707–1748*, New Delhi: Oxford University Press.

——— (1998), 'The Pursuit of Persian: Language in Mughal Politics', in *Modern Asian Studies* 32: 2, pp. 317–49.

——— (2000), '*Akhlāqī* norms and Mughal Governance', in M. Alam, F.N. Delvoye, and Marc Gaborieau (eds), *The Making of Indo-Persian Culture: Indian and French Studies*, Delhi: Manohar.

——— (2003), 'The Culture and Politics of Persian in Precolonial Hindustan', in Sheldon Pollock (ed.), *Literary Cultures in History: Reconstructions from South Asia*, Berkeley: University of California Press.

Alam, Muzaffar and Sanjay Subrahmanyam (2004), 'The Making of a Munshi', in *Comparative Studies in South Asia, Africa and the Middle East* 24:2, pp. 61–72.

Ali, Daud (2004), *Courtly Culture and Political Life in Early Medieval India*, Cambridge: Cambridge University Press.

Ali, M. Athar (1966), *The Mughal Nobility Under Aurangzeb*, London: Asia Publishing House.

——— (1985), *The Apparatus of Empire: Awards of Ranks, Offices and titles to the Mughal Nobility, 1574–1658*, Delhi: Oxford University Press.

——— (1999), 'Translation of Sanskrit Works at Akbar's Court', in Iqtidar Alam Khan (ed.), *Akbar and His Age*, New Delhi: Northern book Centre, pp. 171–80.

——— (1999), 'Pursuing an Elusive Seeker of Universal Truth—the Identity and Environment of the Author of the *Dabistān-i Mazāhib*' in the *Journal of the Royal Asiatic Society* 3:9:3 (November).

'Allami, Abu'l Fazl (1997), The *A-In-I Akbari* I [trans. H. Blochmann], New Delhi: Low Price Publications.

Alvi, Sajida Sultana (ed. and trans.) (1989), *Advice on the Art of Governance: Mau'izahi Jahāngīrī of Muhammad Bāqir Najm-i Sānī: An Indo-Islamic Mirror for Princes*, Albany: State University of New York Press.

Andrews (1977), 'P.A. The Tents of Timur: An Examination of Reports on the Quriltay at Samarqand, 1404', in Philip Denwood (ed.), *Arts of the Eurasian Steppelands*, London: SOAS, pp. 143–88.

——— (1999), *Felt Tents and Pavilions: The Nomadic Tradition and its Interaction with Princely Tentage 2 volumes*, London: Melisende.

Bibliography

Anok Singh (ed.) (1992), *Maskīn jī de Laikchar: Bhāg Pahilā* (6th edition), Amritsar: Singh Brothers.
Archer, W.G. (1966), *Paintings of the Sikhs*, London: Her Majesty's Stationery Office.
—————— (1973), *Indian Paintings from the Punjab Hills: A Survey and History of Pahari Miniature Painting* II, Delhi: Oxford University Press.
Asher, Catherine (1992), *Architecture of Mughal India*, Cambridge: Cambridge University Press.
—————— (1993), 'Sub-Imperial Palaces: Power and Authority in Mughal India', in *Ars Orientalis* 23, pp. 281–302.
Ashok, Shamsher Singh (ed.) (1968), *Gurbilās Pātshāhī 10 krit Kuir Singh*, Patiala: Punjabi University Press.
—————— (1971), *Prāchīn Vārān te Jangnāme*, Amritsar: SGPC.
Ashta, Dharampal (1959), *The Poetry of the Dasam Granth*, New Delhi: Arun Prakashan.
Asiri, F.M. (1951), 'Chandar Bhan Brahman and His Chahar Chaman', in the *Visva-Bharati Annals* 4, pp. 51–6.
Askari, S.H. (1975), 'Baba Nanak in Persian Sources', in the *Journal of Sikh Studies* II:2 (August), pp. 112–16.
Baagha, Ajit Singh (1969), *Banur Had Orders* (Delhi: Ranjit Printers and Publishers.
Badauni (1869), *Muntakhabuttavārīkh* [edited by Ahmad Ali and Nassau Less], Calcutta: Bibliotheca India.
Badawi, M.M. (1980), 'From Primary to Secondary Qasīdas: Thoughts on the Development of Classical Arabic Poetry', in the *Journal of Arabic Literature* 9, pp. 1–31.
Bajwa, Kulvinder Singh (ed.) (2004), *Mahimā Prakāsh (Vārtak)*, Amritsar: Singh Brothers.
Banga, Indu (1978), *Agrarian System of the Sikhs*, Delhi: Manohar.
Basu, Kunal (2003), *The Miniaturist*, London: Orion Books.
Bayly, C.A. (1993), *Rulers, Townsmen and Bazaars: North Indian Society in the Age of British Expansion 1770–1870*, Delhi: Oxford University Press.
Beach, Milo Cleveland (1992), *Mughal and Rajput Painting*, Cambridge: Cambridge University Press.
Beach, Milo C. and Ebba Koch (1997), *King of the World: the Padshahmana, an Imperial Manuscript from the Royal Library, Windsor Castle* [trans., Wheeler Thackston], London: Azimuth Editions, Sackler Gallery.
Bedi, Harmahendr Singh (1993), *Gurmukhī Lipi men Upalabdh Hindī Bhakti Sāhitya kā Ālochnātmak Adhyayan*, Amritsar: Guru Nanak Dev University Press.

Bibliography 295

Bedi, Tarlochan Singh (ed.) (1994), *Sikhān dī Bagatmālā*, Patiala: Punjabi University Publication Bureau.

Begley, W.E. and Z.A. Desai (comp. and trans.) (1989), *Taj Mahal: The Illumined Tomb An Anthology of Seventeenth-century Mughal and European Documentary Sources*, Seattle and London: The University of Washington Press.

────── (1990), *The Shāh Jahān Nāma of 'Ināyat Khān*, Delhi: Oxford University Press.

Beveridge, Annette S. (ed. and trans.) (1994), *The History of Humāyūn: Humāyūn-Nāmā by Gul Badan Begum*, New Delhi: Low Price Publications.

Bhagat Singh (1993), *A History of Sikh Misls*, Patiala: Punjabi University Publication Bureau.

Bhalla, Sarup Das (1971), *Mahimā Prakāsh 2 volumes* [ed. Gobind Singh Lamba and Khazan Singh], Patiala: Bhasha Vibhag, Punjab.

Bhatia, Gurbux Singh (1971), 'Persian Writings on Guru Nanak', in *Punjab History Conference Fifth Session (March 8–10, 1970) Proceedings*, Patiala: Punjabi University Press, pp. 52–61.

Bhatia, Uttam Singh (1987), *Gurū Bhagat Bhāī Nand Lāl Goyā*, Patiala: Pavitar Pramanik Prakashan.

Bilimoria, Jamshid H. (trans.) (1908), *Ruka'at-i-Alamgiri or Letters of Aurangzebe [with Historical and Explanatory Notes]*, London: Luzac & Co.

Blake, Stephen (1979), 'The Patrimonial-Bureaucratic Empire of the Mughals', in the *Journal of Asian Studies* 39 (November), pp. 77–94.

────── (1991), *Shahjahanabad: The Sovereign City in Mughal India, 1639–1739*, Cambridge: Cambridge University Press.

Bonazzoli, Giorgio (1983), 'Composition, Transmission, and Recitation of the *Purānas*', in *Purāna* 25 (July).

Bosworth, C.E. (1973), *The Ghaznavids: Their Empire in Afghanistan and Eastern Iran, 994–1040* (2nd edition), Beirut: Librairie du Liban.

────── (1977), *The Later Ghaznavids: Splendour and Decay*, New York: Columbia University Press.

Boyce, Mary (1957), 'The Parthian Gōsān and Iranian Minstrel Tradition', in *Royal Asiatic Society of Great Britain and Ireland* 18.

Brand. Michael and Glenn D. Lowry (1985), *Akbar's India: Art from the Mughal City of Victory*, London: Sotheby Publications.

Brookshaw, Dominic P. (2003), 'Palaces, Pavilions and Pleasure-gardens: the Context and Setting of the Medieval *Majlis*', in *Middle Eastern Literatures* 6:2 (July).

Brotman, Irwin F. (1970), *A Guide to the Temple Tokens of India*, Los Angeles: Shamrock Press.

Brown, Katherine (2000), 'Reading Indian Music: the Interpretation of Seventeenth-century European Travel Writing in the (Re)Construction of Indian Music History', in the *British Journal of Ethnomusicology* 9:2.

────── (2006), 'If Music be the Food of Love: Masculinity and Eroticism in the Mughal *mefil*', in Francesca Orsini (ed.), *Love in South Asia: A Cultural History*, Cambridge: Cambridge University Press.

────── (2007), 'Did Aurangzeb Ban Music? Questions for the Historiography of His Reign', *Modern Asian Studies* 41:1, pp. 77–121.

Browne, Edward G. (ed. and trans.) (1900), *The Chahár Maqála ('Four Discourses') of Nidhám-ı-i-'Arúd-ı-i-Samarqand-ı*, London: Luzac & Co.

────── (1924), *A History of Persian Literature in Modern Times (AD 1500–1924)*, Cambridge: Cambridge University Press.

Bryant, Kenneth (1978), *Poems to the Child-God*, Berkeley: University of California Press.

Burhanpuri, Bhimsen (1972), *Nuskha-i Dilkusha* [Jadunath Sarkar (trans.)] in V.G. Khobrekar (ed.), *Sir Jadunath Sarkar Birth Centenary Commemoration Volume: English Translation of Tārīkh-i Dilkasha (Memoirs of Bhimsen Relating to Aurangzeb's Deccan Campaigns)*, Bombay: Maharashtra State Archives.

Busch, Allison (2002), 'The Courtly Vernacular: The Transformation of Braj Literary Culture, 1585–1675', Ph.D. dissertation, University of Chicago.

────── (2004), 'The Anxiety of Innovation: The Poetic Practice of Literary Science in the Hindi/*Riti* Tradition', in *Comparative Studies of South Asia, Africa and the Middle East* 24:2, pp. 45–59.

────── (2005), 'Literary Responses to the Mughal Imperium: The Historical Poems of Keśavdās', in *South Asia Research* 25:1.

Callewaert, Winand M. (1992), 'Singers Repertoires in Western India', in R.S. McGregor (ed.), *Devotional Literature in South Asia: Current Research 1985–1988*, Cambridge: Cambridge University Press, pp. 29–35.

Canfield, Robert (1991), *Turko-Persia in Historical Perspective*, Cambridge: Cambridge University Press.

Chakravarti, Chintaharan (1946), 'Muslim Patronage to Sanskrit Learning', in D.R. Bhandarkar *et al.* (eds), *B.C. Law Volume part 2*, Poona: Bhandarkar Oriental Research Institute.

Chaturvedi, Parashuram (ed.) (1954), *Mirānbāī kī Padāvalī*, Allahabad: Hindi Sahitya Sammelan.

Chaudhari, Bharat Bhushan (1976), *Ālam aur unkā Kāvya* [Alam and His Poetry], Delhi: Sahitya.

Chejne, G. Anwar (1965), 'The Boon-Companion in Early 'Abbāsid Times', in *Journal of the American Oriental Society* 85, pp. 327–35.

Chetan Singh (1991), *Region and Empire: Panjab in the Seventeenth Century*, New Delhi: Oxford University Press.

Chopra, P.N. (1976), *Life and Letters Under the Mughals*, New Delhi: Ashajanak Publications.

Clinton, Jerome W. (1972), *The Divan of Manūchihrī Dāmghānī: A Critical Study*, Minneapolis: Bibliotheca Islamica.

Cohn, Bernard (1996), 'Cloth, Clothes, and Colonialism: India in the Nineteenth Century', in his *Colonialism and Its Forms of Knowledge*, Princeton: Princeton University Press.

Corrie, Rebecca Wells (1975), 'The Paisley', in *The Kashmir Shawl*, New Haven: Yale University Art Gallery.

Craven, Jr., Roy C. (1990), 'The Reign of Raja Dalip Singh (1695–1741) and the Siege of Lanka Series of Guler', in *Mārg: Ramayana: Paintings from the Hills* (September).

Crooke, William (1968), *The Popular Religion and Folk-Lore of Northern India* I, rpt, New Delhi: Munshiram Manoharlal.

Dale, Stephen F. (1990), 'Steppe Humanism: The Autobiographical Writings of Zahir al-Din Muhammad Babur, 1483–1530', *International Journal of Middle East Studies* 22, pp. 37–58.

———— (1996), 'The Poetry and Autobiography of the *Bâbur-nâma*', in *Journal of Asian Studies* 55:3, pp. 635–64.

———— (2000), *Indian Merchants and Eurasian Trade, 1600–1750*, Cambridge: Cambridge University Press, 1994 (paperback edition).

———— (2004), *The Garden of the Eight Paradises: Bābur and the Culture of Empire in Central Asia, Afghanistan and India (1483–1530)*, Leiden and Boston: Brill.

Darling, Linda T. (2002), '"Do Justice, Do Justice, For That is Paradise": Middle Eastern Advice for Indian Muslim Rulers', in *Comparative Studies of South Asia, Africa and the Middle East* 22:1–2.

Dasti, Humaira Faiz (1998), *Multan: A Province of the Mughal Empire (1525–1751)*, Karachi: Royal Book Company.

de Bruijn, J.T.P. (1983), *Of Piety and Poetry: The Interaction of Religion and Literature in the Life and Works of Hakīm Sanā'ī of Ghazna*, Leiden: E.J. Brill.

De, Sushil Kumar [with notes by Edwin Gerow] (1963), *Sanskrit Poetics as a Study of Aesthetic*, Berkeley: University of California Press.

De, S.K. (1960), *History of Sanskrit Poetics II* (2 volumes in 1, second revised edition), Calcutta: Firma K.L. Mukhopadhyay.

Dehkhoda, A.A., *Lughat-nāmah*, CD-ROM edition.

Delvoye, François Nalini (1994), 'Indo-Persian Literature on Art-Music: Some Historical and Technical Aspects', in Delavoye (ed.), *Confluence of Cultures*, New Delhi: Manohar.

Deol, Jeevan (2001), 'Eighteenth Century Khalsa Identity: Discourse, Praxis and Narrative', in Christopher Shackle, Gurharpal Singh, and A.S. Mandair (eds), *Sikh Religion, Culture and Ethnicity*, London: Curzon, pp. 25–46.

―――― (2003), 'Illustration and Illumination in Sikh Scriptural Manuscripts', in Kavita Singh (ed.), *New Insights into Sikh Art* 54:4, Mumbai: Marg.

Desai, Vishakai N. (1990), 'Painting and Politics in Seventeenth-Century North India: Mewār, Bikāner, and the Mughal Court', in *Art Journal: New Approaches to South Asian Art* 49:4, Winter.

Dhillon, Balwant Singh (1979), 'Some Unknown Hukam-namas of Guru Gobind Singh', in *Punjab History Conference Proceedings* 13 (March).

Dhillon, Dalbir Singh (1982), 'Development of Illustration on the Sikh Sacred Writings', in *Punjab History Conference, Sixteenth Session, March 12–14, 1982, Proceedings*, Patiala: Punjabi University.

Digby, Simon (1986), 'The Sufi Shaikh as a Source of Authority in Mediaeval India', in Marc Gaborieau (ed.), *Purushārtha*, vol. 9, *Islam et société en Aise du sud*, Paris: Ecole des Hautes études en sciences sociales.

Divakar, Krishna (1969), *Bhonsla Rāj-darbār ke Hindī Kavi*, Varanasi: Nagari Pracharini Sabha.

Doniger, Wendy and Brian K. Smith (ed. and trans.) (1991), *The Laws of Manu*, New Delhi: Penguin Books.

Drake, Hubert (trans.) (1960), *The Book of Government or Rules for Kings: the Siyāsat-nāma of Siyar al-Mulūk of Nizām al-Mulk*, New Haven: Yale University Press.

Dyal, Ram (1923), *The Life of Bhai Nand Lal Goya*, Amritsar: The Sikh Tract Society.

Eaton, Richard (1994), *The Rise of Islam and the Bengal Frontier 1204–1760*, New Delhi: Oxford University Press.

Elias, Jamal J., 'The Sufi Robe (*Khirqa*) as a Vehicle of Spiritual Authority', in Stewart Gordon (ed.), *Robes and Honor*, pp. 275–89.

Elliot and Dowson (ed.) (2001), *The History of India as Told by Its Own Historians: The Muhammadan Period*, Delhi: Low Price Publications.

―――― (2001), *The History of India as Told by its Own Historians* VII, Delhi: Low Price Publications.

Elias, N. and E. Denison Ross (trans.) (1973), *The Tarikh-i Rashidi of Mirza Muhammad Haidar Dughlat A History of The Moghuls of Central Asia*, Patna: Academia Asiatica.

Norbert Elias (1983), *The Court Society* [trans. Edmund Jephcott], Oxford: Basil Blackwell.

Fane, Henry (1970), *Five years in India; comprising a narrative of travels in the Presidency of Bengal, a visit to the court of Runjeet Singh, residence in the Himalayah mountains, an account of the late expedition to Cabul and Affghanistan, voyage down the Indus, and journey overland to England* I, rpt, Patiala: Language Department.

Faruqi, Shamsur Rahman (2004), 'A Stranger in the City: The Poetics of Sabk-e Hindi', in Naqi Husain Jafri (ed.), *Critical Theory: Perspectives From Asia*, New Delhi: Creative Books, pp. 180–285.

Fauja Singh and G.S. Talib (1975), *Guru Tegh Bahadar: Martyr and Teacher*, Patiala: Punjabi University Press.

Fauja Singh (1979), *Guru Amar Das: Life and Teachings*, New Delhi: Sterling Publishers.

Fenech, Louis E. (1994), 'Persian Sikh Scripture: the Ghazals of Bhai Nand Lal Goya', in *International Journal of Punjab Studies* I:1, pp. 49–70.

——— (2000), *Martrydom in the Sikh Tradition: Playing the 'Game of Love'*, New Delhi: Oxford University Press.

——— (2001), 'Martyrdom and the Execution of Guru Arjan in Early Sikh Sources', in the *Journal of the American Oriental Society* 121:1, pp. 20–31.

——— (2003), 'Conversion and Sikh Tradition', in Rowena Robinson *et al.* (eds), *Religious Conversion in India: Modes, Motivations, Meanings*, New Delhi: Oxford University Press, pp. 149–80.

——— (2004), 'Bhāī Nand Lāl "Goyā" and the Sikh Tradition', in Pashaura Singh and N. Gerald Barrier (eds), *Sikhism and History*, New Delhi: Oxford University Press, pp. 111–34.

——— (forthcoming), 'Maharaja Ranjit Singh (1780–1839 CE): A Diamond in the Rough', in Kate Brittlebank (ed.), *Tall Tales of the Raj*.

Findly, Elison (1987), 'Jahāngīr's Vow of Non-Violence', in the *Journal of the American Oriental Society* 107, pp. 245–56.

Foucault, Michel (1972), *The Archaeology of Knowledge and the Discourse on Language* [trans. A.M. Sheridan Smith], New York: Pantheon Books.

Frye, Richard (1975), *The Golden Age of Persia: The Arabs in the East*, New York: Barnes and Noble Books.

Ganda Singh (ed.) (1949), *Ma'ākhiz-i Tavārīkh-i Sikhān jild avval: 'Ahd-i Gurū Sahibān*, Amritsar: Sikh History Society).

——— (1963), *Kulliyāt-i Bhā'ī Nand La'l Goyā*, Malaka, Malaya: Sikh Sangat.

——— (ed. and trans.) (1975), *Amar-nāmā: Fārsī mūl, Panjābī Utārā te Arath*, Patiala: Sikh History Society.

——— (1985), *Hukamnāme: Gurū Sāhibān, Mātā Sāhibān, Bandā Singh ate Khālsā jī de*, Patiala: Publication Bureau Punjabi University.

——— (1987), *Kavī Saināpati Rachit Srī Gur-Sobhā*, Patiala: Punjabi University Press.

——— (1989), *Bhāī Nand Lāl Granthāvalī*, Patiala: Punjabi University Press.
Garja Singh (1961), *Shahīd-bilās (Bhāī Manī Singh) krit Sevā Singh*, Ludhiana: Punjabi Sahit Academy.
Gerow, Edwin (1977), *Indian Poetics*, Wiesbaden: Otto Harrassowitz.
Ghani, Muhammad Abdul (1929), *A History of Persian Language and Literature at the Mughal Court: part III–Akbar the Great*, Allahabad: The Indian Press Ltd.
——— (1930), *A History of Persian Language and Literature at the Mughal Court: with a brief survey of the growth of Urdu [Babur to Akbar] volume 2, Humayun*, Allahabad: the Indian Press Ltd.
'Gharib', Bhai Megh Raj ji (1912), *Prem Phulvarī arthat Srī Gurū Gobind Singh jī de annanay Sikh Bhāī Nand Lāl jī krit 'Dīvān Goyā'*, Amritsar: Bhapedi Hatti.
Gian Singh (1993), *Tavārīkh Gurū Khālsā 2 vols*, Patiala: Bhasha Vibhag Punjab.
Gill, Inder Singh (ed.) (1968), *Kavi Sohan jī krit Srī Gur-bilās Pātshāhī Chhevīn Tipanīān Samet* 5:55, Amritsar: Vazir Hindi Press.
Glynn, Catherine (1983), 'Early Painting in Mandi', *Articus Asiae* XLIV: 1.
——— (1995), 'Further Evidence for Early Painting at Mandi', *Articus Asiae* LV:1/2.
——— (2004), 'Mughalized Portraits of Bilaspur Royalty in the Second Half of the Seventeenth Century', in Rosemary Crill, Susan Stronge, and Andrew Topsfield (eds), *Arts of Mughal India: Studies in Honour of Robert Skelton*, London, New York, Ahmedabad: Victoria and Albert Museum and Mapin Publishing.
——— (2004), 'A Rājasthānī Princely Album: Rājput Patronage of Mughal-Style Painting', in *Articus Asiae* LX: 3/4 (2001), abad: Victoria and Albert Museum and Mapin Publishing.
Gold, Daniel (1987), *The Lord as Guru: Hindi Sants in the Northern Indian Tradition*, New York: Oxford University Press.
Gommans, Jos (1998), 'The Silent Frontier of South Asia, c. AD 1100–1800', in *Journal of World History* 9:1 (Spring).
Gopal Singh (1979), *A History of the Sikh People*, New Delhi: World Sikh University Press.
Gordon, Stewart, 'Legitimacy and Loyalty in Some Successor States of the Eighteenth Century', in John Richards (ed.), *Kingship and Authority in South Asia*.
——— (1994), *Marathas, Marauders, and State Formation in Eighteenth-Century India*, Delhi: Oxford University Press.
——— (2003), 'Introduction: Ibn Battuta and a Region of Robing', in

Stewart Gordon (ed.), *Robes of Honour: Khil'at in Pre-Colonial and Colonial India*, New Delhi: Oxford University Press.

Goswamy, B.N. (1980), 'A Matter of Taste: Some Notes on the Context of Painting in Sikh Punjab', in *Mārg: Appreciation of Creative Arts under Maharaja Ranjit Singh* (December).

Grewal, J.S. and S.S. Bal (1967), *Guru Gobind Singh: A Biographical Study*, Chandigarh: Panjab University Press.

Grewal, J.S. and Indu Banga (ed. and trans.) (1975), *Early Nineteenth Century Panjab: From Ganesh Das's Chār Bāgh-i-Panjāb*, Amritsar: Guru Nanak Dev University.

Grewal, J.S. (1976), *Guru Tegh Bahadar and the Persian Chroniclers*, Amritsar: Guru Nanak Dev University Press.

———— (1980), 'Dissent in Early Sikhism', in *Punjab History Conference Fourteenth Session March 28–30, 1980 Proceedings*, Patiala: Punjabi University Press.

———— (1982), *From Guru Nanak to Maharaja Ranjit Singh*, Amritsar: Guru Nanak Dev University Press.

———— (1988), *The Sikhs of the Punjab*, Cambridge: Cambridge University Press.

Grewal, J.S. and Irfan Habib (eds) (2001), *Sikh History from Persian Sources: Translations of Major Texts*, New Delhi: Tulika.

Guha, Sumit (1999), *Environment and Ethnicity in India c. 1200–1900*, Cambridge: Cambridge University Press.

———— (2004), 'Transitions and Translations: Regional Power and Vernacular Identity in the Dakhan, 1500–1800', in *Comparative Studies of South Asia, Africa and the Middle East* 24:2, pp. 23–31.

Gulchin-i Ma'ani, Ahmad, *Kārvān-i Hind: dar ahvāl va āsār-i shā'irān-i 'asr-i Safavī keh beh Hindūstān raftah and 2 vols* (Mashhad: Astan-i Quds-i Razavi, 1369/1990–1).

———— *Tārīkh-i Tazkirah-hā-ye Fārsī*.

Gupta, Hari Ram (1984), *History of the Sikhs I*, Delhi: Munshiram Manoharlal Publishers.

G.B. Singh (1972), *Gurmukhī Lippī dā Janam te Vikās* (2nd edition), Chandigarh: Panjab University Press.

Gurcharan Singh (ed.) (1971), *Ādi Granth Shabad-anukramnikā* I, Patiala: Punjabi University Press.

Gurmukh Singh (ed.) (1997), *Gur-bilās Pātshāhī Chhevīn krit Bhagat Singh*, Patiala: Punjabi University Publication Bureau.

Habib, Irfan (1992), 'Formation of the Sultanate Ruling Class of the Thirteenth Century', in Irfan Habib (ed.), *Medieval India 1: Researches in the History of India, 1200–1750*, New Delhi: Oxford University Press.

——— (2002), *The Agrarian System of Mughal India 1556–1707* (second revised edition), New Delhi: Oxford India Paperbacks.
Haksar, A.N.D. (trans.) (1994), *Dandin Tales of The Ten Princes (Daśa Kumāra Charitam)*, New Delhi: Penguin Books.
Hambly, Gavin R.G., 'The Emperor's Clothes: Robing and "Robes of Honour" in Mughal India', in Stewart Gordon (ed.), *Robes of Honour: Khil'at in Pre-Colonial and Colonial India*.
——— (2001), 'From Baghdad to Bukhara, from Ghazna to Delhi: the *khil'a* Ceremony in the Transmission of Kingly Pomp and Circumstance', in Stewart Gordon (ed.), *Robes of Honor: The Medieval World of Investiture*, New York: Palgrave.
Hans, Surjit (1987), *B-40 Janamsakhi Guru Baba Nanak Paintings*, Amritsar: Guru Nanak Dev University Press.
——— (1988), *A Reconstruction of Sikh History From Sikh Literature*, Jalandhar: ABS Publications.
Haq, Mahfuzul (1931), 'The Khan Khanan and His Painters, Illuminators, and Calligraphists', in *Islamic Culture* 5, pp. 627–9.
Haq, S. Moinul (ed.) (1975), *Khafi Khan's History of Alamgir*, Karachi: Pakistan Historical Society.
Harbans Singh (1985), *The Heritage of the Sikhs*, Delhi: Manohar.
——— (ed.), *The Encyclopaedia of Sikhism*, Patiala: Punjabi University Press, 1992, 1998.
Hardy, Peter (1978), 'Growth of Authority over a Conquered Political Elite: Early Delhi Sultanate as a Possible Case Study', in J.F. Richards (ed.), *Kingship and Authority in South Asia*, Madison: South Asian Studies, University of Wisconsin.
——— (1986) 'The Authority of Muslim Kings in Mediaeval India', in *Purushārtha*, vol. 9, *Islam et société en Aise du sud*, Marc Gaborieau (ed.), Paris: Ecole des Hautes études en sciences sociales.
Haribhajan Singh (trans.) (1989), *Sāchī Prīti: Ghazalān Bhāī Nand Lāl jī 'Goyā' ate 'Ganj-nāmā' chon 'Salatanati Dahamm' Satīk*, Amritsar: Singh Brothers.
Hasrat, *Dārā Shikoh*.
Hawley, John Stratton 'Mirabai at the Court of Guru Gobind Singh.' Unpublished paper.
Herrli, Hans (1993), *The Coins of the Sikhs*, Nagpur: Indian Coin Society.
Hiltebeitel, Alf (1990), *The Ritual of Battle: Krishna in the Mahābhārata*, Albany: State University of New York Press.
Hodgson, Marshall G.S. (1974), *The Venture of Islam: Conscience and History in a World Civilization* I*: The Classical Age of Islam*, Chicago: University of Chicago Press.

Hoyland, J.S. (trans.) [with annotations by S.N. Bannerjee] (1922), *The Commentary of Father Monserrate, S.J., on his Journey to the Court of Akbar*, London, Bombay: Oxford University Press.

Hutchison, J. and J. Ph. Vogel (1933), *History of the Panjab Hill States* II, Lahore: Superintendent, Government Printing, Punjab.

Ingalls, Daniel (ed. and trans.) (1965), *An Anthology of Sanskrit Court Poetry Vidyākura's* Subhāshitaratnakosha, Cambridge, Mass.: Harvard University Press.

Irvine, William (1995), *The Later Mughals* vols 1 and 2 bound in one [Jadunath Sarkar (ed.)], Delhi: Low Price Publications.

Isfandyar, Mobad Kaykhusrau (1362/1983), *Dabistān-i Mazāhib* I [ed. Rahim Rizazadah-'i Malik], Tehran: Kitabkhanah-'i Tahuri.

Jaggi, Gursharan Kaur (ed.) (1989), *Gurbilās Pātishāhī Dasvīn*, Patiala: Bhasha Vibhag, Punjab.

Jaggi, R.S. (ed.) (1972), *Kesar Singh Chhibbar dā Bansāvalīnāmā Dasān Pātshāhīān kā* in S.S. Kohli (ed.), *Parkh: Research Bulletin of Panjabi Language and Literature*, Chandigarh: Panjab University.

Jakobsh, Doris (2003), *Relocating Gender in Sikh History: Transformation, Meaning and Identity*, New Delhi: Oxford University Press.

Jan Arek, (1968), 'Persian Literature in India', in Jan Rypka, *History of Iranian Literature*, Dordrecht: D. Reidel Publishing Company.

Keene, Manuel (2004), 'The *Kundan* Technique: the Indian Jeweller's Unique Artistic Treasure', in Rosemary Crill, Susan Stronge, and Andrew Topsfield (eds), *Arts of Mughal India: Studies in Honour of Robert Skelton, London*, New York, Ahmedabad: Victoria and Albert Museum and Mapin Publishing.

Khalsa, Gurdharam Singh (1997), *Guru Ram Das in Sikh Tradition*, New Delhi: Harman Publishing House.

Khan, Iqtidar Alam (2005), 'Martial and Political Culture of the Khalsa', in Reeta Grewal and Sheena Pall (eds), *Five Centuries of Sikh Tradition: Ideology, Politics, and Culture*, Delhi: Manohar.

Khan, Kunwar Refaqat Ali (1976), *The Kachhwahas Under Akbar and Jahangir*, New Delhi: Kitab Publishing House.

Khan, Muhammad (1978), *Iranian Influence in Mughal India*, Lahore.

Khwandamir (1966), *Qanun-i-Humayuni (Also known as Humayun Nama)* [Baini Prashad (trans.)], rpt, Calcutta: The Asiatic Society.

Kinsley, David R. (1979), *The Divine Player: A Study of Krsna Līlā*, Delhi: Motilal Banarsidass.

Kirpal Singh (ed.) (1963), *A Catalogue of Punjabi and Urdu Manuscripts*, Amritsar: Sikh History Research Department, Khalsa College.

——— (1976), 'Saif Khan and His Relations with Guru Tegh Bahadar', in *Punjab History Conference Tenth Session February 28–29, 1976 Proceedings*, Patiala: Punjabi University Press.

Kolff, Dirk H.A. (1990), *Naukar, Rajput and Sepoy: The Ethnohistory of the Military Labour Market in Hindustan, 1450–1850*, Cambridge: Cambridge University Press.

Laine, James W. (2003), *Shivaji Hindu King in Islamic India*, New York: Oxford University Press.

Lal, Magan and Jessie Duncan Westbrook (trans.) (1913), *The Diwan of Zeb-un-Nissa: the First Fifty Ghazals*, New York: Dutton.

Lal, Ruby (2005), *Domesticity and Power in the Early Mughal World*, Cambridge: Cambridge University Press.

Lambton, Ann (1962), 'Justice in the Medieval Persian Theory of Kingship', in *Studia Islamica* 17, pp. 91–119.

Latif, Muhammad (1989), *History of the Panjáb: From the Remotest Antiquity to the Present Time*, New Delhi: Kalyani Publications.

Lawrence, Bruce (1978), *Notes from a Distant Flute: The Extant Literature of pre-Mughal Indian Sufism*, Tehran: Imperial Iranian Academy of Philosophy.

Leach, Linda York (2004), 'Pages from an *Akbarnama*', in Rosemary Crill, Susan Stronge, and Andrew Topsfield (eds), *Arts of Mughal India: Studies in Honour of Robert Skelton*, London, New York, Ahmedabad: Victoria and Albert Museum and Mapin Publishing.

Lentz, Thomas W. and Glenn D. Lowry (1989), *Timur and the Princely Vision: Persian Art and Culture in the Fifteenth Century*, Los Angeles: Los Angeles County Museum of Art.

Levi, Scott C. (2002), *The Indian Diaspora in Central Asia and its Trade, 1550–1900*, Leiden: Brill.

Levy, Reuben (trans. and ed.) (1951), *A Mirror for Princes: The Qābūs Nāma by Kai Kā'ūs ibn Iskandar Prince of Gurgān*, London: Cresset Press.

Lewis, F.D. (1995), 'Reading, Writing and Recitation: Sanā'ī and the Origins of the Persian Ghazal', unpublished Ph.D. dissertation, University of Chicago.

Lutgendorf, Philip (1991), *The Life of a Text: Performing the Rāmcaritmānas of Tulsidas*, Berkeley: University of California Press.

Macauliffe, M.A. (1909), *The Sikh Religion: Its Gurus, Sacred Writings and Authors* 6 vols, Oxford: Clarendon Press.

Machariar, M. Krishna (1970), *History of Classical Sanskrit Literature*, New Delhi: Motilal Banarsidass.

Mackenzie, John (1984), *The Empire of Nature: Hunting Conservation and British Imperialism*, Manchester: Manchester University Press.

Mann, Gurinder Singh (1996), *The Goindval Pothis: The Earliest Extant Source of the Sikh Canon*, Cambridge, Mass.: Harvard University Press.

────── (2001), *The Making of Sikh Scripture*, New York: Oxford University Press.

Manucci, M. Niccolao (1907–9), *Storia da Mogor; or Mughal India, 1653–1708*, 4 volumes [William J. Irvine (trans.)], London: J. Murray.

Mansukhani, Gobind Singh (1979), *Guru Ramdas: His Life, Work and Philosophy*, New Delhi: Oxford and IBH Publishing Company.

McGregor, R.S. (1968), *The Language of Indrajit of Orcha: A Study of Early Braj Bhāshā Prose*, Cambridge: Cambridge University Press.

────── (1984), *Hindi Literature From its Beginnings to the Nineteenth Century*, Weisbaden: Otto Harrassowitz.

McLeod, W.H. (1968), *Guru Nanak and the Sikh Religion*, Oxford: Clarendon Press.

────── (1980), *Early Sikh Tradition: A Study of the Janam-sākhīs*, Oxford: Clarendon Press.

────── (trans. and ed.) (1980), *The B40 Janam-Sakhi*, Amritsar: Guru Nanak Dev University Press.

────── (ed. and trans.) (1984), *Textual Sources for the Study of Sikhism*, Manchester: Manchester University Press.

────── (ed.) (1987), *The Chaupa Singh Rahit-Nama*, Dunedin, New Zealand: University of Otago Press.

────── (1989), *Who is a Sikh? The Problem of Sikh Identity*, Oxford: Clarendon Press.

────── (1991), *Popular Sikh Art*, New Delhi: Oxford University Press.

────── (1997), *Sikhism*, New York and London: Penguin.

────── (2003), *The Sikhs of the Khalsa*, New Delhi: Oxford University Press.

────── (trans.) (2006), *The Prem Sumārag: The Testimony of a Sanatan Sikh*, New Delhi: Oxford University Press.

────── (2007), 'Reflections on the Prem Sumārag', in *Journal of Punjab Studies* 14:1 (Spring).

Mehta, Shirin (1999), 'Akbar as Reflected in the Contemporary Jain Literature in Gujarat', in Iqtidar Alam Khan (ed.), *Akbar and His Age*, New Delhi: Northern Book Centre.

Metcalf, Barbara (1995), 'Too Little and Too Much: Reflections on Muslims in the History of India', in *Journal of Asian Studies* 54:4, pp. 951–67.

Meisami, Julie Scott (1987), *Medieval Persian Court Poetry*, Princeton: Princeton University Press.

Miller, Barbara Stoler (ed.) (1984), *Theatre of Memory: the Plays of Kālidāsa*, New York: Columbia University Press.
——— (ed. and trans.) (1984), *The Gītagovinda of Jayadeva: Love Song of the Dark Lord*, New Delhi: Motilal Banarsidass.
Mohiuddin, *The Chancellery and Persian Epistolography*.
Moosvi, Shireen (1999), 'Making and Recording History—Akbar and the *Akbar-nāma*', in Iqtidar Alam Khan (ed.), *Akbar and His Age*, New Delhi: Northern Book Centre.
——— (2005), 'Economic Profile of the Punjab (sixteenth-seventeenth centuries)', in Reeta Grewal and Sheena Pall (eds), *Precolonial and Colonial Punjab: Society, Economics, Politics and Culture*, New Delhi: Manohar.
Mukhia, Harbans (1999), 'The Celebration of Failure as Dissent in Urdu Ghazal', in *Modern Asian Studies* 33:4, pp. 861–81.
Nabha, Kahn Singh (1981), *Gur-shabad Ratanākar Mahān Kosh*, Patiala: Bhasha Vibhag Punjab.
——— (1988), *Gurmat Sudhākar* (5th edition), Patiala: Bhasha Vibhag Punjab.
Naiar, Gurbachan Singh (ed.) (1995), *Gur Ratan Māl: Sau Sākhī* (3rd edition), Patiala: Punjabi University Publication Bureau.
Naik, C.R. (1966), *Abu'r-Rahim Khān-i Khānān and His Literary Circle*, Ahmedabad: Gujarat University Press.
Nasrabadi, Muhammad Tahir (1938), *Tazkirah* [ed. Vahid Dastgirdi], Tehran: Armaghan.
Nayyar, Gurbachan Singh (1998), *Guru Hargobind in Sikh Tradition (Based on Acknowledged Conventional Sources)*, New Delhi: National Book Organisation.
Nesbitt, Eleanor (1999), 'Sikhism', in Peggy Morton and Clive Lawton (eds), *Ethical Issues in Six Religious Traditions*, rpt, Edinburgh: Edinburgh University Press.
Nicholson, Reynold A. (ed. and trans.) (1970), *The Kashf al-Mahjūb: The Oldest Persian Treatise on Sufiism* (1911; 2nd edition 1936. Rpt), London: Luzac.
Nikky-Guninder Kaur Singh's (2005), *The Birth of the Khalsa: A Feminist Re-Memory of Sikh Identity*, Albany: State University of New York Press.
Nizami, Khaliq Ahmad (1997), *Royalty in Medieval India*, Delhi: Munshiram Manoharlal.
Nripinder Singh (1990), *The Sikh Moral Tradition*, Columbia, MO: South Asia Books.
Onkar Singh (1993), *Kabitt Savaiye Bhāī Gurdās: Pāth, Tuk-Tatkarā, Anukramnikā ate Kosh*, Patiala: Punjabi University Press.

Oberoi, Harjot (1994), *The Construction of Religious Boundaries: Culture, Identity and Diversity in the Sikh Tradition*, Delhi: Oxford University Press.

O'Hanlon, Rosalind (1997), 'Issues of Masculinity in North Indian History: The Bangsh Nawabs of Farrukhabad', in the *Indian Journal of Gender Studies* 4:1.

——— (1999), 'Manliness and Imperial Service in Mughal North India', in the *Journal of the Economic and Social History of the Orient* 42:1.

Orsini, Francesca (2006), 'Introduction', in Francesca Orsini (ed.), *Love in South Asia: A Cultural History: A Cultural History*, Cambridge: Cambridge University Press.

Parikh, Dwarakadas (ed.) (1959–60), *Go. Shrī Hari Rāy jī Pranīt Chaurāsī Vaishnavan kī Vartā [Tīn Janam kī Līlā Bhāvanā Vālī]*, Mathura: Shri Bajrang Pustakalay.

Parkash, Ved (1981), *The Sikh in Bihar*, Patna: Janaki Prakashan.

Pashaura Singh (2000), *The Guru Granth Sahib: Canon, Meaning and Authority*, Delhi: Oxford University Press.

——— (2005), 'Understanding the Martyrdom of Guru Arjan', in the *Journal of Punjab Studies* 12:1 (Spring), pp. 29–62.

Pashaura Singh (2003), *The Bhagats of the Guru Granth Sahib: Sikh Self-definition and the Bhagat Bani*, New Delhi: Oxford University Press.

——— (2006), *Life and Work of Guru Arjan*, New Delhi: Oxford University Press.

Pearson, M.N., 'Recreation in Mughal India', in the *British Journal of Sports History* 1(3), pp. 335–50.

Petruccioli. Attilio (1985), 'The Geometry of Power: The City's Planning', in *Mārg: Akbar and Fatehpur Sikri* XXXVIII:1 (March).

——— (1985), 'The City as an Image of the King: Some Notes on the Town-Planning of Mughal Capitals in the Sixteenth and Seventeenth Centuries', in *Mārg: The Mughals and the Medici* XXXIX:1 (December), pp. 57–68.

Pettigrew, Joyce (1991–2), 'Songs of the Sikh Resistance Movement', in *Asian Music* (Fall/Winter).

Piara Singh Padam (1976), *Srī Gurū Gobind Singh jī de Darbārī Ratan*, Patiala: New Patiala Printers.

——— (ed.) (1991), *Gurū kīān Sākhīān krit Bhāī Svarūp Singh Kaushish* (2nd edition), Amritsar: Singh Brothers.

P.S. Padam (1991), *Rahit-nāme* (5th edition), Amritsar: Bhai Chatar Singh Bhai Jivan Singh.

Carla Petievich (1992), *Assembly of Rivals: Delhi, Lucknow, and the Urdu Ghazal*, New Delhi: Manohar.

Piara Singh Padam (ed.) (1997), *Bhāī Kesar Singh Chhibbar krit Bansāvalīnāmā Dasān Pātshāhīān kā*, Amritsar: Singh Brothers.

Pollock, Sheldon (1996), 'The Sanskrit Cosmopolis, 300–1300 CE: Transculturation, Vernacularization, and the Question of Ideology', in Jan E.M. Houben (ed.), *Ideology and Status of Sanskrit: Contributions to the History of the Sanskrit Language*, Leiden: E.J. Brill.

—————— (1998), 'The Cosmopolitan Vernacular', in the *Journal of Asian Studies* 57, pp. 6–37.

—————— (2000), 'Cosmopolitan and Vernacular in History', in *Public Culture* 12:3, pp. 591–625.

—————— (2006), *The Language of the Gods in the World of Men: Sanskrit, Culture, and Power in Premodern India*, Berkeley: University of California Press.

Pope, A.U. and P. Ackarman (eds) (1964–5), *A Survey of Persian Art From Prehistoric Times to the Present IX*, reissue London and New York: Oxford University Press.

Porter, Yves (1994), *Painters, Paintings and Books: An Essay on Indo-Persian Technical Literature 12–19th Centuries* [trans. S. Butani], Delhi: Manohar.

Rai, Gurmeet and Kavita Singh (2003), 'Brick by Sacred Brick: Architectural Projects of Guru Arjan and Guru Hargobind', in Kavita Singh (ed.), *New Insights into Sikh Art*, 54:4, Mumbai: Marg Publications.

Rajindar Singh (1974), 'Historical Accounts of the Childhood Days of Guru Gobind Singh', in *Punjab History Conference Eight Session December 15–16, 1973 Proceedings*, Patiala: Punjabi University Press.

Randhawa, Mahinder Singh (ed.) (1965), *Pūran Singh Jīvanī te Kavitā*, New Delhi: Sahit Akadami.

Rangarajan, L.N. (ed. and trans.) (1992), *Kautilya: Arthashastra* 3:1, New Delhi: Penguin Books.

Rao, V.N. (2003), David Shulman, Sanjay Subrahmanyam, *Textures of Time: Writing History in South India 1600–1800*, New York: Other Press.

Randir Singh (ed.) (1964), *Bābānī Pīrhī Chalī Guru-Pranālīān*, Amritsar: Shiromani Gurdwara Prabhandak Committee.

—————— (1985), *Shabadārath Dasam Granth Sāhib (pothī pahilī)*, Patiala: Punjabi University Publication Bureau.

Richards, J.F. (1984), 'Norms of Comportment among Imperial Mughal Officials', in Barbara D. Metcalf (ed.), *Moral Conduct and Authority*, Berkeley: University of California Press.

Rinehart, Robin (2004), 'Strategies for Interpreting the Dasam Granth', in Pashaura Singh *et al.* (eds), *Sikhism and History*, Delhi: Oxford University Press, pp. 135–50.

Rizvi, S.A.A. (1983), *A History of Sufism in India* 2 vols, Delhi: Munshiram Manoharlal.

Rizvi, S.A.A. and V.J.A. Flynn (1975), *Fathpur-Sikri*, Bombay: Taraporevala.

Rose, H.A. (1990), *A Glossary of the Tribes and Castes of the Punjab and North-West Frontier Province*, rpt. Patiala: Language Department, Punjab.

Rypka, Jan (1968), *History of Iranian Literature*, Dordrecht: D. Reidel Publishing Company.

Sachdeva, Veena (1993), *Polity and Economy of the Punjab During the Late Eighteenth Century*, Delhi: Manohar.

Sagar, S.S. (2002), *Hukam-namas of Guru Tegh Bahadur: A Historical Study*, Amritsar: Guru Nanak Dev University Press.

Sarkar, Jadunath (1925), *History of Aurangzeb Based on Original Sources* vols I and II (second edition), Calcutta: M.C. Sarkar & Sons.

——— (1928, 1930), *History of Aurangzeb Based on Original Sources* III, IV (second edition), Calcutta: M.C. Sarkar & Sons.

——— (trans.) (1925), *Anecdotes of Aurangzib (English Translation of Ahkam-i-Alamgiri ascribed to Hamid-ud-din Khan Bahadur) with A Life of Aurangzib and Historical Notes*, Calcutta: M.C. Sarkar and Sons.

——— (trans.) 1947), *Maāsir-i 'Ālamgiri: A History of the Emperor Aurangzib-'Alamgir (reign 1658–1707 AD) of Sāqi Must'ad Khan*, Calcutta: Royal Asiatic Society of Bengal.

Saxena, R.K. (2002), *Karkhanas of the Mughal Zamindars: A Study in the Economic Development of 18th Century Rajasthan*, Jaipur: Publication Scheme.

Schimmel, Annemarie (1975), *Mystical Dimensions of Islam*, Chapel Hill: University of North Carolina Press.

——— (1982), *As Through a Veil: Mystical Poetry in Islam*, New York: Columbia University Press.

——— (1988), 'Persian Poetry in the Indo-Pakistani Subcontinent', in *Ehsan Yarshater, Persian Literature*, New York: Columbia University Press.

——— (1988), 'The Genius of Shiraz: Sa'di and Hāfez', in Ehsan Yarshater (ed.), *Persian Literature*, New York: Columbia University Press.

Schokker, G.H. (1983), 'Keshavadasa's Method of Basing Braj Krishna-lyrics on the Sanskrit Tradition of Literary Aesthetics', in Monika Thiel-Horstmann (ed.), *Bhakti in Current Research 1979–1982*, Berlin: Dietrich Reimer Verlag.

Schomer, Karine and W.H. McLeod (eds) (1987), *The Sants: Studies in a Devotional Tradition*, New Delhi: Berkeley Religious Studies Series and Motilal Banarsidass.

Schwartz, Susan (2004), *Rasa: Performing the Divine in India*, New York: Columbia University Press.
Scott, Jonathan (trans.) (1800), *Tales, Anecdotes, and Letters. Translated from the Arabic and Persian*, Shrewsbury: J. and W. Eddowes for T. Cadell and W. Davies, London.
Seigel, Lee (1987), *Laughing Matters: Comic Tradition in India*, New Delhi: Motilal Banarsidass.
Seyller, J.W., E. Koch, A. Owen, and W.M. Thackston (eds) (2002), *The Adventures of Hamza: Painting and Story Telling in Mughal India*, Washington, DC: Freer Gallery of Art and Arthur M. Sackler Allery.
Seyller, John (1987), 'Scribal Notes on Mughal Manuscript Illustrations', in *Artibus Asiae* XLVIII.
———— (1997), 'The Inspection and Valuation of Manuscripts in the Imperial Mughal Library', in *Artibus Asiae* 57:3/4, pp. 243–335.
———— (2001), 'For Love or Money: The Shaping of Historical Painting Collections in India', in Mason *et al.*, *Intimate Worlds: Masterpieces of Indian Painting from the Alvin O. Bellackj Collection*, Philadelphia: Philadelphia Museum of Art.
———— (2000M), 'A Mughal Code of Connoisseurship', in *Muqarnas* 17.
Shackle, Christopher (1978), 'Approaches to the Persian Loans in the *Ādi Granth*', in the *Bulletin of the School of Oriental and African Studies* 4:1.
———— (1983), *An Introduction to the Sacred Language of the Sikhs*, London: School of Oriental and African Studies.
Sharma, Sunil (2000), *Persian Poetry at the Indian Frontier Mas'ud Sa'd Salman of Lahore*, New Delhi: Permanent Black.
Siddiqi, Iqtidar Husain (1995), 'Social Mobility in the Delhi Sultanate', in Irfan Habib (ed.), *Medieval India 1. Sikh Rahit Maryādā*, Amritsar: SGPC.
Sinopoli, Carla M. (Fall 1994), 'Monumentality and Mobility in Mughal Capitals', in *Asian Perspectives* 33:2, pp. 293–308.
Sital, Jit Singh (ed.), *Srī Gur-panth Prakāsh*.
Snell, Rupert (1983), 'Metrical Forms in Braj Bhāshā Verse: The *Caurāsī pada* in Performance', in Monika Thiel-Horstmann (ed.), *Bhakti in Current Research 1979–1982*, Berlin: Dietrich Reimer Verlag.
———— 1992), *The Hindi Classical Tradition: A Braj Bhāshā Reader*, London: School of African and Oriental Studies.
Soucek, Priscilla P. (1987), 'Persian Artists in Mughal India: Influences and Transformations', in *Muqarnas* 4, pp. 166–81.

Streusand, Douglas E. (1989), *The Formation of the Mughal Empire*, New Delhi: Oxford University Press.

Subtelny, Maria Eva (1978), 'The Poetic Circle at the Court of the Timurid, Sultan Husain Baiqara, and its Political Significance'. (Unpublished PhD thesis, Department of Near Eastern Languages and Civilizations, Harvard University.

────── (1983), 'Art and Politics in Early 16th Century Central Asia', in *Central Asiatic Journal* 27.

────── (1986), 'A Taste for the Intricate: The Persian Poetry of the Late Timurid Period', in *Zeitschrift der Deutschen Morgenlandischen Gesellschaft* 136:1, Stuttgart: DMG, pp. 56–79.

Sukha Singh (1989), *Gur-bilās Pātishāhī 10* 16:171–2 [ed. Gursharan Kaur Jaggi], Patiala: Bhasha Vibhag Punjab.

Surinder Singh (2004), *Sikh Coinage: Symbol of Sikh Sovereignty*, Delhi: Manohar.

Syed, Anees Jahan (trans.) (1977), *Aurangzeb in Muntakhab-al Lubab*, Bombay: Somaiya Publications Pvt. Ltd.

Talib, Gurbachan Singh (1967), 'The Zafar-Namah', in Prakash Singh (ed.), *The Saint Warrior Guru Gobind Singh*, Amritsar: Khalsa College.

Tasbihi, M.H. (ed.) (1967), *The Persian-English Gulistan or Rose Garden of Saʻdi* [trans. Edward Rehatsek], Tehran: Shargh's Press.

Thackston, Wheeler (1974), 'The Poetry of Abu-Talib Kalim Persian Poet-Laureate of Shahjahan Mughal Emperor of India'. Harvard University, Dept. of Near Eastern Languages and Civilizations.

Thackston, Wheeler H. (trans.) (1999), *The Jahangirnama: Memoirs of Jahangir, Emperor of India*, Washington, D.C.: Smithsonian.

Thackston, Wheeler M. (2000), *A Millennium of Classical Persian Poetry*, Bethesda, Maryland: Ibex Publishers.

Thackston, Wheeler (2002), 'Literature', in Zeenut Zaid (ed.), *The Magnificent Mughals*, Karachi: Oxford University Press.

Thackston (2002), Wheeler (trans. and ed.), *The Baburnama: Memoirs of Babur, Prince and Emperor*, New York: The Modern Library.

Thiel-Horstmann, Monika (1983), *Crossing the Ocean of Existence: Braj Bhāshā Religious Poetry from Rajasthan: A Reader*, Weisbaden: Otto Harrassowitz.

Tikku, G.L. (1971), *Persian Poetry in Kashmir 1339–1846*, Berkeley: University of California Press.

Trilochan Singh and Anurag Singh (2002), *A Brief Account of the Life and Works of Guru Gobind Singh* (3rd revised edition), Amritsar: Bhai Chattar Singh Jiwan Singh.

della Valle (1989), *Pietro, The Pilgrim: The Travels of Pietro della Valle* [George Bull (trans.)], London: Hutchinson.
Vedanti, Joginder Singh (ed.) (1998), *Gur-bilās Pātshāhī Chhevīn*, Amritsar: Dharam Prachar Committee of the SGPC.
Vedi, Bhagat Singh (ed.) (1989), *Mahimā Prakāsh krit Sarūp Dās Bhallā (Bhāg Dūsrā)*, Chandigarh: Bhasha Vibhag Punjab.
Wade, Bonnie (1998), *Imaging Sound: An Ethnomusicological Study of Music, Art, and Culture in Mughal India*, Chicago and London: University of Chicago Press.
Wagoner, Phillip P. (1996), '"Sultan Among Hindu Kings": Dress, Titles, and Islamicization of Hindu Culture at Vijayanagar', in the *Journal of Asian Studies* 55:4, pp. 851–80.
Welch, Stuart Cary (1978), *Imperial Mughal Painting plate* 14, New York: George Braziller.
White, Charles S.J. (1977), *The Caurāsī Pad of Shri Hit Harivamsh: Introduction, Translation, Notes, and edited Braj Bhāshā text*, Honolulu: University of Hawaii Press.
White, Hayden (1992), *The Content of the Form: Narrative Discourse and Historical Representation* (Paperback edition), Baltimore: John Hopkins University Press.
Wickens, G.M. (trans.) (1964), *The Nasirean Ethics*, London: George Allen and Unwin Ltd.
Yule, Henry and A.C. Burnell (eds) (1969), *Hobson-Jobson* (1st edition 1886), London: Routledge & Kegan Paul.
Vir Singh (ed.) (1966), *Ganj-nāmah*, New Delhi: Bhai Vir Singh Sahitya Sadan.
────── (1990), *Kavi Chūrāmani Bhāī Santokh Singh jī krit Srī Gur Pratāp Sūraj Granth VII*, Patiala: Bhasha Vibhag, Punjab.
────── (1997), *Srī Gurū Granth Sāhib jī dī Kunjī: Vārān Bhāī Gurdās Satīk Bhāv Prakāshanī Tīkā Samet Mukammal*, New Delhi: Bhai Vir Singh Sahit Sadan.
────── *Bhai Gurdās jī dī Yarvhīn Vār dā Tīkā Arthāt Sikhān dī Bhagat Māllā Rachit Sacchkhand Vasī Srī Bhāī Sāhib Shahīd Bhāī Mani Singh jī Gayānī*.
Zaehner, R.C. (ed. and trans.) (1973), *The Bhagavad-Gita with a Commentary Based on the Original Sources*, London: Oxford University Press.
Zakhmi, Karam Singh (1930), *Srī Gurū Gobind Singh jī de Annanay Sikh Bhāī Nand Lāl jī krit Tausīfo Sanā*, Amritsar: Bhape di Hati.
Ziauddin, M. (trans.) (1935), *A Grammar of the Braj Bhakha by Mīrzā Khān (1676 AD) The Persian Text critically edited from original MSS. with an*

Introduction, Translation and Notes together with the contents of the Tuhfatu-l-Hind, Calcutta: Visva-Bharati Book Shop.

Zilli, Ishtiyaq Ahmad (2000) 'Development of *Inshā* Literature to the End of Akbar's Reign', in Muzaffar Alam, N. Delvoye, and Marc Gaborieau (eds), *The Making of Indo-Persian Culture: Indian and French Studies*, New Delhi: Manohar.

Zipoli, Ricardo (1993), *The Technique of Ğawāb: Replies by Nawā'ī to Hāfiz and Ğamī*. Quaderni del dipartimento di Studi Eurasiastici 35, Venice: Universita degli Studi di Venezia.

Zielgler, Norman P. (1978), 'Some Notes on Rajput Loyalties During the Mughal Period', in J.F. Richards (ed.), *Kingship and Authority in South Asia*, Madison, Wisconsin: South Asian Studies.

Index

Abdul, Mir (dhadhi) 96, 97
Abdur Rahim Wuzarat (see also
    Bikrami) 126
Abu'l Fazl 'Allami 5, 30, 56, 88, 91,
    92, 130, 183, 235
Abu'l Fazl Fayzi 130
Adha (poet) 139
Adil Shah, Ibrahim 131, 140
Adi Granth also Guru Granth Sahib
    4, 10, 12, 13, 14, 17, 24, 55, 56,
    59, 63, 64, 65, 66, 67, 73, 75, 99,
    142, 146, 153, 155, 156, 158, 190,
    191, 194, 197, 198, 200, 201, 203,
    205–7, 209, 211, 239, 245, 248,
    257, 268, 271, 280, 284, 285, 286
    intratextuality within 153
    basis of court 162
    its 'courtly structure' 163–4
    Sikh etiquette before 24, 284
advice literature 92
afzū 149
Aghapur 224
ahl-i qalām (men of the pen) 29, 144
ahl-i saif (men of the sword) 29,
    143, 144
Ahmadnagar 132
Ā'in-i Akbārī 235
Aj, Raja 158
Ajai Singh (Yudhishthira's
    successor) 159

Ajit Singh (Mata Sundari's
    adopted son) 207, 208
Akal Takht 95, 96, 97, 285
Akāl Ustati 13, 137, 159, 243–4, 245
Akbar, Jalaluddin 25, 58, 60, 62, 67,
    218, 228, 235, 255–6, 264
    meeting with Guru Arjan 25, 37,
        60–1, 62, 68, 155, 213
    hunting 91
    enticing poets from Iran, 128–9
    and court poets 134, 218
    as a child 144
    his camp 85
Akbār-nāmah 235
akhand path 201, 249
Akhbārat-i Darbār-i Mu'alla 17
Alam (poet) 134, 201, 209
Alam, Muzaffar 52
Alankua 235
Ali, Daud 159
Amar Das, Guru 56, 61, 94, 164, 284
Amar-nāmah 219
Amir Timur 4 51, 52, 101, 237
Amritsar 62, 65, 66, 67
'Amuli, Muhammad Talib 130
Anandpur-Makhowal 7, 122, 136, 137,
    159, 160, 164, 180, 277–81, 288
    court at, 132–6
    praise of in poetry 140–1
Angad, Guru 245

Index 315

Ani Rai (poet) 22, 138, 201
Arabic 242
Ardas 285
Arjan, Guru 5, 13, 24, 25, 26, 65,
    66, 134, 155, 162, 191, 194, 198,
    200, 212, 213, 268
  his court 5, 55, 59, 62, 63, 64,
    66, 68, 162
  courtly acitivites 68
  granting turbans 64
  construction plans 66
  and the Adi Granth 163
  Mughal execution of 212
armed peasantry 61, 90
Arora Sikhs 281
Aruzi see Samarqandi, Nizami-i
  Aruzi-i
'arz-dīdah 67-8
'arz-dasht 42, 280, 285, 290
Ārzulalfāz 234
Asad Khan 214
Ashta, Dharampal 105, 122, 154–5
Asman Khan 94
Atal Rai Tower 95
Aurangzeb also 'Alamgir 1, 8, 10,
    11, 19, 28, 43, 47, 48, 51, 68, 99,
    100, 101, 104, 123–8, 131, 132,
    133, 134, 136, 143, 148, 155, 208,
    209, 212, 215, 216, 219, 220, 223,
    226, 227, 232, 234, 252, 256, 257,
    263, 264, 271
  and Guru Tegh Bahadar 123, 143
  and Ram Rai 143
  iconoclasm 131
  appreciation of painting 124–5
  appreciation of music 126
  appreciation of poetry 125–8
  banning chronicles 125
  as a cultured emperor, 126–7
  in *Pakhyān Charit* 155
  interest in Quranic interpretations
    214, 215
  image in Sikh accounts 220
  and Guru Gobind Singh 279–81

Azam Shah, Muhammad (d. 1707)
    226–7
Azim, Shahzada (son of Bahadar
    Shah) 148

B40 Janam-sakhi 284, 284
Babur, Zahiruddin 51, 52, 58, 68,
    76, 77, 78, 86, 91, 129, 138, 171,
    212, 214, 215, 216, 223, 251
  as a poet, 129
Bachitar Nātak 8, 9, 19, 123, 136,
    148, 149, 151, 153, 160, 161,
    204, 205, 218, 253, 254
  apnī kathā portion 149
Bachitar Nātak Granth 149, 157
Bahadar Shah, Emperor (d. 1712)
  also known as Prince Mu'azzam
  and Shah 'Alam 17, 99, 112, 139,
    147, 160, 209, 212, 213, 216, 219,
    222, 228, 238, 252, 253, 258, 260,
    265, 282, 286
  and Guru Gobind Singh 147,
    216, 219
  and Nand Lal Goya 148, 208–11,
    214–15, 219, 222, 223
Bajpei, Hans Ram 21, 22, 140, 180
Bakhtawar Khan 125, 126, 127
Bal, S.S. 19, 104, 161, 279
Bali, Raja 142, 181
Balkhi, 'Unsuri 50, 51
Balwand, Rai 55, 56
Banda Bahadar 16, 17, 222, 281,
    282, 290
  possible darbar 282
Bandagī-nāmah
  title changed by Guru Gobind
    Singh 217
bānī also *gur-bānī* 78, 153, 157–8,
    200, 210, 213, 218, 233, 239,
    240–2, 245–8, 251, 267, 272,
    273, 274
*Bansāvalī-nāmā Dasān Pātshāhīān
    kā* 90, 133, 156–8, 207–8
baraka (blessing) 64

Index

Batha, Bhai 104
Badauni, 'Abd al-Qadir 130
Bedil, Mirza 128, 132
bhaddan/bhaddar 230, 236
Bhāī Nand Lāl Granthāvalī 223, 225
Bhagavad-Gita 152, 211, 243
Bhalla, Bawa Kirpal Das (Singh) 90
Bhalla, Hirda Ram 2
Bhalla, Sarup Das 91, 135, 210, 211, 212, 213, 214, 217, 231, 246, 253, 257
Bhandari, Sujan Rai 99
Bhangu, Ratan Singh 58, 212, 222–3
Bhattān de savaīe 56, 57, 58, 59, 98
bhatts 55, 56, 57, 58, 59, 60
Bhavishya Purana 220
Bhav Panchāshikā 20
bhet 65
Bhim Chand 23, 142, 160, 218
Bidhita [Bhidia] 96
Bihari (poet) 138
Bijapur 132, 140
Bikrami 126
Bilaspur-Kahlur 9, 133
bir-ras(i)/bir-rass (heroic sentiment) 2, 157
Brahma (*chaturānan*) 122, 158
Brahmā Avtār 149, 158
Brajbhasha poetry 59, 77, 78, 239–40
performative nature 154
Brajbhasha courts 149
Brind/Vrnd (poet) 20, 134
Browne, E. 231
Buddha, Baba 209–10
Bulakidas 142
Burhanpuri, Bhimsen, 10

Chāhar Chaman 226
Chāhar Muqalah 213, 231
Chamkaur, Battle of 278, 279, 287
Chānākā Rājnītī also *Chānākā Shastr* 136–7
Chand (poet) 44, 134
Chand, Debi 96, 115

Chandan (poet) 23
Chandar Bhan Brahman 226
Chandi 151
Chandī Charitr 149, 155, 158
Chandī Charitr Ukti Bilās 149, 158
charitr 150–1
historical character 151
Chaubīs Avtār 149, 158
Chaupa Singh Rahit-nama 242
chaurī/chavar (royal whisk) 8, 56, 285
Chetan Singh 61
Chief Khalsa Diwan 247
Chima Khan 94
Chhabila, Bhai (dhadhi) 44
Chhajju Mall 224
Chhand Vichār Pingal 137
chhatrī (royal canopy) 8, 55–6, 142
chhatrdhārik/chhatrdhārī 158
chhatarpati 14
Chhibbar, Chaupa Singh 20–1, 144, 242, 245, 266, 270, 275, 284
Chhibbar, Dargah Mal 44
Chhibbar, Kesar Singh 17, 44, 90, 156–7, 163, 207–8, 229, 242, 243, 245, 274, 284
Chhotah Mall 226
Chinggis Khan (d. 1227 CE) 51, 52, 53, 237
Chishti, Muinuddin 58
comportment 4, 13–14, 18, 28, 35, 36, 48, 59, 99, 146–7, 285
courtly jewels 49

Dabistān-i Mazāhib 58, 61, 63, 64, 74, 87, 96, 98
Daia Ram Abrol 284
Dai Lado 146
Dalia, Janaji 227
Damaghani, Manuchhihri 50
Damdama 277, 280
Dara Shikoh (d, 1658) 99, 100, 123, 224
darbār (term) 205

Index 317

darshan 147
 and the Mughal emperors 147
Das Gur Kathā 2
Das, Dayal 101–2
Das, Hari 164, 278
Das, Keval 164
Das, Narina 91
Das, Pandit Devi 140
Dasam Granth 1, 6, 122, 142,
   148–62, 156, 199, 206, 207, 242,
   243, 245, 248, 270, 271, 280
 and courtly poetry 150
 dates within 150
 conventional imagery in, 151–2
 intertextual resonances with
   Sanskrit literature 152
 intratextual echoes 153
 performative dimensions of 154–5,
   157, 158
 courtly references within 158–60
Dasaratha, King 46, 153, 158
Dasturulinshā 225–7
Daya Singh Rahit-nama 242, 243–4,
   245
Ded Mal, Bhai 104
Dehradun 99, 118, 143
Deol, Jeevan 229
Desa Singh Rahit-nama 230
Devanagiri 26, 122, 152
Devī-mahātmya 151
Dhanna Singh 23
Dhaul, sangat of 148
dhadhis 44, 116
dhadhi recitals 154
dhādhī sangīt 96, 158
Dhiāu Guhaj Ustat Dasam Shabad
   211
Dhir Mal 24
Dhuni Chand (of Kabul) 142
Digby, Simon 57
Dina 277, 279
Dīvān-i Goyā 206, 231, 233, 234,
   239, 251, 259, 263, 267, 270
 title given by tenth Guru 218

Eaton, Richard 244
elephant 49, 56, 69, 142

Farhatulnazarin 232
Farrukh Siyyar, Emperor (d. 1719)
   58, 208, 216–17, 282
Fatehpur Sikri 61, 66, 67
Fateh Shah 23, 160
Fazil Ali Khan, Nawab 209
Ferdausi 50
Fifty-two poets 1
Fighani, Baba 164
Fitrat (Mu'azzuddin Muhammad
   [d. 1690]) also see 'Muswi'
   128

gaddī (cushion, throne) 62
Ganda Singh 146, 225, 282
Ganj-nāmah 201, 225, 231, 234,
   235, 238, 239, 259, 268
Garhwal 161
Ghani, Muhammad Abdul 129
ghazl 129, 137
Ghazna 49, 50, 70, 71, 82, 224
Ghaznavids 49–51
Giān Prabodh 158
Gian Singh 216
Gibb, E.J.W. 217, 231
Girdhar Lal (poet) 43
Gītgovind 151
Glynn, Catherine 9, 101
Gobind Singh, Guru, 1, 2, 4, 5, 6,
   13, 21, 153, 219
 images of 5, 6–9;
 hukamnamas of 18, 22, 45,
   142–3, 146–8, 160, 280
 court of 51, 105, 159–60, 201,
   214–15, 237, 277–82
 kavi-darbar 135
 as safe refuge 136
 poetic imagery of 138–40
 praise of his sword 141
 childhood narratives of, 143
 understanding of darbar 161–4

Index

associations with Nand Lal Goya 205, 230–1, 236–7
relations with Aurangzeb 279–81
Goindwal Pothis 53
Golconda 126, 132
Golden Temple (also Harimandir) 67, 285
Gordon, Stewart 103
Goya, Nand Lal 20, 134, 148, 200–47
jack-of-all-trades 201–2
tenth Guru's emissary 203–3, 222, 223
Persian *baits* 202
and brahmans 203, 222
as image of first Guru 204, 211, 212–13, 222
erudition 207–8, 213, 219, 231–2
sobriquet 'Goya' 208,
interpreting Quranic ayat 208, 214–15
as *mīr munshī* 209, 225
childhood narrative 209–11
sacred thread investiture narrative 211
as *sevādar* 212, 233–4, 246
association with Mughal court 211–16
arriving at tenth Guru's court 216–17
possible military career 227–8
as tenth Guru's boon companion 221–2
and Farrukh Siyyar 222
account by ancestors 223–5
dates of death 228
Persian works attributed to 229, 231
Brajbhasha/Punjabi works attributed to 229, 230
questions regarding his identity 233–8
transformation of poetry into bani 238–47
as *viākhīā* 239, 272

and *langar* 246
and Bahadar Shah 148, 208–11, 214–15, 219, 222, 223
Grewal, Jagtar Singh (J.S.) 19, 104, 161, 279
Guha, Sumit 9, 10
Gulistān 280
Gurbakhsh Singh 227
gur-bānī see *bānī*
gurbilās literature 242, 282
Gurbilās Pātshāhī Chhevīn 91, 95, 96
Gurbilās Pātshāhī Dasvīn (Sukha Singh) 218
Gurbilās Pātshāhī Dasvīn (Koer Singh) 219–21
Gurdas Bhalla, Bhai 12, 13, 15, 16, 57, 58, 59, 67, 88, 200, 207, 239, 240
vars 14–15, 89, 233
kabitts 14, 233
Gurditta, Baba 117
Gurmukhi script
within Dasam Granth manuscripts 152–3
within manuscripts of Nand Lal's poetry 206, 241–6
rahit-nama attitude towards 242–3
Gur-pādhantī 199, 201, 229
Gur-panth Prākash 58, 222
gurpranālī/gurpranāvalī 9
Gurpratāp Sūraj Granth 3, 93, 133, 135, 216, 220, 247
Gur-sobhā 17, 18, 136, 139, 205, 229, 236, 281, 282
Guru Darbar 205
Guru Granth/Guru Panth/Khalsa doctrine 205, 284
Gurū kīān Sākhīān 2, 245
gur-ustati 138
Guru Granth Sahib see Adi Granth
gutkā (breviary) 64

Habib, Irfan 65, 66
Hafez Shirazi 51, 127

Index 319

halemī-rāj (rule of the meek) 66
Hamzah-nāmah 67
Hans Ram (poet) 140–1
Hans, Surjit 60
Hanuman 2
Hanuman-Nātak 2, 191
Hardy, Peter 50, 53, 93
Hargobind, Guru 15–16, 61, 64, 87–8, 91, 101, 132
hukam-namas 87–8
hunting 89–94, 95, 161
as king, 95–8
robing Guru Hari Rai, 98
Bhai Gurdas' description of, 89–90
Dabistān's description of, 90, 94, 96
Kesar Singh Chhibbar's description of, 90
Jahangir and, 92, 93–4
Shah Jahan and, 92, 94
court of, 88, 94, 96–8
birth heralded, 95
Hargobindpur 95–6
Hari Krishan, Guru 97, 98
hukam-nama of, 22, 104, 116
Hari Rai, Guru 63, 64, 89, 97, 98, 117–18
courtly image of, 98
comportment 99
and Dara Shikoh, 99
Hari Sen of Mandi, Raja 114
hasbulhukam 19, 280
Hashim (court painter) 124
hawks 94, 114
Hazin, Muhammad bin Abi Talib 132
hazūr 146–7
Hitopadesha 122, 123, 133, 145, 156
Hujwiri Data Ganjbakhsh, Shaikh 50
hukum 24
hukam-namas 16, 87–8
Humayun, Emperor 128, 129, 138, 171, 284

as a poet 129
Iranization of Mughal court 129
hundī 88
hunting 161
animals 91, 94
symbols 91

ihām 129
Indo-Timurids
also see Mughal 4
'Inayatullah Khan 19
inshā 225
Islamicate 69
itihāsa 151
Itimaduddaula, Ghiyasuddin 130
izzat 161

Jahandar Shah, Emperor (d. 1711)
also Muhammad Ma'azuddin Bahadar 241, 79
Jahangir, Emperor (d. 1627)
also Prince Salim 7, 43, 61, 65, 75, 76, 77, 79, 89, 92, 93, 94, 110, 111, 112, 113, 115, 124, 130, 132, 134, 155, 166, 170, 173, 174, 176, 183, 235, 251
court poets of 134
Jahāngīr-nāmah 92
Jai Singh Kacchawaha 101
jāmah 7, 32
Janak, Raja 57
janam-sakhis 6, 17, 52, 57, 98, 210, 282
Jang-nāmā Gurū Gobind Singh jī kā 22, 141
Jāp 153
Japji 153
javān-mardī 25, 48
Jhanda, Bhai 96
jharokā 83–4, 185
Jograj manuscript 98
joti 89
Joti Bigās 234
justice 161

Kabir 26, 153
kalgī (aigrette) 285
kalgīdhar 2, 285
Kalidasa 145
Kalim, Abu-Talib 97, 131, 235
Kaliyuga 201–2
Kalu the Khatri 15
Kāmasūtra 156
kammarband (cummerbund) 6
Kangra 133
Kahn Singh of Nabha 105, 122, 206, 247
Kal, Bhatt also Kal Shar 120
Kankan (poet) 2
Kans, Raja 158
Kanshi Ram (poet) 134
Kapur Singh, Nawab 17, 284
Karan Singh (Rajput) 113
Karna Parab 21–2, 140
Kartarpur 65
Kartarpuri bir 4, 96
Kaushish, Seva Singh 2, 26
Kashf-ul-mahjūb 50, 70
katar 6
kathā 154
kathākar 95, 149, 207
kavi-samaja (society of poets) 59
khaimah/khemā (tent[s]) 2, 102
Khafi Khan, Muhammad Hashim 125, 126, 127
khālsā 24, 88
Khalsa 6, 139, 229, 234, 278, 280, 281, 282, 283, 284, 286, 287, 288, 289, 291
khanaqah 52
Khanda 284
Khan-i Khanan, Abdurrahim (Rahim) 228
khānzādī 25, 47–8
Khara, sangat of 148
Kharag Singh 2
Khatri(s) 61, 207–8, 210, 211, 219, 224, 229, 230, 232, 233, 236, 243, 253, 264, 265, 266, 274, 281, 282

Khiala, Lal Das (poet) 279
khil'at (robe of honour) see also *siropā* 2, 64, 98, 103, 117
given to Guru Gobind Singh, 147–8
khirqah 117
Khulāsatuttavārīkh
kirtan 154, 158, 239
kitāb-khānah 62, 67, 96, 99
Kirat, Bhatt 57
Kirpal Singh (tenth Guru's maternal uncle) 104, 142, 208
Kirpan 284
Koer Singh 18, 220
Koka-shāstra 20, 145
Kolff, Dirk 90, 134
Krishna/Krishan 145–6, 151, 157
Krishanavtār/Krishan Charit 2, 145–6, 151, 152, 158
Kulliyāt-i Bhā'ī Nand La'l Goyā 223, 225
kundan 6
kurnīsh 235
Kuvaresh; also Kuvar (poet) 20, 135

Lauhari, Tansukh (poet) 178
Lahore 5, 85
Lakkhi Jungle 138, 139, 178, 179, 278, 287, 288
darbar at 138, 278–80
poetry of 138, 139, 279
Lakhnaur 143
Lakkhan Rai (poet) 122, 133
līla 156–7
Lohgarh fort 95

Ma'āsir-i 'Ālamgīrī 127, 147
Macauliffe, Max Arthur 211, 221
Macchiwara 277
Madu, Bhai (rababi) 44
Mahabharata 21, 22, 151, 158, 221, 246
mahāfil 59
mahākavyā 150

Index 321

mahalla 84
Mahimā Prakāsh [Kavitā] 91, 133, 135, 142, 201, 210, 214, 216, 219, 223, 246
Mahimā Prakāsh Vārtak 90
Mahmud of Ghazna 49–51, 70, 71, 137
māiki Sikhs 283
majālis (sing: *majlis*) 23, 46, 50, 58, 59, 77
Majhān Gurū Gobind Singh kīān 138
Majhān Sassī dīān 139
maleccha-bhākhā 243
malfūzat 52
malikushshu'arā' (poet-lauerate) 51, 127, 221
Mallia 15
Mandi 9
Mangal Rai 22, 23, 140, 141
Mani Singh 2, 280
manjī 61, 94
mansab 37
mansabdar 48, 94, 99, 100
Manucci, Niccolo 124
manuscript 124–5, Guru Nanak Dev Univeristy 4, 5
manuscript 115, 123, Punjabi University 206
manuscripts
 Persianite 5, 67–9
 autographing 68
 Sikh 68
 of Nand Lal Goya's works 201–6, 207
 corrections 68
 size of 206
Mardana 58
Markandeya Purana 152
masands 15, 62, 63, 64, 88, 94, 96
masnad/masnad-i 'ālī 62
masnavi 137
Mati Das, Bhai 105
Māvarā'annahar 51
Mazandaran 220

McLeod, Hew (W.H.) 87, 146, 214, 229, 239, 240, 242, 247, 281
Medini Prakash 23, 160
Mira Bai 200
Mir'at-i 'Ālam 125, 127
miri-piri 60
Mir Jumla (Mir Muhammad-Amin Shahrastani Ruhalamin 131
Mir Mushki (dhadhi) 44
mirzā 101
Mirzā-nāmah 11, 36
misls 17, 283
morcham 8
Moti Ram 225
Mubarak, Shaikh 130
Mughal court
 ambiguous Sikh attitude to, 3, 4, 10
 kitāb-khānah 68
 symbols 10, 49, 64
 Persian terminology of 10
 character of, 14, 63
 movements 68, 93
 hunting 93
 and patronage of artists and poets, 124–6, 128–32
Muhammad, Prophet 19, 137
Muhammad Saqi Musta'idd Khan 147–8
Mukhalis Khan 126
Multan 224, 225, 226, 233
munshis
 training 224
Muntakhabullubāb 125
Muntakhabuttavārīkh 130
muqaddam 233
Murshid Quli Khan 132
musicians also see *rabābīs* and dhadhis 12, 58, 96, 126
Muswi 128

nadīm 222
nagārā/naqqārā (kettledrums) 2, 91, 97, 116, 284

Nanak, Guru 13, 14, 49, 52, 60, 64, 164, 203, 204, 210–14, 216, 219, 220, 222, 233, 234, 241, 243, 246, 250, 257, 258, 265, 267, 269, 275
   bestows Mughals with rule 212
Nand Ram (poet) 134
Nand Lal (see Goya)
Nand Lal (Mughal courtier) 232
naqīb 281
Nasīhat-nāmā 230, 286
Natha (dhadhi) 96, 97
Nath Mall, Dhadhi 219
naubat 113, 142, 286
naubat-khānah 113
nav ras or the nine sentiments 3
Ni'amat Khan 126
niāz 148
nindak (detractor) 63
nishān (drum) 97, 116
Nishan Sahib 284
Nizami 52
Nizamuddin Auliya 52
nūr 5

Oberoi, Harjot 240

Padam, Piara Singh 1, 2, 134, 138, 164, 209, 236, 278
Pahari region 133
   arts and ateliers 133
Painda Khan 94
Pakhyān Charitr 43, 112, 118, 149, 151, 152, 153, 154–6, 158
palkī 6
Panchatantra 156
panch pīrs 89
Pashaura Singh 55, 58, 67, 68, 244
patkā 7
Patna 18, 143
   sangat of, 103, 104
pātishāh 54–5, 60
Pattan (i.e. Pak Pattan)
   sangat of, 104

Paunta Sahib 137, 160, 161, 190, 194, 195, 279, 280
Persian language 52, 240, 246
   eighteenth-century Sikh literature attitude towards 241–3
Persianite values
   transferral to India 51–2, 53
   terminology of royalty in Sikh literature 53–5
Perso-Arabic script 244
phalashruti 151
Phattmall (poet) 139
pigeons 88
pigeon flying (*'ishqbāzī*) 88
Pirana Jat 96, 116
Pingalsār 43
poets
   emigrations to India 128–30
   qualities of 213, 235
   introductory etiquette 217
Pollock, Sheldon 150–1
pothī-mahal 62, 67, 96, 98
Prakash Asthan 32, 83, 284, 287
Prashan-uttar 204, 212, 249, 250
Prem Abodh 164, 200, 278
Prithi Chand 24
Punjab
   frontier 49, 61, 69
Puranas 145, 246
Puratan Janam-sakhi 98, 216

Qur'ān 5, 30, 127, 243
   Quranic verses 127
   script of 242

rabābīs 12, 44, 55
radīf 234
rahīl 137, 220
rāgīs 20,
Rahim see Khan-i Khanan, Abdurrahim
rahit-namas 17, 32, 92, 230, 285, 286
   denunciation of Persian 230
Rai Kot 282

Index 323

Rai Singh Khatri 281–3
Raja, Bhai 102, 103
Raja Raghunath Rai Rayan 134
Rajputs
  courtly art 6–9, 125
rājnīti 145
rāj-yogī 60
Rama (Ramchandra) 143, 150, 151, 156
Rāmavtār 150, 152, 156
Ramayana 151, 246
Ramcharitmanas
Ram Das, Guru 60, 62, 63, 64, 94
Ramdaspur 60, 63
Ram Rai (son of Guru Hari Rai) 24, 99
Ram Rai, Bhai (disciple of Guru Gobind Singh) 146
Ram Singh Kacchawaha 100
  relations with Guru Tegh Bahadar 100–1
Ranjit Nagara 181
Ranjit Singh, Maharaja of the Punjab 16, 17, 21, 284
Rati Rahass Kok 20
ravatī (tent) 102
Richards, John 58
rītigranths 145, 151
Rose, H.A. 99
Rudaki 235
Rudra 2
Rudr Avtār 149
rumāl 7
Rumi, Jallaluddin 51, 52, 127
Rypka, Jan 130, 225

sabk-i hindī (also *shīvah-'i tāzah*) 129
Sadhu, Bhai 96
Sadhu Ram 21
Sa'di, Shaikh 52, 127, 280
Sadu, Bhai (rababi) 44
Safavids 129
  and Humayun 129
Saharu 15

Sahazadpur 102
sahī see manuscript corrections
Sahib, Mata Devi 282
Sagar, S.S. 105
Sa'ib, Mirza Muhammad Ali 131
Saif Khan, Nawab (d. 1685) 100
  relations with Guru Tegh Bahadar 100
Sainapati 17, 132, 135, 230, 236, 281, 282
Sākhī Bhāī Nand Lāl jī 157, 202
Salman, Masud Sa'd 50
Samanid court 235
Samarqandi, Nizami-i Aruzi-i 213
samvād 152
sanad 19
Sana'i, Hakim 50
Sanghu, Bhai 283
Sanskrit 'cosmopolis' 150–1
Santokh Singh 3, 21, 93, 135, 140, 142, 211, 212, 215, 231, 245, 247, 252, 253, 254, 256, 257
sarab-loh 145
Sarab-loh Granth 1
Saraswati, Kavindracharya 134
sarkār 65
Sarkar, Jadunath 128
Satta the Dum 55, 56
Sau Sakhīān 221–2, 242, 245
scribes also *likhārīs* 5, 12. 20, 21, 31, 37, 44, 45, 51, 53, 54, 67, 80, 84, 96, 97, 105, 117, 118, 121, 147, 148, 149, 164, 171, 184, 186, 196, 197, 201, 209, 225, 226, 232, 243, 248, 250, 255, 262, 264, 267, 280, 282
sevā 12
Shabad Hazare 159
Shackle, Christopher 53, 146, 233
Shahīd-bilās 2
Shah Jahan, emperor 100, 124, 131, 134, 155, 167, 169, 173, 174, 176, 183, 185, 216, 226, 227
  poets of, 131, 134

Shāh Jahān Nāmah 131
Shahjahanabad 61, 66, 67
<u>Sh</u>āh-nāmah 50, 68
Shah Tahmasp (d. 1576) 129
Shalya Parab 22
shamsa 4
shastrdhārī (learned in weapons) 29, 145
shāstrdhārī (learned in scripture) 29, 145
Shirazi, Shah-Nawaz Khan 131
Shiromani Gurdwara Prabhandak Committee (SGPC) 82, 285
Shivaji Bhonsale 100, 145
shutrī (drum on camel's back) 97
Sikh art
  contemporary 60
  eighteenth century
  nineteenth century
Sikhān dī Bhagat-mālā 203, 222
Sikh coins 16
  Gobindshahi couplet upon, 16
Sikh court
  basics of membership 13–14
  conspicuous images of, 14
  poetic images of 159
  character of earlier courtiers 14–15
  narrativizing 16–25
  courtly symbols of 19, 62, 66, 142
  kitāb-khānah/pothī-mahal of, 62–3
  kār-khānah 63
  list of poets 134
  reasons for poets coming to, 135–6
  at Paunta Sahib 137–8
  at Lakki Jungle 138, 139
  'Mughalization' 154
Sikh Rahit Maryādā 200, 238, 247
Singh Gaū kī Kathā 140
Singh Sabha movement 200, 224, 238, 240, 241, 247, 249, 261, 273, 276

Sirhindi, Nasir 'Ali (d. 1696) 133
Siri Dhar 100
Sirmur 98
siropā (robe of honour) 2, 21, 50, 98, 103, 285
Srī Gur-sobhā, see *Gur-sobhā*
Srī mukhvāk pātishāhī dasvīn 149
Sri Rann Khambkala 153
Sobha Chand 146
sudh see manuscript corrections
sudh kichai see manuscript correction
sudhār (improvement) 152, 199
Sufis 50, 51, 52, 57, 58, 64, 72, 76, 77, 83
Sukh Dev (poet) 137, 209
Sukha Singh 218
Sultanat Dahamm 234, 235
Sundari, Mata 207, 208, 222, 223, 282
Sūraj Prakāsh (see *Gurpratāp Sūraj Granth*)
symbols of court 4
  see also *naqqārah*, <u>kh</u>aimah, *siropā*, *khil'at*
  poets of, 20–4

Taj Mahal 97
takhat (throne) 55
Talwandi Sabo 277, 280
tan<u>kh</u>āh 229
Tan<u>kh</u>āh-nāmā see also *Nasīhat-nāmā* 229, 230
Tarn Taran 65
Tarī<u>kh</u>-i Dil-kushā 10
Tasnīfat-i Goyā 225
tasvīr-<u>kh</u>ānah 124, 173
Tat Khalsa 247
tazkīr 52
tazkirah/tadhkirat 57, 59
Tegh Bahadar, Guru 13, 88, 96, 101, 103, 105, 122, 132
  courtly associations 100, 101, 105

courtly symbols 101–2, 103
hukam-namas of 22, 30, 100–4, 146
hunting 104
community-strengthening activities of, 103–4
possible poets of, 105, 122, 123, 132–3
and Aurangzeb, 123
martyrdom narrative of, 135–6, 154, 212
Tentage 102–3
Thapal 98
tikkā (coronotion mark) 55
Tikke dī vār 55, 98
Timur see Amir Timur
trade routes
Mughal concern with 226
'Triumph over Islam' theme 214
turhī 95, 115
turk akhar 242

'Urfi, Jamaluddin Muhammad 130–1, 235

'unvān 30
Uzbek courts 237

Valajah court 132
vernaculars 151
viākhīā 239, 272
Vidyā Sagar 1
Viro, Bibi 90
Vir Singh 247
Vishnu 122
Vyasa 158

Wakā'i (Battles) 126
Wassaf Khan, Nawab 224

Zafar-nāmah (Guru Gobind Singh) 30, 43, 160, 196, 197, 279, 280
Zafar-nāmah (Sharafuddin Yazdi's) 167
Zebunnisa 167, 220, 258
Zindagī-nāmah 206, 209, 217, 231, 234, 239, 248, 257, 263, 266, 267, 270
Zuhuri, Nuruddin 140